History of the Royal Regiment of Artillery

WESTERN FRONT 1914–18

by

General Sir Martin Farndale, KCB

ISBN 1 870114 00 0

The Royal Artillery Institution
Old Royal Military Academy
Woolwich, London SE18 4DN

Printed in Great Britain by Henry Ling Limited The Dorset Press, Dorchester.

Contents

Annexes

Appendices

Illustrations

Introduction

This is a story of a regiment at war. But it is no ordinary regiment. By 1918 the strength of the Royal Regiment of Artillery in France was 548,780 officers and men organised into 2161 batteries. These figures became even greater, surpassing the million mark in men, when all those of the British Empire were added to the total, as indeed they must be since all bore the same cap badge and belonged to the same great Regiment.

The story is essentially that of the guns—the Colours of the Regiment—and the dominant part they played in a war which was in effect a great artillery duel. It is the story of the artillery in the Great War in France from August 1914 to November 1918. It does not cover those other members of the Royal Regiment of Artillery who fought on land and sea elsewhere in the World. That still needs to be done. It is a great human story of the men who served the guns, and in this great cause 48,949 officers and men gave their lives and countless others nursed their wounds for years afterwards.

The story is about the part the artillery played in the war. It certainly does not do—nor does it attempt to do—justice to the other Arms and Services. Their stories are told elsewhere but, if the reader feels that their part has been underplayed, this is not intentional. It is certainly not the intention to claim more for Gunners than are their just deserts, but rather to record in more human terms than is normally the case the enormous part played by the Regiment in the Great War.

At this stage I must pay tribute to Brigadier General Edgar Anstey, who wrote the history between the wars which reached galley proof stage in 1950. That excellent work is the basis of this book. For many months I checked the detail of Anstey's work against official histories and war diaries and, apart from the most minor detail, I could not discover an error. His work was of the very highest order. I have therefore accepted it as an authority in itself. The reader will not find pages of references and notes, for there is but one—Edgar Anstey. In adjusting his style I have, however, added to it in places, but again only from the Official History of the war, which lay beside me throughout, individual war diaries which I consulted at length in the library at Woolwich (there is still a fund of material in those diaries), from Becke's Order of Battle of the British Army in France, which was also always by my side, and finally from my own visits to the battlefields themselves. Anstey produced the facts and details—I have tried to retain these but to bring them to life from the sources listed above yet leaving the story historically accurate.

Here too I must pay tribute to the work of Alix Bremridge SGA FRSA who has drawn the maps so carefully, so accurately and so beautifully. The positions of the batteries on these maps were taken from contemporary maps and traced from them so the position shown are relatively accurate to their positions at the time. However a reader who wishes to see these positions on the ground will first need to consult the maps themselves in the Imperial War Museum.

Throughout the fifteen years of research into this book I have consulted many people many times, and I could not list them all. However I have had wonderful help and encouragement from General "Bil" Hughes, Brigadiers John Codner, John Lewendon, and Peter Mead, Colonels Maxwell Macfarlane, and Roscoe Turner, Major Denis Rollo, and, latterly Brigadier Paddy Ryan. I have also had help from many members of the staffs of the Royal Artillery Library and Museum (remembering in particular Mrs Bridget Timbers), of the Imperial War Museum, who were particularly helpful over maps and photographs, of the Staff College Library, and of the War Office Library who helped so much with Orders of Battle. I visited many of the battlefields themselves where I always had enormous help from the Commonwealth War Graves Commission who keep the graveyards and memorials in such beautiful condition. They also have my sincere thanks. Finally I thank my wife and many personal assistants and secretaries who, over the years, have typed and retyped the 26 chapters of this book.

My major problem has been the enormous quantity of material available. I therefore set myself two limitations. First, this is not a technical book. It does not trace the development of technical gunnery in detail, though there are many references to technical developments. Second, the book covers the war in France only. Third, I am conscious of not doing full justice to air defence but this is to be covered more fully in another volume of this series. But, in addition, it seemed to me that every battery that fought in France had a right to be mentioned, even if it is only a record of the day it arrived or left. I have told part of the story of many batteries, but in all cases too briefly I fear, and for every one included there are a dozen similar contenders. As one walks the battlefields today, where so much blood was shed, where fear haunted the hearts of men, and where the guns so often saved the day, one realises the immensity of the debt we owe to the men who fought there. No account such as this can do the fullest justice to them. I have tried to report what happened without too much hindsight, and only in the last chapter—the Epilogue—have I allowed my pen to wander into the lessons of it all.

So this book is both memorial and story, and, with luck, a history for the future. If it had a title it would be taken from a picture by Snaffles, inspired by the action of 114th Battery, Royal Field Artillery, as they charged forward into action in front of the hard pressed infantry on the Marne, which he called,

"THE GUNS! THANK GOD, THE GUNS!".

ACKNOWLEDGEMENTS

The author and publishers are grateful to the following for their support and permission to reproduce illustrations:

The Trustees and Director of the Imperial War Museum for numbers 1, 2, 3, 18, 20, 25, 33, 37, 41, 43; John Kemp Welch, Esq., for number 35; Climene Brunker for numbers 4, 5, 12, 13, 27, 28, 45, 47; H. A. Power, Esq., for numbers 34 and 44; B. Matania, Esq., for numbers 17, 32 and 38, Terrence Cuneo, Esq., for number 8; Messrs Fores Ltd., for numbers 11 and 14.

Many illustrations appeared in *The Royal Artillery War Commemoration Book* which was published on behalf of the R.A. War Commemoration Fund by G. Bell and Sons Ltd., London in 1920.

Grateful acknowledgement is also due to K. M. White, Esq., for the preparation of the Index.

The 18-pounder QF gun mark 1.

CHAPTER 1

Mobilisation for War — August 1914

The batteries of the Royal Artillery which mobilised for war in August 1914 were highly trained and efficient; annual firing camps and tactical training had just ended and war was half expected. Mobilisation had been ordered at 1600 hours on the 4th August 1914—the Army was not unprepared, small though it was. Mobilisation plans were ready; after all, the Army had been preparing to fight in France and, for the first time in history, it was to go to fight a war for which it had trained specifically; morale was very high. The regular horse and field batteries were ready, they were up to strength and there was no hasty re-organisation or improvisation so often a feature of the early days of war. Indeed one can read of almost leisurely activity in the batteries destined for France, most had eight to ten days in which to mobilise and most had tested their plans only a short time before. Extra mobilisation stores were available and ready for issue and there was time for quick exercises and route marches to toughen and harden men and horses; but let us pause! What were they like, how were those Gunners of 1914 equipped and organised, how did they assemble for war and move with the British Expeditionary Force—the BEF—to France as the rest of England hurried home from summer holidays?

First, the guns. Regular units were armed with four equipments. The 13-pounder Q.F. gun Mark I and the 18-pounder Q.F. gun Mark I were the armament of all the Royal Horse Artillery and most of the Royal Field Artillery. Well handled, each could fire up to 20 rounds a minute to a maximum range of 6,500 yards. That range could in fact be increased to 7,800 yards by digging in the pole trail. A proportion of the field batteries were armed with the 4.5-inch Q.F. howitzer Mark I, a useful equipment which fired a 35 pound shell to 6,600 yards. Lastly, the Divisional heavy batteries were armed with the 60-pounder B.L. gun Mark I with a maximum range of 10,300 yards.

Territorial field batteries were armed with the 15-pounder B.L. gun, inferior to the 18-pounder in the rate of fire and shell power but with the same maximum range, and with the even older 5-inch B.L. howitzer.

Siege batteries of the Royal Garrison Artillery—RGA—were armed with the much outdated 6-inch 30-cwt B.L. howitzer, the maximum range of which was 5,200 yards.

The whole of the ammunition of the field guns was shrapnel which was fitted with a powder burning fuze set by hand. The adjustment of the critical height of burst was made by visual observation and verbal orders, and required much experience and skill. There was no high explosive shell for field guns. Howitzer batteries carried a small allotment of shrapnel shell but relied primarily on high explosive shell with a direct action fuze which burst on impact. The guns were

1

organised into batteries, and batteries into brigades. The Royal Horse Artillery—
the RHA—was organised into brigades of two batteries (each of six guns and
twelve wagons and an ammunition column. There were two such brigades in the
Cavalry Division and the 5th Independent Cavalry Brigade had its own—J
Battery RHA. The Royal Field Artillery—the RFA—was organised into brigades
of three batteries (each of six guns and twelve wagons) and an ammunition
column. A brigade was commanded by a lieutenant colonel with an adjutant, an
orderly officer and a very small staff.

The brigade signal section was capable of producing line communications to
two batteries only, on the grounds that the brigade commander would always be
close to at least one of his batteries! A divisional artillery consisted of three
brigades of 18-pounders, one brigade of 4.5-inch howitzers and a battery of 60-
pounders. In September 1914, a section of Pom-Poms (one pound shell) was
added to each divisional artillery to act in the anti-aircraft role but it was not a
very effective weapon. In addition there was a divisional ammunition column, an
artillery unit which carried ammunition for all arms. A divisional artillery was
commanded by a Commander Royal Artillery—CRA—a brigadier-general. He
had a Brigade-Major Royal Artillery—BMRA—to help him. The post of CRA
in a division had only been created in 1912 and that of BMRA in 1913, so there
was little experience in handling artillery at this level. What is more, the CRA had
no artillery communications to his brigades and had to manage with whatever the
divisional signal company could spare for him or by sending liaison officers to his
brigade commanders on horseback.

There was no corps artillery as such. At Corps Headquarters the Brigadier-
General, Royal Artillery—BGRA—was an adviser and not a commander. At
Army level there were six siege batteries Royal Garrison Artillery each of four 6-
inch howitzers. These were clumsy out of date weapons but sixteen of the new 9.2-
inch B.L. howitzers had been ordered to replace them just before the declaration
of war.

So much then for the guns and their organisation; now for techniques. The
artillery doctrine for engaging targets in 1914 can be summarised as follows: Gun
positions were either in the open, semi-covered or covered (Covered referred to
being covered from the enemy's view, while semi-covered implied that, though the
guns were covered from view, the gun flashes were not). Voice control of guns by
the battery commander from his observation post (or OP) was deemed essential,
thus, since the battery commander had also to see the enemy, open or semi-covered
positions were more normal. The introduction of the Number 7 Dial Sight and the
Number 3 Director (survey instrument) had however made the occupation of
covered positions easier but observers tended not to be far forward of the gun line.
Though the need for forward observing officers (FOOs) was recognised,
techniques to enable them to operate were not yet fully developed. Indeed, the
only communications which an OP officer had to his guns was a telephone line
reeled out as he moved forward or by using signalling flags or even runners; radio
was not yet available. The OP officer was trained to register his zone (fire a few
shells at known bearings and ranges to see their relative positions to likely targets)
on initially occupying his OP which in any case was close to his guns, and to help
him in this task he had a range finder. Fire discipline was strict and great emphasis
was given on maintaining parallel lines of fire from all six guns.

The 4.5-inch QF howitzer. Unaltered during the war, it was a magnificent field howitzer firing a 35-pound shell to 6,600 yards, and, with its five different charges, capable of firing from behind almost any cover.   *(I.W.M.)*

When a target was seen, a section of two guns was selected to 'range' for the rest. Two opening rounds were fired and a one hundred yard bracket on the target established; when this was split the remaining guns joined in. Targets could be engaged very quickly by well trained batteries using this technique. If the target was infantry attacking in mass, they were stopped by establishing a belt of fire through which they must pass.

In attack, batteries were employed at close range to support the final stages of the assult—there was no preliminary bombardment. Battery commanders selected their gun positions, but artillery brigade commanders often sent patrols forward to reconnoitre areas containing suitable positions and to advise battery commanders accordingly. It was also taught that guns must be fought to the last and that it was most important to provide support to the cavalry or infantry to the last possible moment, even if it did mean the loss of the guns. This occurred many times in the opening battles of 1914 and was to account for great gallantry in the service of the guns.

Ammunition supply was a major problem but a system of re-supply had been perfected in 1914 just before the war started. The system was based on a scale of ammunition being carried with the guns and in the brigade and divisional ammunition columns. This was backed by a scale in the Divisional Ammunition Park and another in the Ordnance Depots. Ammunition was carried forward to re-filling points where it was met by guides from the next echelon and led forward to the next and so on to the guns. The scales in rounds per gun in 1914 were:

	13-Pounder	18-Pounder	4.5-Inch	60-Pounder
In gun limbers	24	24	12	—
In battery wagons	152	152	96	80
In brigade ammunition columns	220	76	48	40
In divisional ammunition columns	—	126	44	60
Total Forward:	396	378	200	180
In divisional ammunition parks	150	150	80	70
In ordnance depots	454	472	520	250
Total in Theatre:	1000	1000	800	500

The ammunition columns were only formed in 1914, indeed some were only formed ten days before embarkation, and it was a highly creditable fact that within a period of a few weeks each division was provided with an ammunition column consisting of 15 officers, 563 men, 723 horses and 113 vehicles. They had to carry ammunition for the cavalry and infantry as well as for the guns. Few of the men had met or trained before and many were unfamiliar with horses. One can imagine the activity as these units trained, fitted harness, teamed up horses and carried out driving drill; they had many more problems than the batteries themselves. The units worked round the clock to be ready for war and were soon to prove their worth in battle.

The 60-pounder BL gun Mark I. Like the 18-pounder gun it was redesigned during the war, but remained the standard medium gun throughout. *(I.W.M.)*

A word here on the problem of providing some 120,000 horses needed for the artillery, the five cavalry brigades and six divisions destined for France. This was one of the most successful features of the mobilisation plans. Some years before 1914, the War Office had carried out a horse census of the UK: lists of suitable horses and remounts were made by specially appointed officers together with their allocation to units in time of war. These were kept up to date and it was this that made the process of mobilisation go far more efficiently than would otherwise have been possible.

What of the state of training? By July 1914 all field artillery batteries had completed their annual practice camps and were in a high state of technical training. Much had been done to improve artillery co-operation with the cavalry and infantry. Officers of these two Arms had attended the artillery practice camps, and batteries had taken part in brigade exercises. Commanders of all Arms had studied the problems of the use of artillery in battle. By 1914 the controversy which had continued since the Boer War on the grouping of artillery had been more or less resolved. The custom was developed of allotting the same artillery brigades to support the same cavalry and infantry brigades whenever possible. For the first time we read of infantry brigade commanders complaining if they were not allotted "their" batteries. The result was that in 1914 the Army had developed a considerable sense of confidence and understanding between Arms; this was to prove invaluable and was to develop throughout the War.

One problem remained unsolved. Training had revealed the disadvantage of having separate gun and howitzer brigades. It was planned to re-organise field brigades to consist of two gun batteries and one howitzer battery, but this fell through. Ultimately the experience of battle resulted in an organisation of four batteries per brigade, three gun and one howitzer.

The heavy artillery had not fared so well. Due to a shortage of funds prior to 1914, heavy batteries had been reduced to twelve horses only. Extra horses had to be hired once per year for manoeuvres, and this had happened in 1914. Batteries of siege artillery fared even worse and had last manoeuvred in 1912, and then only with a number of hired horses. There had, however, been a practice camp in 1913 when trials were conducted in observation of fire using aircraft! Heavy and siege artillery procedures had, nevertheless, been brought into line with those of field branch, and the new Number 2 Director, a great improvement, had been introduced.

Lastly, the commanders. The regular Gunner officers of 1914 were experienced and well trained. Artillery officers fell into that special group of men who were professional, intelligent and fighting leaders. They fell into the socially acceptable gap between the pure warrior who fought with his hands and the military technician who was beginning to appear in the armies of 1914. They were skilled not only in gunnery but also in cavalry and infantry tactics, and most had battle experience from South Africa and India. It is interesting to see how so many of those early artillery commanders in 1914 reached high rank. Milne, CRA 4th Division in 1914, was to become Army Commander in Salonika and later Chief of the Imperial General Staff (CIGS); Horne, Brigadier-General Royal Artillery (BGRA) I Corps, became Commander First Army; Du Cane started as Brigadier-General General Staff (BGGS) III Corps, became Quartermaster General and ended the war commanding XV Corps. Montgomery went to France as a Major, a grade two staff officer in 4th Division and left as Major-General General Staff (MGGS) Fourth Army. Holland was CRA of 8th Division in 1914 and ended the war commanding I Corps. Perhaps none were to rise as far as Ironside. He graduated from the Staff College in August 1914, went to France as a Major, and ended the war as Army Commander in Russia!

Some were not to rise so far but contributed much to artillery doctrine, like Birch, who started the war as Commander 7 Brigade RHA and ended as GOC RA, Fourth Army. Few men contributed more to artillery tactics except perhaps Uniacke, who started commanding 5 Brigade RHA and ended as Inspector General of Training for British Armies in France.

So mobilisation was complete. It had gone smoothly and well. There was excitement in the air; after all, it would be over by Christmas! The BEF had been training specifically for war in Europe alongside the French, and it had come. Preparations had been sound and training thorough; there was a sense of excitement and confidence everywhere. Britain's best ever regular army left her shores; formations from Britain sailed from Southampton and those from Ireland (5th and 6th Divisions) from Dublin, Cork and Belfast. They landed at Le Havre, Rouen and Boulogne and concentrated around Maubeuge, near the French frontier with Belgium and some twenty miles south of Mons where advance parties had prepared billets for them. News of the violence of the German attack through Belgium reached the men as they arrived. News of the gallant defence by the Belgian Army inspired them but the Germans were still ruthlessly advancing— time was short, battle was near. They had aimed to concentrate by 14th August, but it was the 20th before all was complete. Such was the atmosphere in 1914 that delays were caused by congestion on the British railways; it was, after all, bank holiday in England!

The Order of Battle of the Artillery of the BEF which was to fight at Mons was:

The Cavalry Division
Commander Royal Horse Artillery—Colonel B.F. Drake.

3 Brigade RHA—Lieutenant Colonel R.W. Breeks.
  D Battery RHA—Major G. Gillson.
  E Battery RHA—Major A.S. Forman.
  Brigade Ammunition Column.

7 Brigade RHA—Lieutenant Colonel N.F. Birch.
  I Battery RHA—Major W.G. Thompson.
  L Battery RHA—Major The Honourable W.D. Sclater-Booth
  Brigade Ammunition Column.

5th Independent Cavalry Brigade
  J Battery RHA—Major H.S. Seligman.
  Brigade Ammunition Column—Captain C.D.W. Uniacke.

1st Divisional Artillery
  CRA—Brigadier-General N.D. Findlay.
  25 Brigade RFA—113th, 114th, 115th Batteries.
  26 Brigade RFA—116th, 117th, 118th Batteries.
  39 Brigade RFA—46th, 51st, 54th Batteries.
  43 Howitzer Brigade RFA—30th, 40th, 57th Batteries.
  26th Heavy Battery RGA (60-pounders).

2nd Divisional Artillery
CRA—Brigadier-General E.M. Perceval.
34 Brigade RFA—22nd, 50th, 70th Batteries.
36 Brigade RFA—15th, 48th, 71st Batteries.
41 Brigade—9th, 16th, 17th Batteries.
44 Howitzer Brigade RFA— 47th, 56th, 60th Batteries.
35th Heavy Battery RGA (60-pounders).

3rd Divisional Artillery
CRA—Brigadier-General F.D.V. Wing.
23 Brigade RFA—107th, 108th, 109th Batteries.
40 Brigade RFA—6th, 23rd, 49th Batteries.
42 Brigade RFA—29th, 41st, 45th Batteries.
30 Howitzer Brigade RFA—128th, 129th, 130th Batteries.
48th Heavy Battery RGA (60-pounders).

5th Divisional Artillery
CRA—Brigadier-General J.E.W. Headlam.
15 Brigade RFA—11th, 52nd, and 80th Batteries.
27 Brigade RFA—119th, 120th, 121st Batteries.
28 Brigade RFA—122nd, 123rd, 124th Batteries.
8 Howitzer Brigade RFA—37th, 61st, 65th Batteries.
108th Heavy Battery RGA (60-pounders).

CHAPTER 2

Into Battle — Mons!

See maps 1, 2, 3, 4 and 5

The French knew of the Schlieffen Plan and expected a major German flanking movement through Belgium; their plan to counter this was threefold. First, they would attack strongly on their right to Lorraine, with two Armies and, at the same time, they would attack with three Armies in the centre to dislocate any possible German movements there. Next, the left of the centre Armies, the Fifth under Lanrezac, would swing round the German right in Belgium. The BEF would join with Lanrezac on the left and link up with the Belgian Army. Lanrezac had ten French divisions plus the British (four infantry, one cavalry division and one cavalry brigade). These, coupled with the six Belgian divisions, gave Lanrezac twenty-one divisions to turn the German flank on the Meuse.

The BEF advanced into Belgium from its concentration area near Maubeuge on the morning of 21st August. Meanwhile, further south the French plans were already going wrong. The attack in Lorraine on their right was severely defeated by the Germans, mainly due to the French mass attack technique and their over reliance on the effect of their 75mm field guns—the famous '75s'. In the centre they pushed into the Ardennes, met the Germans head on, were thrown back and a threat developed towards Namur. Meanwhile on the left, the Belgian Army had been driven back into Antwerp and already Lanrezac's Fifth Army was in a salient; *two German Armies, the Third under Hausen and the Second under Bülow* were converging onto it; *the German First Army (von Kluck)* was to the north passing through Brussels and swinging south as the British approached Mons. Such then was the situation as the BEF marched into battle. Captain Brownlow writes in his book "The Breaking of the Storm"—"I have seen Sordet's cavalry march through Inchy on the eve of Le Cateau; I have seen the Iron Corps of France march through the square at Ypres; I've seen the 1st Canadian Division marching to St. Julien before the gas attack; I've seen Indian troops going into action for the first time on European soil; I've seen the Australians on their way to the attack of Pozières; but I have no remembrance to equal in any way that of the old regiments of the BEF marching to the Battle of Mons".

Although the German wheel through Belgium had extended much further north and west than had been expected, the French did not alter their plans. It was assumed that, when von Kluck swung his armies south, his right would be to the east of Mons and that the British would overlap him to the west. Sir John French was therefore ordered to put his centre on Mons and wheel his left flank north east towards Nivelles. The 1st Division of I Corps under Major General S.H. Lomax was on the right, with the task of closing the gap with the French Fifth Army, and by 0200 hours on the 23rd August the extreme right—1st Guards Brigade—were at Grand Reng and trying to contact the French. Meanwhile II Corps under General Sir H.S. Smith-Dorrien took up positions along the Mons-Condé Canal. On their right was 3rd Division under Major General H.I.W. Hamilton, in the centre 5th Division under Major General Sir C. Fergusson and on the left the 19th Independent Infantry Brigade under Brigadier General P.R. Robertson, which linked with the French 84th Territorial Division.

During the 22nd August, the Cavalry Division under Major General E.H.H. Allenby had been covering the left flank and while doing so had made first contact with the enemy advance guard. C Squadron 4th Dragoons drew first blood and it was at 1100 hours on the 23rd August that E Battery RHA, commanded by Major A.S. Forman, came into action at Bray some four miles north east of Harmignies and fired the first artillery round of the War from C sub-section, the Number 4 gun. The German guns replied and succeeded in wounding one horse of the Battery, in the head.

During the night 22–23 August bad news arrived. Two of the French corps of the Fifth Army had been thrown back, although the XVIII Corps on the French left held firm. An alarming gap, some nine miles wide, now existed between the British right and the French. Moreover, during the 22nd, no less than five German corps had been identified heading south from the area of Charleroi. As a result, Lanrezac requested Sir John French to attack east and relieve the pressure on the Fifth Army. This was clearly impossible, it would have been suicidal to attack across the front of the advancing Germans. Sir John French therefore ordered his I Corps to consolidate its position on the right of II Corps. 2nd Division moved to carry out this order during the night. The initial deployment of the BEF was nevertheless risky, all divisions were committed, there was no real reserve, the front was extended and thinly held for the tactics of 1914, nor was it well suited to defence; it was certainly unsuitable for the use of artillery by the methods then in use. In front of I Corps, under Lieutenant General Sir Douglas Haig, the ground was open and undulating and good fields of fire were possible, but no attack developed there. The story was very different in the II Corps sector; its right was thrust forward into a small salient at Nimy to include the bridge at Obourg and its centre strung out along the Condé canal with its left at the bridge at Le Petit Crepin, a front of nearly twenty miles. The most prominent feature on the right was Bois la Haut, a steep partly wooded hill offering good observation to the north east in the 3rd Division's area. Next, and holding the centre as far as Le Petit Crepin road bridge, was the 5th Division.

The ground in front of 5th Division was dreary in the extreme, the approaches were masked by rows of houses, factories and slag heaps, and a complex system of drains and streams dotted with clumps of trees made observation and movement along the canal extremely difficult. The canal itself was no real obstacle, being little more than twenty yards across and six feet deep. There were at that time some eighteen bridges across the canal in this sector, and these were to affect the shape of the first day's fighting. We must not forget too that the full horror of war has not yet been felt, few civilians had left the area, indeed trains were still running and families were on their way to Mass as the first shells crashed into the Summer countryside on that fateful Sunday morning—23rd August, 1914.

Troops moving up to the concentration area by train in 1914. From a painting by Captain Gilbert Holiday RFA. *(Royal Artillery Institution)*

It was hard to find either gun positions or observation posts which could cover properly the approaches to the main defensive positions, or indeed protect the outpost line. Few guns could cover properly more than the narrowest arcs of fire; the line selected had the gravest shortcomings for the use of artillery. True, Sir John French did not realise the strength of the German forces about to be unleashed upon him, but it was nevertheless a mistake to deploy an army in such a way that its guns could not be brought to bear properly.

August 23rd started with a misty dawn, it then drizzled for a while but by mid-morning the sun came out again. The fighting on that day can be considered in three parts; first, the attack on the extreme left of I Corps; second, the assault on the Nimy Salient and third, the attack on II Corps. Little occurred on I Corps front throughout the day. 1st Divisional Artillery under Brigadier-General N.D. Findlay was deployed in fairly open positions in depth behind the foremost infantry, the nearest gun positions being only 1,700 yards behind them. The guns of 2nd Division under Brigadier-General E.M. Perceval were similarly deployed on the left, with 50th and 70th Batteries of 34 Brigade RFA in semi-covered positions just behind the infantry firing line. They opened fire on German cavalry patrols causing some casualties but in so doing drew fire onto themselves from German guns near Binche. The flashes from the British guns made them easy to locate and they were soon heavily shelled, only saving themselves from heavy casualties by their gun pits. Thus even on the first day the weakness of open or semi-covered positions was demonstrated. Later in the day, 70th Battery, with two sections well forward and one in the rear, was engaged by two German howitzer batteries while it was engaging infantry at 2,300 yards—the Germans put three guns out of action with splinters through the outer buffer cases. 34 Brigade RFA, suffered two officers and three men killed (all in 70th Battery) and twenty-seven wounded. During the night 23–24th August, 70th Battery was withdrawn and replaced by 22nd Battery of the same brigade. The 41 Brigade RFA was in action with 16th and 17th Batteries engaging enemy infantry and cavalry; its 9th Battery was in reserve with 6th Infantry Brigade. Nevertheless no real attack developed on 2nd Division's front.

Meanwhile on the II Corps front the Germans were pressing home their attacks. 3rd Divisional Artillery under Brigadier-General F.D.V. Wing had a particularly knotty problem. The Bois la Haut, while it gave good observation, made the selection of gun positions particularly hard. Whereas it sloped gently from the north and east, it dropped precipitously on the west and south. 40 Brigade RFA got into action somewhat precariously, between 1000 and 1100 hours. The 6th Battery was in a covered position on the eastern shoulder facing north east; the 23rd Battery was in a semi-covered position on the top of the hill facing east and only a few hundred yards behind the infantry firing line. The 49th Battery had one section on Point 62 facing north (at the northern end of Mont Panisel) and two sections on Bois la Haut facing north east. It is significant to note that 6th Battery opened fire at enemy guns and infantry at 3,200 yards, 23rd Battery at infantry at 3,000 yards and the section of 49th Battery on Point 62 at 1,500 yards! 42 Brigade RFA (Lieutenant Colonel G.H. Geddes) prepared positions in the area of Nouvelles but was not engaged on 23rd August. The 23 Brigade RFA (Lieutenant-Colonel A.T. Butler) was similarly only slightly engaged; 107th Battery had a section on Mont Erebus, due south of Mons, to cover one of the

Field Artillery moving to the front by line of march. From a painting by Gilbert Holiday.   *(R.A.I.)*

canal bridges. 108th Battery (Major H.E. Carey) was not engaged, while the 109th Battery had two sections in action on the outskirts of Mons, and a third in the rear of them. The 30 Howitzer Brigade RFA (Lieutenant-Colonel W.C. Staveley) did not arrive at Bavai from Valenciennes until 1500 hours. Thus, although there was fierce fighting in the Division's front, the artillery were unable to help much. The batteries on Bois la Haut could do little to assist the hard pressed 8th Infantry Brigade fighting to repel two German divisions converging on the eastern side of the salient. To the north the German guns were concentrated on the Brigade and on the section of 49th Battery, the only British guns firing north. By 1600 hours the infantry fell back on the guns and this section, notably well handled, helped for a time to check the enemy swarming after them.

The situation in the salient at Nimy was now critical. The 8th Infantry Brigade had withdrawn to the Bois la Haut and were being hard pressed by the *German 17th Division*. This left the right flank of 9th Infantry Brigade, the 4th Middlesex and the 4th Fusiliers, exposed and by 1515 hours these two battalions were withdrawn. As Mons was evacuated so the rear of 8th Infantry Brigade and all the guns on the Bois la Haut became exposed. The Lincolns gallantly checked the German pursuit through the town and the guns of 109th Battery (Major S.F.Metcalf) did some execution. Some Germans, however, worked their way south from the town and under the sheer slopes of the Bois la Haut; consequently, when 23rd Battery was ordered to withdraw down a sunken lane, it ran unexpectedly into them. The Battery had its leading teams and drivers shot down but, using its rifles and together with its escort of Gordon Highlanders, drove the enemy into Hyon.

Meanwhile, more Germans attacked the Bois la Haut, but were driven off. The firing alarmed 6th Battery in its exposed position on the south eastern slopes and its Commander, Major E.W.S. Brooke, ordered his battery into a position of all round defence since it would soon be dark. It was clear that Bois la Haut must be given up, and at last light 8th Infantry Brigade was ordered to evacuate it. Accordingly, 6th Battery man-handled its guns down the slope, hooked in and withdrew at 2300 hours. 23rd Battery, having cleared the lane to Hyon, withdrew under the very noses of the Germans just before midnight, and moved to Nouvelles via Spiennes. 49th Battery had already withdrawn and by 0300 hours 24th August, 41 Brigade RFA was in Nouvelles with 8th Infantry Brigade. By dusk 9th Infantry Brigade had withdrawn to Frameries and all 3rd Divisional Artillery was in action between the two villages, among the slag heaps, mines and factories.

We must now turn to the fortunes of 5th Division, next in the line, and located further west of Mons itself along the canal. Here conditions were very different, though no easier, and the CRA, Brigadier-General J.E.W. Headlam, was able to take a firmer grip of his artillery than were the other artillery commanders. Fields of fire and observation were almost impossible along the canal and the divisional commander had seen the very real possibility of having to give up the line of the canal in favour of the higher ground to the south. Consequently, the CRA reconnoitred gun positions south of the river Haine, but north of a line through Dour and Wasmes. This line was to be held by 14th Infantry Brigade on the left, and 15th Infantry Brigade on the right. Accordingly, Brigadier Headlam deployed his artillery as follows:

a. Left:

28 Brigade RFA (Lt Col E.C. Cameron)
122nd Battery RFA (Major G.S. Sanders)
123rd Battery RFA (Major G.H.W. Bayley)
124th Battery RFA (Major G.R.V. Kinsman)

b. Right:

27 Brigade RFA (Lt Col W.H. Onslow)
119th Battery RFA (Major E.W. Alexander)
121st Battery RFA (Major C.N.B. Ballard)
37th Howitzer Battery RFA (Major E.H. Jones)

c. Under the CRA:

120th Battery RFA, 27 Brigade RFA
(Major C.S. Holland) deployed forward.

15 Brigade RFA (Lt Col C.F. Stevens)
11th Battery RFA (Major P.W.B. Henning)
52nd Battery RFA (Major A.C.R. Nutt)
80th Battery RFA (Major R.A. Brierley)

8 Howitzer Brigade RFA (Lt Col E.J. Duffuss)
61st Battery RFA (Major F.A. Wilson)
65th Battery RFA (Major J.E.C. Livingston-Learmouth)

All batteries selected their own positions, moved into action and dug in.

Meanwhile the foremost guns of the Division, those of 120th Battery, came under heavy rifle and shell fire during the morning of 23rd August, but their return fire, coupled with the fire of the infantry, repulsed the Germans. They were deployed, dug in, on the canal towpath at St. Ghislain. Nevertheless by 1200 hours, due to heavy enemy pressure, the Battery had to be withdrawn having suffered a number of casualties. One section came into action on the side of a slag heap at 1400 hours, and fired on enemy guns to good effect all afternoon. It was at this section's observation post that the Battery Commander, Major C.S. Holland, was killed by a rifle bullet during the afternoon. He was a popular, competent officer well known through the Regiment for his love of practical joking; a sad loss to the Battery on its first day of battle. By 1900 hours parties of enemy had worked round behind this section and were firing at the detachments from the rear. Accordingly, the section was withdrawn with the rest of the Battery to Bois de Boussu. During the withdrawal a gun was lost, as was another from another section, which had been brought into action independently. This was how the end of the first day's fighting came about for 120th Battery; almost the only one of the Divisional Artillery to be engaged.

119th Battery was in action near the Bois d'Hamme. It opened fire on the infantry in Ville Pommerouel and during the afternoon "searched" for enemy guns. It was joined in this task by the guns of 108th Heavy Battery RGA (Major

C. de Sausmarez) firing from a position near Dour. There was great jubilation on the guns as a huge explosion occurred with the third round indicating a hit on some ammunition. At 1700 hours the 52nd (Major A.C.R. Nutt) and 124th Batteries (Major G.R.V. Kinsman) were ordered forward to assist, but were too late to be of use.

So ended the first day of the battle of Mons. The BEF had had its baptism of fire, and had proved its fighting qualities. The Germans got a shock; they had despised the British and were astonished as they closed to the canal at the accuracy and concentration of their fire. They had never experienced the "mad minute" of concentrated rifle fire which the British infantry had perfected. To achieve it, every man aimed to get off 15–20 rounds and some experts managed 30! Walter Bloem, a German novelist, was commanding a company of the *Brandenburg Regiment* that day, and reports how his battalion commander said to him "Our first battle has been a heavy, an unheard of heavy defeat, and that against the English; the English we laughed at!" The British were amazed to hear the German bugles sounding "cease-fire" as the evening shadows gathered.

The result was essentially favourable to the British. They had survived their first day of the shattering crash of modern war and, apart from the withdrawal of 8th Infantry Brigade in the Nimy salient, they still held the ground they started with. Nevertheless, the BEF was now confident that, man for man, it was superior to its enemies. There was, however, one sad result in that the events of the day bred a distrust of the French who gave on the right.

The Gunners, on the other hand, were disappointed with their first day of battle. True, they had fought gallantly, displaying coolness, skill and courage wherever they did fight, but so few guns ever really came to grips with the enemy. True, also, that the conditions for their employment could scarcely have been worse. Little of their training could have been put into practice amongst the pit heads, factories and slag heaps of the battlefield. Some guns had been fought in the infantry firing line at ranges of only a few hundred yards, others had been fought in the streets, with their detachments fighting off the enemy with their rifles. Batteries were often fought as separate sections, these were frequently surrounded and only crept away under the noses of the enemy. There were two reasons for this failure to use the guns properly. First, Sir John French chose to fight his main action forward along the canal without due consideration of the ability of his guns to strike at the enemy as he closed to it, and second, the concept for the use of artillery was to hold it well forward and to fight it by batteries. There was as yet no way of concentrating the guns of a divisional artillery deployed further back, so keeping them relatively free from direct fire from enemy infantry. The reason for the second factor was purely one of organisation and training, and this was quickly put right during the next few months of the war. Why, however, did Sir John French fail to consider his guns? Was he not properly advised? It is hard to find any record of any artillery advice he did get, yet there is no evidence to show that there was any dispute between himself and his senior gunner, Major-General W.F.L. Lindsay. The reason was, in effect, more simple. On the morning of 23rd August, Sir John French assumed that his task was to check the leading elements of a relatively weak enemy force and then to resume his advance on the 24th and it was only during the day that he realized the size of the enemy forces opposing him. By 1700 hours, reports reaching GHQ, at Bavai, indicated that *von Kluck's First Army* would reach Valenciennes well outside the British left and not as was expected, directly opposite it. The British 4th Division was moving up on the left but could not be in action for a further forty-eight hours. By this time, too, disturbing reports of withdrawal began to come in from the French Army on the right. Accordingly at 2400 hours, Sir John changed his plan for the morrow and told II Corps, ". . . to stand the attack on ground now occupied, and to strengthen your positions by every means possible during the night". There was no talk yet of withdrawal, nor was there a full appreciation at GHQ of the troops' desperate need for rest rather than protection.

At midnight on 23rd August, Sir John French's liaison officer to Lanrezac, Lieutenant Spears, arrived at GHQ with the surprising news that the French Fifth Army had been roughly handled and were going to withdraw to a line twenty-two miles south east of Mons, running through Maubeuge to Solre le Chateau. This would leave a wide gap between the BEF and the French, and leave the former dangerously advanced beyond the French left. A withdrawal from Mons now became inevitable. The news from Lanrezac also confirmed Sir John's developing distrust of his neighbour, who had taken no action to inform the British of his intentions; Spears had been acting on his own initiative!

As the staffs at Army and Corps HQ began feverishly to turn their minds to withdrawal plans, they realised the precarious position of the BEF. It was unbalanced. Its four divisions were all in the line facing in two directions; I Corps, with 1st and 2nd Divisions, was in line facing east from Grand Reng to Harmignies while 3rd and 5th Divisions of II Corps faced north from Nouvelles to Thulin. Moreover, during the day's fighting a gap had occurred between these two divisions, and 5th Infantry Brigade of 2nd Division had been moved in to fill it.

It is astonishing now to read how the lack of contact between the British and the French was allowed to continue, and how the only messages were cryptic comments between Sir John and Lanrezac. Yet it is equally astonishing to read of the vague plan for withdrawal put forward to Sir John. He appears to have chosen a line through Bavai and told his two Corps Commanders that I Corps was to cover II Corps, otherwise they must get on as best they could. This is probably an over simplification, but in essence it accounts for the confusion and lack of control which existed during the subsequent withdrawal. This was particularly so since the two Corps Commanders were unable to meet until mid-day 24th August, by which time the withdrawal had been in progress some seven hours! It is difficult to understand how Sir John French failed to realise the threat to his left flank; had he done so and ordered I Corps to withdraw first, less confusion might have followed. At it was I Corps stood fast during the day under no threat of attack, while II Corps tried to execute the most complex of all military manoeuvres, that of withdrawing while in close contact with the enemy.

The events of 24th August are confused; the withdrawal plan and its execution had little in common. It was, however, a better day for the guns. They started in better positions and had some excellent shooting.

3rd Division of II Corps began to withdraw at 0600 hours 24th August. 8th Infantry Brigade got away without much trouble, but the rear guards of 7th Infantry Brigade (2nd South Lancashires) and of 9th Infantry Brigade (1st Lincolns) did not fare so well. 23 Brigade RFA was in its overnight positions with 109 Battery at Frameries and with 9th Infantry Brigade and 107th and 108th Batteries close by. The latter two opened fire at 0415 hours on enemy infantry and guns massing north of Frameries. The enemy then assaulted after a quick bombardment and all the batteries found excellent targets among the attacking Germans, whose action failed due to the combined fire of the guns of the Brigade and the rapid small arms fire of the infantry. At 1000 hours the infantry withdrew, and the batteries accompanied them, frequently coming into action to give cover. Both infantry and artillery finally went into bivouac near Bavai. Meanwhile 42 Brigade RFA withdrew covering the new rearguard—the Worcesters—but, at 1030 hours, had to begin to engage enemy infantry approaching Frameries. The Brigade finally retired to St. Waast. The remainder of 3rd Divisional Artillery withdrew without incident.

The German artillery opened fire on 5th Division before dawn on 24th August and soon their infantry followed it up. It will be recalled that the CRA, Brigadier Headlam, had divided the divisional defensive position into two sectors. First, the right sector. One section of 121st Battery was in the infantry firing line of 1st Dorsets under Lieutenant H.C. Chapman. He had one of his guns in the firing line itself and another a little further to the rear. At 0300 hours the enemy appeared between the buildings and slag heaps to his front. The range was 750 yards! His forward gun immediately engaged and silenced the enemy machine guns. At 0600 hours an enemy battery opened fire on the section and the rear gun, being exposed, was withdrawn. At 0700 hours the infantry were relieved by a fresh battalion, who were unable to get forward to Lieutenant Chapman and his now isolated, remaining gun. He nevertheless fought the gun until 0800 hours when the position became untenable. He decided to send the breach block to the rear, and then to manhandle the gun to a nearby burnt-out cottage, and try to get it back from there. In spite of close-aimed small arms fire, he managed this almost impossible feat. On his own initiative Driver Busket came forward to the cottage with a team and the limber, and together they limbered up and galloped across 200 yards of fire-swept ground to safety. Meanwhile, the rest of the battery was dug in further back, alongside the four remaining guns of 120th Battery who had arrived from their battle on the canal at midnight. Just in front of the two field batteries was 37th Howitzer Battery, which carried out some very accurate shoots against enemy infantry debouching from Hornu; at ranges of up to 2,000 yards the howitzer shells tore the enemy to pieces. So impressive was this shooting that the Dorsets sent a message of congratulation to the Battery. By 1400 hours the two 18-pounder batteries were under both shell and rifle fire. At 1430 hours a staff officer of 14th Infantry Brigade galloped up with an order for the 1st Manchesters to retire, and he told Lieutenant Colonel W.H. Onslow of 27 Brigade RFA that orders for the withdrawal of the guns had been issued. Onslow, however, refused to withdraw without a written order, and both the Manchesters and the 1st KOYLI refused to leave the guns. A brisk battle ensued until written orders arrived and, with the help of men from the Manchesters, the guns were manhandled back under fire.

28 Brigade RFA was dug in by batteries on the left sector around Bois de Boussu. At 1000 hours, when there was still no contact there, four guns per battery were withdrawn without having fired. By mid-day enemy infantry were seen approaching and were engaged at 3500 yards but the weight of fire was small since most of the guns had gone. Indeed, the German infantry could be seen dodging the shelled areas! Soon a German battery galloped up and was unwise enough to attempt to come into action in the open. It was quickly silenced by the section of 122nd Battery. The sections eventually retired at about 1230 hours when the enemy were on slag heaps only 600 yards away. Meanwhile 15 Brigade RFA and the 8 Howitzer Brigade RFA had few targets and withdrew without incident. 108th Heavy Battery RGA was in action near Dour but did not fire.

While 3rd and 5th Division were withdrawing in the centre, there developed on the left a dramatic cavalry and artillery battle which, when the story became known, swept the headlines in Britain.

The Germans had been trying since before dawn to conduct an enveloping movement round the British left flank, but they did not know where that flank was, or what it contained. They thus conducted a wide sweep to the west through Quiévrain. General Allenby advanced the 1st Cavalry Division in the early hours of the day to look for the enemy but he found no one, since the Germans were still wheeling further to their right. However, by now the attack on 5th Division's left, described earlier, was developing and its commander, Sir Charles Fergusson, quickly ordered a rearguard, composed of the 1st Norfolks, 1st Cheshires and 119th Battery RFA, all under command of Lieutenant Colonel C.R. Ballard of the Norfolks, to occupy some high ground facing west towards Quiévrain; he also asked the Cavalry Division to conform and to assist in covering this open flank. The position was good with good fields of fire. The 2nd and 3rd Cavalry Brigades withdrew to the area west and south of Audregnies, and 3 Brigade RHA conformed, with D (Major G. Gillson) and E Batteries RHA (Major A.S. Forman) taking up positions just east of Angres; L Battery (Major The Honourable W.D. Sclater-Booth) of 7 Brigade RHA galloped into action behind the Norfolks and just behind the railway, north of Audregnies.

At 1230 hours German attacks began from the area of Quiévrain and Baisieux. To give Colonel Ballard time to get his blocking force into position, Brigadier De Lisle, commanding 2nd Cavalry Brigade, ordered the 9th Lancers and two troops of the 4th Dragoon Guards to make a mounted attack, covered by the guns of L Battery RHA. The attack was promptly executed, and the cavalry charged across the enemy front straight towards nine German batteries in action east of Quiévrain. They began to suffer heavily and, realising the impossibility of pressing home their attack, they wheeled across the front of the Norfolks and Cheshires to reform. The charge achieved little, but it did surprise the Germans and delayed their advance, thus gaining time for the hard pressed Colonel Ballard. Shortly after the charge all twelve battalions of the *German 8th Division* began to attack the rearguard from Quiévrain in mass formation. L Battery did great execution, bursting its shrapnel low with terrible effect. Almost unaided, the Battery drove this mass of German infantry back into the village. Machine gun and rifle fire from the Norfolks and Cheshires did much slaughter to those who escaped the guns; a section of 119th Battery joined in but came under very heavy fire and was forced to withdraw. As it came out of action it became involved with the cavalry retiring after its charge. The section commander, Lieutenant C.O'D. Preston, managed to extricate his guns and wagons and come into action again firing first on German cavalry, and then on infantry and machine guns, at ranges of 200 yards! The section was in action about 400 yards to the right of the rest of the Battery but the fire was now so intense that it had to be withdrawn.

Sergeant Macartney, the Number 1 of the first gun, manhandled his gun to safety and then ran back to assist with the other. The fire was so intense and losses to horses so severe that one wagon had to be abandoned. Lieutenant Preston, although four times wounded, attempted time and again to save it before he fell, unable to stand, and had to be put into an ambulance. Sergeant Macartney then took command of the section and led it to the rear having lost its commander, one sergeant, and ten men. Meanwhile, the rest of the Battery was engaged in a duel with two German batteries near Quiévrain which it silenced. Thus the German attempt at outflanking the left of the BEF was thwarted. They tried again further left but ran into the fire of D and E Batteries RHA and 1st and 3rd Cavalry Brigades. Again they failed with heavy losses. Major Tom Bridges of the 4th Dragoons, escaping from the German lines after the cavalry charge, wrote that he noted "two British guns firing away at the advancing German hordes as steadily as if they had been on the range at Okehampton". These must have been guns of L Battery. All laurels for the day would by now be with the British except for one failure; orders to 1st Cheshires to retire failed to reach the battalion. Three separate messages failed to get through and the gallant battalion, with its commanding officer hit, the enemy closing in on three sides and all its ammunition expended, was forced to surrender late in the evening. Only about two hundred all ranks escaped.

When 2nd Cavalry Brigade began to withdraw, the two remaining sections of 119th Battery came under enfilade fire from fresh German batteries, and soon from a machine gun at close range. Sergeant-Major F. Smyth of the Battery organised all spare gunners along the railway embankment alongside the position. Here they were joined by two machine guns of the 9th Lancers. Captain J.C. Walford moved the Battery wagons back some 300 yards under cover of the embankment, and then took over the OP while the Battery Commander, Major E.W. Alexander, reported to Colonel Onslow who ordered him to withdraw, but it was too late to get the teams up to the guns. By this time the Germans were on a mine dump only a few hundred yards away in force, and bullets were falling thick and fast among the guns. Major Alexander accordingly ordered them to be manhandled back the 300 yards to the shelter of the embankment. However, the soil was so heavy that only one gun could be moved at a time. The situation was indeed grave when Captain Francis Grenfell of the 9th Lancers came up with forty or fifty men and offered assistance. Together with the gunners and under the cover of the gunners on the embankment and the dismounted Lancers, they got all the guns and most of the wagons back under cover; a gallant and fine effort. Their troubles were not yet over, for the level crossing behind them was blocked by a blazing wagon; however the guns found another way out and thundered off to safety within 300 yards of the enemy on the mine dump; the day had been saved by the steadiness of the drivers. The Battery lost one officer, one sergeant, twenty-eight men, and thirty-six horses, but both Major Alexander and Captain Grenfell earned the Victoria Cross for their exploits in saving the guns at Elouges. Major

The action at Elouges. From a watercolour by J C Walford. Captain Walford painted a collection of over forty watercolours during the course of the war on the Western Front. The collection was presented by his family to the Regiment, and may now be seen in its museum. (*R.A.I.*)

Alexander's citation read, "... Major Alexander handled his battery against overwhelming odds with such conspicuous success that all his guns were saved, notwithstanding that, owing to heavy casualties, they had to be withdrawn by himself and three other men—all that were left available. This action enabled the retirement of the 5th Division to be carried out without serious loss. Subsequently, Major Alexander rescued a wounded man under heavy fire with the greatest gallantry and devotion to duty". This was the first of eighteen Victoria Crosses to be won by the Royal Regiment before November 1918.

Though the Norfolks lost over two hundred men and the Cheshires nearly six hundred, the cavalry, these two battalions, L Battery RHA and 119th Battery RFA had checked the advance of a German Corps, so saving the left flank of the British Army! Such was the indomitable spirit of the Regiments and Batteries of the BEF.

Reports of the heavy fighting at Elouges caused the CRA of 5th Division to prepare a rear guard position just north of Athis. This was occupied by most of the artillery of 5th Division but, as nothing materialized, at last light the artillery again fell back to positions near Houdain covering Bavai. 15 Brigade RFA took up positions between St. Waast and Bavai, and 108th Heavy Battery RGA was at Wargnies-le-Grand with 27 Brigade RFA. There is no doubt that 5th Divisional Artillery had been well handled and many lessons were learnt that day. In retrospect it is clear now that it was a mistake to put only one battery in support of the blocking force—but then such thoughts are always easy in retrospect! So ended the second day's fighting at Mons. More severe than the first, but not altogether a failure. Nevertheless, the withdrawal had begun; it was not yet a retreat but the men were tired—very tired indeed.

Three lessons had now clearly emerged. First, open or semi-covered positions were dangerous; they meant that the guns inevitably became involved in the same fighting as the infantry they were supporting, thus depriving the latter of maximum support at the most critical periods. Second, the British doctrine to burst shrapnel low was extremely sound. It was noticeable how the high bursting German shrapnel lost much effect whereas the low burst of the 13 and 18-pounders was devastating amidst the massed German infantry. Third, it was now abundantly clear that CRAs must have better communications in order to be able to influence the battle. The concept of a corps artillery had not yet been born. Had it been, massed guns might well have stopped the German right hook. As it was, 3rd and 5th Divisions had between them four artillery brigades which, although within a few miles of the threatened sector, did not fire a shot. The Germans had learnt this lesson and later at Le Cateau they sent the whole of their reserve 4th Corps artillery to support their cavalry.

Both British Corps continued their withdrawal starting early on 25th August and Sir John French decided to send them one each side of the Forêt de Mormal, a thick wooded area across his rear. He decided to stand again at Le Cateau. It was to be a frustrating day for the BEF; delays occurred due to masses of refugees and to confusion with the French. The men were tired and tempers were not improved by the passage of Sordet's Cavalry Corps across the BEF's withdrawal route. Nevertheless, 4th Division was beginning to arrive and moved into positions around Solesmes, to cover the British left. The bulk of 4th Divisional

Nº 1.
On the Mons-Condé Canal.
Aug. 23ʳᵈ 1914. The Fifth
Division Sector. A section
of the 119th Battery R.F.A. in
action behind the Norfolks.
J.C.W.

AUGUST, 1914.

Guns in action at the beginning of the war; the elementary camouflage is noteworthy. From a watercolour by
Captain J C Walford, RFA.   *(R.A.I.)*

Artillery under Brigadier-General G.F. Milne, began to take up position around Ligny. It consisted of:

14 Brigade RFA—39th, 68th, 88th Batteries.
29 Brigade RFA—125th, 126th, 127th Batteries.
32 Brigade RFA—27th, 134th, 135th Batteries.
37 Howitzer Brigade RFA—31st, 35th, 55th Batteries.
31st Heavy Battery RGA (60-pounders).

Meanwhile, 5th Division continued its withdrawal and 15 Brigade RFA had some brushes with the enemy, notably near Bavai. 61st Howitzer Battery had the memorable experience of watching a shrapnel shell, fired in error at an incorrect line, burst neatly above a German company crossing a viaduct, and eliminating nearly all of them! 52nd Battery was detached to cover the rear battalion as it withdrew south west down the Roman road to Le Cateau. In turn it detached a section to cover the rearguard which was continually dropping into action but the Germans were not following up closely and they did not have to fire south of Bavai. 28 Brigade RFA was placed in support of the two battalions holding a covering position just north of Montay. The Brigade had 11th Battery of 15 Brigade RFA attached to replace 123rd Battery, which had become detached in the withdrawal. The position was not attacked and the guns withdrew at sunset. At 1730 hours it began to rain and it was 2330 hours before the tired 5th Divisional Artillery had assembled near Reumont, after a third long exhausting day.

Meanwhile, 3rd Division also had to contend all day with blocked roads, refugees and confusion, together with a series of minor delaying actions. 41st Battery of 42 Brigade RFA were covering the 2nd Irish Rifles—the rearguard—but were not engaged. As the Division neared Le Cateau and Caudry, the confusion and congestion were alarming. Had the Germans pressed hard, disaster might have resulted. However, 23 Brigade RFA reached its bivouac area near Troisvilles at 1730 hours, came into action and dug in. So during the day the two British Corps had withdrawn round the Forêt de Mormal; I Corps to the east, and II Corps to the west. There was now some confusion about the requirements of the Le Cateau position. Certainly the men arriving there knew that they were going to stand and fight, and word got round that there would be no more retreat. Meanwhile in the closing hours of the day more confusion occurred on the I Corps front. Some Germans broke through the forest and blundered into a troop of 1st Division's cavalry, the 15th Hussars, at the bridge near Maroilles. The Germans drove off the Hussars and advanced on to Landrecies where they met outposts of 4th Guards Brigade. The confusion can be imagined, since HQ 2nd Division was at the time in Maroilles, only two miles away! Meanwhile at Landrecies, the 3rd Coldstream and 2nd Grenadiers held the Germans until they approached the village again, this time with a field gun. This gun fired down the street at short range, with considerable effect until midnight, and the Germans looked like making progress. By 0100 hours a howitzer of 60th Battery of 44 Brigade RFA was brought into action by hand, and with its third round destroyed the enemy gun, whereupon the Germans withdrew. The situation was quiet by 0400 hours 26th August. The battle of Mons was over, the retreat had begun, but there was more to follow. Indeed, the 26th was to prove one of the most glorious in the history of the Royal Regiment as the two armies came to grips at Le Cateau.

CHAPTER 3

Le Cateau — The Great Artillery Duel

See map 6

Confused reports reached GHQ during the afternoon of 25th August. It was first decided to stand and fight at Le Cateau along a line from there to Caudry, and orders to this effect were issued. Then, in the late afternoon, Sir John French changed his mind and new orders were issued at 1930 hours to continue the withdrawal, but these orders did not reach GOC II Corps until 2230 hours. General Smith-Dorrien, having learnt that the enemy was too close to permit his tired men to withdraw beyond the reach of the enemy before dawn, reluctantly came to the decision that he must stand his ground. So he issued orders that the Corps would fight at Le Cateau and then continue to retire but his orders were not made clear and many units remained convinced that there was to be no further withdrawal. Indeed, many units did not receive the order at all!

So without reconnaissance and in heavy rain and mist during the evening of 25th August, II Corps began to prepare for battle. General Smith-Dorrien also took command of the 4th Division in the area of Quiévy, the 19th Infantry Brigade at Le Cateau itself and the Cavalry Division. The ground was open and rolling chalk land; on the right and running through Le Cateau it was split by the steep valley of the River Selle, narrow but unfordable; this river running from Solesmes to Le Cateau formed the British right flank. Running west from Le Cateau was a low ridge stretching to Esnes with a series of valleys running up to it from the north. The Montay spur jutting north just to the west of Le Cateau was also significant, as it gave the enemy a covered approach to the town.

The line was thirteen miles from Esnes to Le Cateau. The layout of divisions was, from the right, 5th Division holding from Le Cateau to Troisvilles inclusive, some four and a half miles; 3rd Division to include Caudry; and 4th Division from Fontaine-au-Pire to Esnes facing north-west. Behind 4th Division was 4th Cavalry Brigade. 1st Cavalry Brigade now moved to protect the rear and right flank at Escaufourt and 19th Infantry Brigade became Corps reserve.

The Artillery of 5th Division were obsessed by the need to give the infantry the closest possible support and, since all three infantry brigades were in line covering the road Le Cateau-Inchy, the CRA, Brigadier Headlam, put one artillery brigade with each; 27 on the left supporting 15th Infantry Brigade; 28 in the centre with 13th Infantry Brigade and the 15 Brigade RFA supporting 14th Infantry Brigade on the right. He put 65th Howitzer Battery near Le Fayt (in 3rd Division's area) south of Troisvilles to cover the Division's left flank, and 37th Howitzer Battery to reinforce his right with 15 Brigade RFA. He kept 61st Howitzer Battery and 108th

Heavy Battery in reserve under his own command near Divisional HQ at Reumont. Brigadier Headlam ordered his brigade commanders to bring their guns into action at once, to give the closest possible support to the infantry. Accordingly, Lieutenant Colonel C.F. Stevens, commanding 15 Brigade RFA, brought 52nd, 37th Howitzer, 80th and 11th Batteries into action in a line within a few hundred yards of the leading infantry positions. He told the batteries that there would be no retirement. 37th Howitzer Battery came into action astride the road in a covered position, the Battery Commander, Major E.H. Jones, ordered the guns to be camouflaged, and he himself prepared to control their fire by flag and telephone from an open crest just to the front. 11th Battery covered the extreme right with their muzzles almost over the trenches overlooking Le Cateau railway station (the Battery had detrained here from England only five days before!). 80th Battery was in a covered position but could not clear its crest at very short ranges. Accordingly at 0430 hours it was ordered right forward and to the right of the 37th, though even this was not considered forward enough by Lieutenant Colonel Stevens and the guns were run further forward by hand. Thus the whole of the 15 Brigade was deployed in a long line in the open. It is easy to be critical of this exposed layout now, but with the primitive signalling equipment of the time it is doubtful if the really close support which had been ordered could have been given from positions further back. We must remember, too, that the Brigade thought that it was to be a fight to the finish!

The situation was very similar in 13th Infantry Brigade area further to the left. The guns of 28 Brigade RFA, 122nd, 123rd and 124th Batteries, were well forward and close to the leading infantry; 124th Battery was directly behind 123rd Battery. The guns of 27 Brigade RFA supporting 15th Infantry Brigade were deployed differently. The position north of Troisvilles was on a reverse slope; this enabled 119th and 121st Batteries to deploy well forward but in covered positions. 120th Battery was in support of 3rd Division and had a section forward in Troisvilles. 65th Howitzer Battery (from 5th Division) was well sited in a covered position about one mile south west of Troisvilles and was never located by the Germans.

Deployment of 3rd Divisional Artillery was better. Delayed during the night 25–26 August by congestion at Solesmes, the units arrived late, tired and piecemeal. However, the position itself was better than that of 5th Division, and mercifully the German attacks did not develop here until mid-day 26th August. However, Brigadier-General Wing, the CRA, was concerned that he was not giving the best support to his infantry and ordered 23rd Battery to put four guns out in front and to be well dug in and stocked with ammunition. He then allotted 42 Brigade RFA to 7th Infantry Brigade in Caudry. The Brigade had only two batteries, since 41st Battery had become detached, and spent the night near Le Cateau and moved into a reserve position at Montigny next day. To the right of 7th Infantry Brigade was the 8th supported by 40 Brigade RFA, with 6th, 23rd and 49th Batteries in line and with 48th Heavy Battery in a valley just behind them. To their right, the guns of 107th, 108th and 109th Batteries of 23 Brigade RFA were in action, again in line. One section of 107th Battery and one of 108th Battery were dug in on the infantry firing line with orders not to fire until the final assault. All the Howitzer batteries, 128th, 129th and 130th of 30 Brigade RFA, were in action side by side in the Warnelle Ravine, just south of Caudry. The CRA established himself alongside 3rd Division's Tactical HQ just near 48th Heavy

Battery. He retained command of all guns himself, and none were more than a mile from him, and all could be reached under cover.

On the left 4th Division, who had just arrived from England, received orders to deploy along the flank between Fontaine-au-Pire and Esnes at 0600 hours, 26th August. The artillery problem was considerable and complex. The guns could not clear the crests from the bottom of the Warnelle Ravine, the slopes to the south of it were in full view of the enemy and the northern slopes were completely exposed. The CRA, Brigadier G.F. Milne, did not believe in putting his guns on the infantry firing line; he liked his artillery in depth and behind it. The Division had 11th and 12th Infantry Brigades forward with 10th in reserve. Brigadier Milne therefore decided to concentrate 14 and 29 Brigades RFA south of Harcourt and he dispatched 32 and 37 Brigades RFA to prepare areas east of the Idris stream near Ligny. This deployment was still being carried out when heavy enemy artillery and machine gun fire fell on the 1st Battalion, The King's Own, who were digging in just north of Longsart and who suffered 400 casualties in a few minutes. 32 Brigade RFA deployed immediately with 27th Battery in the open just west of Ligny and 134th and 135th Batteries echeloned back behind cover. The battle of Le Cateau had started. Meanwhile 14 Brigade RFA had come quickly into action with 68th Battery in the open to the west of Harcourt. 29 Brigade RFA had all its batteries in good covered positions to the south-west of the village, and ideally placed to shoot across the front of 11th Infantry Brigade. 37 Howitzer Brigade came into action just east of Selvigny, some 4,000 yards back from the Longsart Ridge.

The Horse Artillery batteries of the Cavalry brigades were deployed with E and L covering the right flank from positions south of Le Cateau in the bed of the Escarts stream. D was further to the right, just south of Bazuel supporting 3rd Cavalry Brigade, while I Battery had a section at Caudry.

The German attack began at 0600 hours from the north-east. *Their 4th Corps (7th and 8th Infantry Divisions) and 2nd Cavalry Corps (2nd, 4th and 9th Cavalry Divisions)* began to close onto the 4th British Division, still hurriedly preparing its positions. The attacking divisions were supported by the artillery of five infantry divisions, three cavalry divisions and sixteen 5.9-inch howitzers. The Germans had already learnt the value of concentrated artillery fire. They had sent this mass of artillery forward under a cavalry escort to positions ahead of their assaulting infantry and arranged for its fire to be concentrated onto the right of the 4th Division, the unfortunate British 11th Infantry Brigade, which was to bear the brunt of the first attack.

On the British right the first German shells smashed into 13th Infantry Brigade positions shortly after 0600 hours; the gun flashes could be detected near Neuvilly some 5,000 yards away. The guns of 15 Brigade RFA and 37th Howitzer Battery quickly silenced many of the German batteries, but more (the whole of the *German 7th Divisional Artillery*) came into action in the same area. This mass of guns began to pour shells onto 13th Infantry Brigade still digging in. The British were now to learn a vital lesson—it is not possible to provide effective counter battery fire from guns in forward positions sited to support the infantry. Not only are the guns themselves under direct fire but enemy gunfire directed at them falls on the infantry with whom they are fighting; this now happened and the 2nd Suffolks suffered many casualties as a result. Guns so far forward cannot carry out both tasks, particularly in the final phases of an enemy assault. The Germans were quick to exploit this weakness and the artillery duel that began illustrated well the differences between the British Gunners trained to deploy forward and to kill infantry with shrapnel and the heavier German guns—"five-nines"—designed to pound guns and defences with their HE. At 0615 hours a German shell burst over 15 Brigade RFA observation post killing Bombardier Johnson and wounding all officers present, including Lieutenant Colonel Stevens (in the spine) and 37th Battery Commander, Major E.H. Jones, but somehow they remained at their posts. By now the guns of 27 Brigade RFA were hotly engaged and 123rd Battery suffered heavily under the converging fire of three enemy batteries. Soon a direct hit on Number 2 gun wounded all the detachment and the Battery Commander, Major G.H.W. Bayley. Captain A.G. Gillman immediately took command. 124th Battery swung north to assist but collected all the "overs" aimed at 123rd Battery; 122nd Battery, from its covered position, was not located throughout the battle. Similarly, the guns of 119th and 121st Battery began to pound the enemy but were well enough concealed to escape punishment. 65th Howitzer Battery located a German battery just before 0800 hours which was shelling their area; at 3,500 yards it engaged it and silenced it. The advantage in this duel was with the Germans. They had a wide choice of good positions, their targets were for the most part fully exposed, their HE shell gave them an advantage over the British shrapnel in such a duel, and from their observation post on the top of Le Cateau Church they could see the entire British position. It is therefore remarkable that so many German guns should have been silenced so quickly. The British proved to be quicker in ranging, their fire was more accurate, and their gunners steadier in serving the guns.

Moving further left, the guns of 3rd Division were well concealed. The artillery of the *German 4th Cavalry Division* opened fire on men of 9th Infantry Brigade at 0600 hours. The fire was so ineffective that the men went on digging! Infantry of the *German 8th Division* were cut to pieces by the four forward guns of 23 Brigade RFA as they closed on Inchy, then 6th Battery of 40 Brigade RFA joined in. Those that got into the village were pinned down by accurate fire from 65th Howitzer Battery, and accurate small arms fire from the Royal Scots and the Lincolns. However, further west the position in the exposed salient of Caudry soon became difficult. The guns of 29th and 45th Batteries and of I Battery RHA were in action to the north of the village where they were in front of the infantry. The village was attacked by *German Jäger battalions* and a dismounted cavalry regiment at 0700 hours. This attack was repelled by the Gunners, but it was clear that the position was already untenable. At 0800 hours all guns were withdrawn to the area of Montigny where they joined up with 41st Battery. The artillery of 3rd Division was now well disposed in depth to fight a delaying action.

We left the artillery of 4th Division, on the left, already in action as it was deploying. 27th Battery, deployed among stooks in a stubble field with its observation post forty yards to its right front, was soon hotly engaging the enemy attack onto 11th Infantry Brigade. It and 134th Battery soon drew most of the enemy gun fire off the infantry and onto themselves. At this point Major H.E. Vallentin, commanding 27th Battery, detected a German battery near Caudry firing at 11th Infantry Brigade and engaged it. The German battery instantly began to engage 27th Battery, but Major Vallentin was too quick for the Germans. He ranged so quickly that his effective fire knocked out five of the six German guns before they could finish ranging on the British. This was another of the many examples that day of the superiority of the British gunnery. So accurate was the fire of 4th Division Artillery that the Germans were never able to press home their attacks and the Division held its own without difficulty.

Battle had now been joined right across the British front, so let us look again at the exposed right flank of 5th Division. At 1000 hours German infantry began to appear from Le Cateau advancing towards 14th Infantry Brigade. 15 Brigade RFA and 37th Howitzer Battery immediately engaged them, opening at 2,000 yards and dropping range steadily to 800. By this time the combined fire of guns, machine guns and small arms began to take heavy toll of the Germans. By then the German artillery, now just east of Le Cateau and at Rambourlieux Farm to the north, began to provide accurate close support to their infantry. 11th Battery began to suffer heavily, although one gun temporarily silenced enemy guns to the east of Le Cateau. Shortly afterwards German infantry began to assualt the 2nd Manchesters from the Selle Valley who helped to manhandle the left section of 11th Battery across the rear of the position so enabling it to engage the enemy at point blank range. This fire was so deadly that the Germans withdrew. Major P.W.B. Henning, the Battery Commander, wounded in the knee, now switched the remaining gun of the right section onto targets on the Montay Spur, and continued to do so until noon. Two German howitzers then located the gun and silenced it with a direct hit. Meanwhile 80th Battery continued to burst its shrapnel low over infantry attacking from the area of Rambourlieux Farm and, in spite of massive enemy fire, it prevented all attacks from developing. 108th Heavy Battery RGA and 37th Howitzer Battery kept up a hail of fire taking very heavy toll of the Germans and the latter soon fired away most of its ammunition. 52nd Battery to the left punished two German batteries with rapid fire so swiftly that they never fired again. However, the gallant 52nd was then located, and its number five gun was knocked out by a direct hit with HE and the centre section was soon out of action due to casualties. Nevertheless, the remaining guns continued to fire; the centre section got back into action and three more wagons of ammunition arrived. Accurate fire down to 1,000 yards was kept up on German infantry trying to cross the Le Cateau-Cambrai road. All wire was cut but orderlies lay out in the open in a chain relaying fire orders.

Further left, 27 Brigade RFA took a heavy toll of German infantry advancing by platoons, shoulder to shoulder, at ranges down to 800 yards. One round of gunfire would cause a platoon to go down "like a target at practice camp when the rope is cut". To their right, however, the exposed 123rd and 124th Batteries suffered heavily. Guns were hit, wagons were on fire and ammunition ran low, yet the Batteries fought on. The masses of German infantry never reached the Cambrai Road while the guns were in action and suffered the most terrible casualties. The British Gunners had been told that it was to be a fight to the finish, and they proved their determination to do so.

On 3rd Division front, the attacking infantry of *8th German Division* were the ones who attacked L and 119th Batteries at Elouges on the 24th. They had already learnt their lesson and paid dearly when attacking British artillery! They came on in very open order, using cover, and supported by their own guns. The German artillery was not very effective, the British guns were well hidden and, though the enemy closed to 2,000 yards, they never crossed the main road by Inchy. Caudry still held and until noon the situation in 3rd Division caused no special concern.

The artillery duel continued in 4th Division's sector. But 4th Division was under no delusion about fighting to the finish! They realised that they must fight to halt the enemy but also that they were then to withdraw. However, the tactical importance of Ligny was realised; its loss would split the Corps, and threaten all withdrawal routes. Orders were given to 11th Infantry Brigade to organise a close defence of the village and 32 Brigade RFA was to assist. 27th Battery, already in action to the west of the village, supported the infantry as they retired across the Warnelle Ravine and again as it fired it drew the German guns onto it. Number 5 gun was hit and a wheel blown off but, incredibly, and under aimed fire it was replaced by a wagon wheel and the gun got back into action. With great sacrifice the guns continued to fire until all ammunition was exhausted, and the detachments were withdrawn. 37 Howitzer Brigade, in action near Selvigny, silenced a German battery as it came into action just north of the Warnelle Ravine. The observation post had watched a German officer lay out the position, waited, and then caught the battery as it came into action and unlimbered! Practice camp training was well justified!

So far the Germans had been held right along the front but by 1400 hours the crisis of the battle developed. Let us turn again to the British position on the Montay Spur. By now 11th Battery was taking heavy punishment and 52nd Battery was suffering fearfully; with great gallantry the Battery Commander, Major A.C.R. Nutt, shot through the throat, continued to whisper his orders from his observation post; his second Captain, Captain Barber-Starkey, relayed them to the guns. At this point, Sergeant Woolgar of the Battery staff was killed, and Sergeant Crabtree and Corporal Dennet were wounded. The enemy concentrated more and more guns onto the exposed British position; the impact was so great that the ground trembled, it seemed impossible that anyone could live there. The steadiness of the Gunners had a great effect on the infantry morale in that terrible position. The Commanding Officer of the 2nd Battalion, the Suffolk Regiment said ". . . their behaviour throughout was magnificent and the morale effect on us was terrific. In spite of being defiladed first from the left, then from the right, they continued to fire, and their coolness under the most trying conditions was inspiring to us all". Nevertheless, the weakness of the position was soon to show itself. With 11th Battery crushed, only two guns left in 52nd and 80th Batteries, all with almost all ammunition expended, it was decided to withdraw. So insistent had been the orders forbidding retirement that when Lieutenant Colonel C.F. Stevens, 15 Brigade RFA, received a message through his signallers to withdraw, he refused to do so without a written order. Meanwhile, Lieutenant Colonel E.P. England, commanding the 5th Division Ammunition Column, was frantically organising the move forward of more ammunition. Supplies began to arrive in lorries from the Corps Ammunition Park; this is the first recorded incidence of lorries appearing on the battlefield during combat. But the guns were desperately short. 80th Battery had expended almost all it had, 37th Howitzer Battery was now without any and 52nd Battery had fired 1,100 rounds.

The German infantry were slow in assaulting. They had learned to respect the accuracy of the British guns and rifle fire. However, by 1315 hours the position

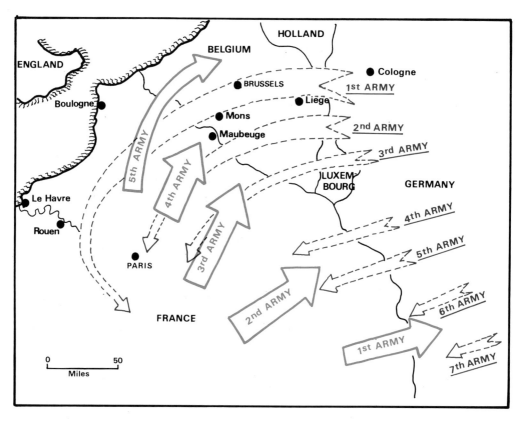

Map 1   The Schlieffen Plan to attack France and the French defence plan

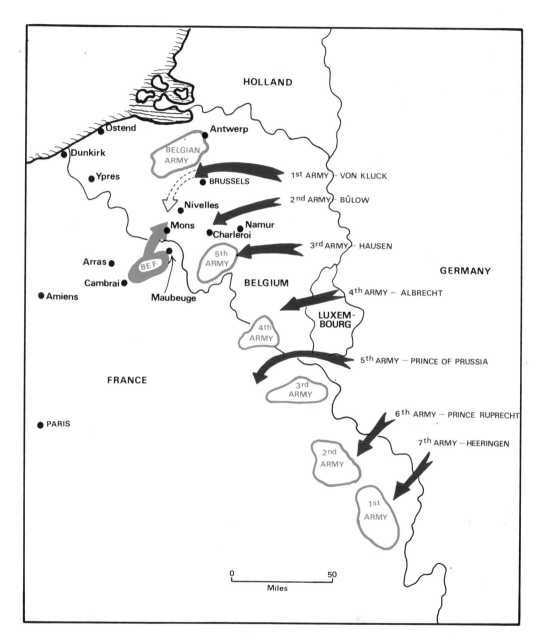

Map 2 The Situation on 21 August as the BEF advanced to Mons

Map 3 Divisional Artillery layout at the start of the Battle of Mons—23 August 1914

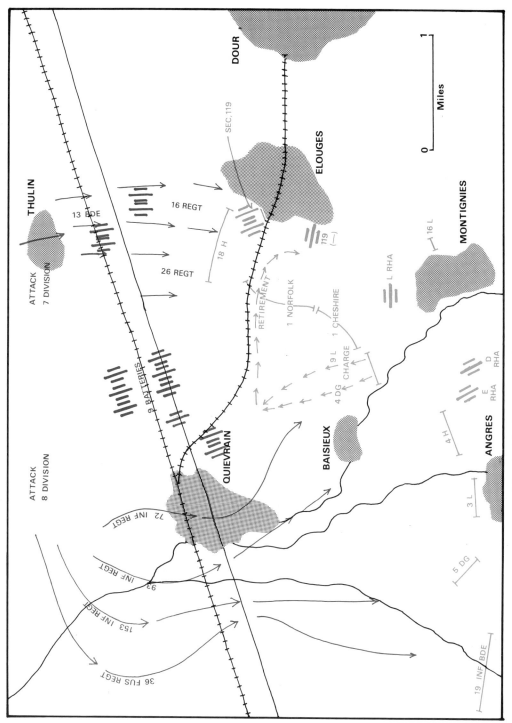

Map 4 Flank attack at Elouge—24 August 1914

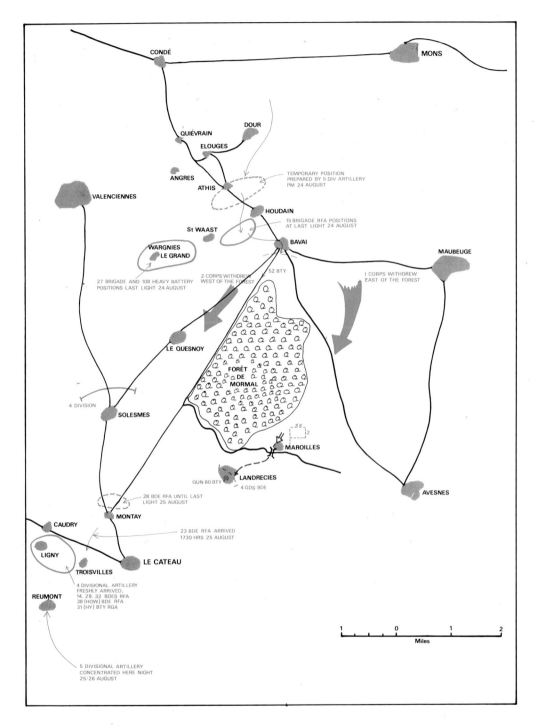

CONDÉ

MONS

DOUR

QUIÉVRAIN

ELOUGES

ANGRES

ATHIS

TEMPORARY POSITION
PREPARED BY 5 DIV ARTILLERY
PM 24 AUGUST

VALENCIENNES

HOUDAIN

15 BRIGADE RFA POSITIONS
AT LAST LIGHT 24 AUGUST

St WAAST

BAVAI

WARGNIES
LE GRAND

MAUBEUGE

52 BTY

27 BRIGADE AND 108 HEAVY BATTERY
POSITIONS LAST LIGHT 24 AUGUST

2 CORPS WITHDREW
WEST OF THE FOREST

I CORPS WITHDREW
EAST OF THE FOREST

LE QUESNOY

FORÊT
DE
MORMAL

4 DIVISION

SOLESMES

MAROILLES

2

GUN 60 BTY

LANDRECIES

4 GDS BDE

AVESNES

28 BDE RFA UNTIL LAST
LIGHT 25 AUGUST

MONTAY

CAUDRY

23 BDE RFA ARRIVED
1730 HRS 25 AUGUST

LIGNY

TROISVILLES

LE CATEAU

REUMONT

4 DIVISIONAL ARTILLERY
FRESHLY ARRIVED.
14, 29, 32 BDES RFA
38 (HOW) BDE RFA
31 (HY) BTY RGA

1   0   1   2

Miles

5 DIVISIONAL ARTILLERY
CONCENTRATED HERE NIGHT
25/26 AUGUST

Map 5   Withdrawal from Mons to Le Cateau—25/26 August 1914

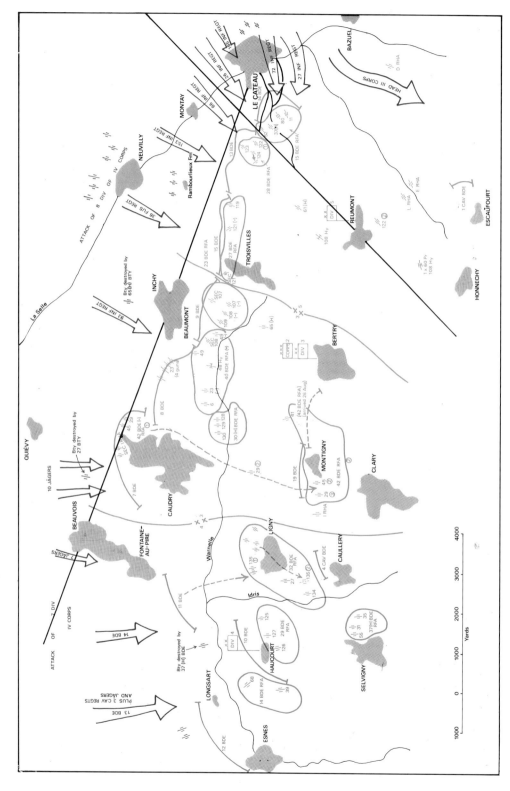

Map 6 The layout of II Corps Artillery at the start of the Battle of Le Cateau—26 August 1914

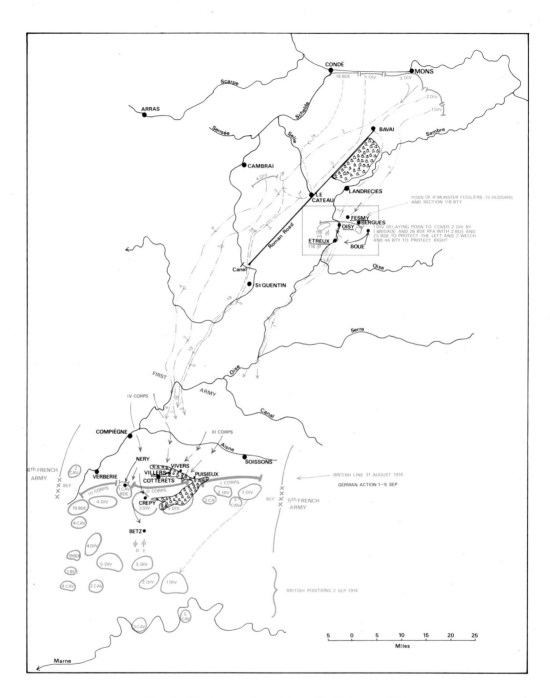

Map 7   The Retreat from Mons, 24–31 August 1914

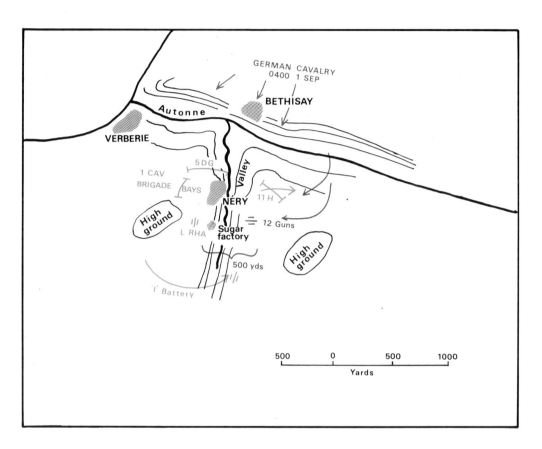

Map 8   Sketch map of Néry—1 September 1914

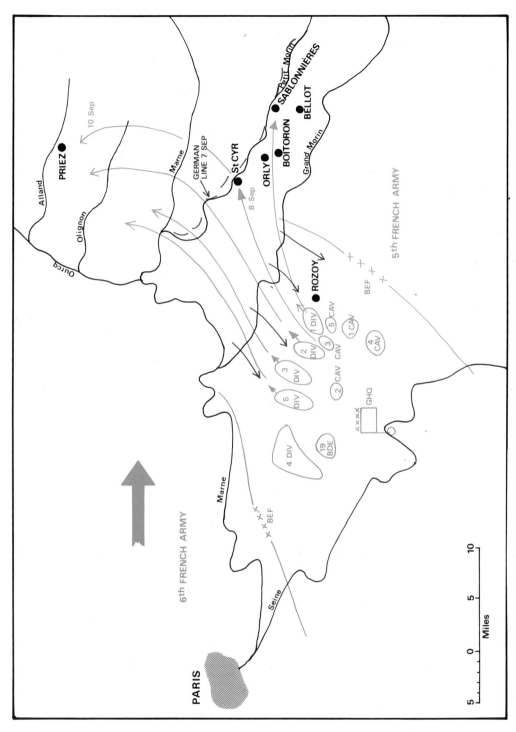

Map 9 Situation at limit of retreat 5 September 1914 and the start of the Allied Offensive on 6 September 1914

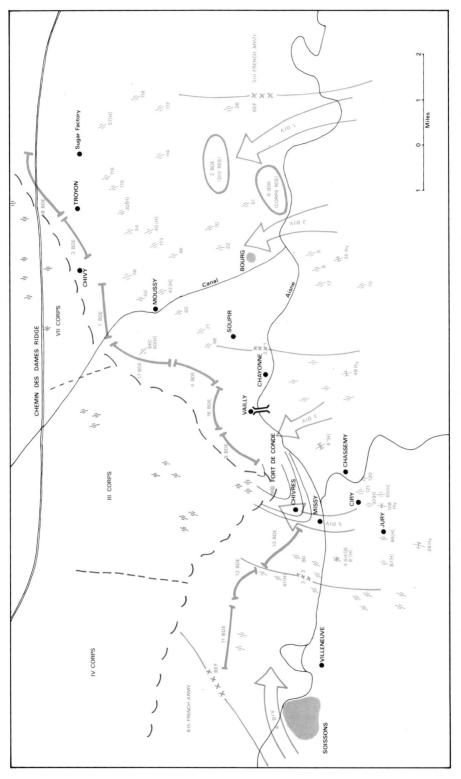

Map 10 The crossing of the Aisne 13 September 1914 and subsequent operations until the move of the BEF to Ypres

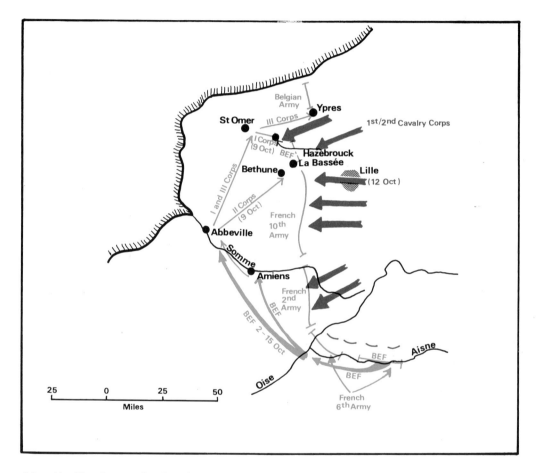

Map 11   Sketch map showing the move of the BEF to Flanders to stop the German race to the
sea—2–15 October 1914

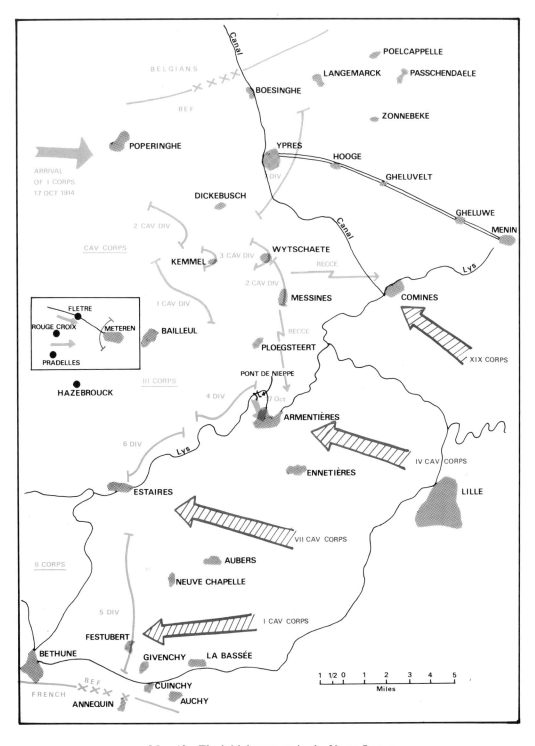

Map 12 The initial contacts in the Ypres Sector

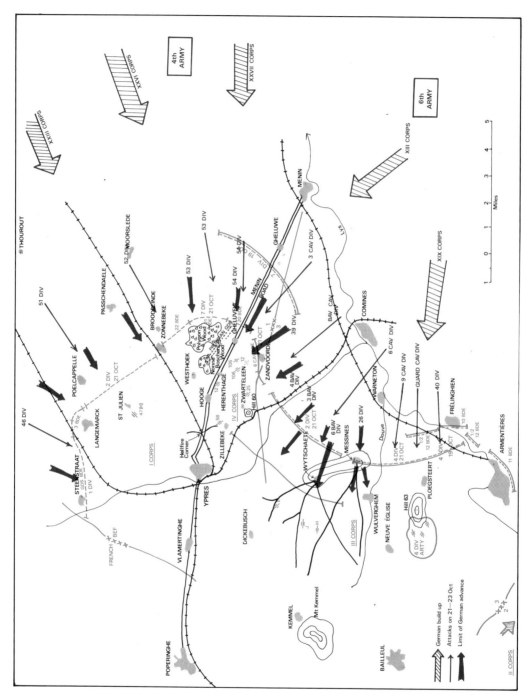

Map 13 The First Battle of Ypres—19 October–11 November 1914 (Only batteries mentioned in the text are shown)

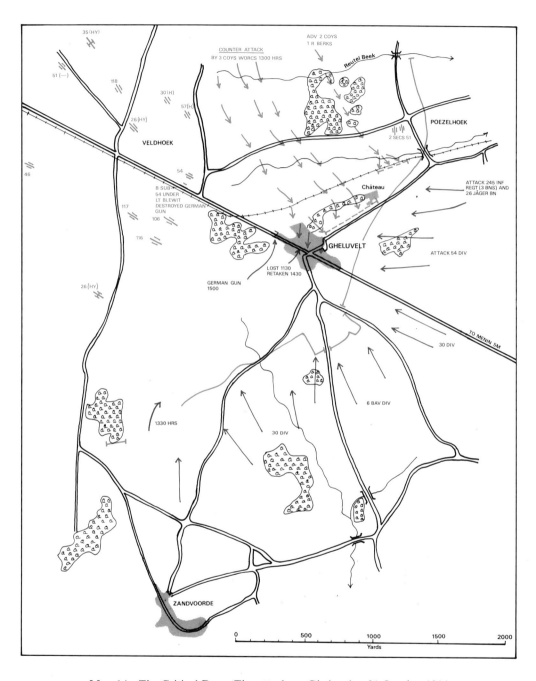

Map 14 The Critical Day—The attack on Gheluvelt—31 October 1914

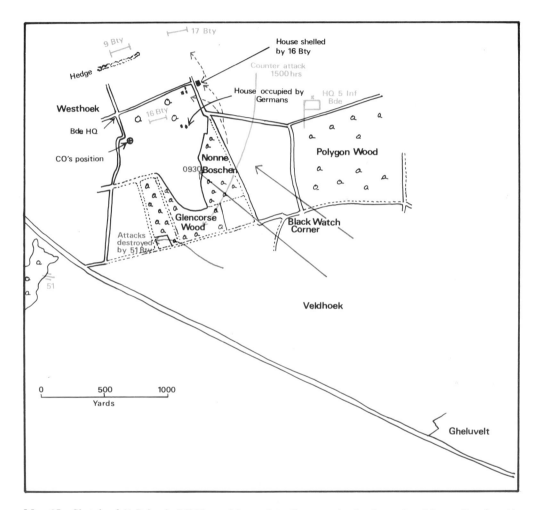

Map 15 Sketch of 41 Brigade RFA's positions when Germans broke through at Nonne Boschen 11 November 1914

was hopeless, and Commander 5th Division asked permission to withdraw. Now the lack of artillery in depth and of reserve battalions to cover the operation was felt. Only 61st Howitzer Battery, 108th Heavy Battery RGA and E and L Batteries RHA were in a position to help. By 1340 hours General Smith-Dorrien said that two reserve battalions were on the way, and the Division could withdraw but that it should hold as long as possible. 3rd Division were to move next, followed by 4th Division. When this order reached HQ 5th Division, the CRA and BMRA were out visiting Brigades. Not knowing that an order to retire had been given, Major Tailyour, the BMRA, realised the importance of getting some guns back to support such an order, if and when it did arrive. The remaining guns of 52nd Battery were badly exposed. The wagon lines had been hit and half the drivers and horses had been killed or wounded. The end was drawing near for 11th Battery—11th Battery which had also fought so well at Minden so long before—German infantry were using covered approaches and sunken roads, and were slowly out-flanking the position. Captain Buckle swung four guns round to meet the new threat and controlled rounds of gun fire at the enemy until he fell, across a gun, mortally wounded. Lieutenant Coghlan took command only to be killed by rifle fire and one after another Lieutenants Maxwell and Stanford fell wounded. By now only Major Henning remained and he was already wounded. The gallantry of the NCOs and men was supreme, they were under fire from the front right and left and yet they continued to blast the enemy at point blank range forcing them off the position. Men of the 2nd Manchesters helped to swing two guns around and the gallant Major Henning controlled their fire—but the end was very near now. All officers lay dead or dying; only one gun was able to fire and Sergeant Hopper, the senior NCO left, ordered up the horses to save the guns. They came up at a gallop led by Farrier Quarter Master Sergeant Watts but were caught in the open by German shell fire. One team was blown to pieces as it was about to move off and one gun turned over but four were driven out under a hail of fire with such wounded, gunners and infantry alike, as could be carried. As they passed the support trenches the 2nd Manchesters stood and cheered them—and how well they deserved it. Both Hopper and Watts earned a DCM that day. Major Henning, too badly wounded to ride, followed on foot, the last man to leave the position. 80th Battery to the left of 11th fared little better, soon they were all but out of ammunition when Captain Higgon brought up three wagons but they could not be driven forward and suffered many casualties to men and horses. Meanwhile, one gun received two direct hits and by now there were only two or three men per gun left. Ammunition was carried forward to the guns where the few remaining men fired steadily at the closing enemy. Lieutenant McLeod was wounded, as was Lieutenant Hewson, but both remained on duty. Major Birley remained by his guns calmly directing their fire and encouraging his men, but soon he too was wounded—several times. Five more DCMs were awarded to this gallant Battery after Le Cateau. Major Tailyour himself drove up the teams of 80th Battery, still ignorant of any order to retire, but determined to get one battery out to cover any subsequent withdrawal. Five guns got away and Major Birley tried to reach the Brigade observation post to report to Lieutenant Colonel Stevens, but was again seriously wounded in doing so. Major Tailyour then reported to Colonel Stevens himself but he had no order to withdraw so the latter refused to leave his post. Shortly afterwards the observation post was surrounded

The recovery of the howitzers of 37 Battery RFA towards the end of the battle of Le Cateau. From an oil painting by Terence Cuneo.   *(R.A.I.)*

and all, including Major Jones the gallant commander of 37th Howitzer Battery, were captured.

Four guns from 37th Howitzer Battery were withdrawn by the remaining teams of the Battery and those remaining from 52nd and 80th Batteries. Captain D. Reynolds, Captain of the 37th, searched for teams to withdraw the remaining two howitzers but failed, so he disabled them and withdrew with the remaining men. Arriving at Reumont he came across two teams, and decided to try and rescue the howitzers. Together with Lieutenant Earle, who was already wounded, they led the teams back to the gun position. To onlookers it seemed a crazy, hopeless task; the German infantry were already within a hundred yards of the position when, trotting through a volley of shrapnel, Captain Reynolds ordered his teams, one commanded by 2nd Lieutenant Morgan with Driver Luke as 'Wheel' and the other by the wounded Lieutenant Earle, to gallop! They stretched themselves forward and, with limbers bouncing behind them, swept up to the astonished masses of German infantry now on three sides of the guns. It seemed incredible that such large targets could escape total destruction at point blank range but, with surprise on their side, they did. They wheeled up to the abandoned howitzers, swung round and limbered up as the astonished Germans, at last realising what was happening, opened fire on them. By his skilful driving Luke brought the limber hook right over the 'eye' of F sub-section and, with two gunners, limbered up; but as they left, the centre Driver was shot, throwing his whip into the air; this was caught by Captain Reynolds who galloped alongside the centre team and kept them going as they charged down some astonished Germans and got clean away! The other team was less fortunate. Having hooked in and moved some fifty yards the centre horses were both killed; Lieutenant Earle and Sergeant Bower (already wounded four times during the day) dismounted to unhook the lead and centre horses, but then both wheelers were shot and the howitzer had to be abandoned. Sergeant Bower helped Lieutenant Earle, again wounded, and both got back to Reumont. Gunner Fraser, at the last minute, dashed back to the limber to get his great coat and, as he turned to watch Lieutenant Earle, was hit in the forehead and eye and his comrade Sergeant Bower helped him from the field. For their bravery, Captain Reynolds and Drivers Luke and Drain were awarded the Victoria Cross, Lieutenant Earle the DSO, and Sergeant Bower and Trumpeter Waldron the DCM. Later, much later, this gallant battery was authorised the Honour Title "Le Cateau". Few units of any Arm have earned their Honour Title so well as did 37th Battery on 26th August 1914.

In a sense the death of 52nd Battery was no less glorious. The two flank guns were now all that were left. Slowly and painfully Captain Barber-Starkey and a sergeant, both wounded, kept the guns firing. Two more wounded sergeants struggled to carry forward ammunition. The German attack now enveloped the Suffolks and it was impossible for the guns to fire at the mixture of friend and foe. Aided by some unwounded gunners, the gallant band under Lieutenant Neve and Sergeant Campbell removed their breech blocks and sights and withdrew and sadly all the guns of the 52nd—later the Bengal Rocket Troop—were lost. The battery lost 96 men that day, but only two officers, four sergeants and eight men, all severely wounded, fell into enemy hands! Of these two officers, Major Nutt eventually recovered from his throat wound, but Captain Barber-Starkey died on 10th September 1914.

We must now look to the fate of 28 Brigade RFA supporting the 13th Infantry Brigade to the left. The CRA, Brigadier-General Headlam, himself rode up and decided that an attempt must be made to save the guns. Captain R.A. Jones of 122nd Battery called for volunteers and at once got six teams. At 1430 hours they moved forward and, as they passed the trenches of the Royal West Kent Regiment, the infantry rose to their feet and cheered the Gunners on their way. But as they topped the rise, a storm of fire hit them, Captain Jones and eight men were killed. Second Lieutenant R.W. Macleod and fourteen men were wounded and twenty horses fell. The remainder galloped on towards the guns. They reached the left half of the Battery, one team was shot down at once, a second limbered up one gun and got clear away, but the third had half its horses down. Lieutenant Macleod, already wounded, unhooked the traces off the dead 'leaders' and the 'centres', hooked in another 'lead' and mounted it himself; he then had a riding leader, a centre and two wheelers. As he galloped the team up the slope he was again wounded, but he had saved the gun and to a Gunner what else mattered? Again an exploit in the highest traditions of the Royal Regiment. The Battery Quartermaster Sergeant of 124th Battery now galloped up to attempt to save his guns, but was only stopped from charging forward by the CRA himself. The CRA then had to order Captain Gillman of 123rd Battery to abandon his guns, an order that was obeyed only with the greatest reluctance. Battered and torn, with dead and wounded everywhere (right section had received three direct hits), the spirit of the men of 123rd was unshaken. Captain Gillman ordered the remaining sixteen rounds to be fired; he ordered all the sights to be smashed and the breech blocks to be removed. The men then carried their wounded back; Captain Gillman, the last to leave his beloved guns, himself carried a wounded soldier of the KOYLI. Further left, the two Batteries of 27 Brigade RFA covered each other's movements in a classic withdrawal to positions just north of Reumont. They all got out leaving only three burning wagons.

Meanwhile, 15th Infantry Brigade had itself begun to withdraw covered by the guns of E and L Batteries RHA, 61st Howitzer and 108th Heavy Batteries. The Germans, reckless from success, advanced in mass across the Cambrai Road straight into the rapid fire of 2nd KOYLI. This battalion fought off the enemy until 1630 hours and undoubtedly prevented the withdrawal turning into a retreat. Similar German advances down the Selle Valley south of Le Cateau were checked. Another mass of infantry rushed forward straight into the fire of 61st Howitzer Battery and suffered heavily. Another large body appeared in full view of 108th Heavy Battery RGA and one section blew this enemy concentration to pieces. The heavies then began once again to pound the German artillery and continued to do so until 1530 hours when all ammunition was expended. A fall back position was now created around Honnechy, with E and L Batteries on the right flank. The Germans, however, had had enough. They had already paid too high a price and had learnt not to close with the deadly fire of the British guns and infantry. Thus ended 5th Division's battle at Le Cateau. As darkness fell, the weary troops were unmolested as they packed up to continue the withdrawal, but in a sense they had won; their training, their professionalism, their devotion, gallantry and their accurate fire had prevented their withdrawal turning into a defeat.

Returning now to the centre. After a lull from noon to 1300 hours, the German guns came to life again. An infantry attack on Inchy was virtually halted in its tracks by the hidden section of 108th Battery. At 1500 hours the Division was ordered to retire. 107th and 108th Batteries each left one section to cover the infantry with one hundred rounds per gun, and the remainder got away without loss. The sections left behind then used all their ammunition destroying a German assault south from Inchy. They then disabled the guns and the men withdrew with the infantry. The rest of the artillery and the Divisional Ammunition Column got away without incident. Once again the Germans did not follow up for fear of the accuracy of the British fire.

On the extreme left, 4th Division was now heavily engaged. By mid-afternoon 27th Battery in its open position could neither be supplied with ammunition, nor could it be withdrawn. The trails were buried by intensive firing and would need digging out and the guns themselves were red hot. When 55th and 31st Howitzer Batteries engaged enemy guns advancing over Longsart ridge, the Germans replied with some accuracy using aircraft as spotters for the first time. 12th Infantry Brigade now began to withdraw and were well covered by 39th and 68th Batteries. At 1630 hours 29 Brigade RFA withdrew by batteries in succession, and got away with only light casualties. By now 32 Brigade RFA were in a most exposed position west of Ligny. Commander 11th Infantry Brigade issued orders to abandon the guns of 135th Battery but Major C.H. Liveing, the Battery Commander, judged differently. His battery was well dug in on the northern edge of the village and as long as he was there no enemy could approach it. As the last infantry left, 135th Battery ran both guns and wagons back by hand and got them all out save one wagon—no mean feat under observed enemy fire. By now 27th Battery was in a desperate position. There was no ammunition and the men had been withdrawn. Lieutenant-Colonel M.J. MacCarthy, commanding 32 Brigade RFA, called for volunteers to save the guns by hand. The whole Battery responded to a man and rushed forward. Gradually the trails were dug out and four guns and limbers were run back. The Germans now realised what was happening and poured such a concentration of fire onto the position that the last two guns had to be abandoned. But yet again, the Germans failed to pursue the British and the last two batteries, 126th and 127th of 29 Brigade RFA, placed to be sacrificed to cover the rear, got away without loss.

Thus ended the battle of Le Cateau. There were many lessons. The most important one was that, if guns are to guarantee to destroy enemy attacks, they themselves must not be engaged by the same enemy who are engaging the infantry. Still, with the limited communications of the day, with the confusion over the aim of the battle, and with the techniques of gunnery in use, there was little alternative. It must be remembered too that the positions were occupied in great haste in the rain, mist and darkness and by men who were *very* tired. Nevertheless, where guns were concealed and sited in depth, they gave the best support, and got away to fight again. Where they were in the firing lines they suffered heavily and many were lost. However, the British proved that their gunnery was sound if their tactics were faulty; they ranged more quickly and fired more accurately than the Germans. Their shrapnel was superior and they burst it at a more effective height. On the other hand, the Germans had HE shells for field guns, ideal for counter battery work; they used aircraft to spot the fall of shot and they had learned how to concentrate masses of guns onto single targets. It was this last factor that won them the day on the Montay Spur.

Von Kluck had, however, completely misunderstood the battle. He captured forty guns. He thus told von Moltke that he had won a great victory, chasing the British from the field and getting back to their gun lines. He thought he had swamped the British, and only a rabble was fleeing to the south. Pursuit was not necessary; having smashed the British, they could be left while he turned on the French. How wrong he was, but it is important to understand this fact since it explains the ease with which the British escaped and why the Germans got such a shock on the Marne later on. Perhaps the loss of forty guns was not so fatal after all?

Le Cateau was an artillery battle fought with twentieth century weapons by men used to nineteenth century methods. It was the Royal Regiment's first real test of the War. Though mistakes were made, there was no shortage of gallantry. Deeds of great heroism occurred right across the front; the guns were fought with cool, steady courage and there is no doubt that the Germans suffered appalling losses from them. But it was not only the gunners on the guns who were gallant. There was the magnificent dash of the drivers who, on 5th Division's front alone, snatched sixteen guns from under the very noses of the Germans. It needed great courage to suffer shelling for hours on end in the wagon lines, then to gallop forward with a limber full of ammunition right up to the trail eye of a gun firing from the infantry trench line and, in full view, gallop back again. Most important, the Gunners proved their worth to the infantry. It was at Le Cateau that the co-operation learnt in training was turned into respect, admiration and trust. This combined esprit de corps, born on the slopes around Le Cateau, was to remain between the two Arms throughout the War. Brigadier Headlam, CRA 5th Division, wrote in his diary after Le Cateau, "That the help afforded by the artillery at Le Cateau was appreciated by their comrades of the infantry was touchingly shown next morning. Exhausted as they were by the long night march, many men stepped from the ranks as they marched passed to give a silent pat to the guns drawn up in action by the roadside to protect their progress".

Though it is hard to call Le Cateau a victory, since it was an action in a retreat, it did stop the Germans, and it did so mainly by the violent pounding given to them by the Gunners. It enabled the British to break action in broad daylight when disaster seemed otherwise inevitable.

"Went the day well? We died and never knew". An incident at the battle of Le Cateau. From a painting by C Clark. *(R.A.I.)*

CHAPTER 4

The Retreat to the Marne

See maps 7 and 8

II Corps began its retreat to the Marne on 27th August. It is remarkable that the British were allowed to break contact so easily and in relatively good order, but now it is possible to see why. First, the Germans completely misunderstood the significance of the Battle of Le Cateau and they were certain that the British were in utter confusion. Second, the German soldiers had learnt to respect the accuracy of the British artillery and rifle fire, and were loathe to close. Third, the Germans had already suffered a very large number of casualties.

It was after Le Cateau that the high morale of the BEF once again showed up. The men were tired, beaten and wet, yet there are countless stories of small pockets holding out until they could break clean. We read of stragglers getting back to their units and of men singing and whistling as they marched south; yet fatigue was very great. At halts the infantrymen could rest immediately, but the Gunners had to water and feed their horses, check the guns, refill with ammunition and check the harness before they could snatch a few minutes of rest themselves.

We must now look quickly back to I Corps, who had not been involved at Le Cateau. On the morning of the 26th August, Sir Douglas Haig signalled to HQ II Corps to ask how he could help, adding "We are well able to co-operate with you today". This message was ignored by II Corps and GHQ, who failed throughout the day even to keep I Corps informed of the situation. Even Sir John French did not appreciate the true state of affairs. He allowed a message to be sent to Marshal Joffre saying the British had been defeated! This, when I Corps had not even been involved, and even 3rd and 4th Divisions of II Corps were unaware that a significant battle had taken place! However, I Corps continued to withdraw, even though the gap between the two Corps was widening. Although not involved in the fighting, the men had been marching and digging constantly and were reacting to false rumours of the approaching Germans, thus they too were weary. 1st Division was ordered to cover the withdrawal of 2nd Division at Oisy, and 1st Infantry Brigade and 26 Brigade RFA were given this task; 2nd Infantry Brigade and 25 Brigade RFA were ordered to protect the left flank, and 2nd Welsh with 46th Battery RFA were to protect the right. 1st Infantry Brigade deployed the Royal Munster Fusiliers at Fesmy covering the approach to the Canal. The rear party was commanded by Major Charrier and he was given a section of 118th Battery, and two troops of the 15th Hussars to help. This section came into action in the centre of the Munster's position, right up in the firing line. Major Charrier was told to hold the position until he was forced to retire. At 1030 hours a

German attack was beaten off, then the right flank force, now east of Bergues, retired. At 1220 hours the road through Etreux was reported clear and Commander 1st Infantry Brigade issued the order that all units were to retire. This message failed to reach the Munsters who at 1230 hours came under attack supported by artillery. Major Charrier drew in his flanks to the village of Fesmy but soon a few Germans got into the village and shot down two artillery wagon teams—they in turn were all killed or captured. Meanwhile, the remaining two sections of 118th Battery came into action on the high ground north of Etreux in support of the Black Watch, and 117th Battery was in action to the south, with 116th Battery also in action on the Etreux-Guise road. It seems that no steps were taken to protect the right flank and to cover the approach from Boue, nor were steps taken to defend Etreux itself. During the afternoon, the Munsters slowly and skilfully withdrew from Fesmy but, as they neared Etreux at about 1930 hours, they came under close and accurate enemy artillery and rifle fire. This enemy force had got into Etreux from the east. One enemy shell destroyed the gun team of one gun in the section of 118th Battery but the other—D sub-section—came into action at 300 yards range. The Germans were now firmly in the houses, and this gun was ordered to demolish them. The range was so short that the detachment was shot down as they were getting the gun into action. A gallant charge by one company of Munsters was wiped out to a man. Nevertheless, the rest of the force continued to resist till 2115 hours when, surrounded on all sides with all ammunition gone, the 250 survivors surrendered to six battalions of Germans. The two guns were without ammunition, both officers, Major A.R. Bayly and Lieutenant A. Stewart-Cox and ten men lay wounded and twelve men had been killed. This gallant section had ceased to exist as a fighting unit.

By the morning of 28th August, II Corps were south of the Somme, thirty-five miles from Le Cateau, exhausted and footsore, but confident that they could handle the Germans given a chance. 52nd Battery for example, who had lost their guns at Le Cateau, had turned themselves into a company of mounted infantry. The withdrawal continued; by evening 3rd Division had covered sixty-eight miles in fifty hours' marching and was almost at the end of its endurance. The defence of the Munsters at Etreux had undoubtedly delayed the Germans but, apart from two engagements by 114th and 57th Batteries, there was no other incident. Far out on the left flank, 5th Cavalry Brigade saw German cavalry advancing and a section of J Battery RHA galloped into action in the open under small arms fire to cover a charge by the Scots Greys. They got off their first round some fifteen seconds after the order "Halt Action Front" in true Horse Artillery style. The Greys charged and cleared the enemy with lance and sabre but then came under heavy fire themselves. The rest of J came into action and silenced the enemy, allowing the Greys to withdraw. The combined charge and gunfire accounted for some three hundred enemy killed or wounded, a classic example of the excellent co-operation which existed between cavalry and gunners. A similar action was a combined ambush set up by 4th Hussars and E Battery RHA of 3rd Cavalry Brigade on the right flank. These actions were typical of the withdrawal and of the last few days of August. By the end of the month III Corps, under Lieutenant-General W.P. Pulteney, and consisting of 4th Division and 19th Infantry Brigade, came into existance. By 31st August, the BEF was behind the Aisne; I Corps on the right near Soissons, II Corps in the centre near Villers Cotterêts and III Corps on the left near Verberie. There was a five mile gap between II and III Corps, and Ist Cavalry Brigade were to fill it at Néry!

The Commander of the *German 2nd Cavalry Corps* decided to press on into the forest of Villers Cotterêts through the night 31st August/1st September and before the British could consolidate; this proved a justifiable though rash move. By 0400 hours, as the weary German cavalry were closing on the steep valley of the river Automne, just north of Nery, they did not realise that they were almost on top of the outposts of the British 1st Cavalry Brigade. This Brigade had been told that it was "to bivouac at Nery in the II Corps area". This order implied that Nery itself was covered by II Corps outposts. As a result, Brigadier General C.J. Briggs, the Brigade Commander, only had local outposts in position and none watching the crossings over the Automne. There were many alarms during the night, including a French farmer who rode into Néry to warn of the German approach, but all went unheeded. Brigadier General Briggs had allotted his regiments sectors of the village, the 5th Dragoon Guards faced north, the 11th Hussars faced east, with the Queen's Bays on the west. L Battery RHA was placed in a field on the south side of the village and was given the sugar factory for billets. Their task was to cover the approaches from the east and south. So the Brigade turned in for a well earned rest with orders to be ready to march at 0430 hours next day.

At 0230 hours on 1st September, the men of L Battery woke, rubbed down the horses, breakfasted, harnessed up and hooked in. The battery formed up facing north east but the mist was very heavy so the start of the move was postponed. Major W.D. Sclater-Booth, the Battery Commander, ordered poles to be lowered and sections to be led off to the sugar factory, in turn, to water. He then walked up the village street to Brigade Headquaters for orders. Meanwhile, a patrol of the 11th Hussars rode east and turned south where they ran into approaching German cavalry; they turned and escaped in the mist and regained Néry at 0525 hours. The 5th Dragoons refused to believe their report, but the 11th Hussars lined the eastern edge of the village. At 0540 hours German shells crashed into the village and into L Battery with devastating effect. Major Sclater-Booth ran towards the guns but a shell burst immediately in front of him knocked him unconscious where he fell.

At the guns, the left (rear) section was watering at the sugar factory as the first shells burst right among the massed horses of the rest of the Battery. Captain E.K. Bradbury was standing near the haystacks with the subalterns (J.D. Campbell, J. Giffard and L.F.H. Mundy); he shouted, "Come on, who's for the guns?" The officers and a number of men raced towards them and began to unlimber B and D sub-sections. They were sorely hampered by the horses tied to the wheels, and the rest plunging terrified, many wounded, as the German shells crashed into the field. Eventually they freed the two guns and turned them to face twelve German guns lining the edge of the high ground some 500 yards away to the east. D sub-section, with Lieutenant Campbell laying and Bombardier Perrett (later Captain F.M. Perrett) loading, was first to fire. It opened at 800 yards but dropped to 500 and soon got results with fuzes set to $1\frac{1}{2}$. As a detachment gathered round the gun, Lieutenant Campbell and Bombardier Perrett ran to C sub-section, they cut free the dead and dying horses, dropped the trail and swung into action. Again Lieutenant Campbell acted as layer but, after a round or two, a direct hit struck the shield, killing or wounding all serving it. A second direct hit killed the wounded Campbell, whose gallant efforts had done so much to bring the two guns into action.

Meanwhile Captain Bradbury and the other subalterns had got B-section into action. They began to fire at the enemy guns but soon used up the ammunition in the limber beside the gun. They then had to carry rounds forward through a hail of fire. Then D sub-section under Lieutenant Giffard was hit, leaving only B sub-section in action. Lieutenant Mundy acted as section commander, Captain Bradbury continued as layer while Sergeant Nelson acted as range setter. Gunner Darbyshire and Driver Osborn crossed and re-crossed the shell swept field to bring up ammunition. The German guns were now being hit but concentrated all their fury on the remaining guns of the gallant, dying L Battery.

Ammunition was now almost expended and more German guns were coming into action. Lieutenant Mundy was seriously hit and Sergeant Nelson was also badly wounded; somehow they kept on firing and, in so doing, drew almost all the enemy fire onto themselves. Captain Bradbury saw that more ammunition must be brought up; at that moment Battery Sergeant-Major Dorrell arrived at the gun and Captain Bradbury went for the ammunition. As he left the gun, this gallant officer, whose example had triggered off the whole action, was hit by a shell and mortally wounded. With only the Sergeant-Major and the brave, wounded Nelson left, the gun was served until the last round was fired, then it was silent—the end had come. Yet help was at hand; Major W.G. Thompson, commanding I Battery, selected a position for Captain Burnyeat's four gun battery (two sections of I Battery) about 2,000 yards from the German guns. The guns soon took heavy toll of the Germans caught in enfilade. As the mist cleared, the machine guns of the Middlesex caught the German gunners with rapid fire. Their teams were caught in the open. With costly gallantry, four of their guns were withdrawn but were later abandoned, the remainder were left where they stood; five were useless but three were taken. L had lost five officers, forty two men and one hundred and fifty of its two hundred and twenty-eight horses. Captain Bradbury died after the action and was posthumously awarded the Victoria Cross. His example and courage had inspired all, and his was the greatest share of the imperishable glory won that day. Lieutenant Campbell was killed, and Lieutenant Mundy died two days later. Lieutenant Giffard was wounded but recovered. Battery Sergeant Major Dorrell and Sergeant Nelson, both wounded, were also awarded the Victoria Cross. (Sergeant Nelson later rose to the rank of Major but was killed in 1918).

While this now famous action at Nery was being fought, another clash occurred at Crépy further east. 13th Infantry Brigade of 5th Division supported by 27 Brigade RFA was attacked by cavalry and infantry. Each battery of the Brigade was deployed in depth, but each had one section in the infantry firing line. One section of 119th Battery was only two hundred yards behind the front firing line of the King's Own Scottish Borderers, the KOSB. When the KOSB front line was withdrawn to the gun position, this section fired one hundred and fifty rounds at attacking infantry and halted it. The KOSB and the section then withdrew under the fire of the rest of the Battery. The whole brigade was withdrawn by the skilful use of artillery covering fire; another reminder of the high state of training and co-operation which had been achieved by the BEF.

Meanwhile the rearguard of 2nd Division, 4th Guards Brigade supported by 41 Brigade RFA, came under heavy attack in their position on the northern edge of

The one remaining 13-pounder gun of L battery **RHA** in action at Néry. From the original by Fortunno Matania in the possession of the Royal Artillery. *(R.A.I.)*

the forest of Villers Cotterêts between Puisieux and Vivers. 9th Battery effectively engaged German infantry in lorries but by 1000 hours it was decided to withdraw. Heavy fighting occurred in the forest but the batteries came into action covering its exits to the south. 2nd Division now faced north and east and did not appreciate that a strong German attack was developing from the north west. When it materialised the guns were ordered not to fire as the attackers were taken for British! However, when two German batteries opened fire, 41 Brigade RFA replied and silenced them. The guns were now seriously threatened and a battalion was ordered forward to protect them and cover their withdrawal. At this moment more German guns opened fire with such ferocity that a staff officer ordered the teams not to be sent forward, but this was too much for the drivers, who dashed forward before they could be stopped. They galloped through the shell fire and got to the guns. All were saved with remarkably few casualties. A gunner of 17th Battery and two of 9th Battery received the DCM for their courage that day.

These actions at Néry, Crépy and Villers Cotterêts were the last serious clashes with the enemy during the withdrawal to the Marne. The enemy would not close with the rearguards—usually the cavalry brigades. On 1st September, south of Betz, D and E Batteries drove off six German squadrons with their fire. On 2nd September, J Battery slaughtered more enemy while, on the 4th, E Battery caught a hostile battery in action and totally destroyed it.

On 5th September the withdrawal, often called the retreat to the Marne, stopped. The BEF had covered 140 miles in thirteen days not counting the two days advance to Mons to begin with. The infantry managed about four hours rest in twenty four, the Gunners only got two or three. First reinforcements began to arrive but replacement guns had not yet reached the battle area. 5th Division still had only about one-third of its artillery.

The retreat had once again shown the shortcomings of the high level control of artillery. The shortcomings in communications forced guns to be put too far forward, and the effect of concentrated fire was still to be learned. On the other hand, the technical handling of the guns and the bravery and courage of the Gunners were beyond praise. They still proved to be more accurate and quicker than the Germans, who usually fared worse in a gun duel, and few enemy infantry survived in a mass attack when caught by the murderous fire of the 18-pounders. The German fire lacked accuracy and they seemed unable to burst their shells to achieve maximum effect. On the other hand, their use of 5.9-inch howitzers and 8.2-inch mortars as medium artillery to support their field guns gave them a great advantage.

Yet, all in all, the Gunners had done superbly well, constantly in action, constantly in the rearguard, often in the foremost firing line, they had never failed and they earned great praise from their cavalry and infantry comrades in those memorable days. So they welded the respect built up at Le Cateau, a respect for the Guns which has never died in any war since those days of great glory, in the story of the Guns.

CHAPTER 5

The Battles of the Marne and the Aisne

See maps 9 and 10

At 1400 hours on 5th September, General Joffre arrived at the British GHQ at Chatillon-sur-Seine to beg, in the name of France, the intervention of the British Army in a battle into which he had decided to throw his last man. Visibly moved, Sir John French gave his word that the BEF would not fail. So it was that, on the 6th September, the Allied armies turned and advanced north eastwards. The Germans had advanced due south and were facing the British south of the Grand Morin river. They suddenly realised the peril of their position as the French Sixth Army advanced from Paris in the west. Von Kluck ordered a withdrawal and told *2nd and 9th Cavalry divisions with four Jäger battalions,* two in lorries, to advance to Rozoy to cover the operation. Accordingly early in the morning of the 6th September, this force struck the advancing British Army. 3rd Cavalry Brigade was without guns and fell back onto 1st Divisional Artillery, 26 and 43 Brigade RFA and 26th Heavy Battery. These guns silenced the German batteries and with this the Germans withdrew.

On 7th September, the Germans fell back to the Petit Morin; as they did, D Battery RHA caught a German battery in action and silenced it, otherwise the British advance continued unopposed. Von Kluck strengthened the Petit Morin to hold the British so that he could concentrate against the French along the Ourcq River. But he underestimated the British offensive power; on the 8th September the 3rd Cavalry Brigade drove in the German outposts and occupied St Cyr. However, a German counter-attack forced the detachments from the guns of D and E Batteries but, on the right, 1st Division cleared Sablonnières supported by the fire of 118th and 119th Batteries. 2nd Division had a harder job; the guns could not hit the enemy on the reverse slope of the Petit Morin valley; it was close infantry country and, apart from 9th Battery silencing some guns and manhandling a gun down the valley to support a crossing, the Gunners could do little to help. In the confusion, one battery mistook some Guards for Germans and opened fire on them, one disadvantage of the British decision not to use telescopes. It was here that 36 Brigade RFA was halted in column of march near Boitoron when Germans appeared two hundred yards away to the west. The Gunners seized rifles and lined the bank, and an officer, realising the Germans wanted to surrender, ran forward. The men, thinking he wanted help, charged; one of the rare occasions of gunners charging enemy infantry! The Germans were captured. At Bellot, the German cavalry counter-attacked but were smashed to pieces by six batteries of 1st Divisional Artillery. At 1600 hours the Germans withdrew right along the line and the guns took heavy toll of them. Most of the defenders of Orly were accounted for. It was at the crossing of the Petit Morin that the need for mortars was felt. They were needed to give close rapid support when the enemy clung to reverse slopes.

At 0800 hours on 9th September, the British crossed the Marne. I Corps had no enemy in front of it and pressed on. 5th Division struck a large mixed force of Germans which 3rd Division had by-passed when moving to the east. A great chance was now lost as both British divisions halted, not realising how successful they had been. The artillery "searched" for and destroyed some German guns; indeed, 65th and 80th Batteries saved 14th Infantry Brigade from disaster during a German counter-attack. 107th and 129th Batteries each silenced a German battery which was later captured by the infantry. However, no co-ordinated attack was made and the guns were used piecemeal on opportunity targets only. Had the 2nd, 3rd and 5th Divisional Artilleries been concentrated to support a rapid advance by the infantry, the Germans would not have been left to withdraw unmolested. But such techniques were not yet known to the British.

On 10th September, 1st Cavalry Brigade contacted a strong enemy force with heavy artillery support. L Battery, formed from two sections of I to replace the losses at Néry, engaged them but was itself silenced. However, the action lasted long enough to enable the French to come up and deal with the enemy. Further west, 1st Division came up against a strong enemy position near Priez. It was raining hard and the infantry of 1st Division were wearing ground sheets as they began to attack. The guns were left to fire on any likely target during the assault, when one battery, mistaking some infantry for retreating Germans, shelled them heavily causing them to fall back. The CRA, Brigadier Findlay, rushed 41 Brigade RFA into action to cover their withdrawal and silence German guns now opening fire. At this action, Brigadier Findlay was killed by German gun fire and his place was taken by Brigadier Horne, BGRA I Corps. This unfortunate action illustrated the weakness in British doctrine for artillery-infantry co-operation in attack; there was no fireplan, no co-ordinated observation or control and binocular observation from a distance was insufficient.

By the evening of 12th September the Allies had closed up to the Aisne. There was by this time a twenty-five mile gap between Rheims and Ostel in the German line but this was not located by the British. Both sides were very tired and the weather was very bad; the impetus of the British advance was lost and only one crossing was attempted on the 12th, by 11th Infantry Brigade.

The Battle of the Aisne began on the 13th September. It was doubly notable, for it saw the start of trench warfare and it saw the fire of British Artillery being directed by an aerial observer for the first time in battle. This was tried because the guns south of the river could not get far enough forward to find targets using the then normal methods. Two RFC—Royal Flying Corps—subalterns, Lewis and James, were the pioneers of the methods adopted for aerial observation of artillery fire and continued throughout this war. Observations were reported by means of a 'clock-code' system and transmitted by morse to the engaging batteries. The Regiment owes much to these young officers, both of whom were killed by enemy anti-aircraft fire; James in 1915, while observing for artillery, and Lewis in 1916.

Again British attack philosophy was wanting. Divisions were strung out and on 13th September were told to pursue an enemy who was not in flight. No priorities were given, no fireplan was made, no reserves were held with which to influence the battle; indeed, most troops attacked not even knowing their objectives. The advance was thus leisurely, as no sense of urgency was created by the higher command. It is remarkable that so many crossings were achieved so quickly. Only one bridge was standing and the Aisne, between sixty and seventy yards wide, was unfordable. Nevertheless, by last light the whole of 1st Division with its Artillery was across and took up position south of the Chemins des Dames ridge. Meanwhile, 2nd Division crossed on foot unopposed and built a pontoon for vehicles. The guns remained on the south bank and 35th Heavy Battery RGA shelled German infantry on the Soupir ridge. But again a chance was missed. There were few Germans on the Chemin des Dames ridge and those that were there were tired and dispirited. 1st and 2nd Division could have captured it on 13th September and subsequent German reports show that this would have rolled back the whole Aisne position and forced a general withdrawal. Instead, the British stopped and found billets, while the Germans rested and reinforced the ridge. Meanwhile, 3rd Division got infantry across but its artillery was two miles away on the south bank. Indeed, even when 49th Battery came into action, it was located, shelled and lost two guns. Most of the German guns were out of range of the rest of the divisional artillery. There was insufficient cable to link OPs on the north bank with guns on the south. Flag signalling was tried but it was not very successful, thus the infantry were denied the support of artillery without which they could not advance.

Opposite 5th Division, the German defences came right down to the river so a crossing was made after dark at Missy. The crossing was well supported by the divisional artillery from the south bank, still short of twenty-six guns lost at Le Cateau. The Germans, however, started to use some 5.9-inch and 8-inch howitzers which could only be reached by the British 60-pounders. These guns silenced the 5.9s but then were forced to move themselves. On 4th Division front, the British left flank, 11th Infantry Brigade, had crossed during the previous night, 68th Battery also got over and 12th Infantry Brigade crossed early on the 13th. Later in the morning these two brigades attacked but had almost no artillery support. In fact, these attacks could have been supported by the guns of 5th Division, a different division and a different corps, but this technique was still not developed.

The 14th September dawned cloaked in mist which blindfolded the artillery. The orders to I Corps were to advance in column and continue the pursuit. In fact, the enemy were on high ground, dug in and rested. The plan necessitated the decentralisation of artillery to infantry brigades. The infantry advance guards blundered into the enemy in the mist and units drifted into battle piecemeal. As the mist cleared some batteries were very exposed though, by luck, 46th and 113th Batteries found themselves ideally sited to drive back an enemy counter-attack onto 3rd Infantry Brigade. Throughout the day the battle became very confused as the British struggled up the spurs running south from the Chemin des Dames ridge. The guns were controlled by battery commanders doing what they could; affiliations were broken up and guns were moved to suit themselves rather than the infantry. All this was the result of bad orders, indeed wrong orders—"to pursue" when they should have been "to attack!". The result was no fireplan, units coming into battle piecemeal, and confusion. But there were successes. As 2nd and 3rd Infantry Brigades fought their way uphill at Troyon, 113th Battery was ordered forward in close support and, as it reached the crest with the infantry, the Battery Commander, Major Ellershaw (later drowned in 1916 as a Brigadier-

General with Lord Kitchener en route for Russia), saw a German attack developing and engaged it at 900 yards inflicting terrible slaughter on them. It was here that Bombardier Harlock continued to lay his gun after being twice severely wounded. For this action he was later awarded the Victoria Cross, the eighth such award to the Royal Regiment thus far in the war. During the subsequent fight two machine guns were knocked out and Major Ellershaw and eight Gunners raced forward to capture them, only to come suddenly face to face with two German officers and fifty men! Drawing his pistol, Major Ellershaw yelled "Charge" and the gallant band rushed the Germans who all surrendered! Suddenly, another call came from the area of the sugar factory on the Chemin des Dames feature. This time 114th Battery were dispatched. It was this battery galloping through the infantry into action which inspired the painting "The Guns! Thank God, The Guns!".

The stories were the same right across the front, though in places commanding officers and battery commanders were creating the basis of future attack planning. The Commanding Officer, 1st Royal Berkshires, directed his attack from 50th Battery's observation post and a form of covering fire was organised during the operation. Many batteries, however, did not fire at all and some only a few rounds when the infantry were hard pressed. Just when the CRA of 2nd Division, Brigadier E.M. Perceval, was beginning to realise the need to co-ordinate the fire of his brigades, he was sent to take command of 4th Guards Brigade, which was unfortunate for the Gunners as he was fast developing new techniques. The German artillery being particularly well handled, destroyed the only bridge at Vailly, thus isolating 40 Brigade RFA north of the river. Lieutenant Colonel R. J. G. Elkington, commanding it, eventually got back through 2nd Division but his brigade was moving all day and did not fire. 42 Brigade RFA had two batteries in action at Chassemy, with 23 Brigade RFA further east, where 109th Battery was neutralised. 30 Howitzer Brigade did all it could to silence some German 5.9-inch guns at 6,000 yards but failed. Meanwhile, 5th Division attacked the Chivres spur supported by their divisional artillery. However, since Le Cateau losses had still not been made up, only three field batteries and one heavy battery were available. 13th Infantry Brigade began to suffer heavily from two German batteries near Fort de Condé. 121st Battery, from positions near Ciry and at 3,500 yards, engaged them and assisted by 120th Battery and later 65th Howitzer Battery, the German guns were silenced. The observation post officer of 61st Howitzer Battery, often ahead of the infantry trenches, used his guns with great effect and soon dominated the whole spur. On the left of the British line, 4th Division crossed the river to the west of Soissons. The guns got across but could do little to help. 31st Heavy Battery RGA was spotted by an enemy aircraft and lost seventeen men and thirty-five horses to a German 8-inch gun.

However, 14th September was notable for another reason for it was on that day that aerial photographs were taken for the first time. These disclosed most of the German gun positions and resulted in the first really successful counter-battery fireplan at night.

Although the British crossed the Aisne, they could not gain the high ground—they held their positions but could not advance. The Germans dug themselves in on their dominating positions and, as the days went by, they reinforced their artillery with more heavy guns and repulsed all attempts to dislodge them. Trench

"The Guns! thank God, the Guns!". From a painting of guns on the Marne by Snaffles (Charles J Payne). *(R.A.I.)*

warfare had begun. The British guns had no covered positions nearer than 4,000 yards and soon all 3rd Division's guns across the river were located and silenced by the German heavy guns. The Germans enjoyed wonderful observation and concentrated their gunfire with skill, but the British gunners did well. On 16th September a German report stated "the attack of *VI German Corps* to drive the British into the river never started because of their overpowering artillery fire". On 20th September a German commander, explaining the failure of his attacks, said "the enemy is too stubborn and uses his artillery too skilfully". Once again the British guns were being well handled in defence. They found that they could not locate the enemy guns and so began to work more and more with aircraft, and began too to shoot more off the map, checking the results from the air.

On 19th September the first 18-pounder replacements arrived. On 23rd September, 1st, 2nd, 3rd and 4th Siege Batteries RGA arrived with old pattern 6-inch 30 cwt BL howitzers. Their range was only 6,000 yards and they were inferior to the German 5.9s; however, it was a help. A week later 5th and 6th Siege Batteries RGA arrived, each with four 6-inch BL 26 cwt howitzers. These batteries had been formed from 23rd, 39th and 107th Companies RGA.

On 20th September the rain stopped and German attacks began; there were bitter infantry struggles at close range, with the guns only playing a small part. However, lessons were being learned. On 25th September, the combined fire of the thirty-three guns and howitzers of 1st and 2nd Divisions were concentrated on Germans in the Chivy valley. The German report of the action states how their *14th Division* came to a complete standstill under heavy concentrated artillery fire. On 26th the enemy, when ordered to attack, refused to leave their trenches—the British had at last learnt the effect of concentrating their artillery. For the first time, at the insistence of General Haig, a "Group" of artillery was placed directly under orders of HQ I Corps. This Group consisted of 27 Brigade RFA, one battery of 12 Howitzer Brigade RFA, 3rd Siege Battery and one section of 35th Heavy Battery. The fire of this group was swung across the Corps front with devasting effect. By now too the 6th Division had arrived with its artillery under Brigadier-General W.L.H. Paget consisting of: 2 Brigade RFA—21st, 42nd and 53rd Batteries; 24 Brigade RFA—110th, 111th and 112th Batteries; 38 Brigade RFA—24th, 34th and 72nd Batteries; 12 Howitzer Brigade RFA—43rd, 86th and 87th Batteries; 24th Heavy Battery (60 pounder). Before the BEF withdraw from the Aisne to move to the Ypres sector, it may be useful to summarise the lessons and new techniques learned in this first month of war.

First it was clearly proved that properly made fireplans were indispensible in attack. This was a change of immense significance and led to the vast expansion of the Regiment in the next four years. Second it was again shown that open positions were fatal and voice control was unreliable, and these facts resulted in a renewed demand for improved artillery communications. Third was the need for cover and concealment both from enemy ground and aerial observation; again, following from this, came the use of alternative and dummy positions. 47th Battery had used both on 23rd September, having been located from the air, with great success. Fourth came the urgent need for anti-aircraft guns. Early in September some small QF pom-poms arrived for this purpose but they were of little use. It was now necessary to design a proper anti-aircraft weapon. Fifth, Divisional and Corps Artillery Commanders began to learn the value of co-ordinated, concentrated fire. Last was the problem of supply of ammunition. Guns were firing many times the expected rates of fire, so stocks had to be built up.

The major effect of all these lessons was a new study of the techniques of attack. Even so, it was a process of costly evolution rather than a simple re-think. British Commanders were still obsessed with the problems of defence. One effect of recognising the need to site guns further back and to improve communications to them was to realise the need for longer range and the ability to allow higher elevations to be used.

The design of the British guns was good. The 18-pounders and 4.5-inch howitzers had done well. The carriages needed strengthening and the spring recuperators, which sometimes failed, were replaced by 'air' versions. The 60-pounder carriages also needed strengthening, but had well proved themselves.

So ended the battles of the Marne and the Aisne, a period of transition for the Gunners. In defence, they had proved the soundness of their training, but in attack they had much to learn, and learn it they did and fast. It is interesting to note how, even in those early days, the need for all the major branches of the Regiment was demonstrated; field, medium and heavy guns working together; locating and counter battery and anti-aircraft. The vital role of communications and aircraft were realised, as was the need for co-ordinated centralised control of artillery.

CHAPTER 6

Ypres — The First Battle and the Expansion of the Artillery in 1914

See maps 11, 12, 13, 14 and 15

By early October 1914 Lord Kitchener was forecasting a long war; reports from the Front indicated the success of the German heavy guns and howitzers. The result was a realisation that many, many more guns would be needed. Accordingly, orders were placed for thirty two 12-inch howitzers, forty-eight 9.2-inch howitzers, sixty 6-inch howitzers and eight hundred and ninety–two 18-pounders. A build up of the Army to twenty four divisions was now foreseen. The War Office soon saw that even these figures were not enough and that three thousand 18-pounders, or five hundred six gun batteries, would be needed by May 1915. More serious, however, was the slow rate of manufacture of shells, only ten thousand per month for the 13 and 18-pounders and 4.5-inch howitzers, and one hundred for the 60-pounders. The shortage was already becoming apparent on the Aisne and it was vital to take action.

But more guns were urgently needed in France. Eighty more 6-inch howitzers, twenty 4.7-inch guns and one prototype 9.2-inch howitzer were sent to France in October 1914. This latter became affectionately known as "Mother". Meanwhile in the Empire, artillery units were preparing to fight. 22 Brigade RFA from South Africa joined the new 7th Division, and the divisional artilleries of the Lahore and Meerut divisions were on their way to France from India. These consisted of 5, 6 and 18 Brigades RFA (64th, 73rd, 81st; 83rd, 84th, 85th; 59th, 93rd and 94th Batteries) of the Lahore Division and 4, 9 and 13 Brigades RFA (7th, 14th, 66th; 19th, 20th, 28th; 2nd, 8th and 44th Batteries) of the Meerut Division. 7th Division disembarked at Zeebrugge on 6th October. The Artillery, under its CRA, Brigadier H.K. Jackson, consisted of 14 Brigade RHA, (C, F and T Batteries), 22 Brigade RFA (104th, 105th and 106th Batteries), 35 Brigade RFA (12th, 25th and 58th Batteries) and 3 Heavy Brigade RGA (111th and 112th Batteries of 4.7-inch guns). There were unfortunately no howitzers. The units of the 7th Division had nearly all come from overseas, having been relieved there by territorial units. There had been three weeks of training as a division before landing in Belgium.

The early weeks of October saw much movement in Belgium without a great deal of fighting. However, a major German threat was now developing and it was decided that the BEF should hand over its position on the Aisne to the French and march north to stem the enemy advance. On 9th October II Corps advanced from Abbeville to Bethune and III Corps moved to Hazebrouck. By 12th October the Germans had taken Lille and on the 11th October General Foch assumed command of the Northern Group of Armies.

The wheel driver of a gun team. From a sketch by Gilbert Holiday.   *(R.A.I.)*

The country around Ypres is undulating, flat and featureless. The roads are straight, lightly metalled and tree lined. There are small fields bounded by hedges themselves lined with trees, water is just below the surface and streams, dykes and canals are everywhere. To the east lies Mont Kemmel and a low range of hills. Towards Bethune, slag heaps provided some rather poor observation. The country was in no way suited to the British method of providing artillery support.

II Corps came up on the left of the French at La Bassée, to be opposed by *four German cavalry divisions and twenty-four Jäger battalions.* On 13th October the Germans attacked strongly and the British 5th Division bore the brunt. It was only on that same morning that the Divisional Artillery was made up to strength with guns, replacing those lost at Le Cateau. At Givenchy, 11th Battery was giving close support to the infantry and was severely mauled by enemy guns and infantry. Soon every man in the two forward sections lay dead or wounded, the enemy closed to 200 yards and, getting between the guns and their teams, prevented them from getting forward. With almost all their men either dead or wounded and the teams cut off from the guns the two sections were abandoned. The third section was withdrawn. The close country had forced CRAs to decentralise all guns to brigades and the still poor communications forced battery commanders to deploy their guns well forward. Near Annequin 28 Brigade RFA came into action alongside two French batteries and, together with 65th Howitzer Battery, the group did much execution in support of 13th Infantry Brigade. 27 Brigade RFA had 120th Battery in action as a battery but 119th Battery had one section in the line with the East Surreys, one also in the line with the Manchesters and a third alongside HQ 13th Infantry Brigade. 37th Howitzer Battery had a section with the Duke of Cornwall's Light Infantry and the other two in reserve. The Gunners still had little opportunity to do other than decentralise to this extent; they desperately needed better communications.

Co-ordination of effort was however improving; on 14th October, General de Maistre visited II Corps to thank the British for their artillery support. He said that his own officers stated that the British fire was distinctly more effective than their own!

On 15th October the guns had a busy day silencing enemy guns and destroying houses containing snipers and observers. 119th and 120th Batteries supported an attack by the Manchesters and East Surreys, with forward observers moving with the infantry—fire-planning was beginning. Co-operation with the French continued—they lacked howitzers to support their 75s, so 65th Howitzer Battery and 2nd Siege Battery moved to Annequin to support French attacks on Vermelles by their 58th Division. Later the French 24th, 25th and 26th Batteries came under command of 5th Division. During the month also the British and French artillery commanders discussed the best means of supporting the infantry in attack. The British believed in fire and movement, with bursts of fire whenever targets presented themselves. The French practice was to fire a violent "rafale" and then stop as the infantry rose to assault. This frequently failed, as the enemy were left free to man their guns during the assault. It was from these discussions that the idea of a moving barrage of fire was born, based on the British technique.

Meanwhile, further north the British cavalry and III Corps were advancing from Hazebrouck. On 12th October, D Battery RHA closely supported a highly successful attack by the 16th Lancers, driving the Germans from the Mont des

Cats. The cavalrymen were dismounted and D Battery kept up its fire to the very last moment, contributing greatly to the success of the attack. Strong German positions were encountered at Meteren, and air reconnaissance reported more Germans arriving. The Corps halted to prepare for its first attack of the war.

The conditions were most difficult, especially for the artillery. It was wet and misty, and the country was close, flat and gave poor observation. The flàt ground was dotted with farms—each a strong point. The only observation points were on the German side. The enemy consisted of *two cavalry divisions, four Jäger battalions and three batteries of field artillery*. On the British left II Corps, and on the right the French were unable to make progress. Such was the setting for III Corps' attack on Meteren. It is interesting here to record the exact wording of 4th Divisional Artillery orders:

"1.   The Divisional Artillery will come under orders of the Divisional Artillery Commander.

2.   29th FAB (Field Artillery Brigade) will support and supply SAA (small arms ammunition) to 12 IB (Infantry Brigade) from north slopes of Klite Hill ($1\frac{1}{4}$ miles E. of Pradelles, B9).

3.   32nd FAB will support 10 IB from W. of Fletre, advancing if necessary to hill 1,500 yards E. of that village.

4.   14th FAB will also support and supply SAA to 10 IB on the left of 32nd FAB.

5.   37th FAB will be distributed.

6.   31(H) (Heavy) Battery RGA will assemble at Rouge Croix ($1\frac{1}{2}$ miles SE. of Fletre)".

Though the idea of concentrating artillery is announced in paragraph one, subsequent paragraphs then distribute it out to brigades and give it the additional task of supplying small arms ammunition for the infantry.

To the right of 4th Division, 6th Division concentrated the fire of 12, 24 and 38 Brigades RFA to support the assault brigade. It added, "2nd Infantry Brigade and the Heavy Battery are to remain in reserve at Pradelles".

No targets were ordered, as nothing was known of the enemy positions in detail. It was in fact an ideal situation for a barrage, but the technique was not yet ready. The guns were concentrated and little was known about the enemy; all that was needed was a programme of covering fire. As it was, the attack developed into an infantry fight with such support as the gunners could give on opportunity targets. Forward observers did move forward with the infantry but they had acute communication problems, using flags and reeling out line. Meteren was eventually occupied but the Gunners were not happy with their inability to help at close quarters. The story was repeated on the 14th and 15th, as the Germans slowly fell back.

Meanwhile, a tenuous line now extended north to the sea. I Corps were moving up from the Aisne, II Corps under heavy attack lost Givenchy and the enemy opposite III Corps increased his pressure. The cavalry became bogged down in the close country and the RHA batteries with their 13-pounders felt the lack of high explosive shell. Their shrapnel had little effect against buildings. On 16th October,

4th Division seized a bridge at Pont de Nieppe over the Lys. 31st and 125th Batteries assisted, giving close support. On 17th October, III Corps occupied Armentières and 2nd Division of I Corps occupied Poperinghe. The scene was set for a major attack right along the line and this was ordered by Sir John French for 18th October. But this was too soon; there was not time for proper planning and, though gallant attacks were launched at mid-day on that day by both 5th and 6th Divisions, little progress was made. However, once again a vital lesson was learned. Some attacks were launched without proper artillery support and these failed. 12th Infantry Brigade of 6th Division, however, had close artillery support and gained most success, while 15th Infantry Brigade in 5th Division was supported by 11th, 52nd, 61st, 80th, 123rd and 108th (Heavy) Batteries and again was successful. The day as a whole was a success, for it again strengthened the line. Behind the three Corps, the newly formed IV Corps was coming into position. Sir John French had very little information about his enemy at this time. He had no idea of the massive build up going on in front of him. The newly arrived *German 4th Army* of four corps was now preparing for a stroke to end the war and seize Calais. But the Germans had their problems. The men were new, many were recruits and few of their officers had experience, especially in the artillery. They did not lack gallantry and they had massive superiority in numbers but their military knowledge was poor and they proved no match for the hardened, experienced regulars of the BEF.

Both sides were preparing for attack and both did attack, head on, in what has now become known as 'The First Battle of Ypres'.

The battlefield of Ypres needs description, for it features many times in this story. Map 13 shows the positions and shape. Ypres stands in a shallow saucer. The rim stretches from Wytschaete in the east to Hill 60 and on to Hooge, Polygon Wood and Passchendaele. Ypres is about 7,000 yards from Wytschaete and Polygon Wood. Zonnebeke is slightly higher giving some observation, with Messines Spur being the most important secondary feature. To the south across the Douvre stream lie Ploegsteert Wood and Hill 60. There was, in early 1914, an almost continuous line of woods stretching from Wytschaete to Zonnebeke, with gaps of flat open stretches between them. Inside the rim of this bowl the ground was drained by many streams and ditches. Fields were small, bounded by high ditched hedges, there were many houses and the roads were mud tracks. The country did in fact aid the defender as concentrated fire made the open spaces untenable. However, as winter approached and the effects of gunfire tore down the trees, the area became more open, but worse, it became soft and boggy, particularly in the British positions at the bottom of the saucer.

On 19th October, *eighteen German divisions* faced sixteen allied divisions. Against the British, who, between La Bassée and Langemarck had seven infantry and three cavalry divisions, were *ten German infantry and six cavalry divisions*. A period of probing actions next occurred, starting on the 19th October when 7th Division of IV Corps began an attack across the German front to Menin. As it did so, reports of a massive German thrust against its left flank began to arrive. IV Corps stopped in its tracks and fell back without attacking. 111th and 112th Heavy Batteries had great difficulty getting their guns back through the mud. On the 20th, 10th Infantry Brigade closely supported by 12 Brigade RFA successfully attacked Frélinghein without any knowledge of the approach of the *German 4th*

Army in the north. I Corps advanced into Ypres and reconnoitred forwards, as did the Cavalry Corps, but the latter was forced to retire. On 6th Division front the Sherwood Foresters were almost wiped out at Ennetiers. Still, however, the British had no idea of the size of the enemy advancing towards them and, on 21st, Sir John French ordered the Army to dig in and I Corps to attack Thourout. The advance of I Corps against Thourout really started the main battle of Ypres.

The battle followed five phases. First the encounter battle from 19th to 21st October, described above in very broad outline. Second the battle of Langemarck involving I and IV Corps from 26th to 28th October. Third the battles of La Bassée and Armentières which lasted up to 2nd November. This phase coincided with renewed allied offensives and the battle of Gheluvelt. Fourth came a final German effort culminating on 11th November at the battle of Nonne Boschen and finally the petering out of the battle up to 21st November.

On 21st October, II Corps on the right held its positions against repeated enemy attacks and great execution was again achieved by the guns. III Corps attacked, supported by the 4th Divisional Artillery. A section of 25th Battery caught an enemy attack in the flank with such devastating effect that it stopped. The German guns were notably ineffective all day, sweeping and searching from the map. The guns of I Corps were still well forward with the infantry; 2nd Division advanced towards Passchendaele and 1st Division towards Langemarck. 41 Brigade RFA supported 1st Guards Brigade, with 27 Brigade RFA and 47th Howitzer Battery supporting 5th Infantry Brigade. In 1st Division, 3rd Infantry Brigade was leading, supported by 39 Brigade RFA. I Corps met the Germans on an eleven mile front between Menin and Steenstraat and the guns again had a field day, 9th Battery firing at ranges of 1,000 yards, with 47th Howitzer Battery hotly engaged at St. Julien. 46th Battery caught German infantry advancing in the open and mowed them down with well burst shrapnel. The advance was halted at 1500 hours and I Corps was ordered to dig in where it stood. The guns kept up their fire with shrapnel on German infantry. Observation was difficult but helped by observation ladders which were first used here. Now that the battle had settled down, arrangements began to be made to concentrate the field guns with the heavy batteries. All were well forward. Telephone lines linked CRAs, and divisional artilleries were given tasks right across the front irrespective of the division they were supporting. The Commander Corps Royal Artillery—the CCRA—could, however, still do little. He had one clerk, no communications and a half share in a motor car with the Chief Engineer. A breakdown in radio on 21st October made aerial observation ineffective so all shooting was either from the map or controlled by forward observers. However, the arrival of gridded French maps made map shooting much more effective, enabling the divisional artilleries to be used more efficiently against enemy infantry and leaving counter-battery tasks to the heavies. There were fifty-four heavies at Ypres in 1914 (Twenty 60-pounders; sixteen 4.7-inch guns; sixteen 6-inch howitzers; one 6-inch gun and 'Mother', the 9.2-inch howitzer). In addition, there was an armoured train of six 4.7-inch guns.

The most serious factor now emerging was the shortage of ammunition. By the end of October, a limit had to be placed on daily expenditure. Despite desperate messages for more, none came forward, and the situation was just not understood in England. The War Office simply said that no Army or Nation could maintain the supply at the rate requested. This shortage did, however, have one side effect; the Gunners had to get the very best out of each round and as a result their accuracy, already good, improved further.

In spite of this acute shortage, for the next few days the guns were constantly firing. On 22nd October, a mass of Germans attacked 21st Infantry Brigade of 7th Division. This was almost annihilated to a man by twenty-eight 18-pounders and four 60-pounders of 2nd Divisional Artillery. On this day came a significant message from the Camerons to say that they had been driven back because they had advanced without artillery support; slowly, lessons were being learnt. On 23rd, the 1st Division attacked, supported by the concentrated fire of 25, 26 and 43 Brigades RFA and 26th Heavy Battery RGA, a notable concentration in 1914. The fire was controlled by forward observers reeling out telephone wire and, on this occasion, this was most effective. It was on this day, too, that 49th Battery near Aubers fired the first 18-pounder HE shell sent to the front for trials. During 23rd October, 2nd Divisional Artillery expended 3,572 rounds of all types.

24th October was notable, for it saw the transfer of the whole of 2nd Divisional Artillery to support 7th Division. 7th Division were desperately holding on to Polygon Wood and again the ammunition shortage became critical. Sir John French sent a message to the War Office saying, " Unless the supply of gun ammunition can be maintained, the troops will soon be forced to fight without the support of artillery". Indeed, on that day there were only some 150 rounds per gun in France! The seriousness of the situation was followed by a report which said that the massed German attacks could only be broken up by artillery.

Phase 2 of the battle began on 26th October, when the British and French tried to resume the offensive. They failed primarily because they still provided no proper fireplan to get the infantry onto their objectives; the guns, still right forward, were engaging opportunity targets only. An attempt at a rudimentary fireplan was made on 27th October for the attack on the Keiburg Spur. It failed because the exact location of the enemy was not known and there was insufficient ammunition. A similar attack on Neuve Chapelle by II Corps was supported by four British and nine French batteries. The bombardment opened at 1100 hours and lifted 500 yards at 1115 hours. The infantry (British, Indian and French) did not, however, follow up closely and again the attack failed.

On 29th October, it is reported for the first time that batteries fired "on their night lines" and a German night attack was stopped by artillery alone.

The Indian Corps had now arrived in the Ypres Sector. It consisted of the Lahore and Meerut Divisions, and, in addition to their own artillery listed earlier, came the 10, 11 and 18 Brigades, RFA.

As the days wore on and the tired infantry were relieved in the line, the practice began of leaving the guns constantly in action. The control of guns in defence was improved and soon guns in mass could be switched quickly onto any target along the front. Infantry Brigades had the call on some named battery at all times and on all else if available. The battles of La Bassée and Armentières struggled on, neither side achieving much. But on the 29th the Germans brought up massive reinforcements, including *2nd Bavarian Corps* of regular,tried troops and some two hundred and fifty guns and mortars. The German plan was to attack Gheluvelt with *two Corps* on 29th October and Ypres on 30th.

The British position at Gheluvelt was desperate. The infantry were tired and wet and bogged down in thick muddy ditches. The guns were down to seven rounds each per day, with orders to engage enemy guns only. The trenches of 7th Division were on forward slopes in full view of this mass of German guns. The Germans fired with all they had onto these forward trenches and, as the mist cleared, their infantry in mass broke through. They had, however, failed to touch the British guns. In the afternoon the fire of 14 and 26 Brigades RFA was concentrated to support a counter-attack by 1st Division. This attack was entirely successful, completely restoring the position by last light.

On 30th October, the main German attack started with a massive bombardment of Zandvoorde. This part of the line was held by the Cavalry Corps, having only their light 13-pounders and one section of 6-inch howitzers behind them. The British line gave between Messines and Zandvoorde but it did not break. At 0900 hours the Germans got two batteries up onto the Zandvoorde Ridge but these were seen by 105th and 106th Batteries, who engaged them in enfilade at 2,500 yards from positions just west of Gheluvelt and drove the detachments from the guns with shrapnel. Somehow, these two batteries kept their guns in action all day, sandbagging them in after dark. Meanwhile, 7th Divisional Artillery was hotly engaged supporting counter-attacks. 22 Brigade RFA was split up, 35 Brigade RFA fell back in depth, with 12th Battery near Herenthage, 25th Battery at Zwarteleen and 58th near Zillebeke. 12th Battery was pushed right forward to support a counter-attack to re-take Zandvoorde and became heavily engaged at short range, losing four officers. Three guns were hit and all the rest disabled. The battered but gallant Battery was then withdrawn to Hooge to refit. Later that day, a German battery caught the 1st Battalion Royal Welch Fusiliers and almost wiped them out. Try as they would the British Gunners could not locate this German battery.

Further south, south that is of Messines, the Germans could make no progress. 5th Divisional Artillery fired through the mist on fixed lines with great success. Known enemy batteries were kept quiet by the heavies. The Artillery Brigade group system developed by CRA 3rd Division, Brigadier Short, worked well. He brought down very heavy concentrations of fire wherever the enemy appeared.

On 31st October, the Germans were certain that they would break through the British lines. The Kaiser himself came forward to witness his armies destroying "the most hated enemy in the field"—the British. It is true to say that 31st October was perhaps the greatest day of crisis ever to face the British army. The men were tired, the line was thin, the artillery at the most threatened point disorganised and all reserves had been committed; ammunition was critically short. However, the ebb and flow of battle on the previous days ensured that the Germans did not know the exact British layout and the ground itself favoured the defenders. The Germans poured massive artillery concentrations onto areas they were sure contained British reserves—but they fell on empty ground—there were no reserves! Also the deadly accuracy of the British gunnery and rifle fire was beginning to tell on the untried German infantry, who had already sustained the most terrible losses. Stories of them attacking in mass with arms linked and being destroyed in mass shows the state they were in. There was, however, only one prepared British counter attack—south from Polygon Wood by 2nd Division's meagre reserves. This was to be covered by 41 Brigade RFA and its commander,

Ammunition Column passing through the ruins of Ypres. From a painting by Gilbert Holiday.   *(R.A.I.)*

Lieutenant-Colonel Lushington, set up in a cottage in the south west corner of the wood, and waited.

The defence of the Messines Ridge fell to the dismounted cavalry supported by E,H and J Batteries RHA. However, 4th Division Artillery on Hill 63 was able to cover the southern and south eastern approaches. The concentrated fire of this divisional artillery prevented any German advance from this direction. Further north, although the Germans managed to enter Messines, they could get no further throughout the day.

In the north 2nd Division, well covered by its artillery, managed to hang on to its ground all day.

It was again at Gheluvelt that the enemy made its main effort with some success. Thirty-eight 18-pounders, twelve 4.5-inch howitzers and eight 60-pounders, excluding Colonel Lushington's 41 Brigade RFA, were able to fire onto the Gheluvelt sector. These guns were all located around Veldhoek and Zandvoorde. Two sections of 51st Battery were dug in at Poezelhoek and were able to fire directly onto enemy approaching Gheluvelt. The rest depended on forward observers in Ghuluvelt itself. Soon, most of these were killed or wounded or their telephone lines were cut. No pre-arranged defensive fireplan existed, nor was the artillery co-ordinated under one commander so, with the observers killed or wounded and cut off, the guns were unable to fire on massed German infantry attacking the village. At 1130 hours the Germans occupied Gheluvelt but were unable to exploit north. 116th and 117th Batteries came under rifle fire at 500 yards range but continued to rake the Germans with shrapnel. The sight of the guns in action acted as a rallying point to the disorganised infantry falling back from the village. 54th Battery covered the exits to the north and west. The Gloucesters rallied to the guns and dug in round them. At 1330 hours the Worcesters counter-attacked, supported by 41 Brigade RFA as planned. The attack was almost entirely successful, driving the Germans from the village north of the road. At this moment, a German aircraft saw the staffs of 1st and 2nd Divisions assembled at Hooge and accurately shelled them. General Lomax was wounded and Captain F.M. Chenevix-Trench, BMRA 2nd Division, was killed, together with six other officers—a shattering loss just as the battle reached its peak. By 1500 hours 116th and 117th Batteries came under close rifle fire and began to withdraw with some losses. Meanwhile the Germans worked one gun forward of the village on the road. Lieutenant R. Blewitt of 54th Battery was sent forward with a gun to silence it, which he did with his second round of HE shell recently arrived in France. Meanwhile, the guns kept up a heavy fire on the Germans who could get out of the village. After dark it was evacuated and a stronger line constructed to the north.

Two hours after the attack on Gheluvelt had begun, the whole of the 7th Division sector was attacked after a massive bombardment. Soon, Zandvoorde Ridge had fallen and a gallant section of 106th Battery lost almost half their men. They had kept on firing down to ranges of 1,000 yards but, as the infantry fell back and passed them, the survivors took the sights and breech blocks and withdrew. Although the guns were overrun, a quick counter-attack enabled the teams to gallop up and the guns were saved. As the line fell back, 25th Battery found itself in the firing line, with 58th Battery actually in front of it! 58th Battery withdrew to Hooge but 25th Battery stuck it out with the Irish Guards until 1600

"TEAMS STOOD PATIENT."
By "Snaffles."

"The teams stood patient". From a painting by Snaffles.   (*R.A.I.*)

hours. Then an incredible thing happened. 2nd Infantry Brigade suddenly counter-attacked, led by Brigadier E.S. Bulfin, and swept all before it. Encouraged by this gallant attack, the whole of 7th Division moved forward, regaining most of its lost ground. As the British were consolidating, two German machine guns hidden in a house began to do much damage. A gun of C Battery RHA was manhandled forward and knocked them out—the final action of the day. The crisis was over, the line had held, but not without heavy loss in men and horses. Ammunition was again critically low, there being only some 320 18-pounder rounds per gun left in France.

We must now look further south where we left the Germans just entering Messines. The line held all day but after dark the British withdrew. Elsewhere, the exhausted enemy was held everywhere. Although unknown at the time, the two sides had at that moment occupied positions that were to remain almost unaltered for the next three years.

There now came a period of ten days of minor actions, until the Germans made their final bid to break through on 11th November. Again, the most critical factor was the shortage of ammunition; guns were restricted to twenty rounds 18-pounder and ten rounds 4.5-inch howitzer per gun per day. Minor incidents occurred; centralised control of guns was practised and developed until, on 11th November on a nine mile front north east from Messines, 17,500 Germans rose to attack 7,800 British.

On the British right, the concentrated fire of 4th Divisional Artillery, backed up by 7th Divisional Artillery and controlled by Brigadier Headlam, held the Germans in their trenches and for some time no attack developed. The French, holding the line between Messines and Zillebecke, held. Except just north of the Menin Road where the *Prussian Guards Division* attacked Nonne Boschen Wood, the Germans were held right along the front. A German history states that the attacks all failed "owing to the deadly fire of the British artillery". The British system of developing strong points in depth did much to absorb the German attacks but, even so, on 2nd Division's front the situation against the *Prussian Guards* was critical. It was here, on that Wednesday 11th November 1914, that the Scots Guards, Black Watch and Cameron Highlanders were overwhelmed and the Germans entered Nonne Boschen Wood, pushing through to its western edge. Here they came face to face with 41 Brigade RFA (9th, 16th and 17th Batteries) who were in action to the east of Westhoek only 400 yards away. The Batteries were echeloned back, in good cover but on lower ground, and were facing south east. Lieutenant Colonel Lushington, the Brigade Commander, had his HQ in a shelter by the Chapel just to the south of the Westhoek crossroads. Brigade HQ was connected by telephone to CRA 2nd Division and HQ 5th Infantry Brigade, which was in the north west corner of Polygon Wood. 9th Battery was sited along a hedge with only the muzzles of the guns visible. Slit trenches were dug for the detachments and the command post. The guns of 16th Battery were in action in order, A, B, C, D, E and F sub-sections in a grass field but along a wire fence and under some apple trees. Again slit trenches were dug and overhead cover improved. Polygon Wood could be seen about 1,000 yards to the east. To the front was Nonne Boschen Wood. 17th Battery faced south east behind a line of willows, with a barn on its right flank protecting it from Nonne Boschen. A French "75" battery was near Brigade HQ. Further to the east was HQ 39 Brigade

RFA (Lieutenant Colonel G.G.S. Carey) but nothing else lay between the Brigade and HQ 2nd Division.

As the stragglers of the three infantry battalions passed through the gun lines, Major W.E. Clark, commanding 16th Battery, opened fire on Nonne Boschen Wood. He and Captain C.R.B. Carrington and two signallers dashed through enemy shell fire and rapidly organised the close defence of the battery, getting every possible man into action with rifles at either side of the guns. Lieutenant O.M. Lund, Brigade Orderly Officer, was sent back to warn 2nd Division of the situation. On the way, he collected a few gunners from 16th Battery officer's mess, armed them with some French rifles, showed them how to use them and put them in action covering left section where they fired all day at the enemy infantry! By 0915 hours Major H.C. Rochfort-Boyd, commanding 9th Battery, was in his observation post in Nonne Boschen Wood. Soon he was surrounded by Germans but, putting on his old pattern dark blue overcoat, he slipped through the leading Germans who mistook him for one of themselves in the smoke and mist and reached 16th Battery, confirming that there were now no British infantry in front of the guns. The gap through which the enemy were coming was some 1,500 yards wide between the Menin Road and Polygon Wood.

At 0930 hours the enemy moved out of the wood towards 16th Battery, which itself was out of sight from them in a hollow. Major Clark opened fire with all guns at 300–400 yards, shrapnel, fuze 1/2. The effect was devastating. At the end of the day, three hundred Prussians lay dead and wounded in front of 16th Battery. Nevertheless, the Germans had continued to close on the battery from the flanks. Corporal Richardson and four men were covering the left flank and reported a party of Germans only eighty yards away. Lieutenant H.O.C. Anne, commanding left section, immediately ordered Number 5 gun to swing round and at fuze 0 it destroyed the enemy party. Corporal Richardson then took four men, Cook, Ware, Radson and Eustace and occupied a building where they did great execution with rifles on the attacking Germans. Corporal Ware acted as observer, using a biscuit tin in the wood as a reference point. Meanwhile, another party were seen entering a house just in front of 17th Battery. With its second round, Number 5 gun of 16th Battery hit the house just as the Germans entered, destroying all but one. Major Bond, commanding 17th Battery, sent Second Lieutenant R.T.W. Glynn and six gunners to a barn to his right front. Here he found a sergeant of the Cameron Highlanders and he spread his force out along the hedge around the barn. Taking the sergeant he went off to reconnoitre. They saw Germans closing in and returned to the barn in time to engage the enemy at close range and drive them off, so saving the flank of the Battery. Later in the day, Lieutenant Glynn was wounded in the face by a rifle bullet.

This party, together with that of Corporal Richardson on the left of 16th Battery, effectively prevented any further German penetration. Throughout the day the Germans closed on 17th Battery but, with British shrapnel bursting low, all their attempts were stopped. At this point Lieutenant P.H. Murray of 39 Brigade RFA galloped up to find out what was going on (he had no saddle!). Major Clark told him but said he was not clear of the situation on the edge of Nonne Boschen Wood. Lieutenant Murray yelled "All right I'll clear it up for you!" and galloped off. Shortly afterwards he re-appeared, hatless and pursued by rifle fire, shouting that German infantry were closing on the guns of 16th Battery.

He said he had come in a hurry because his horse was an excitable brute and disliked bullets and he was sorry he had lost his hat! He then galloped off, saying he must go and find it! Soon he re-appeared with accurate details of the position, which were of great value to the Battery. He was extremely angry because, though he had found his cap, some German had dared to remove his badge from it. He then turned to return and report the position to his Colonel. This extremely gallant young officer was later killed in action on 25th September 1915. By now, however, the 16th Battery position was the British firing line. At the end of the day a Prussian was found dead, killed by shrapnel, only two hundred yards from 17th Battery guns. Gradually odd parties of men, including some from Brigade HQ, some sappers and infantry, reinforced the position. But it was the fire of the guns and gunners with small arms that had finally halted the Prussian Guards. To the south of the German break-through the guns of 51st Battery of 39 Brigade RFA, in action at the eastern edge of Sanctuary Wood, engaged targets to the front of 7th Infantry Brigade. This Brigade records how, time after time, these guns broke up attack after attack as the enemy emerged from Glencorse Wood. The gallantry of 9th, 16th and 17th Batteries on that memorable day has seldom been surpassed in the annals of the Royal Regiment.

At 1300 hours on 11th November, the 2nd Battalion the Oxfordshire and Buckinghamshire Light Infantry some three hundred strong, arrived at 16th Battery position. A counter-attack was planned. When this went in at 1500 hours, supported by 41 Brigade RFA and 46th and 54th Batteries of 39 Brigade RFA, the Prussians were swept from the field and the line between the Menin Road and Polygon Wood was safe. The Gunners had few losses, due to the excellence of their positions and the fact that they had not been located by German artillery. After the war the Germans acknowledged the destruction of the *2nd Guard Grenadier* and *1st Foot Guards Regiments* on 11th November at Nonne Boschen, a total of thirty officers and one thousand three hundred men, almost entirely due to the deadly fire of the guns of 41 Brigade RFA! The Brigade expended 1,744 rounds on that day and held a vital gap which undoubtedly saved the line. General Monro, commanding 2nd Division, sent the following message to 41 Brigade RFA at 1700 hours 11th November: "My best congratulations to the splendid 41 Brigade RFA. They have behaved today as they have on every occasion in this war. I am proud to have the honour of serving with them". Other than this, the action appears to have been overlooked, for no honours have ever been awarded for Nonne Boschen—perhaps now they should be? Nevertheless, it had been the Gunners day, almost entirely. After the battle an infantryman led a wounded German officer who, seeing Major Clark, saluted and, as they walked along the line of guns, said, "And where were your reserves?" To this Major Clark pointed to his guns; unbelieving, the German said, "But what troops stood behind?" Major Clark's curt reply was "Divisional Headquarters!"

So ended the first battle of Ypres. The German "thrust to the Channel" was stopped, primarily by the tough quality of the B.E.F. The German conscripts were no match for the British regulars—quality had defeated quantity. The Gunners had every reason to be proud of themselves after the first battle of Ypres. They earned warm admiration from the French, respect and fear from the Germans, and again strengthened the confidence of the British infantry. They proved they could fight with great gallantry and accuracy but, as before, they were best in defence. The lessons of command and control in attack, though known, were yet to be practised.

First Ypres was possibly one of the greatest defensive battles fought by the British in the war. There is no doubt that the skill, courage and gallantry of all Arms was superb but let it be recorded here that, in all German accounts explaining their failure, they say that "it was due to the devastating British artillery".

CHAPTER 7

March 1915 – Neuve Chapelle

See map 16

By 17th November, the Germans had abandoned all hope of renewing the offensive in 1914. The winter had set in and conditions were appalling. Minor attacks did continue but these were easily stopped. Meanwhile, 8th Division had arrived in France with 5 Brigade RHA (G, O and Z Batteries); 32 Brigade RFA (32nd, 33rd and 36th Batteries); 45 Brigade RFA (1st, 3rd and 5th Batteries) and 8 Heavy Brigade RGA (118th and 119th Heavy Batteries with 4.7-inch guns). The latter was the first heavy brigade to arrive in France and its CRA was Brigadier A.E.A. Holland.

The period of minor actions which now began saw further consolidation of the line. A gun of 54th Battery was run up into the trenches and blew some Germans out of some forward positions. A section of 3rd Heavy Battery destroyed buildings at point blank range, but the need for many more medium guns was felt. A heavy bombardment of Neuve Chapelle on 10th November by field batteries had done little damage to the buildings, leaving them to be re-occupied by the enemy. But these were isolated incidents, ammunition of all kinds was still very short and, as winter arrived, the fighting decreased and artillery commanders began to take stock. The main problems were the need for better communications, and development of air observation techniques, the need for mortars and better map shooting methods to improve the local defence of gun positions.

Demands for new and more telephones were made to give all artillery commanders direct control of more guns. It is interesting to note that it was on 2nd December that 7th Divisional Artillery reported that telephone communications between HQRA and all brigades were working well, the first indication that such a network existed.

The need for air observation and radio, particularly for the heavy batteries, had been well proved. Without it, it was impossible to be really effective. On 8th December a young artillery captain, Captain H.C.T. Dowding (later Air Chief Marshal Lord Dowding), commanding 9th Squadron RFC, was assigned to aerial artillery observation. A system was devised of using a template running north to south representing a clock face with 12 o'clock north and 6 o'clock south. Range rings of 50, 100, 200, 300, 400 and 500 yards were inscribed and corrections were given by using a clock hour, for example "2 o'clock 200 yards". The radio he used weighed 75 pounds and its inclusion in an aircraft meant ousting the observer; nevertheless, the system was now ready for trial. The urgent need to improve observation was making many commanders turn their eyes to the RFC.

A trial mortar of 5-inch calibre firing a 50-pound shell was sent to the trenches but it was much too big, clumsy and inaccurate and was not introduced.

The art of map shooting was born during the winter of 1914/15. It was realised that, provided the guns were level, accurately located and calibrated and there was no wind, there was a very good chance of shooting accurately from the map. A paper by a Captain G.W. Baron suggested that accurate allowance be made for "the temperature of the charge, the density of the atmosphere and the force and direction of the wind". But how? As with so many of the 1914 problems, that was the question.

The importance of well dug in guns was realised but such digging must not impede the elevation and traverse of the gun. Zones of 180 degrees had to be expected but cover from the air was now vital too and the requirements of these conflicted. Policy instructions were issued on siting trenches, establishments of rifles per battery, camouflage and concealment.

One of the most significant advances came on 13th December 1914, when the first full artillery operation order for an attack was issued by HQRA 3rd Division. The important document is repeated below.

"3rd Division Artillery Operation Order No 1

Reference Artillery Map   December 13th, 1914

1. The French Corps on our left attacks tomorrow Wytschaete from the North. The 3rd Division co-operate by attacking from the West, first objective Petit Bois and point 73—Fine de Medlestede; the 8th Infantry Brigade carrying out this task.

   Portions of the 5th and 4th Division Artillery from positions between Mont Kemmel and Square K4 co-operate by fire to assist 3rd Division.

2. The attack will be preceeded by a preliminary bombardment and details regarding this are shown in Appendix I.

3. Appendix II details the names by which certain localities will be referred to during the operation.

4. The Artillery in their present positions will be grouped as follows:

   (a)   Under CRA
          23rd Brigade RFA

   Howitzer   { 1 Battery 30 Brigade RFA }   under Lieutenant Colonel Staveley
   Group   { No 1 Siege Battery   }   of 30 Brigade RFA
              { No 3 Siege Battery   }

   (b)   Under GOC 8th Infantry Brigade
          42nd Brigade RFA
          But during preliminary bombardment this Brigade will conform to instructions in Appendix I.

5. The 40 Brigade and 2 Batteries 30 (Howitzer) Brigade will be in reserve.

6. The Trench Howitzers will fight under instructions issued separately.

7. The Artillery will comply with Appendix I during preliminary bombardment but Battery Commanders will act on their own initiative if, during this period, they get a favourable target in their usual zone.

8.   After preliminary bombardment no unit will fire on Petit Bois or point 73—Fine de Medelstede without orders. Batteries will be ready to engage targets communicated on the 12th to Brigade Commanders and the Heavy Battery. There will be no actual cessation of fire at 7.45, batteries turning on to targets communicated to Brigade Commanders tonight by CRA.

9.   The Brigade and Batteries in Reserve will remain harnessed up at their billets from 8 a.m. ready to move on short notice. An officer from 40 Brigade and each Howitzer Battery will report to Division Artillery HQ at 8 a.m.

10.   The ammunition expended by units during the 14th should not, and, in the case of 4.5 in Howitzer, will not, exceed the amounts in Appendix I.

11.   Ammunition supply will be carried out so far as possible during the hours of darkness.

12. Division Artillery HQ will be at Schoepenberg from 630 a.m. Orderlies from Brigades and Heavy Batteries to be there at that hour.

Copies to   23 Brigade   (Signed)   E. N. TANDY
             30 Brigade   Major RA
             40 Brigade   Brigade Major
             42 Brigade   3rd Division Artillery
             48 Heavy Battery

Issued at 9.45 p.m.

APPENDIX I (to 3rd Division Artillery
Operation Order No. 1)

1.   Ammunition allotment per gun for 14th.

	For preliminary bombardment	For rest of day	Total
18-pounder	60	165	225
4.5-inch howitzer	50	130	180
6-inch howitzer	10	18	28
60-pounder	As fast as possible	As may be required	

2.   Preliminary Bombardment to last from 7 a.m. to 7.45 a.m. in bursts of intense fire during the following periods:—

    7 a.m.–7.10 a.m.
    7.20 a.m.–7.23 a.m.
    7.30 a.m.–7.35 a.m.
    7.40 a.m.–7.45 a.m.

3. Targets during Preliminary Bombardment.

German support trench N.E. corner of C15 b N. of Petit Bois	} 1 Battery, 23rd Brigade
Petit Bois	{ 3 Batteries, 42nd Brigade 5 6in Howitzers 1 Battery, 23rd Brigade
German trenches just W. of Farm Medelstede Road Junction Point 73	{ 2 6in Howitzers 4 4.5in Howitzers 1 Battery, 23rd Brigade 2 4.5in Howitzers
Wytschaete Cross Roads	1 Section 48 Heavy Battery
Working with aeroplane or as ordered	1 Section 48 Heavy Battery

4. Official time is $3\frac{1}{2}$ minutes ahead of the time given to Brigade Commanders tonight.

(Signed)   E. N. TANDY
Brigade Major"

This first artillery operation for an attack in the war covered the allocation of guns, timings, supply of ammunition and communications. It was followed by an elaborate timetable, not reproduced here. CRA 5th Division issued a similar order on this occasion, the occasion being an attack on Messines which, though it failed, saw a great advance in command and control of artillery.

On 18th January, it was proposed to change the status of the Corps Artillery Adviser to that of 'Commander'. This was hotly opposed by the CRAs of the day. It was also decided to group all heavy batteries into 'groups' at Army level commanded by brigadiers. Medium guns were similarly grouped at Corps level. The controversy over the organisation of field brigades was again opened, all CRAs wanting mixed field and howitzer brigades. Also the old four or six gun battery argument was re-opened at this time; this was the result of casualties and shortages and the various organisations then in existence. The War Office issued new training pamphlets in February 1915 summarising these lessons but, strangely, they did not highlight the artillery drills to be used in attacks.

At the beginning of 1915, the British held a front of only twenty-one miles from Wytschaete in the north to Givenchy in the south. Ypres had been handed over to the French. Meanwhile, the 1st and 2nd Indian Cavalry Divisions had arrived with 1 Indian Brigade RHA (The Chestnut Troop, Q and U Batteries) and 2 Indian Brigade RHA (N, V and X batteries). The Chestnut Troop fired its first round of the war at Givenchy on 20th December. About the New Year the newly raised 27th and 28th Divisions, formed from the last of the overseas garrisons, landed in France. 27th Division brought 1 Brigade RFA (98th, 132nd and 133rd Batteries; 19 Brigade RFA (95th, 96th and 131st Batteries) and 20 Brigade RFA (57th, 99th and 148th Batteries). 28th Division brought 3 Brigade RFA (18th, 62nd and 365th Batteries); 21 Brigade RFA (69th, 100th and 103rd Batteries) and 146 Brigade RFA (75th, 366th and 367th Batteries). Most of the batteries of these two Divisions had only four guns, had done very little training and had only one or two regular officers and NCOs each. Training started in earnest on arrival in France. On 26th December, the BEF re-organised into two Armies, the First Army under General Haig and the Second under General Smith-Dorrien. The senior Gunner at GHQ under Sir John French was Major General J.P DuCane. He was still an Artillery Adviser. Artillery Adviser at HQ First Army was Major General F.D.V. Wing and at HQ Second Army it was Brigadier G.T. Forestier-Walker. It was, however, during 1915 that these officers gradually became known as MGRAs. In October 1915, Corps Artillery Advisers were re-designated GOCRAs.

But the expansion of the Army was still under way. Lord Kitchener's new army of eighteen divisions was being formed. Raising artillery for such a force in such a short time was a formidable task. Minute nuclei formed into batteries. One artillery brigade was formed around a retired colonel and four new second lieutenants! One battery moulded itself together round a volunteer infantry company and a band sergeant! On 27th February, the first of these Divisions, 46th (North Midland) (NM), landed in France. It had 1 (NM) Brigade RFA (1st, 2nd and 3rd Lincolnshire Batteries), 2 (NM) Brigade RFA (1st, 2nd and 3rd Staffordshire Batteries) and 3 (NM) Brigade RFA (4th, 5th and 6th Staffordshire Batteries) and 4 (NM) Howitzer Brigade RFA (1st and 2nd Derbyshire Batteries). The field batteries each had four 15-pounders and the howitzer battery had four 5-inch howitzers.

By the end of February it was decided to carry out a major attack at Neuve Chapelle. This battle was to be the last with the BEF alone, and the first of the battles which were to characterise the fighting in France for the next three and a half years. The battle will be described in some detail since it became a turning point in artillery tactics. It became a pattern for the use of artillery in attack which was followed right through to the Second World War. General Haig, whose First Army was to carry out the operation, gave his Corps Commanders four tasks for their artillery. He ordered that guns should be allotted to these tasks and, when this was done, all the plans should be co-ordinated into one massive bombardment plan. The tasks were: first, to destroy the enemy fire and front trenches; second, to protect the flanks; third, to form a curtain of fire behind the enemy's front trenches to prevent him reinforcing them and fourth, to neutralise the enemy guns and machine guns. Experiments showed that 18-pounders firing shrapnel were very effective in cutting wire and could do it in thirty-five minutes if the fire was really accurate. A plan was accordingly drawn up between the five CRAs (8th, Lahore and Meerut Divisions and the two Heavy Group commanders).

It is remarkable that they felt that this could be done without an overall Artillery Commander. There was, in fact, some friction and it again showed the need for Artillery Commanders at Corps and Army level. However, a plan was arranged in three phases as follows:

a. *Phase 1—0730 hours to 0805 hours:* Infantry to assault at 0805 hours on a 2,000 yard front and charge across 200 yards to the enemy front trenches while the guns lift to phase 2 targets.

    (1) *13 and 18-pounders* (total of 240 guns or 40 batteries):
        (a) Wire cutting.
        (b) Trenches to right and left of front attack.
        (c) Selected targets.

(2) *4.5-inch and 6-inch howitzers* (60 howitzers and 10 batteries):
    (a) Trenches under attack.
    (b) Selected targets.

(3) *9.2-inch howitzers* (3 howitzers): Neuve Chapelle.

(4) *4.7-inch guns and 6-inch guns* (36 guns): German Artillery.

b. *Phase 2—0805 hours to 0835 hours:* Infantry to clear the enemy front trenches and then clear up to the support trenches 200 yards beyond and pause till 0835 hours. Then attack Neuve Chapelle and pass on to the final objective.

(1) *13 and 18-pounders:* On a belt east of the village and across the front of the attack.

(2) *4.5-inch howitzers:* Enemy strong points.

(3) *6-inch and 9.2-inch howitzers:* Neuve Chapelle.

c. *Phase 3.* Corps Commanders to order targets, depending on the progress of the battle, particularly known strong points at Bois de Biez, Pietre and Aubers. Phases 1 and 2 were to be carried out by the 8th Division and this meant placing all artillery less the heavies under its CRA, Brigadier A.E.A. Holland. He organised it into five groups as follows:

a. *The Horse Artillery Group*
    (1) 5 Brigade RHA (O and Z Batteries)
    (2) 14 Brigade RHA (F and T Batteries)
    (3) 1 Indian Brigade RHA (The Chestnut Troop, Q and U Batteries)
                             Total of 42 × 13-pounders

b. *A Group*
    (1) 32 Brigade RFA
    (2) 45 Brigade RFA
                             Total of 36 × 18-pounders

c. *B Group*
    (1) 2 Indian Brigade RHA (N, X and V Batteries)
    (2) 22 and 35 Brigades RFA.
                             Total of 18 × 13-pounders
                            and 36 × 18-pounders

d. *Siege Howitzer Group*
    (1) 4th and 5th Siege Batteries (6-inch howitzers)
    (2) 59th and 81st Siege Batteries (6-inch howitzers)
                      due 9th March
                         Total of 20 × 6-inch howitzers

e. *Field Howitzer Group*
    37 Brigade RFA—18 × 4.5-inch howitzers

The heavy artillery remained under Army control, consisting of 32 × 4.7-inch guns, 3 × 9.2-inch howitzers and 1 × 15-inch howitzer (part of the armoured train). The arrival of the battery of 9.2-inch howitzers marked the arrival of the first all mechanised battery to see action. The guns were drawn by Holt caterpillar tractors and all other transport was motorised.

The aim now was to concentrate this artillery and to maintain secrecy. The batteries were brought into action by night and registration of targets was completed slowly along with "routine" shooting. The 18-pounders were placed in a large semi-circle facing Neuve Chapelle. They were to engage the wire at ranges of 1,200–2,000 yards. The howitzers and heavies were placed to engage at 3–5,000 yards. A Royal Engineers survey party 'fixed' the heavy and siege batteries and computed accurate firing data to the main targets. Artillery time-tables were first prepared at Neuve Chapelle and detailed objective maps were issued. Gun platforms were prepared and the guns firmly anchored to give accurate fire on the wire.

Observation was a problem in the flat, low lying country. Two "crows nests" were established at Rouge-Croix but these were a mile behind the line. Some haystacks were hollowed out to give semi-protected observation. Some houses at Port Logy offered the best and most forward observation posts. Here it is reported that, just before the battle, there were thirty artillery observing officers in one house!

All guns were in position by 5th March and were well settled and registration complete. All, that is, save 59th and 81st Siege Batteries (6-inch) who were delayed in UK. They were to have the vital role of destroying the enemy front trenches in phase 1 and they did not get into position until 9th March, the day before the assult. The difficulty of bringing a battery direct from England to France, to take part in a main attack the next day, can be imagined.

Ammunition supply was a problem but some stocks had been built up until the following scale was available for the whole operation:

		No. of guns
13-pounder	600 rounds per gun	60
18-pounder	410 rounds per gun	324
4.5-inch howitzer	212 rounds per gun	54
60-pounder	450 rounds per gun	12
4.7-inch gun	437 rounds per gun	32
6-inch howitzer	285 rounds per gun	28
6-inch gun	400 rounds per gun	4
9.2-inch howitzers	333 rounds per gun	3
2.75-inch gun	500 rounds per gun	12
15-inch howitzers	40 rounds per gun	1

Reconnaissance was carried on during the early days of March. The Royal Flying Corps prepared to control artillery fire on a scale hitherto unheard of. Aerial photographs were produced and the data transferred to maps showing the exact locations of enemy trenches and batteries.

So it was that, because of thorough and detailed preparations, complete tactical surprise was gained when the bombardment opened up at 0730 hours on 10th March 1915.

Phase one was remarkably successful. The wire, some fifteen yards thick, was effectively cut by fifteen batteries at fifty rounds per gun. The gaps were, in fact, ready within ten minutes of opening fire. The German defence works were then methodically destroyed by the 4.5-inch howitzers, except for some four hundred

The pilot and his aircraft. Captain B E Catchpole, **RFC**, who was the pilot of an **R.E.8**, and was engaged on the observation of the fire of guns. The **R.E.8** was designed for that purpose, flying more slowly than the enemy fighters could. *(R.A.I.)*

yards, the target of 59th and 81st Batteries brought hastily into action the previous night. The infantry assault, successful everywhere else, failed with heavy losses at this point and demonstrated dramatically how dependent the infantry were on accurate artillery support. However, another feature of the battle was the speed with which 45 Brigade RFA, 35th Heavy Battery and 4th Siege Battery were swung onto this section of the German trench and destroyed it, so enabling the remaining infantry to occupy it with few losses, a technique of control not seen before. Meanwhile, the heavies were engaging the German artillery but with only limited success. The technique of long range map shooting was not yet good enough. During the day and the night the Germans managed to reinforce their artillery considerably.

Phase two followed as planned and was a success almost everywhere. The success of the artillery timed programme was proven; it is of interest to note that the First Army report used the word "barrage" for the first time after Neuve Chapelle. With success in their hands, for some inexplicable reason the British commanders waited five hours before ordering phase three. This gave the Germans time to re-organise and, of course, covering fire was now entirely on call. 7th Division was to carry out phase three. This division, so heavily involved at Ypres, had not perfected the art of command and control of artillery to the extent of the others. Their plan was to control the artillery using one forward observer reporting when 21st Infantry Brigade began its advance; the guns would then fire for twenty minutes—not the most able fireplan!

In fact, the German strong points in depth stopped the British infantry. These had not been registered by the guns and forward observers could not contact their guns, as they were now too far forward. In spite of gallant action by linesmen, the lines were all cut. The ground was flat and, as the forward observers moved to the few vantage points, they became obvious and were killed. The attack bogged down by 1530 hours, visibility was very poor indeed and by the morning of 11th March the chance of victory had passed. The enemy reinforced his forward positions during the night 10th/11th March, but placed his infantry well forward of Bois du Biez and Aubers Ridge. These were heavily shelled by the British to little effect. General Haig was, however, under the impression that the enemy were breaking and he ordered all batteries forward. Obeying this order, N Battery advanced and almost fell into enemy hands; only brilliant driving at full gallop enabled it to get away. It was here that the new trench mortars did good service under Captain R.C. Grosvenor RHA. There were two sections, one of four 4-inch and one of four 3.7-inch mortars. Ammunition supply was the real problem and, though their fire was successful, they soon ran out of bombs.

The greatest problem during the battle was that of forward observers maintaining communications with their guns. Many were killed; indeed, all in 45 Brigade RFA were killed or wounded. A forward observer of 32nd Battery silenced three German guns and a machine gun before his line was cut. He was then shot whilst trying to pass back fire orders by flag signal. 35th, 36th and 55th Batteries, however, each managed to knock out German guns which came into action in the open. The Battery Commander of 36th Battery controlled his guns by megaphone from the top of a house from which he had good observation. Much gallantry was displayed by the officers and their parties working well forward that day.

Early mechanisation of the draught of guns. An 8-inch howitzer and a 9.2-inch howitzer.   *(R.A.I.)*

Meanwhile the Germans, far from being broken, were preparing to counter-attack. They opened with a most inaccurate bombardment in depth which missed the British gun and firing line; they too had their observation problems. Consequently, as the German infantry emerged through the mist at close range, they met the terrible blast of the British infantry's rapid fire. *The Bavarian battalions* were shattered and fled from the field. A rapid follow-up might have carried the day but the High Command ordered a fresh bombardment first. This was not a success due to shortage of time, lack of precise knowledge of the location of British infantry and poor visibility. At this point both guns and infantry were short of ammunition and it was decided to pause to build up stocks.

In one sense, Neuve Chapelle had been a great success. The British demonstrated a new form of attack; they showed how to give a mass of guns specific tasks and how to achieve both tactical surprise and very close co-operation between infantry and gunners during the attack. The failures were almost entirely due to poor communications. Had General Haig realised the success he had achieved in phase one and two, and had he then pressed straight on with phase three, success might have been his. Had the forward observers had reliable links with their guns, the artillery support in phase three would have been much more effective at the critical moments. Nevertheless, progress had been made and a pattern for the future was set. The French, too, were full of admiration for the British techniques at Neuve Chapelle and copied it themselves.

Still, there were some weaknesses which were quickly seen. First, the counter battery fire was not a success at long range. Second, the scope of fire control in battle had to be improved. Third, artillery commanders at each level were shown to be needed to exercise this control. Fourth, full value was still not being made of aerial observation.

CHAPTER 8

The Guns at Second Ypres — 22nd April to 25th May 1915

See map 17

The second battle of Ypres, which was fought at the end of April 1915, illustrated the problems of a very rapid expansion of Armies after war had started. The old BEF was no more. The new Armies were not ready, even though they had begun to take their place in the trenches in France. Britain was not yet geared for war on the scale now developing and the shortages of guns and, in particular, ammunition, were acute. The new batteries arriving in France still had the obsolete 15-pounders and 5-inch howitzers. Medium artillery consisted of aged 6-inch howitzers and 4.7-inch guns of Boer war vintage. Strategically, the decision was taken in May 1915 to give maximum support to the French whose doctrine of "attack, attack attack" still held the day. The new Armies were thus hurled into battle in the spring of 1915 before they were ready. Just as the Gunners of the BEF had learnt the need for co-ordinated artillery fire across the whole front, the new artillery was filled with untrained units and staffs barely capable of carrying out the simplest artillery action, let alone the complexities of engaging divisional, corps or army targets.

The real crime had already been committed. Britain had failed to keep an adequate force trained in peace which could be rapidly expanded in time of war. She had allowed her national insurance policy to sink below the safety level, and the slaughter of 1915 must lie at the feet of those who continually cut the Armed Forces prior to 1914. By unbelievable luck, the Germans were stupid enough to become engaged on two fronts at the same time, thus allowing at least some time to train the Armies of 1916, 17 and 18 while holding the position on the Western front. Britain did not deserve this respite but she made good use of it.

The second battle of Ypres fell into three phases. The first was the German gas attack on the French who were on the left of the Canadians, followed by a similar attack on the Canadians themselves. The second was the attack on Frezenberg Ridge, and the third was the battle for Bellewaarde Ridge which brought both sides to an exhausted standstill on 25th May.

It was in April 1915 at Ypres that the Germans demonstrated their ability to concentrate massed artillery. They had assembled a massive array of medium and heavy guns and, with air superiority, they perfected and demonstrated air observation. On a three corps front running from the Menin Road to Bixschoote, a distance of thirteen miles, they had six divisional artilleries together with one hundred and forty-seven heavy guns and howitzers. They had also developed the command and control techniques necessary to use this mass of guns to blast a

93

path in front of their assaulting infantry. The British had already learned that this technique was essential but still lacked the equipment and doctrine to put it into effect.

Early in April, the British took over the whole of the Ypres salient as far North as the Poelcapelle—St Julien Road. The total British front from Cuinchy in the south near the La Bassée Canal to Poelcapelle was thirty miles in length. It was held by sixteen infantry divisions and the British and Indian Cavalry Corps. The Infantry Divisions were, 1st, 2nd, 3rd, 4th, 5th, 6th, 7th, 8th, 27th, 28th, 1st Canadian, Lahore, Meerut, 46th (North Midland), 47th (London) and 48th (South Midland). 1st Canadian, 46th and 47th Divisions had brought their additional artillery to France as follows:

1st Canadian Division:

1 Brigade RCFA: 1st, 2nd, 3rd, 4th Batteries RCFA, each 4 × 15-pounders.
2 Brigade RCFA: 5th, 6th, 7th, 8th Batteries RCFA, each 4 × 15-pounders.
3 Brigade RCFA: 9th, 10th, 11th, 12th Batteries RCFA, each 4 × 15-pounders.
118 Howitzer Brigade RFA: 458th and 459th Batteries.

47th (London) Division:

5 (London) Brigade RFA: 12th, 13th, 14th Batteries, each 4 × 15-pounders.
6 (London) Brigade RFA: 15th, 16th, 17th Batteries, each 4 × 15-pounders.
7 (London) Brigade RFA: 18th, 19th, 20th Batteries, each 4 × 15-pounders.
8 (London) Howitzer Brigade RFA: 21st and 22nd Batteries, 4 × 5-inch howitzers.

48th (South Midland) Division:

1 (South Midland) Brigade; (1st, 2nd and 3rd Gloucester Batteries)
2 (South Midland) Brigade; (1st, 2nd and 3rd Worcester Batteries)
4 (South Midland) Howitzer Brigade; (4th and 5th Warwick (Howitzer) Batteries)

At Ypres, the British Sector ran from St Eloi in the south, through Hill 60, the West edge of Shrewsbury Forest, through Polygon Wood, past Broodeseinde and Berlin Wood to a point on the St Julien Road half a mile south west of Poelcapelle.

The trench system taken over from the French was not good. Indeed it could not be, since water was just beneath the surface. The defences became breastworks and needed much work to make them effective. The wire was good. There was, unfortunately, no co-ordinated command system between the British and French.

At 1700 hours on 22nd April, the first gas attack of the war fell on the two French territorial divisions to the left of the British-Canadian line. It was accompanied by a violent bombardment of Ypres by German heavies. After five minutes of chlorine gas shelling onto the unfortunate French, the German field guns paused for five minutes to avoid disturbing the gas clouds. At 1710 hours they opened with heavy concentrations of shrapnel onto the French trenches. Enemy infantry followed up at 1720 hours. Soon the bridges over the canal were full of coughing, choking French soldiers, whose will to fight had gone. Totally unprepared and frightened they gave and retreated *en masse*. Only the French 75s held their ground but by 1900 hours they too stopped firing. 1st Canadian Division held the left of the British line and it was soon clear that the whole left flank was in danger of envelopment.

It was here that 10th Battery RCFA was in action some five hundred yards north of St Julien. They were affected by the gas but not too seriously. They soon found the French streaming back onto them. For two hours the Canadian Gunners shelled the enemy when, at 1900 hours, Germans began to advance across the left front of the Battery in large numbers. Left section swung round and poured its fire into the enemy in enfilade at a range of only 200 yards. Their fire not only checked this dangerous penetration but forced the enemy to retire. Meanwhile, the whole Battery was under heavy small arms fire and teams bringing up ammunition were cut to pieces—a truly gallant action in a confused and terrifying situation. By now all four batteries of 3 Brigade RCFA were holding the line, with no infantry between themselves and the Germans. The situation was critical but the steadiness of those Canadians held the day and at 2300 hours they were ordered to withdraw to St. Jean, some two miles back. Meanwhile, the wagons and teams of 459th Howitzer Battery RFA were over-run and lost. Somehow the guns were extricated with ad hoc teams and 459th Battery came into action at Brielen, west of the Canal. 2nd (London) Heavy Battery (4.7-inch guns) was supporting the French and the guns had to be abandoned and were temporarily lost in Kitchener's Wood. Although a counter-attack regained the wood, the enemy defensive fire was so heavy that teams could not reach the guns and they were destroyed. By now there was an 8,000 yard gap between the Canadians and the French.

To the right of the Canadians the line was held by, first, 28th Division facing east at Berlin Wood and onto the centre of Polygon Wood, then by 27th Division as far as Hill 60 and facing south east. Heavy fighting had been in progress for Hill 60 since 17th April, and 27th Division's attention was concentrated onto it. During the 22nd April, however, the real threat was developing in the north, to their left rear. 28th Divisional Artillery could not do much to help the Canadians, though 18th and 365th Batteries who were resting were rushed into action; 27th Division Artillery was facing south-east and could do even less.

During the night a force of some twelve British battalions was rushed into the gap on the left. They had almost no artillery support, since command had become hopelessly mixed, observation was almost non-existent and most of the guns were changing positions. A counter-attack by parts of two of these battalions early on 23rd April was supported by 122nd Heavy Battery of 27th Division, 365 Howitzer Battery of 1st Canadian Division and some ad hoc batteries formed from British, Canadian and French sections which had been out of the line resting and quickly reformed to help stem the tide. The situation was critical.

It is surprising that, under these conditions, the Germans made such poor progress. It appears that they did not really trust their new weapon—gas. They did not like to follow it up and thus it lost its impact when it had achieved complete surprise. Subsequent German accounts of their failure, however, mention the accuracy of the artillery fire on their left flank. Nevertheless, on 23rd April the situation was indeed desperate. A very temporary line was held by this ad hoc force just forward of the canal. Seventeen British and Canadian battalions, supported by half a divisional artillery, faced forty-two German battalions with

A gun position during a gas attack. From a drawing by Fortunino Matania.   *(R.A.I.)*

five times as much artillery, with the Germans holding the high ground and enjoying good observation. During the morning of this fateful day the French requested a counter-attack for 1500 hours to restore the situation. This was planned and the artillery (28th Divisional and 1st Canadian Divisional Artilleries and 122nd and 123rd Heavy Batteries) was ready by 1445 hours. At the last minute H-hour was postponed but no one told the Gunners, who wasted valuable ammunition by opening fire as planned at 1500 hours. Nevertheless, at 1625 hours when the infantry got under way, the fireplan worked well and the attack temporarily restored the line.

On 24th April, a heavy gas attack was launched against the Canadians. This was followed by massed infantry attacks against 2nd and 3rd Canadian Infantry Brigades. It was here that 2 Brigade RCFA broke up attack after attack at ranges of 3,500 yards. 122nd Heavy Battery near Frezenberg, firing at 4,000 yards, kept up a heavy concentration all afternoon until, with no infantry in front of it, it was withdrawn. Some assistance was also given by those guns of 27th and 28th Divisional Artilleries which could reach. The situation in 27th Divisional Artillery was as follows: 148th Howitzer Battery (attached) was in action near Bellewaarde Lake and had guns firing north, east and west simultaneously; 98th Battery was firing north and north east and 132nd Battery was supporting 27th Division; 98th and 133rd Batteries were in a wood and under constant shrapnel and gas attack. Enemy aircraft were always overhead and telephone wires were constantly being cut. At Wieltje, 149th Battery (Captain R.S. Ellis) was in action north of the village facing east. It came under heavy small arms fire but held its own, returning the fire until all its ammunition was expended. The infantry began to fall back past the gallant battery, now holding out with small arms only. At last they too were forced to withdraw and with great difficulty extricated all but one gun and two wagons. After dark that night, Captain Ellis recovered the remaining gun and one wagon; a small but gallant action in the service of the guns.

By 1100 hours on 24th April, a huge bulge had occurred in the Canadian line and it was decided to withdraw to straighten it out. It was noticeable that, as the Canadians withdrew, German 5.9-inch howitzers followed their every move, the fire being directed by aeroplane and balloon observation. The Canadian withdrawal soon affected the position of 28th Division. 37th Howitzer Battery, commanded by Major E. Harding-Newman, was in action north of Frezenberg as the Canadians fell back. Major Harding-Newman ordered Captain E.M. Hutchinson to a flank to see what was happening. He suddenly saw German infantry forming up to attack and engaged them with the battery. Three times the Germans tried to attack and three times they were repulsed by the deadly fire of 37th Battery's 4.5-inch howitzers. Afterwards some five hundred dead Germans were counted in this area; they had been prevented from occupying St. Julien by this gallant action. Meanwhile, a gap developed between the 28th Division and the Canadians; this again was held by the fire of 37th Battery, 122nd Heavy Battery and a section of 6th Battery RCFA. The action becomes the more noteworthy when one remembers that 37th Battery was under field gun fire of about 250 rounds per hour all afternoon. By this time, once again ammunition supply was becoming critical.

The German successes against the French meant that they were now able to concentrate their fire into the salient from three directions. Nearly all gun positions in the Ypres sector were overlooked by enemy observation posts. The Corps Artillery consisted of two batteries of old 6-inch howitzers and three of worn out 4.7-inch guns. On 24th, a 9.2-inch howitzer of 12th Siege Battery RGA arrived, together with 108th Heavy Battery of 60-pounders. Yet it is recorded that throughout this period the precarious situation on 1st Canadian Division front was held mainly by artillery fire. Slowly the situation improved. Command and control, however, lagged and operations often developed into independent actions. A movement by a battalion of the Royal Sussex Regiment to cover the Canadians was stopped partly by the fire of the British batteries, who had not been told that the operation was taking place. Conversely, an attack on St. Julien (temporarily occupied by the enemy) by 150th Infantry Brigade of the newly arrived 50th (Northumbrian) Division was successful almost entirely due to the accuracy of the artillery. This was given by both 5th and 6th Batteries RCFA and the guns of 28th Division firing at ranges of only 1,000 yards. So successful was this attack that the Germans failed to advance again into this key sector.

Later in the day it was decided to mount a major counter-attack to restore the situation. This was to be carried out by 10th Infantry Brigade of 4th Division and fifteen battalions were made available. The fire support was to be by all guns in range under the direction of CRA 1st Canadian Division. H-hour was to be 0330 hours, 25th April, but later it was postponed until 0530 hours. Again this order did not reach the guns of 27th and 28th Division, whose fire was all wasted at 0330 hours. At 0530 hours these guns could not fire as all the ammunition was expended, and the Canadian guns which did, had targets too far away to help the attacking infantry. In the event, only 10th Infantry Brigade attacked, as there had not been time to organise the fifteen battalions. At the edge of St. Julien this whole gallant brigade were almost annihilated by enemy machine guns undisturbed by British artillery fire. However, 10th Brigade had not 'died' in vain, for it forestalled an enemy attack scheduled for the same time and this, as a result, never materialised.

On 26th April a new counter-attack was planned, using the Lahore Division to attack Langermarck together with the French. Fire support was to be provided by the Divisional Artilleries of the Lahore Division, 27th, 28th and 1st Canadian Divisions, 3rd Artillery Group of the Belgian Army, 98th and 102nd Belgian Field Batteries, 11 Heavy Brigade (122nd and 123rd Batteries) and 13 Heavy Brigade (The North Midland Heavy and 459th Howitzer Batteries). To command this Artillery, Brigadier S.D. Browne (son of 'Sam Browne' of "belt" fame), BGRA V Corps, was for the first time appointed Corps Artillery Commander, but the communications problem was acute. Part of this mass of artillery was west of the Canal under Brigadier Gay, CRA 28th Division, and part to the east under Brigadier Stokes. But Brigadier Browne, although appointed Commander, had neither office, staff, communications nor transport. Thus all that could be done was to issue outline orders to the CRAs and rely on them to do the rest. General Plumer ordered the Corps Artillery bombardment to begin at 1320 hours. This was to last until 1400 hours, followed by rapid fire until 1404 hours when the guns would lift 200 yards, forming a barrage while the assault took place. Thus we see for the first time the beginnings of artillery command at Corps level. In fact there were not enough guns, nor was there enough ammunition or observation, for such a complex fireplan and it was not entirely successful. This was particularly so since no counter battery fire was arranged, allowing three German 5.9-inch howitzers to blow the Lahore Division infantry to pieces as they crossed a ridge to attack. Similarly, intimate direct support, always needed in attack, was not arranged and this left many enemy machine guns unlocated until it was too late. It is fair to say that Brigadier Browne had nothing like enough time nor the communications available to prepare a proper fireplan for the attack, and he said so. He was doing the best he could in the time available.

Although the Lahore Division's attack was not entirely successful, 26th April was a great day for the guns. 149th and 366th Batteries closely and successfully supported attacks onto Zonnebeke Ridge. Later, when the Germans counter-attacked, 366th Battery under Captain C.A.R. Scott stopped them dead by firing 1740 rounds at ranges down to 800 yards; 37th (Howitzer) Battery again distinguished itself by destroying enemy infantry from the Gravenstafel Ridge, catching them in the open, driving them into some houses and then destroying the houses. Later on, a heavy German counter-attack against the French was entirely stopped by 118th, 365th and 75th Batteries. The real flexibility and reliability of well handled artillery was truly demonstrated that day.

Nevertheless, the situation in the salient was critical, and units had become hopelessly mixed up and confused. All forces inside the salient were grouped together under General Plumer and known as "Plumer Force". This ad hoc arrangement lasted until 7th May when Plumer replaced Smith-Dorrien as Commander Second Army. Within the salient the German guns were intensely active. Most British guns had to be well back, some west of the canal if they were to survive at all. On 28th April, 4th Battery RCFA was accurately located and suffered a direct hit on one gun. During the night the Battery moved, leaving dummy guns behind, which deceived the Germans so well that three were subsequently destroyed!

On 1st May the withdrawal to a shorter line began, and continued throughout the 2nd May. At 1600 hours 2nd May the Germans put in a gas attack. 366th and 367 Batteries immediately opened fire behind the gas cloud to catch the attacking infantry and did much execution. Primitive gas masks had now been issued and the infantry stood their ground and dealt with any remaining enemy with small arms fire. The most difficult phase of the withdrawal was the final one when, on the night 2nd/3rd May, most of the guns had to fall back across the canal. The new line ran from Sanctuary Wood through Hooge, Frezenberg to Mouse Trap and Turco Farms. The line was still forward of the canal but not far enough to provide space for artillery to the east of it. Consequently the guns had to be to the west, just too far away to provide maximum close support. Desperate fighting now began on the new line as three German Corps attacked 27th and 28th Divisions. Many guns were, however, pushed back (to the east) over the canal to give closer support. Nevertheless, the British were seriously outgunned and artillery shortages now became a critical factor in the battle. The Germans supported their attacks with tremendous concentrations of fire, and on Frezenberg Ridge the shell craters touched each other. Nevertheless, as the attacking German infantry rushed up the ridge, they were totally destroyed by small arms fire and shrapnel from 39th Battery of 14 Brigade RFA. As the Germans closed, Major M.J.F. Fitzgerald, commanding 39th Battery, ordered his guns to swing round. They then caught the Germans in the open and did great slaughter—some engineers helped to bring up ammunition for the rest of the day. There were now no infantry between the guns and the enemy so after dark the Battery withdrew, but yet again the guns had helped to save the day.

The artillery situation was now becoming really serious. The old guns were fast going out of action. Eight 4.7-inch guns were now so worn as to be useless having exceeded their lives by over a thousand rounds. In 1 Brigade RCFA only seven of their 15-pounders were serviceable. So heavy had the firing been that buffer oil soon boiled, springs were broken or tired and packings were burnt out. The Brigade had to be withdrawn for refit. On 6th May, 4th and 5th (Durham) Howitzer Batteries arrived (5-inch howitzers). 27th Battery had repulsed an attack on 84th Infantry Brigade on 7th May and was withdrawn. 22nd Battery lost two guns by direct hits, and 103rd Battery another. Somehow, the ammunition supply was maintained by extreme gallantry on the part of the Brigade ammunition columns.

This then was the situation when the German attack came in on 8th May. All day the guns fought on; by 2000 hours, 62nd Battery lay silenced and 75th Battery, who replaced it, were badly mauled. At 2030 hours all heavies were ordered back. By 0400 hours on 9th May, nine batteries withdrew through Ypres, leaving 69th and 100th Batteries alone on the east bank of the canal supporting 84th Infantry Brigade. As dawn broke on that warm May morning, the confusion of the night became more orderly and it was seen that 27th Division were still east of Ypres. Accordingly, 65th and 103rd Howitzer batteries were ordered back over the Canal. Both Divisions doggedly held their ground on 10th and 11th May, but the toll was great and the infantry of 28th Division were withdrawn, to be replaced by 1st and 2nd Cavalry Divisions. 28th Divisional Artillery, itself worn out, was ordered to remain in action to support the cavalry. All guns now east of Ypres came under command CRA 1st Cavalry Division.

The ammunition situation was desperate. There was practically no 4.5-inch left on 9th May and the 18-pounder supply was critically low. But on 16th May supplies began to arrive, together with reinforcements. 9th (Scottish) Division, the first of the New Army divisions, moved in on 16th May, followed by 14th and 12th Divisions. On 20th May the first British Kite Balloon Section, manned by the Royal Navy, made its first operational ascent at Poperinghe west of Ypres. Fortunately, German progress was also held up by shortage of ammunition and an attack scheduled for 13th May had to be postponed. There was then a pause in the fighting till 24th May which was most fortunate, as it enabled ammunition to be built up and anti-gas measures to be perfected. Flannel helmets were issued and sprayers to clear out trenches. At this time too, 2 (Northumbrian) Brigade RFA came into action east of Ypres, making a total of forty-two guns in that area. The build up in artillery was now:

50th (Northumbrian) Division

1 Northumbrian Brigade; (1st, 2nd and 3rd Northumberland Batteries)
2 Northumbrian Brigade; (1st, and 2nd East Riding Batteries and 3rd North Riding Battery)
3 Northumbrian Brigade; (1st, 2nd and 3rd Durham Batteries)
4 Northumbrian (Howitzer); Brigade (4th and 5th Durham (Howitzer) Batteries)

9th (Scottish) Division
  50 Brigade RFA; (A, B, C and D Batteries (4 guns))
  51 Brigade RFA; (A, B, C and D Batteries (4 guns))
  52 Brigade RFA; (A, B, C and D Batteries (4 guns))
  53 Howitzer Brigade RFA; (B, C and D Batteries (4 Howitzers))

12th (Eastern) Division
  62 Brigade RFA; (A, B, C and D Batteries (4 guns))
  63 Brigade RFA; (A, B, C and D Batteries (4 guns))
  64 Brigade RFA; (A, B, C and D Batteries (4 guns))
  65 Howitzer Brigade RFA; (A, B and D Batteries (4 Howitzers))

14th (Light) Division
  46 Brigade RFA; (A, B, C and D Batteries)
  47 Brigade RFA; (A, B, C and D Batteries)
  48 Brigade RFA; (A, B, C and D Batteries)
  49 (Howitzer) Brigade RFA; (B, C and D (Howitzer) Batteries)

Meanwhile, progress was made in organising the heavy artillery. The Heavies of 5 Corps were organised into three brigades under Brigadier H.C.C. Uniacke, I Corps Heavy Artillery Commander. He had one 15-inch howitzer, three 9.2-inch howitzers, four 5-inch howitzers, eight 60-pounders and twenty 4.7-inch guns. Progress was made with aerial observation to control the fire of the heavy batteries. The spotting aircraft were given the call sign 'Z' and batteries were given letters. Aircraft flew at three or four specific times per day. During these times the guns stood by for aerial shoots. The system soon began to work well and many direct hits were scored. From this, Brigadier Uniacke began to produce, for the first time, comprehensive rules for arranging counter battery fireplans.

On 24th May fierce German attacks began all along the line opposite Ypres and in two places they broke through the British positions. Artillery control again became difficult but, thanks to the system of grouping all artillery east of Ypres under one brigade, some co-ordination was achieved. On this occasion it was the gallantry of the infantry of 27th Division that saved the day. By evening 25th May, the German infantry had suffered appalling casualties and were so exhausted that the operation was cancelled. This cancellation was fortunate for the Gunners. By the end of 25th May, there was virtually no more shrapnel in France, only 272 rounds of HE (4.7-inch), 1,620 rounds HE (5-inch), 379 rounds HE (60-pounder), nil rounds HE (6-inch Howitzer), nil 6-inch gun, nil 8-inch, 612 rounds 9.2-inch and 10 rounds 15-inch. GHQ informed the War Office on that day that all offensive operations in France must close until an ammunition reserve was created.

So ended the Second Battle of Ypres. The line had held but only just. It held because of the gallantry of the British regiments and because of many German errors; had they but pressed home their attacks on numerous occasions they would almost certainly have broken through.

Apart from numerous acts of great courage, Second Ypres was not a great Gunner battle. It was primarily a hard infantry slog. The slaughter was terrible and the chaos and confusion great. So confused was the situation that close intimate artillery support was very hard to achieve with the communications available at that time. Many of the artillery's needs were now pressing. The

Germans had shown how massed fire power, making maximum use of aerial observation, could blast a path for attacking infantry. To do this the British needed more guns, more ammunition, better communications and more control of the air. Replacement of the 15-pounders, 5-inch howitzers and 4.7-inch guns of the Territorial Divisions with 18-pounders, 4.5-inch howitzers and 60-pounders was now urgent. A really modern effective medium gun was also urgently needed. However, advances in command and control had been made. Artillery Commanders at all levels were issuing orders and co-ordination of fire support at high level was developing fast.

The gallantry of the infantry, much of it untrained, was beyond praise at Second Ypres. The Territorial Divisions acquitted themselves with the greatest distinction and many an attack was broken by rifle fire alone, without any help from the artillery. Also many counter-attacks failed for want of a proper artillery fireplan. It is, however, also true that on many occasions the guns fought on when there was no infantry in front of them and stopped many an enemy penetration by the deadly accuracy of their fire alone. The exploits of 10th Battery RCFA on 22nd April and 37th Howitzer Battery on 29th April, or 39th Battery on 3rd May, all testify to this. Magnificent though the infantry were, the gallantry of the Gunners was not wanting when the occasion demanded and many German reports refer to their accuracy and steadiness with the greatest respect.

CHAPTER 9

The Battles of Aubers and Festubert — May 1915

See maps 18 and 19

On 9th May 1915, the First Army under General Haig began its spring offensive. The first battle was at Aubers on the 9th. On that day the 1st, 8th and Meerut Divisions lost over 11,000 officers and men killed and wounded. It was a terrible failure and the minor gains of ground that were made had to be surrendered. Once again the British High Command failed to realise the strength of well dug in defensive positions. They considered that a short sharp artillery bombardment would see the infantry onto their objectives—they had failed to learn from their experience at Neuve Chapelle. The German defences were very strong indeed; in some cases the parapets were six to seven feet high and fifteen to twenty feet thick. The wire was deepened and the whole position had considerable depth. Machine guns were so strongly emplaced that only a direct hit on the loophole itself would knock them out; they were sited every twenty yards, were protected by steel and were at ground level and invisible to British observers. Rudimentary air photographs and the results of infantry patrols had failed to reveal the strength of the German positions.

The offensive was to consist of huge attacks, from Arras in the south by the French Tenth Army to Aubers Ridge in the north by the British First Army. The French employed eighteen divisions, 780 field guns and 293 heavy guns, with three cavalry divisions in reserve. Sir John French planned to employ ten divisions with 516 field guns, 121 heavy guns and five cavalry divisions in reserve.

The British plan was to deliver two converging attacks; the main thrust being on a front of 2,400 yards from Chocolate Mernier Corner ($1\frac{1}{2}$ miles NE of Festubert) to Port Arthur ($1\frac{1}{2}$ miles south of Neuve Chapelle). This was to be carried out by I Corps and the Indian Corps. The second, a subsidiary attack, was to be launched by IV Corps on a front of 1,500 yards, some 6,000 yards NE of Port Arthur and directed on Fromelle.

The artillery plan was to open at H-40 minutes with a steady bombardment, speeding up at H-10. The 18-pounders were first to cut the wire, then to lift behind the German positions and form a barrage of fire to prevent the movement of German reinforcements. The howitzers were to demolish the parapets and strong points in the front line and two Groups of heavies were to engage the German guns. Unfortunately there were not enough guns for these tasks; First Army asked GHQ for more but none could be spared, due to the heavy fighting then in progress around Ypres.

An analysis of the artillery shows severe defects. Of the field guns, eighty-four were obsolete 15-pounders; twenty of the field howitzers were obsolete 5-inch variety; only thirty-three of the heavies were the effective 60-pounders. The

103

twenty-eight 4.7-inch guns were now so worn that the driving bands stripped off the shell at the muzzle resulting in extreme inaccuracy. The four 6-inch guns were also old and inaccurate. It was planned to try out for the first time the idea of some guns accompanying the infantry to knock out strong points at close range. For this task, batteries of mortars and 3-pounders mounted on lorries were organised. Aircraft were fitted with radio and allotted to 1 and 2 Groups Heavy Artillery; this was to help observation, which was bad due to flat low ground and the growth of the spring foliage. Lastly, the adjustment of targets had been completed in cold, wet weather and 9th May dawned hot and sunny! One more experiment was to be tried. The advancing infantry were to put down coloured strips of linen when they captured successive objectives. Reconnaissance aircraft were to report these to the guns as the attack progressed.

Just before the operation began, a series of pipes began to appear from the German trenches. These were thought to herald the use of gas in defence. An immediate plan was then made that, should this occur, all guns would engage the gas cloud and dissipate it!!

Each Corps was to attack on a one division front with a second, follow-up, division. All Corps Artillery was placed under command of each assaulting divisional CRA. The plan was that 1st Division I Corps was to attack on the right, with the Meerut Division of the Indian Corps on the left. Although these divisions were to attack together as one operation, no overall artillery commander was appointed. All artillery of I Corps was allotted to Brigadier-General E.A. Fanshawe, CRA 1st Division, and all artillery of the Indian Corps to Brigadier-General F.E. Johnson, CRA the Lahore Division (even though the attack was to be by the Meerut Division!).

The Artillery plan for I Corps was:

a. **Wire cutting** (ranges 1,600 yards):

(1)   25, 26, 39 and 91 Brigades RFA; 66 × 18-pounders
(2)   5 (London) Brigade RFA; 12 × 15-pounders
(3)   N, V and X Batteries RHA; 18 × 13-pounders

b. **The German Parapets** (ranges 2,600 yards):

(1)   47th, 60th Batteries and one Section 61st Battery; 14 × 14.5-inch howitzers.
(2)   4 (West Riding) and 8 (London) Brigades RFA; 16 × 5-inch howitzers.
(3)   12 and 14 Brigades RGA; 16 × 6-inch howitzers.

c. **Across Whole Front**

35th Heavy Battery; 4 × 60-pounders.

d. **Bombardment of targets in depth.** No 1 Heavy Group under command Brigadier-General G. McK Franks:

(1)   Royal Marine Artillery; 1 × 15-inch howitzer.
(2)   10th Siege Battery; 4 × 9.2-inch howitzers.
(3)   Right section, 13th Siege Battery; 2 × 9.2-inch howitzers.

e. **Counter Battery**

   (1)   24th Heavy Battery; 4 × 60-pounders.
   (2)   48th Heavy Battery; 4 × 60-pounders.
   (3)   1st Canadian Heavy Battery; 4 × 60-pounders.

The Artillery plan for the Indian Corps was:

a. **Wire cutting** (ranges 2,000 yards)

   4, 8 and 9 Brigades RFA; 54 × 18-pounders.

b. **Barrage behind the German front trenches:**

   5, 10 and 18 Brigades RFA; 54 × 18-pounders.

c. **The German Parapet** (800 yards in width)

   (1)   43 Brigade RFA; 18 × 4.5-inch howitzers.
   (2)   6 Brigade RGA; 8 × 6-inch howitzers.

The plan for the IV Corps attack was for 8th Division to assault, followed by the 7th Division. Both Divisional Artilleries were grouped under Brigadier-General A.E.A. Holland, CRA 8th Division. He was supported by 2 Group Heavy Artillery, under Brigadier-General H.C.C. Uniacke. The plan was differently organised in I Corps, where the artillery was divided into three Groups:

a. **Group A.** (Lieutenant Colonel E.W. Alexander)

   (1)   14 Brigade RHA; 18 × 13-pounders.
   (2)   22 Brigade RFA; 18 × 18-pounders.

b. **Group B** (Lieutenant Colonel A.H.S. Goff)

   (1)   33 Brigade RFA; 18 × 18-pounders.
   (2)   45 Brigade RFA; 18 × 18-pounders.

c. **Group C.** (Lieutenant Colonel H. Rouse);

   (1)   1 Brigade RHA; 17 × 13-pounders.
   (2)   5 Brigade RFA; 18 × 18-pounders.
   (3)   1 (West Riding) Brigade RFA; 18 × 18-pounders.

d. **Not Grouped.**

   (1)   35 Brigade RFA; 18 × 18-pounders.
   (2)   5th Mountain Battery; 6 × 3-pounders.

The tasks given were as follows:

a. **Wire Cutting.** The 90 × 18-pounders.

b. **Rear of German front line.** The 36 × 13-pounders.

c.   **Parapets.**

    (1)   37th Howitzer Battery; 6 × 4.7-inch howitzers.
    (2)   7th Siege Battery; 6 × 6-inch howitzers.

In support were the guns of 2 Group Heavy Artillery. They were to engage targets in depth and enemy batteries. The Group consisted of:

a.   Royal Marine Artillery; 2 × 15-inch howitzers.

b.   One section 12th Siege Battery; 2 × 9.2-inch howitzers.

c.   One Section 13th Siege Battery; 2 × 9.2-inch howitzers.

d.   3 Heavy Brigade; 10 × 4.7-inch guns.

e.   8 Heavy Brigade; 10 × 4.7-inch guns.

f.   1st (West Riding) Heavy Battery; 4 × 4.7-inch guns.

g.   1st (Highland) Heavy Battery; 4 × 4.7-inch guns.

h.   Two Armoured trains;

    (1)   "Churchill" (RN); 2 × 4.7-inch guns.
    (2)   "Deguise" (Belgian); 1 × 4-inch gun.

Let us now turn to the fortunes of I Corps attack, led by the 1st Division and the Meerut Division.

The bombardment opened in full daylight at 0500 hours on 9th May 1915. At 0530 hours the rate of fire was increased and the 18-pounders engaged on wirecutting changed from shrapnel to HE. They then lifted and added their fire to the howitzers shelling the parapets but the result was disappointing. The guns were inaccurate, the meteor had changed and there were not enough of them. The German machine gunners (twenty-two of them) were untouched and were able to open up on the British and Indian infantry almost as they left their trenches. Nor was the British bombardment of the German guns any more effective. In spite of the counter battery fire, the German guns opened up on the British trenches, now packed with a confused mass of wounded men and support troops. The radio in one of the two spotting aircraft failed, though the other gallantly directed the fire of 48th Heavy Battery onto moving targets; its activities were, however, restricted as only two batteries had radios themselves.

In spite of the costly initial failures, General Haig ordered fresh attacks with a repetition of the morning's bombardment. At first H-hour was to be 1200 hours, then it was postponed to 1400 hours and later to 1520 hours; the changes were caused by acute problems in forming up the infantry. Meanwhile, all the guns kept up a steady fire on the German positions to prevent repair work but ammunition was very short and, though the Germans were prevented from moving, little extra damage was done. The attack started as planned and the 18-pounders lifted their fire only fifty yards a time to cover the assaulting infantry onto their objectives but the German positions were too strong and, by 1635 hours, the operation was called off.

On IV Corps front, the 8th Division fared little better. The sequence was the same, not enough guns, too short a bombardment, not enough ammunition. Two guns of 104th Battery were, however, brought up into the firing line during the night 8th/9th May and they did great work next day cutting good paths through the wire and even breaching the enemy positions. Through these the infantry managed to rush and gain a foothold but, in the end, they could not hold on and by nightfall all were back in their trenches.

On that terrible day, 458 officers and almost 11,000 men were killed or wounded. These appalling casualties were mostly due to the decision to assault very heavily prepared positions with only a few minutes pre H-hour bombardment. The French had learnt their lesson and, after a four day bombardment, had considerable success. After the failure at Aubers Ridge, General Haig decided to stop all operations in this sector and to concentrate on the right of First Army opposite Festubert.

The battle of Aubers Ridge marked the end of attacking after a short, sharp bombardment. It ushered in a period of long, heavy, carefully prepared attacks by artillery fire. These were to hold sway for almost two years, until the advent of the heavy surprise bombardment and the tank at Cambrai in 1917. The lessons of the battle were four. First, the importance of accurate information about the enemy's defences (this led to the development of the art of raiding); second, the need for really accurate artillery fire; third, the urgent need for an accurate medium howitzer; four, the need to be able to locate enemy guns accurately.

Improvements were, however, on the way in aerial observation, photography and survey and, on 28th August 1915, the first "Bull-Weiss" sound ranging device was presented for War Office approval. This was approved on 12th September and a section was formed in France in October 1915.

The Battle of Festubert—15th–25th May 1915

The battle of Festubert was undertaken to help the French offensive near Arras, by preventing the movement of German reserves. It coincided with the desperate fighting at Ypres and lasted for eleven days. The battle was fought by the British 2nd, 7th and 47th Divisions, the Canadian Division and the Meerut Division. Late on 11th May, the 7th Divisional Artillery, one RHA Brigade and five 6-inch howitzer batteries received orders to move by night to Festubert to support new attacks on the 13th. The 47th Division, originally the 2nd London Division, had been re-named on 11th May; its artillery, commanded by Brigadier-General J.C. Wray, consisted of:

a. **5 (London) Brigade RFA;** (12th, 13th and 14th Batteries)

b. **6 (London) Brigade RFA;** (15th, 16th and 17th Batteries)

c. **7 (London) Brigade RFA;** (18th, 19th and 20th Batteries) (Each battery had 4×15-pounders)

d. **8 (London) Howitzer Brigade RFA;** (21st and 22nd Batteries) (Each with 4×5-inch howitzers)

General Haig decided to adopt the French plan at a conference at I Corps advanced HQ, held on 12th May. The 2nd Division was to assault by night to occupy the enemy front trenches on a front of 1,600 yards from Chocolate Mernier Corner to Port Arthur and then advance to a final objective 1,000 yards further on, on the Festubert—La Tourelle Road. 7th Division, who did not know the ground, decided to await the dawn. They were to attack on a front of 850 yards just north of Festubert, then join up with 2nd Division on their left. The bombardment was to be on a frontage of 5,000 yards between Festubert and Port Arthur. It was to start on the morning of 13th May and to continue without a pause until the evening of 14th May, some thirty-six hours later.

The artillery amounted to 433 guns and howitzers commanded by the CRAs of 2nd, 7th and Meerut Divisions (Brigadier-Generals W.H. Onslow, J.F.N. Birch, R. St C. Lecky) and 1 Group Heavy Artillery, under Brigadier-General G. McK. Franks. The artillery of 47th, 51st and the Canadian Divisions was available under orders CRA 7th Division. In addition, there was a Brigade of French 75's (These were soon to be reduced from eighteen to seven through prematures, from which the French were at this time suffering heavily). Still no Corps Artillery Commander was appointed and CRA 7th Division had neither staff nor communications to co-ordinate the fire of so many guns.

The bombardment began as planned. It was not strictly continuous, each battery firing for three two-hour periods during the day. Most of the 18-pounders were engaged in steady methodical wire cutting, which they did by accurate observed fire with considerable success, the wire being well cut right across the front. Each 6-inch battery was allotted 250 yards of enemy parapet to demolish. The 4.5-inch batteries engaged support and communication trenches, while the 13-pounder and remaining 18-pounders bombarded the trenches to kill enemy. It was during these bombardments that some of the hastily produced 4.5-inch shells fired failed to explode, a weakness which was not fully overcome until 1917. By night the bombardment continued both to destroy and to kill enemy trying to repair the defences. Ammunition expenditure was 150 rounds per gun for the thirty-six hours. Meanwhile, 1 Group Heavy Artillery had been reinforced by one 15-inch battery (two howitzers), one 9.2-inch and one 4.7-inch battery. These were used against the enemy strong points at Beau Puits, Violaines, the Distillery and selected targets on the defences. Counter battery was directed by air, using 48th and 111th Heavy Batteries and 8th Siege Battery. They were assisted by some French 155 mm guns in action south of the La Bassée Canal. Observation was very difficult and the few buildings available were filled with observers; one is reported to have contained seven.

At the end of the thirty-six hour bombardment, General Haig decided to extend it to sixty hours and to carry out a series of feints to mislead the enemy. Another ruse was tried. The bombardment would reach an intense rate then stop suddenly. The British infantry cheered as if to attack but did not move. The Germans massed in their trenches, whereupon the 13-pounders and 18-pounders fired shrapnel into them; sometimes it worked well.

The battle now took on four phases, the first being the night attacks by 2nd and the Meerut Divisions; the second was the dawn attack on 16th May by the whole Corps; the third was the ejection of the enemy from the "Quadrilateral" by artillery fire and the fourth being the withdrawal of the Germans, and the British consolidation.

The British 2nd Division attack was completely successful. However, prior to the attack, the Meerut Division kept firing their weapons and kept the enemy alert; their attack was not successful. Though 2nd Division's attack did well, by attacking at 2330 hours they gave the enemy all night to re-organise. The guns had fired throughout the attack and had lifted to form a barrage to protect the infantry now in the enemy front trenches. Four 13-pounders of T and U Batteries RHA and two 18-pounders of 12th Battery had been brought up into the firing line and had blasted the enemy with great effect.

In spite of the counter battery fire, the German guns were very active and, as 2nd and 7th Divisions tried to press on, they found strong enemy positions in depth, notably the 'Quadrilateral', and they were 'swept' by accurate enemy artillery. The attacks were unable to make progress on the 16th but the British Gunners wasted no time in registering all known enemy positions, especially the 'quadrilateral'. The British planned an attack at dawn on the 17th to close the gap between the two divisions. Unknown to them, the Germans planned a withdrawal at 0230 hours. The British bombardment started at 0245 hours and caught the Germans in the open and pulling out. Many were killed and some 450 were taken prisoner; the 'quadrilateral' was captured without loss as a result of this gunfire. General Haig thought that this meant that the German resistance was breaking, whereas in fact it was hardening; they had fallen back to strong positions near Ferme du Bois. Accordingly, Haig ordered attacks from 18th May to consolidate his gains. Mist and rain prevented a start during the morning but, at 1355 hours, the guns were ordered to begin bombardment at 1430 hours, continue until 1600 hours, speed up at 1620 hours, then fire intense till 1630 hours, when the assault would go in. The field howitzers now had no ammunition (due to the dispatch of large quantities to the Dardanelles) and could not take part. Insufficient time had been given for the passage of orders and the exact location of the enemy was not known. As a result, the bombardment did not start until 1500 hours and many enemy escaped. The assault failed and was broken up by the German guns and machine guns.

That night, I Corps was relieved by the 51st Division and the Canadian Division under General Alderson. Brigadier-General J.F.N. Birch now commanded the artillery of "Alderson's Force", as it was called. He had three divisional artilleries, 7 Siege Brigade, 8 (London) Brigade RFA, 36 Brigade RFA and a section of mountain guns. He thus had seven subordinate commanders to deal with, more than his staff could handle. During the next few days the new divisions consolidated and even extended their gains. The guns kept up their fire incessantly, supporting attacks by both 47th and the Canadian Divisions. On 27th May, for the first time, an artillery kite balloon took part in the battle with considerable success. Slowly operations came to an end, primarily due to the almost total lack of ammunition. On 26th May, the total quantities available were pathetic:

13-pounder	2 rounds
15-pounder	4 rounds
18-pounder	40 rounds
4.5-inch	12 rounds
5-inch	14 rounds
6-inch howitzer	27 rounds
6-inch gun	nil
9.2-inch howitzer	36 rounds
15-inch howitzer	7 rounds

So ended the battle of Festubert. Though it must be classed as a failure, it had pinned down many enemy and enabled the French to consolidate, and there had been some gains. It did once again demonstrate the superiority of artillery and machine guns in defence. It showed the need for more guns and much, much more ammunition if artillery attacks were to be successful. It showed, too, the dire need to locate and deal with enemy guns and machine guns. Finally, it demonstrated the need for a corps artillery commander with a staff capable of co-ordinating the fire of two or more divisional artilleries and the heavies. The British artillery was still evolving to cope with the new demands of a new war; the Gunners knew what they needed, many strove hard to achieve it; now more than anything they needed time to perfect new drills and equipment to make it possible. Industry needed time, too, to produce new and better guns and the vast quantities of ammunition without which the guns could not function.

CHAPTER 10

The Summer of 1915 — No Rest for the Guns

From an artillery point of view, the battle of Aubers Ridge and Festubert had raised above all the question of command at corps level. Major General J. Du Cane, Artillery Adviser at GHQ, discussed the problem with Sir John French. In IV Corps, Lieutenant General Sir H.S. Rawlinson was already acting. He directed that Brigadier-General Birch, CRA 7th Division, should also act as IV Corps Artillery Commander. Brigadier-General Birch called himself, "Commander Artillery IV Corps" and began issuing "IV Corps Artillery Operation Orders". These were signed by Major S.W.H. Rawlins (BMRA 7th Division) as "BM to CRA IV Corps". The first of these orders, an historic document, is reproduced at the end of this Chapter. This arrangement existed until June, when IV Corps were withdrawn from the line.

Meanwhile at GHQ, Major-General Du Cane quoted the IV Corps arrangement to back up his arguments with the General Staff, but they remained unconvinced—they would not accept the need for artillery command at corps level. So time slipped away, each corps making ad hoc arrangements which were unsatisfactory. It was not until October 1915 that the first Commander Corps Royal Artillery was to be appointed.

In May 1915, the first divisions of Kitchener's New Army began to arrive in France. 9th (Scottish), 14th (Light) and 12th (Eastern) landed in France on the 9th, 18th and 29th May respectively. There was then a pause until July, when the real build-up began. Thirteen new divisions arrived between July and September. The artillery order of battle of these divisions is given in the Annexes. All the new batteries had six 18-pounders or four 4.5-inch howitzers. Although excellent material, these new divisions were not fully trained. In particular, their staff work and junior leadership, mainly through inexperience, were weak; they needed at least six months work-up but this was not allowed them. Politically, a new offensive was imperative. The Dardanelles expedition had failed, the German pressure on Russia was increasing—something had to be done and quickly. Four new corps were formed in France:

14th July

VII Corps, BGRA Brigadier-General H.A.D. Simpson-Baikie
X Corps, BGRA Brigadier-General F.E. Johnson

29th August

XI Corps, BGRA Brigadier-General G.G.S. Carey

6th September

XII Corps, BGRA Brigadier-General W.H. Onslow

111

Before the battle of Loos began in September 1915, there were operations at Givenchy on 15th/16th June, at Bellewaarde on 16th June and at Hooge in July and August, which are important.

Givenchy—15th–16th June

General Haig was ordered to carry out a minor operation to assist Marshal Foch's offensive further south. After some postponements the French decided to attack on 15th June. The IV Corps operation was to be carried out by 7th and 51st Divisions. Brigadier-General Birch used the artillery of three divisions plus 1 Group Heavy Artillery to precede the attack with a 48 hour bombardment. This lifted at H-hour and left the enemy in no doubt as to the direction and size of the attack, surprise was lost and the attacking British suffered enormous casualties. Even so the enemy trenches were reached but, in spite of great gallantry, they could not be held. No artillery covering fire had been arranged and by last light, and with great difficulty, the two divisions were extricated. Not a good day. The guns had done well but the concept was not yet right. The tools of the trade were taking shape but the full complexity of artillery planning was still not understood.

Bellewaarde—16th June

The aim of this operation was to improve the situation at Ypres and to straighten out the British line. There were three objectives; phase one, the German front line which lay some 50–200 yards away; phase two, the Hooge-Bellewaarde farm road close behind the enemy front line trench, and phase three, a trench on the edge of Bellewaarde Lake some 200 yards beyond the road. The operation was to be carried out by V Corps, under General Allenby, consisting of the 3rd and 50th Divisions and two brigades of the 14th Division. The guns available were:

Divisional Artilleries

(1)	18-pounders	66, total of 12,000 rounds
(2)	4.5-inch howitzers	12, total of 2,000 rounds
(3)	5-inch howitzers	6, total of 500 rounds
(4)	2.75-inch howitzers	4, total of 400 rounds

2 Group Heavy Artillery

(1)	9.2-inch howitzers	3, total of 300 rounds
(2)	6-inch guns	2, total of 100 rounds
(3)	6-inch howitzers	8, total of 450 rounds
(4)	60-pounders	8, total of 1,200 rounds
(5)	4.7-inch howitzers	6, total of 2,000 rounds

Detailed arrangements were made to guarantee communications, three separately routed lines being laid, a system of signals organised and a pigeon service arranged. 6 Squadron RFC was allotted for reconnaissance and artillery spotting.

The fireplan started at 0230 hours, 16th June, with all guns bombarding the phase one objectives. This continued with pauses until H-hour at 0415 hours, when the guns lifted to the phase two objective. The 9th Infantry Brigade assault was entirely successful and the phase one objective was captured with very little resistance. The artillery fire had been extremely successful.

At this stage the infantry allotted to the phase two and three objectives rushed forward before being ordered, with disastrous results, for they ran into artillery fire coming down on the phase two and later phase three objectives. Again the problem of co-ordination failed when success was so near. At this point they were in full view of the Germans who had some excellent shoots with their guns; owing to the confusion, dust and smoke, no-one could see at the time what was happening, even so, the phase three objectives were reached, although they could not be held. 42nd Infantry Brigade of 14th Division attacked to restore the situation with a fresh fireplan but even after the most gallant attempts, particularly by the 3rd Worcesters, they were forced back. Though gains were made, the coveted Bellewaarde Ridge remained in enemy hands. 3rd Division lost 73 officers and 3,391 men in this operation, mostly due to the accurate defensive fire of the German guns which the British heavies had been unable to locate, but in any case, even had they done so, they had inadequate ammunition to deal with them. However, lessons had been learnt. Had the infantry moved according to plan, casualties would have been less, for the fireplan had been successful. Communications worked throughout but again counter-battery fire was in-effective and aerial observers could not distinguish friend from foe.

Hooge—19th and 30th July and 3rd–9th August

On 19th July, the Royal Engineers succeeded in exploding a huge landmine under the German positions at Hooge. Immediately, 4th Middlesex of 8th Infantry Brigade of 3rd Division seized the crater. German gun fire became intense and for some reason the British had not arranged a fireplan for the operation. Slowly the Middlesex had to give ground until the artillery of 3rd and 46th Divisions, together with 2 Group Heavy Artillery, attacked the enemy guns and succeeded in getting the upper-hand sufficiently to allow the infantry to consolidate and link the crater with the British trench system. It was the use of artillery at its best—it was the fire of the guns which enabled the Hooge salient to be held.

On 30th July, the enemy made a surprise counter-attack to recover the crater, itself almost untenable because of enemy mortar and gun fire. In places the trenches were only fifteen feet apart! Suddenly, at 0315 hours, a ferocious bombardment came down on all British positions including Sanctuary and Zouave woods. Then out of the darkness came long jets of liquid fire spraying the front trenches. This was the first use of flame-throwers in battle. Surprise was complete, the British fell back but the enemy did not follow up, although severe fighting followed, and the line was consolidated after giving up some ground.

The British counter-attack on 3rd August was a model of its kind. The enemy was completely misled as to its time and place by a series of ruses, including the digging of assault trenches in various sectors along the Second Army front.

The artillery plan was carefully made by CRA 6th Division. He was assisted by two "groups" of French guns and 2 Group Heavy Artillery, consisting of 5, 9, 11 and 13 Heavy Brigades. The infantry were to advance close to the gun fire and they did. The guns fired at various times before 3rd August; they fired too on 3rd August, ending in a very rapid concentration at 0315 hours. They then stopped, the leading infantry being almost in the leading enemy positions as they did. The Germans were completely surprised and all the trenches lost to the flame-thrower attacks on 30th July were quickly re-taken. A heavy enemy bombardment caused a few evacuations around the crater but the British guns in their turn denied the area to the Germans. The operation was very successful. At last, the technique of providing intimate covering fire was being learned. The action was also notable for being the first time that an effort was made, though only partially successful, to maintain contact between Brigade and Divisional Headquarters by portable radios. A few steel helmets were also tried out experimentally and their value was immediately evident.

So the scene was set for the battle of Loos. New British divisions were fast arriving in France, though they were not yet ready for battle. The war was settling-down to a static slog of trench warfare. The use of guns was paramount and artillery techniques were developing, though the equipment to make them possible was still not available. Ammunition was critically short but it too was beginning to improve. Command and control was improving but there was still some way to go; new communicating equipment was urgently required. Gunners now knew what was needed to develop techniques for providing really effective fire power in both attack and defence. The problem lay in the inability to retain control once an operation had started. Where it had worked, operations had been successful; where it had not, loss of life had been enormous.

IV Corps Artillery Operation Order No 1

by

Brig. General J.F.N. Birch, A.D.C., Commanding Artillery IV Corps

3rd June, 1915.

Intention 1.   The Artillery of the IV Corps will prepare the assault of the 20th Inf. Bde. (7th Div.) on the German salient at I.4.

The assault will take place at 9.40 p.m. to-night.

General Plan 2.   At 9.40 p.m. a mine will be exploded under I.4 at which hour the assault on this point will take place.

The assault will be made in two columns, the right column working down the German trench through I.2 to H.3, and the left column up the German trench through I.3 to I.9.

The position will then be consolidated.

Communication trenches will be dug back from the captured trenches and a trench dug from I.2 to I.3.

Should H.3 be reached, the Canadian Division is to dig a communication trench from that point back to our present line.

Artillery 3(a) The hours allotted for registration have already been notified to all concerned.

(b) The 9.2-inch howitzers will fire as already arranged.

(c) Wirecutting will be carried out about I.4 by the Canadian Divisional Artillery. The wire will be inspected at 2 p.m. by O.C. 3rd Can. Arty. Bde. and an officer of 20th Inf. Bde., and a report furnished as to the results obtained.

(d) The Time Table No. 1 for the first bombardment is issued herewith for 7th and Canadian Artilleries (and 3rd Highland Howitzer Brigade).

(e) Further time tables will be issued later.

(f) Separate instructions are issued herewith to Highland Divisional Artillery which will be so employed as to deceive the enemy as to the actual front of assault.

(g) The 14th Brigade R.H.A. and 35th Brigade R.F.A. will be employed as counter-batteries.

Rockets 5. Three white rockets will indicate the capture of I.2, three green rockets that of I.3, and three red rockets that of H.3.

Headquarters 6. The Headquarters of the B.G.C. Artillery IV Corps will remain at Halte W.24.C.

Issued at

(Sd.) S.W.H. RAWLINS,
Major, R.A.,
Brigade Major to C.R.A. 4th Corps.

Copy No. 1–4th Corps.   No. 7-Alexander Group
2–7th Div.   8–14th Bde, R.H.A.
3-Can. D.A.   9-B.G.C., R.A.
4-Highland D.A.   10-Bde. Major.
5-Siege Group.   11–1st Group, H.A.R (Heavy Artillery
6-Nicholson Group.   Reserve).

CHAPTER 11

The Battle of Loos — September 1915

See map 20

The French planned a great autumn offensive in Artois and asked the British to attack in sympathy. General Joffre pressed for a major British operation south of the La Bassée Canal but General Haig was against this. He stated that the German defences at this point were very strong and could only be stormed after a very heavy artillery bombardment. He did not have enough guns or ammunition and, without them, the open ground in front of the German trenches would be swept by machine gun and rifle from high ground. Furthermore, the enemy's superior observation would enable him to concentrate his artillery onto the British infantry all the way from their forming up points to their objectives. Lastly, at this point the German trench systems were in great depth and backed by fortified villages. Again General Haig emphasised his shortage of guns and said that no offensive operations should be launched until at least his supply of ammunition had been built up.

On 19th–20th June 1915, the critical artillery situation was discussed at an important conference at Boulogne between the British and French Minister of Munitions—The British Munitions Minister was Mr Lloyd George. The conference realised that the supply of heavy artillery had now become vital. The proportion of field to heavy guns in the German army was 2:1; in the French Army, 4:1; in the British Army, 20:1! They concluded that, to engage successfully in offensive operations, the proportion should be 2:1, the French stating that they would aim for equal numbers of each. As an example, they quoted Aubers Ridge earlier in the year, when fifteen German companies and twenty-two machine guns strongly supported by artillery had defeated a British attack by three brigades. The next problem was ammunition. The size of the problem was illustrated when they found that the Germans were producing 250,000 rounds of artillery ammunition per day, the French 100,000 and the British 22,000, with no prospect of increasing until early 1916 on present plans. Tactically, the conference stated, at least 1,000 rounds of heavy and 2,000 rounds of field gun ammunition must be constantly available to any sector and a reserve of 200 rounds per gun heavy and 500 rounds per gun field on the remainder of the front. They further deduced that offensive operations must be conducted on a very wide front to avoid the devastating enfilade fire on the flanks. After this conference, General Haig reported that a major offensive would need thirty-six British divisions, 2,400 field guns (400 batteries!) and 1,200 heavy guns and howitzers (200 batteries!). It was clear that such a force could not be available before spring 1916.

Politically the situation was serious. The Russian Armies had collapsed in the East, the Germans were switching troops to the Western front and the French were pressing for an offensive. On 12th July it was agreed that the offensive should begin on ground of General Joffre's choosing at the end of August. The new British Third Army, under General Sir Charles Monro, was to relieve the French on the Somme. The date was later postponed to 25th September to allow the French to complete preparations in Champagne.

The Germans had been shaken by the summer operations. The British attacks had shown them that their lines could be breached; hitherto they had relied on a single very strong position. They now set-to with characteristic thoroughness to construct their defences in depth. They decided to build strong positions, strongly wired, some 4,000 yards behind their front line. This, they argued, would force the enemy to move his guns during the assault should he decide to use them for wire cutting. They were determined to ensure that a quick break-through at a single stroke would be impossible. This build-up was watched by British and French aerial observation but, in spite of some long range bombardment, they had neither guns nor ammunition to prevent it.

The two Armies were now heading for a clash of enormous potential. The British and French were planning a massive assault in great strength, while the Germans were planning a defence in great depth and also in great strength. Unknown to the Allies, it was going to need an enormous superiority to break through. Political pressure, however, dictated speed. So the preparations began throughout that fateful August of 1915.

There was a weakness in the German plan but a weakness which neither General Joffre nor the British Commanders foresaw. To be successful, the Germans must hold both their lines of defence works with separate forces. The second line was too close to the first for the defenders of the first to break clean and fall back to fight again. If kept under constant pressure, the Allies could roll up the defences.

General Joffre decided that his concept would be a massive bombardment followed by waves of assaulting infantry, who would flow like a great human tide over the defences. Divisions would attack on frontages of 1,500 yards and battalions on a single or even half company frontage. The guns would cut the wire but, astonishingly, no orders were given as to how the wire of the second line was to be cut.

General Sir John French ordered First Army (I and IV Corps) to carry out the main attack. Second Army would make diversionary attacks. The artillery of Third Army would support the French. A reserve, held well back under General Sir John himself, consisted of XI Corps, the Cavalry Corps (1st and 2nd Cavalry Divisions) and the Indian Cavalry Corps. A plan was made to bomb the enemy defences by the RFC, and ten flights of four squadrons were allotted for artillery observation.

The ground around Loos is significant. Two spurs run north east from the Artois plateau, with the village at Loos lying between them. The western spur runs just east of South Maroc. It became known as Lone Tree Spur. The edge of South Maroc provided the best possible observation for the British artillery. Indeed, the eastern edge of the village became known as 'Artillery Row'. 'Fosse 5', a large slag heap, provided an excellent view down the Loos valley, in places seeing behind the

German front line. The mining villages of Cité St Pierre and Cité St Edouard occupied the eastern spur which ran, at its north eastern end, into Hill 70. This spur became known as Cité Spur. The Germans had much better observation in the north around Auchy, where their view over the open ground occupied by the British was excellent; in places the opposing front line trenches were only fifty to a hundred yards apart. The two strongest points in the German defences were the village of Loos in the south and the Hohenzollern Redoubt, a group of earthworks on a low rise just south of Auchy. Even so, every village was a fortress and every miner's cottage with its cellar became a dugout. The German second line ran some three miles to the east, in front of Hulluch and Cité St Elie. This trench line was to be the British phase two objective.

The attack was to be carried out by the six divisions of I and IV Corps. The artillery plan provided for nineteen heavy guns per mile of front, though the ammunition situation was far from good; in total there was nothing like enough artillery to establish any form of superiority. The frontage could be reduced and the gunfire concentrated, but experience showed that mass attacks on narrow frontages invited destruction from enfilade fire on the flanks—so here was a dilemma. The ground at Loos demanded an assault on a wide front but there was not enough artillery; there was, however, a possible solution. Encouraging experiments had been carried out with chlorine gas in June as a result of work at the new experimental centre at Porton near Salisbury. There was a good prevailing wind at Loos. The German gas masks were effective for thirty minutes so, if a gas cloud could be made to last for forty minutes, it would compensate for the lack of artillery and ensure a break through. There was not enough gas to cover the whole front but used with the guns it would, it was thought, provide the answer. The gas was to be "fired" from cylinders, on the soda syphon principle, from the British front trenches across to the German trenches. This called for new infantry tactics. They were to go forward in "violent continuous action" without stopping, catching the Germans affected by gas and press on to the phase two objective. Hopes ran high; was there to be a major tactical victory? Was there at last a hope that the German trenches would be completely overrun? As so often with the British, they hoped that at last victory could be won without the great slaughter of earlier battles—they forgot that in the end battles are only won by concentrated fire power co-ordinated with violent, offensive cavalry and infantry action. Nevertheless, they realised that it was possible that the wind might not be right for gas and that two plans must be prepared, one with gas on a six division front and one without on a two division front.

The battle of Loos was a land mark in artillery command and control, though not perfect. For the first time a Commander Corps Royal Artillery (CCRA) was appointed before the battle in each corps; in I Corps it was Brigadier-General J.F.N. Birch and in IV Corps it was Brigadier-General C.E.D. Budworth. HQRA I Corps was formed and the first Brigade Major was Major S.W. Rawlins from 7th Division. Captain K.I. McIver and Lieutenant E.G.W.W. Harrison completed the Staff. HQRA IV Corps consisted of Major H. Young as Brigade Major and Captain G.E. Boscowan as Staff Officer. The heavy artillery of 1 and 5 Groups were not, however, placed under the CCRAs but worked under HQ First Army. This was a mistake, as it meant that the vital counter-battery was not controlled by the HQs controlling the battle.

The artillery line up for the battle was:

I Corps

(1) **Divisional Artillery 2nd Division** (Brigadier General H. Onslow)

34 Brigade RFA—50th and 70th Field Batteries (18-pounders)
36 Brigade RFA—15th, 48th and 71st Field Batteries (18-pounders)
41 Brigade RFA—9th, 16th and 17th Field Batteries (18-pounders)
44 Brigade RFA—47th and 56th Howitzer Batteries (4.5-inch howitzers)

(2) **Divisional Artillery 7th Division** (Brigadier General J.G. Rotton)

14 Brigade RHA— F and T Batteries RHA (18-pounders)
22 Brigade RFA—104th, 105th and 106th Batteries (18-pounders)
35 Brigade RFA—12th, 25th and 58th Batteries (18-pounders)
37 Brigade RFA—31st and 35th Howitzer Batteries (4.5-inch howitzers)

(3) **Divisional Artillery 9th Division** (Brigadier-General E.H. Armitage)

50 Brigade RFA—160th, 161st and 162nd Batteries (18-pounders)
51 Brigade RFA—163rd, 164th and 165th Batteries (18-pounders)
52 Brigade RFA—166th, 167th and 168th Batteries (18-pounders)
53 Brigade RFA—169th, 170th and 171st Howitzer Batteries (4.5-inch howitzers)

(4) **5 Group Heavy Artillery** (Brigadier-General Tancred)

(5) **Siege Group** (Lieutenant Colonel W.J. Napier)

7 Brigade RGA
14 Brigade RGA

This was a simple, direct and cleary defined organisation, but the situation in IV Corps was anything but simple, the whole artillery force being organised in mixed groups as follows:

IV Corps

(1) **1st Divisional Artillery Group** (Lieutenant Colonel F.A.G.Y. Elton)

(a) **Northern Sub-Group**
26 Brigade RFA—116th and 117th Batteries (18-pounders)
C Battery 71 Brigade RFA (18-pounders)
A Battery 119 Brigade RFA (18-pounders)

(b) **Southern Sub-Group**
C and D Batteries 108 Brigade RFA (18-pounders)
30th Howitzer Battery (4.5-inch howitzers)
2nd Siege Battery, 6 Brigade RGA (6-inch howitzers)

(2) **15th Divisional Artillery Group** (Brigadier-General E.W. Alexander)

71 Brigade RFA—A, B and D Batteries (15-pounders)
70 Brigade RFA—A, B, C and D Batteries (15-pounders)
73 Brigade RGA—B, C and D Howitzer Batteries (4.5-inch howitzers)
One section 19th (London) Field Battery attached (15-pounders)
5th Siege Battery, 6 Brigade RGA (6-inch howitzers)

(3) **47th Divisional Artillery Group** (Brigadier-General J.C. Wray)

   (a) **MacNaghten Group**
      25 Brigade RFA—113th, 114th and 115th Batteries (18-pounders)
      39 Brigade RFA—46th, 51st and 54th Batteries (18-pounders)
      21st (London) Battery—40 Brigade RFA (15-pounders)
      C Battery 109 Brigade RFA (18-pounders)
      24th Siege Battery (6-inch howitzers)

   (b) **Massey Group**
      5 (London) Brigade RFA—12th, 13th and 14th (London) Batteries (18-pounders)
      G Battery RHA (13-pounders)
      23rd Siege Battery (6-inch howitzers)

   (c) **Divisional Reserve Group**
      7 (London) Brigade RFA less two batteries
      7 Brigade RHA—H, I and Warwick Batteries

There is no doubt that this was a most untidy grouping, with an excessive use of groups and sub-groups. It was caused by the removal of 1st Division Artillery HQ to act as HQRA IV Corps and by the enormous mixture of equipments between the divisions. It was intended that HQRA IV Corps should revert to 1st Division during the battle! An extraordinary theory which, of course, never happened.

The two Corps Commanders handled their guns quite differently. Brigadier-General Birch issued a simple fireplan which, in outline, ran as follows:

H Hour   Corps artillery engage front trenches
H + 10   Guns lift by stages
H + 20   Guns to have moved their fire 1,200 yards east
H + 21   Guns lift back to front line trenches by stages
H + 30   Guns on front line trenches
H + 40   Guns lift from front line trenches to line 600 yards beyond
H + 50   Guns lift to line c. (ie a further 600 yards)

Brigadier Budworth ordered his "Group" commanders to discuss tasks with divisional commanders. His order stated "Group commanders will allow sub-group commanders the greatest latitude in carrying out their tasks". This suggested that the temporary CCRA did not wish to assert himself unduly over his fellow CRAs! The tasks were selected under the headings:

Wirecutting
Bombardment
Searching and sweeping—trench systems
Special tasks
Concentrations in response to AHQ tasks

Brigadier Budworth did not issue a Corps fireplan, though some were issued within divisions. Lieutenant Colonel Elton formed a temporary HQRA 1st Division, taking Lieutenant J.D.G. Macneece from 26 Brigade RFA and Lieutenant L.R. Fergusson from 25 Brigade RFA. Fireplans were issued by motorcyclist. 15th Division issued normal orders but, surprisingly, in 47th Division the general staff issued the artillery and fireplan orders.

The open nature of the ground and the excellent German observation forced the heavies to deploy on the general line Les Brebis—Mazingarbe—Noyelles—Annequin (south-east of Bethune), some 3–4000 yards behind the front line. The field batteries deployed some 500 yards ahead of them, many in full view of the enemy. Fortunately, German counter battery work at Loos was poor and these batteries did not suffer unduly. Plans were made for all batteries to advance when the attack was successful and each was allotted a bridge over the trenches. Ammunition supply was not good—only 371,000 rounds of HE and shrapnel being allotted to the 18-pounders (Compared to 1,977,000 at Messines in 1917 for a similar task!).

The artillery operations were divided into three phases:

Phase one: Preliminary Bombardment—96 Hours

Phase two: The Battle—48 Hours

Phase three: Subsequent operations (including a move of the guns)—96 hours

Two thirds of the ammunition was allotted to phase one for this and, together with the gas discharge, was the most vital part of the battle. The next complication was the need to produce two plans. The first, without gas, would be an attack by 9th Division of I Corps and 15th Division of IV Corps, attacking Hohenzollern Redoubt and Loos respectively. All possible artillery would support these divisions. Their own divisional artilleries would support the assault. Non-assault divisional artilleries would cover the flanks and the heavies would silence the German artillery. One hour before the assault the bombardment would intensify; the guns were then to lift to "box-in" the objectives with a curtain of fire.

In the second plan, envisaging the use of gas, the gun fire would be spread and dispersed over a six divisional frontage of six miles. The fire would be concentrated on strong points, villages, observation posts, hostile batteries and wire. The most difficult tasks were: first, to site guns to carry out the tasks for both plans in the open undulating country west of Loos and second, the problem of wire cutting at extreme range. The field guns were to cut the wire in front of the phase one objectives and the heavies were to cut wire at extreme ranges in front of the phase two objectives. Many Gunner commanders were much concerned about their ability to do this—but that was the plan or, rather, those were the plans. The choice rested, as so often in military planning, on the state of the weather on D-Day!

D-Day itself was to be 25th September. This meant the pre-H Hour bombardment must start on 21st September assuming that on the 25th the gas attack, that is the attack with six divisions, would be ordered. While the planning had been going on, much preparatory work had gone into fixing the target positions and issuing target lists. Air photographs had been used and a complex observation plan, both ground and air, had been made. All was ready, tension was high, would it work? Would the greatest attack by British forces so far planned in the war be successful?

Harrassing fire started on the 21st, a fine, warm, dry day. The heavies were limited to ninety rounds per gun and the field guns to one hundred and fifty for the first twenty four hours. For hour after hour shells thudded into the German positions. Soon clouds of smoke and dust fell over the battlefield making observation almost impossible. The 23rd dawned wet with variable wind. The heavies started a large fire at Cité St Pierre, which burned for two days and nights. As feared, progress in wire cutting was not good. On the 24th it continued to rain. The intensity of the bombardment grew, visibility improved, but the wind upon which all depended was fickle. During the four days of preparatory fire, feint attacks were made all along the front and, when the Germans manned their parapets, they were engaged with shrapnel. The volume of British fire was relatively slight, however, so much so that the Germans did not deduce that it was the prelude to an attack! Throughout, entry points through the wire were selected for concentrated bombardment by both heavies and field guns and here there was considerable success. Subsequent examination showed the effect of accurate concentrated fire and much damage was done and much wire cut at these points.

The decision facing General Haig at 0500 hours on the morning of 25th September was not unlike that facing General Eisenhower twenty-nine years later, when he too had to "read" the weather. At 0515 hours, a slight breeze got up and General Haig noticed the smoke from a cigarette blew towards the north east. He ordered the gas attack to start as planned at 0550 hours. Unknown to the British, the Germans had captured a deserter, who said the British would attack at 0500 hours. When nothing happened at 0515 hours, they stood down, not really believing it anyway. The scene was set, the die cast for the biggest battle of the war thus far. A few minutes later the wind, slight as it was, died away. General Haig asked if he could stop the attack, but General Gough said it was too late, they must stand by their orders.

So, at 0550 hours on that day, overcast dawn of 25th September 1915, the British launched their first ever gas attack. Haig stood with his ADC in a tower and waited. The guns opened up according to their programmes for gas. Simultaneously, the deadly yellowish chlorine was released all along the British line. It was mixed with the white of conventional smoke to give a false intensity. Soon the smoke, dust, gas and exploding shells formed a thick, grey yellowish cloud along the whole battlefield from Lens to Givenchy. The guns of I Corps swept backwards and forwards across the German trenches but it is the story of the gas that mattered now. Would it reach the enemy trenches? The gun fire was in support of the gas—without it there was not enough artillery to support six divisions. On the extreme right the gas did not reach the German trenches, as the wind was too light; in front of Loos itself and north to the Hohenzollern Redoubt, it carried well and achieved considerable surprise. It contributed greatly to the success of 47th, 15th and 9th Divisions. In the centre, however, astride the Vermelles—Hulluch road it doubled back on the British, causing loss and confusion in the 1st and 7th Divisions. Further north the wind dropped and the chemical detachments did not discharge the gas, as it would endanger their own troops. However, the Divisional Commander of 2nd Division ordered them to discharge, which had disastrous results and it had to be turned off at once.

General Haig and his Corps Commanders were now in a dilemma. They had a situation where three divisions had successful gas attacks and could well proceed, but the other three divisions had no gas support. There was not enough artillery to cope with this situation; command arrangements could not cope—there was little flexibility, the plan could not be changed, or could it? It is hard now to see why not but, of course, such an observation has the benefit of hindsight. The infantry had not yet left their trenches; surely those without gas or adequate artillery should not be committed, surely they should be diverted to reinforce the success of the others—surely? We must not be too harsh. The Commanders did not have good communications nor the hindsight of history and, in the event, the attack was ordered to proceed right across the front.

On the right, 47th Division formed a defensive right flank as ordered and held it. The 15th Division swept into Loos on the track of the gas. They went triumphantly on but lost direction, wheeled right and overran Hill 70. They then advanced against Cité St Laurent, thinking they were attacking Cité St Auguste. They demanded much artillery fire which was most successfully provided. Errors, yes, but success, too. In spite of the failure of the gas and the initial confusion, 1st and 7th Divisions got as far as the German second line on the Lens—La Bassée road west of Hulluch. But the right of 1st Division never got over this initial set back and this widened the gap with 15th Division who were, in any case, too far south by now. 9th Division had varied success. The gas had failed and the division suffered heavily but its right brigade captured the Hohenzollern Redoubt and got as far as the German second line at Haisness. 2nd Division failed all along the line. It never recovered from discharging its gas into an adverse wind!

German counter attacks at last light regained Hill 70 and restored their second line but they did not locate the 1,200 yard gap between 1st and 15th Divisions. On that fateful day, the British lost 15,000 men; by last light the infantry were exhausted. XI Corps (Guards, 21st and 24th Division) was preparing for phase two along with the Cavalry Corps (1st, 2nd and 3rd Cavalry Divisions). During the night 25th/26th September they came into action.

But now we must look back to 25th September. How had the artillery fared?

The attack of 47th Division had been carefully rehearsed on a full scale model of the ground. This was a new approach, to be much copied by later commanders. "Massey" Group fired continuously on German front line trenches, and on Cité St Pierre, while supporting 142nd Infantry Brigade on the right. "Macnaghten" Group supported the successful advance of 140th and 141st Infantry Brigade, the shooting was accurate and good and the wire was well cut. The Divisional Artillery was ordered to form "a strong pivot of manoeuvre", though this mystical task was never defined. Plans were now made for the advance and, for the first time, artillery commanders went to brigade headquarters to co-ordinate this complex maneouvre. Major Peel went to 140th Infantry Brigade and Major Gordon to 141st Infantry Brigade HQ and their orders were "to communicate any special requirements of the Infantry Brigade Commanders to the Group Commanders who will issue the necessary orders to batteries". A forerunner of the present technique of the Gunner Commanding Officer at Brigade HQ.

Meanwhile, 15th Divisional Artillery successfully covered the advance of their division and they were told to "form a strong centre" between Maroc and Lens. Again, this was not defined! At 1000 hours, B and C Batteries of 70 Brigade RFA moved into action about a mile north of Maroc to cover the attack onto Hill 70.

By 1500 hours they were joined by A and D Batteries. These batteries came under enfilade fire from Hulluch and Lens and were unable to advance further. A and C Batteries of 71 Brigade RFA came into action just west of Loos, while B and D were just north of "Fosse 7" (Quality Street). B and C Batteries of 72 Brigade RFA advanced to the north of Loos but found the trenches unbridged, so came into action just near the old British front line. C Battery pushed on boldly into Loos, coming under heavy shell fire, and found retiring German infantry; they came into action. A and D Batteries of 72 Brigade RFA did not move forward. These complex advance manoeuvres were well executed and continuous fire support was maintained. Light rain began to fall during the later afternoon and this, coupled with smoke, made observation almost impossible. Communications to the guns in such mobile operations began to break down. It was almost impossible to maintain the surface laid lines. The infantry then began to report that they were attacking east of Cité St Auguste, when in fact they were attacking south from Hill 70 to Cité St Laurent! This, as can be imagined, caused considerable confusion. Divisional control of the guns was impossible and, as a result, a determined enemy attack on Hill 70 succeeded, since in this situation there was no way to concentrate the gun fire quickly enough. Nevertheless, the Divisional Artillery of the newly formed "New Army" 47th Division had acquitted itself well in its first ever battle.

Further north 1st Division had a harder task. Its more experienced regular Divisional Artillery was well and firmly controlled by Lieutenant Colonel Elton, the acting CRA. 116th Battery of 26 Brigade RFA advanced to Le Rutoire at 1115 hours; 117th Battery joined it by 1200 hours. Lieutenant Colonel G.B. Hinton, commanding the Brigade, went forward with his battery commanders to the German second line. A close link was established with the assaulting brigades and good fire support was given. At 1415 hours, 117th Battery advanced to just north of Haie de Bois Carie to be joined by 30th Howitzer Battery by 1530 hours but observation was bad throughout. Concentrated fire enabled the infantry to capture the "Lone Tree" feature and by last light 39 Brigade RFA were in action alongside Lone Tree itself.

Command at divisional and corps artillery level was not good. Such vague co-ordinating phrases as ". . . to employ artillery in such a manner as will best support their own divisions" or ". . . to afford as much assistance as possible" had virtually no effect. Brigade and battery commanders however established, for the first time, real links with infantry brigade HQs and were thus able to include the guns in the rapidly changing plans. An effort was made on 26th September to co-ordinate the fire of fifteen batteries of 1st and 15th Divisional Artilleries. The guns of 47th Division were later added. This might have been most successful for the attack on Hill 70 had there been enough ammunition. The heavies continued to work on counter-battery tasks and their fire was not really co-ordinated with the rest. Indeed, ammunition soon became so short that rates of two rounds per battery per minute were being imposed! Some 6-inch guns only had fifty rounds for the whole operation!

Further north still the fortunes of I Corps were very different. The CCRA, Brigadier Birch, already experienced in France, exercised a much tighter control over his Corps Artillery. Detailed orders were issued by him for the bombardment and circulated to all interested HQs, including the Royal Flying Corps HQ. CRAs retained good control throughout, though their advances were less spectacular than those of IV Corps. The guns started some 3,000 yards behind the British trenches and could not advance over the forward slopes until the German front trenches were taken. However, both these and his second line had been well registered by air and ground observation, observers being very well forward.

When the attack of 7th Division started, the headquarters of the two leading brigades and the four artillery brigade commanders were close together. A very close and intimate liaison resulted and notably successful shoots were carried out immediately they were requested by 14 Brigade RHA. At 0900 hours the artillery advance began led by T Battery RHA, who galloped down the Hulluch road and raced into action just west of the old German front line. Soon 12th Battery of 35 Brigade RFA and a section of 35th Battery of 37 Brigade RFA were advancing towards Noyelles and Le Borrise (west of Vermelles). As the first section of T Battery advanced again, two lead drivers and thirteen horses were hit by rifle fire but the drills were well known and, only momentarily checked, the section came into action. An observation post was established with the leading infantry and German telephone cable was found and used. By 1030 hours F, T and 59th Siege Batteries were engaging targets with great accuracy. At 0835 hours 22 Brigade RFA, less 106th Battery, advanced in echelon of batteries across open country to positions south of Chapel—"a magnificent sight". They had no casualties. 107th Battery joined them by 1700 hours and were soon engaging enemy columns near Cité St Elie. It is astonishing that none of these forward positions were shelled until the following day.

35 Brigade RFA established an observation post in the German front trenches as they were still being cleared. 12th Battery was ordered forward at 1100 hours but it was 1330 hours before they were in action, so difficult was the going. One section of 35th Battery came into action in the German trenches during the morning. Lines to forward observers remained through all day and some good shooting caused many enemy casualties. During the night 31st Battery's forward observers in "The Quarry" were captured. Next day, the Battery Commander of 35th Battery used a helio to control the fire most successfully from "The Dump", until driven off by German infantry. The forward section of 35th Battery was withdrawn at 0200 hours on 27th September, as it was now suffering heavy casualties. The forward observers did particularly well, being right forward, and many had to use their revolvers during the 26th and 27th. The support they gave to the infantry of 7th Division was of the highest order. Commander 22nd Infantry Brigade in particular said that it was the artillery which got them into their objectives and then kept them there by beating off counter-attack after counter-attack.

Let us turn now to the 9th Division, still further north. The Division had only left England in May. It was the first of the 'New Army' divisions, whose first action had been at Messines on 20th May. They had been out of the line in June, in action with the Indian Corps in July and had joined I Corps on 31st August. All the artillery brigades had four, four gun batteries except the 53 Howitzer Brigade which had three; its A Battery had been transferred to 27th Division on 14th June.

The attack of the 9th Division, checked on the right where the gas was ineffective, was successful on the left. A bombardment was fired between 1130 and 1215 hours in support of 25th Infantry Brigade on the right. On the left 26th Infantry Brigade captured Fosse 8 and at 0930 hours A Battery 52 Brigade RFA advanced, soon to be followed by B, C and D Batteries, then B Battery 50 Brigade RFA and D Battery 53 Brigade RFA. The rest of 50 and 53 Brigades fired a flank barrage to protect the Division's northern, now exposed, flank. By dusk the situation of these very cramped forward batteries was very precarious. Cité St Elie had not been captured and the infantry, enfiladed on both flanks, began to fall back through the guns. By this time the most advanced battery was firing at ranges of less than 100 yards! Accordingly, the CRA ordered the guns to withdraw during the night.

The Germans counter-attacked on 27th when observation was virtually impossible. Telephone lines, laid on the surface during the advance, were constantly cut, so the CRA ordered 50 Brigade RFA to fire a barrage onto the counter-attack, unobserved, to the east of Fosse 8. This was controlled by the CRA from reports from the forward observers of 7th Divisional Artillery to the south who could see it. They reported it most effective in the end and it did much to stabilise a very difficult situation. On 28th September, 9th Division was relieved by 28th Division.

To the north of 9th Division was 2nd Division. They never really recovered from the recoil of the gas onto themselves, so it was a sad day for them. The artillery plan ordered by HQRA in operation order Number 3 of 22nd September was:

a.   Searching fire by the 18-pounders at 12 rounds per gun per minute.

b.   Miscellaneous battery targets as listed (one gun of 45th Battery was given 480 yards of trench!).

The fire was thus spread very thinly and was in no way enough if the gas failed and, as we know, the gas failed disastrously. There was, however, excellent control of the Brigades from HQRA. When the infantry attacks failed with terrible losses, it was the accurate and swift concentrations of gun fire onto the enemy's front trenches which averted total disaster. No advances were made in the Division's front during the day, though the guns were hotly engaged throughout.

So ended the battle of Loos. Though as a battle it was not a success, and the casualties were horrific, it was a landmark in the handling of artillery. The guns did well throughout and were responsible for getting the assaulting infantry onto the objectives and for breaking up the enemy counter-attacks. It was the first British attack on a grand scale, the front being 11,200 yards compared with 1,450 at Neuve Chapelle or 5,080 at Festubert. For the first time, HQRAs at corps were established and co-ordinated the fireplans for their corps' attacks. This was only accomplished with a varying degree of success but it was accomplished. The heavy artillery were not, however, properly controlled. Under HQRA Army they were too remote and they were not properly linked to HQRAs at divisions. The artillery allotted was inadequate in numbers if the gas should fail. 50% of the gas did fail and the shortage of artillery was immediately revealed.

Nevertheless, advances in command and control were made. FOOs performed with great gallantry and the guns were well handled. Communications, when the battle became mobile, were however not good. Ammunition supply was still crucial. However, the first Corps Artillery operation order ever made was issued.

CHAPTER 12

Winter 1915–16 and Operations until June 1916

On 3rd October 1915, GHQ issued a letter in which the Commander in Chief " . . . decided to alter the status of the Artillery Adviser with the Headquarters of a Corps and to appoint him General Officer Commanding Royal Artillery (GOCRA) of the Corps Artillery with the rank of Brigadier-General. The Brigadier-General so appointed will be charged with the co-ordination of the action of the artillery of the corps and the executive and command of such portions of it as the Corps Commander may direct from time to time". So the lessons of battle were sanctioned, the artillery of a corps was to be properly co-ordinated at last. Then came an unfortunate snag. For some inexplicable reason, the War Office insisted on the creation of 'Heavy Artillery Group Commanders' operating under the MGRA at Army HQ with the rank of Brigadier-General. During the 1916 battles, real co-ordination of all artillery at corps level was thus not properly achieved because of this refusal by the War Office to allow the heavy brigades to be correctly grouped. The Heavy Artillery Group Commander was a Brigadier-General, which meant that each corps had two artillery commanders of equal rank. A bid to make the GOCRA a Major-General failed, even though he commanded a similar number of men to a Divisional Commander and, like him, he did it through four Brigadier-Generals. In retrospect it was probably right that this did occur, since it would have meant losing that subtle link which exists between Gunners and their Divisional and Brigade Commanders. This system, unique to the British Army, has ensured that the artillery is always part of the divisional or brigade plan and not superimposed upon it by separate and equally ranked commanders. That was the German system; by the end of the war the British system, which exists to this day, proved far superior (although the Senior Artillery Commander at Corps HQ is now MGRA). Indeed, from it has grown one of the most efficient artillery systems in the world, integrating fire power into commanders' plans in a way which only those Armies who have copied it can achieve. The combat commander's plan grows up with the artillery plan and so the co-ordination of fire power into the plan is included from the start—yet the combat commander's overall authority is never questioned.

The next problem was to provide the new GOCRA with a staff. At first, he was given a BMRA and reconnaissance officer only; this was far from satisfactory but it was a start. It is interesting to note that all Gunner Staff Officers came direct from batteries and none from the Staff College until after the war.

Two significant improvements in artillery equipment were made towards the end of 1915.

The first was the provision of HE shell for field guns; and the second was the replacement of the old 6-inch 30-cwt howitzers by the very serviceable, and newly designed, 6-inch 26-cwt BL howitzer with a maximum range of 9,800 yards. (With

The 6-inch 26 cwt BL Howitzer. After the demise of the 6-inch 30 cwt Howitzer this became the standard, and highly efficient, medium howitzer of the British Army. *(I.W.M.)*

2 c.r.h. projectile. Later marks ranged from 12,500 yards with 5/10 c.r.h.).

At about the same time also, the 6-inch Mk VII BL gun, designed originally for coast defences, was mounted on an improvised field carriage. It had no proper recoil gear, having been intended for a fixed mounting, and ran back up huge ramps to check its recoil. A later Mark XIX was to follow two years later; that was provided with a well-designed new carriage and an efficient buffer and recuperator. The maximum range of the Mark VII was 12,000 yards; of the Mark XIX 19,200.

Some of the 6-inch guns were also bored out to operate as 8-inch BL howitzers with a range of 10,000 yards. Initially they had the same recoil troubles as the 6-inch guns and were similarly modified later, and ranged to 12,500 yards.

By the end of 1915, certain other changes in organisation were recognised as necessary. Field Artillery Brigades were to be changed into mixed Brigades, each of three six gun 18-pounder batteries and one four gun 4.5-inch howitzer battery. Thus each Division of three such Brigades was to have fifty-four 18-pounders and twelve 4.5-inch howitzers. Some Divisional Artilleries had only one brigade with only two 18-pounder batteries. By May 1916, the Brigade Ammunition Columns were also re-organised into an 'A' Echelon of three sections of general service (GS) wagons under brigade control and a 'B' Echelon of one section designed to be detached to under corps control. In this way the flow of ammunition forward to the guns could be better organised and controlled. It is interesting, too, that this system has withstood the test of time.

The next lesson of the 1915 battles was that heavy artillery should be brigaded. That is, batteries should be re-organised into brigades so that whole brigades could be given tasks. The General Staff disagreed and wanted to overrule all artillery commanders who advocated it. Confusion still existed when the battle of the Somme began in 1916. A number of "Lieutenant Colonel's Groups" were produced on a scale of two per Army and two per Corps controlled by the new Heavy Artillery Brigadier-Generals at Corps. It was clumsy, and the Gunners did not want it but they were overruled. It did not, however, last for long. It is worth pursuing this development forward into 1916 at this stage, though a shade out of context.

In June 1916 Major-General J.F.N. Birch, already a most experienced commander in handling guns in action, became Major-General Royal Artillery (MGRA) at GHQ. In a letter to the War Office dated 24th June (see Appendix 1 to Annex E) he proposed to re-organise the whole artillery as follows:

Divisional Artilleries: 48 × 18-pounders and 6 × 4.5-inch howitzers.

Corps Artilleries: All medium artillery.

Army Artillery: The heavies, including railway mountings.

The new thing was the Corps artillery. General Birch asked for and got the following scale:

60-pounders: 2 × 4 gun batteries per division (24 guns in a three division corps)

6-inch howitzers: 5 × 4 gun batteries per division (60 howitzers in a three division corps)

The 6-inch BL gun. The piece of an existing gun, used by the Royal Navy and in Coast Defences, was mounted on a wheeled carriage to produce this heavy equipment. Its violent recoil was checked by two enormous ramps placed behind the wheels. *(R.A.I.)*

8 or 9.2-inch howitzers: 2 × 4 gun batteries per division (24 howitzers in a three division corps)

6-inch guns: 2 × 4 gun batteries per corps of any size.

The Army artillery would vary as to what was available but this enormous increase in medium artillery was a landmark in Gunner history. It was a remarkably accurate forecast and, once achieved, gave at long last something like the correct proportion of field to medium/heavy guns.

Throughout 1915 the need to have guns specifically designed for air defence became apparent. In October, all existing air defence guns were grouped into four gun batteries. In November, an officer was attached to the MGRA's staff to advise on air defence matters. By June 1916, 169 anti-aircraft guns were deployed. Most were the new 13-pounder 9 hundredweight, capable of shooting to 19,000 feet.

Mortars had been used more and more in 1915. They were devastatingly successful in trench warfare. By June 1916 a Divisional Trench Mortar Officer was established—the DTMO. The light Stokes mortars were to be manned by the infantry and be integral to brigades. The medium mortars, and these varied between 1.5-inch, 2-inch, 3-inch or 4-pounders, were to be manned by the Gunners. There were to be three such batteries per division. In addition, the Gunners were to man a battery of four 240mm heavy mortars per division. There was at this time a proposal to form a Mortar Corps but this was, probably quite rightly, refused. The infantry mortars were now organised into one light mortar battery of two four mortar sections per brigade and commanded by a captain.

The early months of 1916 saw two further developments in artillery tactics. First, it was realised how extremely difficult yet important it was to silence the enemy guns during any operation. So counter-battery fire had to be improved. Brigades of 60-pounders and 4.7-inch guns were allotted daily for this task and soon the first hostile battery lists were issued at Army and Corps HQs. Conversely, protection against enemy counter-battery fire was improved and more attention was paid to concealment, track plans and flash cover. Observation posts, too, improved their camouflage and strengthened themselves with concrete. Alternative positions were prepared and wired.

Communications were improved, cables buried, telephone exchanges installed and good links with aircraft established. The Germans have stated that the British infantry successes on the Somme were due to the superior British co-operation between guns and aircraft. The "Zone System" was invented, where all squares of the 1/40,000 map were divided into four and lettered. Then batteries were allotted squares, which gave a very quick response to pilots calling for fire. A call of "General Artillery Action" to pilots called all squadrons to drop all duties and fly, or take off, to control pre-arranged artillery tasks. This proved to be a most successful procedure and showed how aircraft must be permanently allotted to artillery work if they are to be successful. In fact, the increased use of aircraft controlling the heavy artillery in counter-battery work was achieving many successes. On 21st September, Captain Hearne of 2 Squadron RFC scored a direct hit with 13th Siege Battery RGA.

Mr Lloyd-George's promises of more ammunition, for which this new organisation was preparing, did not arrive. This was a severe blow, but what was worse was that the quality of what did arrive was very bad indeed. There were many prematures, fuzes were dangerous and shells were suspect.

Before proceeding with the story of the 1916 battles we must list the new arrivals to France:

January 1916—34th Division, from England. (CRA Brigadier-General A.D. Kirkby).

152 (Nottingham) Brigade RFA; A, B, C and D Batteries (each 4 × 18-pounders)
160 (Sunderland) Brigade RFA—A, B, C and D Batteries (each 4 × 18-pounders)
175 (Staffordshire) Brigade RFA—A, B, C and D Batteries (each 4 × 18-pounders)
176 (Leicestershire) Howitzer Brigade RFA—A, B, C and D Howitzer Batteries (each 4 × 4.5-inch howitzers)

January 1916—35th Division, from England (CRA Brigadier-General W.C. Stavely)

157 (Aberdeen) Brigade RFA— A, B, C and D Batteries (each 4 × 18-pounders)
158 (Accrington) Brigade RFA—A, B, C and D Batteries (each 4 × 18-pounders)
159 (Glasgow) Brigade RFA—A, B, C and D Batteries (each 4 × 18-pounders)
163 (West Ham) Howitzer Brigade RFA—A, B, C and D Howitzer Batteries (each 4 × 4.5-inch howitzers)

February 1916—31st Division, from Egypt (CRA Brigadier-General J.A. Tyler) (The 31st Divisional Artillery in fact joined 32nd Division and went to France with it in December 1915. 32nd Divisional Artillery then joined 31st Division and stayed with it throughout the war. It is this 32nd Divisional Artillery which is listed below).

165 Brigade RFA—A, B, C and D Batteries (each 4 × 18 -pounders)
169 Brigade RFA—A, B, C and D Batteries (each 4 × 18-pounders)
170 Brigade RFA—A, B, C and D Batteries (each 4 × 18-pounders)
171 Howitzer Brigade RFA—A, B, C and D Howitzer Batteries (each 4 × 4.5-inch howitzers)

March 1916—29th Division, from Egypt and the Dardanelles (CRA Brigadier-General G.H.A. White)

15 Brigade RHA—B, L and Y Batteries (each 4 × 18-pounders)
17 Brigade RFA-13th, 26th, 92nd Field and 460th Howitzer Batteries
132 Brigade RFA—369th, 370th, 371st Field and D Howitzer Batteries
147 Brigade RFA—10th, 97th, 368th Field and D Howitzer Batteries

March 1916—1st and 2nd Australian Division, from Egypt.

March 1916—39th Division, from England (CRA Brigadier-General G. Gillson)

174 Brigade RFA—A, B, C and D Batteries (each 4 × 18-pounders)
179 RFA—A, B, C and D Batteries (each 4 × 18-pounders)
184 Brigade RFA—A, B, C and D Batteries (each 4 × 18-pounders)
186 Howitzer Brigade RFA—A, B, C and D Howitzer Batteries (each 4 × 4.5-inch howitzers)

April 1916—New Zealand Division, from Egypt

May 1916—41st Division (CRA Brigadier-General S. Lushington)

183 (Hampstead) Howitzer Brigade RFA—A, B, C and D Howitzer Batteries (each 4 × 4.5-inch howitzers)
187 (Fulham) Brigade RFA—A, B, C and D Batteries (each 4 × 18-pounders)
189 (Hackney) Brigade RFA—A, B, C and D Batteries (each 4 × 18-pounders)
190 (Wimbledon) Brigade RFA—A, B, C and D Batteries (each 4 × 18-pounders)

May 1916—61st (South Midland) Division (CRA Brigadier-General R.C. Coates)

305 Brigade RFA—A, B and C Batteries
306 Brigade RFA—A, B, C Field and D (Howitzer) Batteries
307 Brigade RFA—A, B, C Field and D (Howitzer) Batteries
308 Brigade RFA—A, B, C Field and D (Howitzer) Batteries

May 1916—63rd (Royal Naval) Division: (CRA Brigadier-General C.H. de Rougemont)

 223 Brigade RFA—A, B, C Field and D (Howitzer) Batteries
 315 Brigade RFA—A, B, C Field and D (Howitzer) Batteries
 316 Brigade RFA—A, B, C Field and D (Howitzer) Batteries
 317 Brigade RFA—A, B and C Batteries

June 1916—40th Division (CRA Brigadier-General H.L. Read)

 178 (East Ham) Brigade RFA—A, B, C Field and D (Howitzer) Batteries
 181 (Ashton) Brigade RFA—A, B, C Field and D (Howitzer) Batteries
 185 (Tottenham) Brigade RFA—A, B, C Field and D (Howitzer) Batteries
 188 (Nottingham) Brigade RFA—A, B, C Field and D (Howitzer) Batteries

June 1916—60th Division (CRA Brigadier-General H.A.D. Simpson-Baikie) This Division concentrated in France but soon moved off to Macedonia. It finished the war in Egypt and Palestine and did not serve in action in France.

June 1916—5th Australian Division

June 1916—11th Division, from Egypt (Brigadier General G.S. Duffus)

 58 Brigade RFA—A, B, and C Field Batteries
 59 Brigade RFA—A, B and C Field Batteries
 60 Brigade RFA—A, B and C Field Batteries
 133 Howitzer Brigade RFA—A, B and C Howitzer Batteries

To handle this massive build up, five new corps were created in France:

 XIII Corps, whose BGRA was Brigadier-General R. St C. Lecky
 XIV Corps, whose BGRA was (in February 1916) Brigadier-General A.E. Wardrop
 XV Corps, whose BGRA was Brigadier-General E.W. Alexander
 VIII Corps (from Gallipoli), BGRA—Brigadier General T.A. Tancred.
 IX Corps (from Gallipoli), BGRA—Brigadier-General G. Humphreys.

The first German attack of 1916 opened on 21st February at Verdun against the French. Joffre was slow in realising it was a major operation. When he did, he demanded that the British should relieve the pressure on the hard pressed French Tenth Army. This was done in March by operations of 5th and 14th Divisions of the British Third Army and 23rd, 46th and 51st Divisions of the British First Army. Meanwhile, Fourth Army was formed on 1st March under General Sir Henry Rawlinson, with Major-General A.A. Montgomery (a Gunner) as his chief of staff and Major-General C.E.D. Budworth as MGRA. It took over VIII, X and XIII Corps from Third Army and was soon to prove itself an excellent formation. It held twenty miles of front from the Somme to Fonquevillers (nine miles due north of Albert).

But before we follow the course of these operations, which led to the great Somme battles of the summer of 1916, a few words on the preparations and techniques now developing fast in France.

The first Royal Signals cable detachments were formed for exclusive Royal Artillery use. A grid system of line was laid and buried to give many alternative routes when cable was broken. The pigeon service expanded! However, radio was not yet available to forward troops; the sets that were available were heavy and the batteries cumbersome, with no real method of charging them. Engineer camouflage teams were available and nets were made available to the guns for the first time. The Royal Flying Corps was expanded. Special Squadrons were allotted to artillery work and an even closer co-operation between the two developed.

Meanwhile, this mass of artillery needed a very much bigger and more cohesive supply system to keep it in action. Army and Corps Heavy Artillery Companies, Army Service Corps (ASC), were formed to deal with ammunition supply. ASC workshops were formed. ASC drivers drove the first tractors and lorries beginning to appear in France. GHQ Ammunition Parks were formed on the line of communication, which held large stocks of ammunition. A large veterinary organisation was set up, as losses of horses in the appalling climate and ground conditions were very great. Ordnance Mobile Gun Workshops were established to maintain guns in action. They were kept very busy and without them the massive bombardments of the second half of the war would never have taken place. Finally, in early 1916 steel helmets were made a general issue.

Ammunition supply was still not good—and the quality still left much to be desired. Two 9.2-inch howitzers were destroyed by bore prematures and the 8-inch fuzes failed so often that the battlefield was littered with unexploded 8-inch shells. The 4.5-inch howitzer batteries became known as "Suicide Clubs", so numerous were their prematures. There were driving band problems on the 18-pounders and soon there was an acute shortage of buffer springs. This became so bad at times that guns had to be "run up" by hand, which slowed rates of fire enormously. Nevertheless, in spite of these monstrous equipment failures, the Gunners were about to show for the first time that they were slowly mastering their enemy, slowly out manoeuvring him and coming off best in each battle.

During the first months of 1916 there were nine battles, though "The Bluff", "St Eloi", and "Vimy Ridge" were later classed as actions, leaving "Mount Sorrel" alone classed as a battle and the remaining five as local actions. We will now look again at the story which was, unknown to the actors, to lead to the Somme! Both adversaries were flexing their muscles, both had been appalled at their losses and at their inability to break through. Everyone was searching for new ideas, new tactics, new techniques. The gun was the Queen of the battlefield and, if only we could get enough, it must be possible to succeed. All eyes turned to artillerymen. The infantry could not move without them. The new secret weapon, the tank, was not yet available. Out of it all at last was emerging an artillery force which could do it. As has been so often proved in battle, victory was to come to the side that handled its artillery correctly.

The ground in the British sector was as bad as it could be for offensive operations, whereas the Germans held what heights there were. The British trenches were in low, wet ground and were poorly constructed as a result, and they were generally overlooked. The British were obsessed with the need for a large offensive. Though good for morale, it meant that little attention was paid to improving defences, constructing wire or dugouts. The Germans meanwhile were hard at it, doing just that.

During the night 18th/19th December 1915, warning was received of a German attack at Ypres. At first light the enemy front line trenches were bombarded by 4.5-inch howitzers to explode gas cylinders thought to be there. The attack came. Gas was used. The British were ready and masked. The guns fired shrapnel onto the front trenches with such effect that the enemy never left them. The gas was chlorine, with a 20% phosgene mix, but it spread quickly and was ineffective. The Germans then shelled the whole area with gas which was more effective, but the enemy attack had failed.

Minor patrolling activity occurred throughout the winter. The guns were constantly engaged on defensive fire tasks but it was not until the action on the Ypres—Commines Canal, on 14th/15th February 1916, that a real effort was made. The Germans suddenly attacked 17th Division of V Corps and, in a surprise attack, overran a position known as "The Bluff". Plans were immediately made to recover this important feature. Brigadier-General H.C.C. Uniacke was the new GOCRA of V Corps. In addition to 17th Divisional Artillery, he had some Canadian and British mediums and quite a few mortars. The GOCRA suggested a silent attack but Commander 76th Infantry Brigade, which was to assault, disagreed. A compromise was reached, suggested by Uniacke. He ordered a 60-pounder battery to fire on "The Bluff" trenches at irregular intervals day and night. They would stop, wait two minutes, then invariably fire a further salvo. Punctually at zero hour, 0430 hours 2nd March, the usual series of salvos was fired followed by the two minute pause. This time the salvo did not occur. When the British infantry reached the German trenches, they were still cowering there waiting for it! Complete surprise. During 1st March a comprehensive counter battery plan was prepared and fired with aerial observation. On 2nd March fifty-one enemy batteries were engaged. Though the enemy artillery were not fully neutralised, they seldom achieved better than slow rates of fire all day. For the first time counter battery fire was working. Gun failures were, however, still showing themselves. The 4.7-inch guns of 123rd Battery were firing so wildly that a correction of 1,900 yards was being applied for wear alone! They had to be taken out of action on 1st March. Three guns of 71st Heavy Battery had a 50% zone of 800 yards! Gunners will realise what an enormous effect this would have on accuracy. Nevertheless, the attack on "The Bluff" was successful and due very much to successfully co-ordinated artillery fire.

In March the British assaulted the Hohenzollern Redoubt. XI Corps Artillery prepared a barrage which was fired after the successful blowing of mines, which gained surprise. Though the attack was at first a success, all ground gained was later lost. The Germans brought down such concentrated defensive fire that the assault was literally bogged down in the mine craters. No counter-battery plan had been made. The importance of this aspect of any plan was taking an awful lot of learning by both Commanders and their Gunners.

The Germans retaliated later in April with gas attacks opposite Hulluch. Supporting infantry attacks were repulsed by good artillery work and good gas discipline, but casualties from the gas were noticeably heavy. The Germans were mixing much stronger concentrations and the British helmet masks were not good enough to withstand it, though it was noticeable that the new box masks worn by the Lewis gunners were good. Nevertheless, the excellence of the British defensive fire really stopped all German attacks. Strong concentrations of enemy mortars were destroyed by 9.2-inch and 8-inch howitzers. But still it was policy to use the maximum number of guns on the enemy trenches and relatively few on enemy guns. The Germans too were realising that, if they really could concentrate sufficient guns, they would be successful. In May they made a surprise attack on the "Kink Salient" near Hohenzollern Redoubt. It was accompanied by the

The 8-inch **BL** howitzer. The piece of the 6-inch **BL** gun was shortened and bored out to provide this useful heavy howitzer the carriage of which was made in the railway workshops, and went through several marks during the war. *(I.W.M.)*

heaviest concentration of gun fire yet seen. The smoke and dust prevented the British observers from seeing and it cut their telephone lines. The enemy attack, although very limited, was a success.

It was while engaged in these battles on 26th May 1916 that the Commander-in-Chief, General Sir Douglas Haig, issued the following Special Order of the Day:

"This day 200 years ago the first permanent organisation was given to the Artillery by Royal Warrant.

Today's anniversary of its creation finds the Royal Regiment engaged, as part of the Army of the British Empire, in a great struggle for all that our Race has ever held most sacred: Freedom and Justice.

The Commander-in-Chief knows that all other Arms will join him in congratulating the Royal Artillery on this occasion and in recognising the efficiency with which it has supported other Arms in every action in which it has been engaged. The discipline and devotion to duty displayed by Officers, NCOs and Men of the Artillery throughout this campaign have been in accord with the highest traditions of their Regiment".

At Vimy Ridge in May, the Germans assembled and carefully concealed eighty batteries before the British 25th and 47th Divisions. At 0500 hours on 21st May, a heavy bombardment began and continued until 1100 hours. Then at 1500 hours it was repeated with great violence until 1545 hours, H-Hour for the assault. The guns had lifted onto the British artillery with great accuracy and ferocity. The 47th Divisional Artillery reported heavy shells falling on battery positions at the rate of 150 rounds per hour. The British Gunners, however, settled down and began to engage the German batteries and to answer desperate cries for fire from the infantry. Orders such as "Battery fire 30 seconds, fire!" went on throughout the night 21st/22nd May, with the guns themselves under constant fire and with casualties mounting. Gas shell began falling on the guns during the night but still the defensive fire tasks were engaged. Four 18-pounders of 47th Divisional Artillery were destroyed.

IV Corps Artillery assisted the hard pressed V Corps. Some heavies were re-deployed. Gradually, on 22nd May, the artillery duel swung in favour of the British. Ammunition was short and, if ever they stopped firing, the Germans re-opened fire at once. The system of "one round strikes" by all guns in range firing on each enemy battery was tried with great success. The British commanders were learning at last that an enormous quantity of ammunition has to be fired to destroy enemy guns. The Germans had, however, seized the British front line at Vimy Ridge. They again demonstrated that, if a really powerful, concentrated artillery attack can be launched prior to an infantry assault, the latter can get through.

From 2nd to 6th June, the Germans attacked the British line at Mount Sorrel and Hooge in the Ypres salient and captured a considerable section of the front line positions. The German attack included most effective counter-battery work. The Lahore Divisional Artillery, then supporting the Canadians in this sector, was particularly heavily hit. All cables were cut and all forward observers became casualties; one FOO of the 5th Canadian Battery fought his party to the last until all were killed on Observatory Ridge. It was now vital to recover these positions.

The 9.2-inch BL howitzer, seen here in action, was not mounted on a wheeled carriage and was therefore found to be the most accurate of heavy howitzers. The equipment was split into three loads for movement and its action was stabilized by a large steel box, filled with earth, at the front of the mounting. One of these weapons was in service at the beginning of the war and was nicknamed "Mother". *(R.A.I.)*

More artillery was moved up, including all 3rd Divisional Artillery, 89th Siege Battery (two 12-inch howitzers), 57th, 71st South African and 72nd South African Siege Batteries—all 6-inch howitzers who had just arrived in France. General Plumer ordered a very heavy artillery attack, supported by a minimum use of infantry. The Heavies of both V and IX Corps were brought into range to support. Bad weather on 4th and 5th June prevented this mass of artillery completing its registration. The planned attack for 6th June was therefore postponed. On that day the Germans themselves attacked and captured the British trenches at Hooge.

From 9th to 12th June, four heavy bombardments, including counter-battery tasks, were carried out. The shooting was mostly predicted but much was observed by the RFC. The whole of the British artillery was grouped under command of Brigadier-General H.E. Burstall, GOCRA the Canadian Corps. His plan was:

> **12th June.** Ten hour bombardment on all German positions but overlapping the actual objectives.
>
> **12th June.** From 2000–2030 hours the rate was increased and was so intense and accurate that the assaulting infantry were able to form up close behind it with the German defensive fire coming down raggedly behind them. Smoke was used to blind Hill 60, Sanctuary Wood and Hooge. Corps artilleries on either flank fired diversion attacks to conceal the time and place of attack.
>
> **Counter-Battery.** A complex and progressive plan was made to silence the enemy guns. This proved most effective and many enemy guns were hit. 22nd Siege Battery of 12-inch howitzers was particularly effective.

This attack on Mount Sorrel was a complete success; all objectives were taken with relatively small losses. A German counter-attack formed up, but Brigadier-General Burstall ordered all guns to fire on it as it formed up at 0645 hours and this destroyed the attack in its tracks before it could start. At 0900 hours the Germans tried again, but again the artillery broke up their attacks. Slowly the fighting died away, with the British Artillery the victors. The hard planning and re-organisation of the winter, coupled with the experience of two years fighting, was now paying off. The time had come for a mighty strike to victory!

CHAPTER 13

The Somme and Associated Battles—
June to December 1916

See map 21

The French were pressing the British to take the pressure off their Tenth Army, still under heavy attack around Verdun. General Joffre wanted a massive British thrust on the Somme, and Sir Douglas Haig ordered General Rawlinson and his Fourth Army to prepare such a thrust, on a front of 25,000 yards using twenty-five divisions!

Accordingly in February 1916, General Rawlinson and his MGRA, Major-General Birch, began their planning. The situation was not good, the ground was bad, concentration of such a force under cover would be almost impossible. Roads hardly existed. All diggings and preparations were visible to the enemy. The ground was low-lying and, when it rained, it became a sea of thick, deep mud. However, General Haig was optimistic; he envisaged creating a wide gap through the enemy lines, when cavalry would dash deep into the German positions. But General Rawlinson was more cautious; he recognised the impossibility of infantry moving at all without powerful artillery attacks first and he was right, the German defences were massive; deep shelters built of thick concrete had been constructed in depth, with thick, high wire. He realised also that defences such as these could only be destroyed by lengthy and heavy artillery bombardment, but how long should the guns fire? At what stage could infantry be launched forward with any hope of success? Was it to be simply another head-on clash with appalling casualties? The artillery fire had to be observed to achieve direct hits yet, in many cases, this would not be practicable and much would have to be predicted yet again; this would not be accurate enough, since the survey and meteor data of the day were not up to it. The hastily produced shells varied so much that each performed differently from the other. (Some 6-inch shells were found to vary in length by as much as four inches, with disastrous effects on ballistics). Nor were the guns of the day up to it. The mass produced 18-pounder varied very much in design and the barrels were not equal in performance. Some of the 6-inch guns were made in 1895. An 8-inch howitzer appeared which was a make-shift made by cutting down old coast artillery 6-inch tubes and enlarging the bores: its recoil system consisted of large wooden blocks! The instantaneous fuze was yet to come and wire still had to be cut with shrapnel which only well trained observers could apply effectively. Only very, very few gas shells were available. Nevertheless, the Gunners set to, to plan for this massive attack. Could not the guns fire on the enemy to the last minute? Could not the fire actually creep forward ahead of the infantry? Could it not, indeed? Artillery had proved how it could achieve surprise by its pattern of attack; why not exploit this on the Somme?

General Rawlinson's plan was in three phases:

Phase 1. To capture the line Montauban-Pozières by a simultaneous attack of five divisions.

Phase 2. The left flank to extend from Martinpuich to Miraumont and the advance to continue on the line Montauban-Martinpuich.

Phase 3. Breakout east to seize the Ginchy—Bazentin-le-Grand plateau.

To support this plan, the MGRA produced the first ever Army Artillery Operation Order. It was issued on 5th June 1916, and it was a masterpiece. Its aim was to ensure that all the corps plans were constructed on the same lines. Tasks for the guns were defined, but not targets, and a six day bombardment was ordered; pauses for aerial photography were co-ordinated. The aims of counter-battery tasks were laid down. Deception methods were co-ordinated. Use of gas (fired mostly by the French) was defined. But proportions of guns to tasks, the tasks themselves, fireplans, observation and deployment were, quite rightly, left to GOCRAs at Corps HQs.

The information about the enemy was good. His positions, their construction and his strengths were known with some accuracy; the intelligence staffs had estimated some thirty-two enemy battalions in action. His absolute maximum reinforcement capability over a period of six days was a further sixty-five battalions. The one mis-judgement was that of the physical strength of the German fortifications. All this information was, however, leading to a stereotyped plan based on time-tables and, in war, time-tables kill initiative. A massive aerial support plan was made; four squadrons of aircraft and a kite balloon squadron were allotted to Fourth Army. Thirty aircraft were allotted to counter-battery tasks alone, sixteen for reconnaissance and nine for special missions including photography.

For the first time, massive stocks of ammunition were built up and a properly co-ordinated plan was made to move it forward to the guns as they advanced. Army HQ now controlled its own ammunition supply from railhead forwards. The re-supply plan, the first of its kind of this scale, is interesting. It was:

Dumped at the guns:

18-pounders:	354 rounds per gun
6-inch howitzers:	200 rounds per gun
8-inch howitzers:	90 rounds per gun

Dumped near the guns:

18-pounders	1000 rounds per gun
6-inch howitzers:	650 rounds per gun
8-inch howitzers:	500 rounds per gun

Divisional Dumps: 250 rounds per gun 18-pounder

Corps Dumps: 200 rounds per gun 6-inch

Seven trains a day kept up the work so that by 20th June most was in position. Other natures were delivered direct to batteries by divisional and corps ammunition columns.

Six days water and rations were issued for men and horses.

Observers' positions and some guns were given thick cover made of steel girders, sandbags and trees, and concealment was achieved as far as possible. A number of dummy positions were built. Cables were buried to a depth of six feet for the fire order lines to keep them immune from the 5.9-inch enemy shells: 7,000 miles of underground line were so laid. 43,000 miles of surface line was also laid—the figures are staggering.

It is astonishing that the enemy took virtually no notice of all these preparations, perhaps because the RFC controlled the sky completely and no enemy aircraft ever crossed his line during this period; perhaps the first really effective use of airpower in the land battle.

The tactics to be used were much discussed. The plan was that the Gunners should put down a massive barrage lifting forward at fixed times, with the assaulting infantry creeping forward as close behind it as they could get, at most one hundred yards, some said forty! The infantry were to move forward in waves. The first wave was not to mop-up but to carry on to its objective, taking both its time and direction from the artillery. The fire was to be controlled by forward observers moving with the leading waves, reeling out cable as they went. Second waves were to mop-up and secure objectives. These tactics were laid down by the general staff in a directive dated 8th May 1916, in which no mention was made of other tasks for artillery; a second directive covered this and made the following points:

All artillery in the assault must be under command of divisional commanders.

A co-ordinated plan must be made allotting guns to counter-battery tasks and tasks in depth.

Careful registration of targets is essential and takes time. Close liaison between pilots and Gunners is paramount.

Time-tables need great care in preparation.

Observation posts and alternatives must be carefully concealed and protected.

Potential observation posts in the enemy lines must be pre-allotted.

Single guns well forward could be most successful.

Cables must be buried.

Roads and trench crossing gear must be prepared in advance.

This historic document, issued by Major-General Birch, did much to crystalise the lessons of the war so far. Much more, these directives gave birth to the moving barrage which was, itself, to be a major tactic for the rest of the war. The emphasis was on a rigid programme of continuous, uninterrupted fire. Artillery commanders were obsessed with the need to keep their fire immediately in front of the infantry. In doing so, they again allowed counter-battery tasks, and an ability to switch guns of the barrage to deal with the unexpected, to slip into second priority. But who could blame them—they were feeling their way with new doctrines and new techniques when their equipment was hardly up to it.

The Heavy Artillery Groups were constructed and were all organised with various mixtures of guns; their tasks were either counter-battery or direct bombardment of selected targets. Their fire was co-ordinated with the divisional artilleries so that the fire of a Heavy Group would engage a position and drive the enemy to their shelters; it would then lift to another target and a few minutes later the 18-pounders would engage the same target with shrapnel, so catching the enemy as they came out to repair the damage. This ruse worked time after time. HQs of Heavy Groups were located alongside HQRAs of the divisions they were supporting. Considerable use was to be made of aerial observation, now almost vital for success in counter-battery work.

The artillery power available for the Somme was mighty but still less than what was later assembled for the great battles of 1917. The following guns were available:

Field Artillery

18-pounders	808
4.5-inch howitzers	202

Heavy Guns

4.7-inch	32
60-pounders	128
6-inch	20
9.2-inch	1
12-inch	1

Heavy Howitzers

6-inch	104
8-inch	64
9.2-inch	60
12-inch	11
15-inch	6

French

75 mm guns	60 (gas only)
120 mm long guns	24
220 mm howitzer	16

This gave a total of 1,537 guns and howitzers and a combined density of one field gun per twenty yards of front and one heavy to fifty-eight yards.

The great battles of the Somme lasted from 1st July to 18th November 1916. In outline, the course of events were:

1st July	: The initial assault.
14th July	: Reinforcement of success against the German second line on the right.
22nd–23rd July	: Massive night attacks.
15th–22nd September	: Battle of Flers-Courcelette.
25th–28th September	: Battle of Morval.
26th–30th September	: Battle of Thiepval Ridge.

8-inch howitzers in action.   *(R.A.I.)*

1st–20th October	: Battle of Transloy Ridges (Fourth Army).
1st October–11th November	: Battle of the Ancre Heights (Fifth Army).
13th–18th November	: Battle of the Ancre.

As with any new tactical concept, the idea of the creeping barrage met with a mixed reception. The Artillery Commanders understood what was wanted but in a number of cases they could not convince divisional and brigade commanders of its merits, and many remained unconvinced. They still wanted concentrations of fire on the enemy trenches themselves and missed the point that, to be effective, the fire must start well on the "home side" of the enemy, to protecting the infantry as they moved forward. It was (and still is) a principle that in the last resort the fireplan was a commander's own decision, and thus it was. Of the six corps engaged, VIII Corps ordered a creeping barrage to lift by 100 yards every two minutes; XIII and XV Corps adopted a partial moving barrage and the three remaining corps did not 'creep' and abandoned the idea of a barrage at all.

It is interesting to take each Corps in turn and see what transpired on that July day of 1916 on the Somme.

VIII Corps ordered ". . . The rate of advance of the infantry is to be 50 yards per minute. The divisional artilleries are to lift very slowly, 50 yards a minute. The infantry must make their pace conform to the artillery . . ." In spite of these precise orders, all three attacking divisions prepared lifts of 100 yards. This was disastrous, since no-mans land was so short; it meant that the opening line of the barrage was on, and not in front of, the enemy, thus the guns were lifted zero minus the enemy at the first lift! The heavies lifted off at 10 minutes just as the enormous mine at Beaumont Hamel went off. The enemy could therefore clearly read the battle and the creeping barrage was never tested, since the infantry never reached it. Many complete units were almost annihilated in no-mans land in the first few minutes of the attack.

In XIII Corps the idea of a barrage was, with one exception, abandoned, the guns being ordered to creep from trench to trench in short lifts, which missed the whole point. But in 18th Division (Major-General Maxse), although the early lifts were from trench to trench, the final one thousand yards was covered by a genuine creeping barrage, lifting 50 yards every one and a half minutes, and the attack was most successful, with the artillery fire being very effective and accurate.

In XV Corps the new theory was tested very well. 7th Division's attack was almost entirely successful as far as the second objective, the barrage lifting by 50 yards. In 21st Division the artillery were ordered to search backwards and forwards though the infantry were told to keep close to it. This was not so successful. In 50th Infantry Brigade of 17th Division, the artillery was ordered to lift 500 yards! The consequent attack went in with virtually no artillery and failed. The village of Fricourt in the centre of the Corps attack withstood its bombardment, which was not heavy enough. Consequently, as 7th and 21st Divisions passed on either side of it, the enemy raked the infantry with flanking fire.

In III Corps the whole principle was missed. The guns were given six major lifts and ordered to "rake back" between them! This process of searching backwards and forwards prevented the infantry from staying close to the shells. The whole attack failed.

Likewise, X Corps ignord the creeping technique. The guns were ordered to jump from trench to trench, and a few guns were ordered to "walk up" the communications trenches! However, in one way the principle was tested. Brigadier J.B. Jardine, Commander 97th Infantry Brigade of 32nd Division, ordered his men to creep up to within 40 yards of the bombardment when attacking the enemy's front trenches. The result was most effective and those trenches were taken with little loss. But then the barrage, as ordered, "jumped" away and the Brigade, which could not hold on, had to withdraw.

To the north, VII Corps was ordered to attack Gommecourt on a narrow front as a subsidiary movement. 56th Divisional Artillery lifted from trench to trench and the division got some way. 46th Divisional Artillery swept and searched and failed. The enemy concentrated very accurate defensive fire on this attack and held it.

It was clear by last light on 1st July, where it had been used, the creeping barrage was a success. With plenty of guns, plenty of ammunition and well trained, determined infantry, it was at last possible for the artillery to "transport" them across no-man's land and into the enemy trenches, hold them there and defeat any counter-attacks. But it was essential for the fire to start in front of the enemy's front trenches, where it had to be accurate and the fire intense. At last there was a way of dealing with the enemy tactic of going to ground very deep and coming to his parapet after the barrage had lifted.

It has been said that the idea of a creeping barrage was French but this is not so. The germ of the idea was born at Loos by Brigadier-General E.W. Alexander, CRA of 15th Division. The Germans were onto it and tried it on the Russian front but they never appreciated that it takes a mass of guns and they never really understood the detailed planning required. On the British side, to the end of the war artillery commanders could never convince the infantry that the shape of the defences did not matter and, as a result, complications always arose, since infantry commanders wanted the barrage to wheel to keep its front parallel to the enemy trench line, an unnecessary complication.

But the barrage was only part of the operation; there was also a comprehensive and elaborate counter-battery plan. Army HQ had said that there must be such a plan but BGRAs were left free to plan as they chose. All realised that counter-battery must be planned but at this stage the effort required in guns, ammunition and time to achieve success was not realised. Besides, predicted shooting had not reached the level of accuracy required and the only hope of success was aerial observation, but in July the weather was bad for flying.

The MGRA laid down that counter-battery fire should start on U Day 24th June, six days before Z or Zero Day (in modern terms, D minus six!). VIII Corps allotted four batteries of 60-pounders, one battery of 4.7-inch guns, one battery of 4.5-inch howitzers, four batteries of 6-inch howitzers, one battery of 12-inch howitzers and a section of 6-inch guns to this task. The guns were pre-registered by aircraft with great accuracy and their task was destruction and not neutralisation. Results were excellent. On 26th June, nineteen German batteries were hit and silenced; on 27th, even though the weather was bad, thirteen batteries were hit and many silenced. Then, on 30th June, the weather improved and aerial observation was possible. On that day thirty-two enemy batteries were engaged, even though many had moved. The Germans admit that their batteries in the valleys north of Mametz and Montauban were almost totally destoyed, along with most of their ammunition. They admit that the artillery of the *12th and 28th Divisions* were wiped out, all field guns being rendered unserviceable by the "devastating British Artillery".

XV Corps, to the left of XIII Corps, only allotted four batteries to counter-battery tasks. Attempts at aerial registration were not successful "with so many shell bursts and so many guns firing". The Heavy Artillery Group were swamped with calls for fire from all sources, including aircraft, balloons and forward observers. Fortunately, the front opposite XV Corps was held by the *German 28th Division,* whose artillery had been knocked out by the 8th Divisional Artillery counter-battery plan. The Germans attribute the British XV Corps successes later to the inadequacy of their own defensive fire, as a result of the massive casualties to their guns.

III Corps allotted two Heavy Artillery Groups to counter-battery; a total of eight 60-pounder batteries, two 4.7-inch batteries and three 12-inch howitzers. Co-operation with the RFC was not too good. Efforts to improve it went on until some success was achieved. It is interesting that, when army pilots had been closely linked to guns, all was well. The removal of these pilots to the more rarified atmosphere of the RFC did not help this co-operation. However, on Zero Day 1st July, the enemy guns had not really been silenced and were able to bring down heavy defensive fire on the attacking infantry, enough to wipe out some units. III Corps attack was not a success.

X Corps also allotted two Heavy Artillery Groups to counter-battery; the Northern Group of two and a half 60-pounder batteries; two 18-pounder batteries and one 4.5-inch howitzer battery; and the Southern Group of four and a half 60-pounder batteries and one 4.7-inch battery. Some 6-inch batteries were occasionally added. The snag in X Corps was that far too little ammunition was allotted. We read of six, eight or twelve rounds per target! The need for pinpoint accuracy was not appreciated. It is interesting to note that the counter-battery order was signed by "Major, O.C. Counter-Batteries 10th Corps Heavy Artillery", possibly the first Corps Counter Battery Officer ever. Failure on X Corps sector to silence the enemy guns contributed greatly to the failure of the Corps attack.

The vital importance of counter-battery fire was nowhere made more clear than in VII Corps. Again two 'Groups' of guns were allocated to these tasks. They totalled three batteries of 60-pounders; three batteries of 4.7-inch guns; one battery of 6-inch howitzers; one battery of 9.2-inch howitzers; three batteries of 4.5-inch howitzers; two 6-inch guns and one 9.2-inch gun. A good force, yet ammunition allotted was again far too small, being twenty rounds per gun per day! Only one aircraft was allotted to the whole Corps! By chance, too, the enemy artillery was very strong opposite VII Corps and many more batteries opened fire on the attacking infantry than had ever been located and many were out of range of the British guns. The result was failure to dominate the German guns so that devastating German defensive fire could be brought down on the attacking infantry.

Though an attempt had been made to co-ordinate the counter-battery fire, its effect had varied from being extremely successful to almost non-effective. Nevertheless, much had been achieved in spite of the problems. It is easy to look back with hindsight onto the reasons for failure but the artillery commanders were facing problems of enormous complexity. Never before had such massive amounts of artillery been handled. They were desperately searching for a formula for success, yet unknown to them at the time they had already found it—artillery tactics were right. They were let down by shortages of and inadequate equipment and communications. On the Somme, British counter-battery fire was noticeably ahead of the Germans. Its success in the VIII and XV Corps foreshadowed the growing ascendency which the British artillery was to achieve above all others in the years to come.

While this gun duel raged over the heads of the attacking infantry in the valley north of the Somme, plans were made for the next phase. On 9th July 1916, the Major General Chief of Staff, HQ Fourth Army, Major-General A.A. Montgomery, signed the artillery operation order for the next phase of the battle. In theme it was still as before: loose co-ordination, leaving detail to BGRAs at Corps HQs.

By now, the theme at Fourth Army Headquarters was that "artillery conquers and infantry occupies". This was French philosophy and, although untrue, it does explain the tactics of the day. It was a truth that the infantry alone could not cross no-mans land by day or night without a massive artillery attack. The snag was that, until 1916, the Gunners did not have enough guns or ammunition to guarantee their own part of the doctrine, but they were now getting closer to it. On the other hand, a change in tactics was needed.

The usual half hour bombardment before H-hour acted as a real warning of an impending attack. How to get over the dilemma? The Gunners could now get the infantry into the front trenches and, since the second and third lines were not as strong as the front line, it should be possible to exploit in day-light if sufficient artillery was available.

Brigadier E.W.M. Powell, CRA 3rd Division, and Brigadier H.H.Tudor, CRA 9th Division, proposed that first, wire should be cut to a fixed pattern for some days before an attack and second, the actual attack should be before dawn, when the artillery attack should be not more than five minutes fierce bombardment.

These tactics were used on 14th July by Fourth Army, in the Battle of Bazentin Ridge, with very great success. The wire was cut prior to the attack. Some forward observers had to creep to within 200 yards of the enemy trenches to ensure that this was accurately done. The 6-inch howitzers fired just in front of the enemy trenches to make craters for the infantry covering parties. The 18-pounder and 4.5-inch howitzers fired delayed fuzes only, to avoid air burst in trees over the infantry forming up just behind them, and the infantry did form up just behind the falling shells. The intensive five minutes artillery attack was devastatingly accurate and many of the attacking infantry were into the enemy trenches without a shot being fired at them. They quickly captured forty-two officers and fourteen hundred men, and they found German dead thick on the ground from the gunfire; they quickly secured the Ginchy-Pozières Ridge. It was a huge success but then, for some reason, the infantry stopped; no orders for exploitation were given; the fleeting moment came, went and was lost. The Germans recovered and severe fighting followed for some days. Post war German accounts of the July battles refer to the terrific British artillery fire on 14th July and subsequently, particularly on 19th July at Delville Wood and Longueval.

By now, the Germans had reinforced their artillery so that a tremendous artillery duel developed. Infantry attacks by both sides were broken by the other's guns. Night attacks were tried but defensive fire by flares stopped them all. Again German reports refer to the 'painful' accuracy of the British guns. A moment of truth was at hand. The guns of both sides were making a ferocious bid for supremacy and the British were winning.

Meanwhile, further north, at Fromelles on the Aubers Ridge, First Army carried out an attack on 19th July. But they first failed to master the German guns, which concentrated their fire on the narrow front of the attack and halted it in its tracks. Again it was an artillery battle.

By 23rd July on the Somme, the Australians had captured most of Pozières. This was an operation noticeable for its excellent artillery work. Notably, a single 18-pounder of 6th Battery AFA came up to 200 yards from the enemy on the Bapaume road and brought down deadly accurate fire. Later, a German counter-attack was halted and destroyed by the British and Australian gunners. By now serviceability of the guns was giving trouble but the sweating, weary gunners fought on without rest or respite.

By 25th July, Pozières had fallen and by 29th Delville Wood was captured, largely due to the concentrated fire of 369 guns of two Corps Artilleries. A preliminary barrage almost destroyed Longueval and Delville Wood. A concentrated seven minutes artillery attack preceded the infantry attack. The fire then lifted to form a protective curtain ahead of the objective; the results were terrific. Delville Wood was chaotic, most defenders were killed and the rest were so stunned as to surrender willingly, and the battle rolled on to Bazentin and to High Wood. Major-General Birch issued a memorandum stressing the importance of the new close links between the attacking infantry and the Gunners. He said, ". . . It is therefore of the first importance that in all cases the infantry must advance right under the field artillery barrage, which must not uncover the first objective until the infantry are within 50 yards of it!" An infantry Brigadier ascribed his successes largely to the fact that his men advanced very close to the artillery fire. "On many occasions they have been able to gain the enemy trenches and engage them hand to hand as they emerged from their dug-outs, before they could fire their machine guns".

There was more severe fighting in August. A combined attack on Guillemont, Delville and High Wood started well and, where the infantry kept close to the barrage, there were successes. XV Corps ran into heavy machine gun cross fire and artillery fire which had not been silenced. Bombing and hand to hand fighting followed. In places the infantry got too close to the falling shells and in places guns fired short, and casualties to our own troops resulted, but the lessons were being learned by both gunners and infantry.

In III Corps, one company advanced too soon and was wiped out by the barrage. The lessons were hard to learn. Both gunners and infantry now had a successful doctrine. They needed now to train hard to perfect it.

The Battle of Fleurs-Courcelette—15th–22nd September 1916

Before continuing with the story of the battle of Flers-Courcelette, we should pause to look at life in the batteries at that time. There was no rest or respite for them, day or night; the Gunners did not leave 'the line', they were always in action. Life was a never ending nightmare of meeting streams of fire orders, of constructing and improving dug-outs and of maintaining communications to their forward observers in the front trenches. Tons and tons of ammunition had to be moved, sorted, stacked and prepared for firing; fuzes sorted, tested and fitted to shells. Rations and water had to be brought up at night; roads and tracks built, horses to be attended to. There was little time for rest and, to add to the misery, every time a battery fired the enemy guns would open up on them and there were casualties that needed attention and repairs to be carried out and the whole cycle of living and work and engaging targets began again. New positions were almost impossible to find so, when located, a battery had to sit and take it as enemy shells landed among the guns, dug-outs and ammunition. Batteries were close together and thus a battery would collect the 'overs' aimed at another. There was no respite—no relaxation. But morale was high—only the guns mattered and only the pride in meeting calls for fire whenever they came, day or night, wet or cold, with a speed and accuracy which had become their watch-word.

The subalterns and young captains were the forward observers. They were in the most forward part of the forward trenches, which were evil stinking hell holes, often half full of water and only lightly held by very few infantry. They watched as the battalions in the line were relieved for a rest, they stayed and got to know new men of a new battalion. They did not begrudge them their rest, for in the final analysis, theirs was not an enviable job—to charge to almost certain death in no-mans land. The task of observing was not easy, the view was extremely limited, the problem of map spotting targets on the devastated battlefield was extremely difficult. Indeed, the village of Martinpuich was, in 1916, just a few tree stumps and a heap of rubble. Officers relieved each other in the line for a few days with the guns and occasionally, very occasionally, came a day of rest in Amiens after a long gallop on a battery horse. A day to forget the stink, the death, the killing—a day for a bath and a glass of wine before galloping back in the evening to relieve some other poor devil—if he was still there. Battery commanders were at battalion headquarters and soon built up the closest of liaisons with the battalions as they came and suffered and went. Frequently, Gunner officers found themselves commanding platoons and companies and even battalions when no infantry officer was left. The strain and the fatigue were enormous but the courage, the skill and morale of these small parties of artillerymen in the trenches were an example which none should ever forget. By the end of August, the rain had come and the mud and ooze crept over the battlefield making conditions unbearably difficult.

After the July battles, the merits and demerits of the 'creeping barrage', as it was now called by everyone, were hotly discussed. Was HE better than shrapnel or not? What rates of fire? What distance between lines? How close should the infantry be? But none, gunner or infantry, doubted the principle—there was too much evidence of success. After one barrage which crept from Pozières to Courcelette, a distance of two miles, at the rate of one hundred yards in three minutes, the attacking infantry had found only desolation in front of them, a regular pattern of shell holes and the Germans dead in their trenches.

The British renewed their attack on 15th September but there was to be a difference—for the first time in battle 'tanks' were to be used. Lanes of 100 yards width were to be left in the barrage, along which the new 'tanks' would be able to move. On 13th September the weather was bad but it was better on the 15th—the day of the attack. A strong force of 56 guns and howitzers was used for counter-battery work with considerable success. Aircraft were used to direct the fire and the response from batteries was very quick. The barrage fired that day was extremely successful, the attacking infantry breaking through to the enemy third line on a 4,500 yard front. High Wood fell, as did Martinpuich, then Courcelette and Flers where the tanks had scored a notable triumph. However, the advance beyond Flers was not easy. The British guns had to move and the ground was terrible—the German guns too took their toll of the exposed 18-pounder batteries. Nevertheless, a German counter-attack to recover Flers was stopped and broken by artillery fire. Just east of Ginchy was a strong enemy position called the Quadrilateral which had escaped the bombardment, lying as it did on a reverse slope. No effort could take it and it was not until a forward observer could creep forward and observe artillery fire onto it on 18th September that it finally fell.

As the month passed, the British artillery gradually wore the enemy down. Counter-battery work became a priority—all known enemy batteries were engaged but, although much damage was done, the enemy fire was not suppressed. At this time the British Gunners were suffering considerably from mechanical breakdown. Sometimes up to 30% of field guns were out of action, one of the main problems being a failure of buffer-springs. The hurried expansion of the Army had produced Gunner officers with no shortage of gallantry but with a considerable shortage of technical knowledge. As a result, crash-courses were started to teach officers how to look for signs of equipment failure and straight away an improvement was noticed. Indeed, by 1918 Major-General Birch wrote to the War Office to say that it was rare for 2% of guns to be out of action due to equipment failure, since "officers knew where to look for trouble and in some cases how to put it right".

However, the guns did move forward, in some cases the enthusiasm for victory resulted in wagon lines coming too far forward and then suffering appalling casualties to men and horses. But the real problem by now was fatigue. Men were very, very tired and wet but the determined dogged characteristics of the British soldier somehow kept him going—sometimes only getting two hours of sleep in twenty-four, for days on end. As the guns came into action in the heavily shelled areas which had been the German lines, it was almost impossible to find shelter, the shell holes were lip to lip and tainted with the stench of death.

Technically, now that the battle had moved and the well known layout of enemy batteries had changed, it became extremely difficult to locate them as they moved from position to position. The weather was so overcast that aerial observation was impossible. Nevertheless on 25th September, one hundred and twenty-four enemy batteries were located, forty-seven engaged and twenty-one silenced. Also, as the British slowly but relentlessly pressed forward onto higher ground, observation improved. On 26th September a German counter-attack on Gueudecourt was caught by the fire of some sixty 18-pounders and the Germans fled, throwing away their arms, towards Le Transloy. By 28th September the weather improved, with the Germans under heavy fire and withdrawing.

9.2-inch howitzers in action on the Somme. This is taken from an original by A C Michael and is subtitled "Bringing up Ammunition by Decauville Track". *(R.A.I.)*

The Battle of Thiepval Ridge—26th–30th September 1916

Preparations for Reserve Army's attack of Thiepval Ridge (HQ Reserve Army had taken over the north of the Somme sector) included the assembly of 230 heavy guns, 570 field guns and howitzers, giving one field gun or howitzer to eleven yards of front and one heavy to twenty-six yards. Two new features were to be tried in the attack, first, gas shell was to be fired by 4-inch mortars and then machine gun barrages were to be fitted into the artillery barrages. Although the attack was successful, the infantry lost the barrage in fighting their way through Thiepval. The German defensive fire was heavy and effective but, nevertheless, the ridge fell after more heavy fighting.

The Battle of Transloy Ridges—1st–20th October 1916

On 1st October, the New Zealand Division attacked the Transloy Ridges in heavy rain and mist. The barrage was excellent and carried them right onto their objectives; the mud was appalling and the movement of guns to keep up with the battle was a Herculean task. Sometimes it took ten or twelve hours to shift a single 18-pounder. Guns sank in the mud, fire was inaccurate, positions hard to fix and ammunition was dragged forward on sledges of corrugated iron. The infantry could not keep up with the fire of the guns even when it moved at 50 yards a minute, men drowned in the thick oozing mud or were caught again and again by the German gunners as they floundered in the clinging mire. But the British and New Zealanders kept moving relentlessly forwards. German records state "The British artillery destroys our defences, causes most losses, prevents traffic in our back areas and, by its incessant fire, robs our men of their necessary rest". But the British kept up their attacks. By 5th November, the barrage was moving at only 25 yards per minute and somehow the infantry kept up to it—men of the 50th Division reported how they had to pull one another out of the quagmires.

The Battle of the Ancre—13th–18th November 1916

The battle of the Ancre was the final action of the Somme offensive. A mass of guns was assembled—the guns of the 2nd, 3rd, 32nd, 37th, 39th, 49th, 51st and 63rd Divisional Artilleries amounting to 364 18-pounders, and 108 4.5-inch howitzers. In addition, there were eight Heavy Artillery Groups consisting of two 15-inch howitzers, one 12-inch howitzer, 28 9.2-inch, 16 8-inch and 56 6-inch howitzers, four 6-inch guns, 46 60-pounders and eight 4.7-inch guns. This mass of guns was to support the attack of V Corps (V Corps relieved XIV Corps in October, which had relieved VIII Corps in July). To support II Corps were the guns of 11th, 17th, 18th, 19th, 25th, 1st Canadian, 2nd Canadian and 3rd Canadian Divisional Artilleries and the 4 and 7 Brigades RHA. This force consisted of 30 13-pounders, 405 18-pounders, 100 4.5-inch howitzers, two 15-inch, three 12-inch, 36 9.2-inch, 28 8-inch and 78 6-inch howitzers, four 6-inch guns, 66 60 pounders and four 4.7-inch guns.

The barrage, originally planned to move at 100 yards in ten minutes, eventually moved at 100 yards in five minutes, 25% of the 18-pounders deliberately firing 50 yards short of the remainder across no-mans land. It was to halt for one hour on the first objective and then to move on.

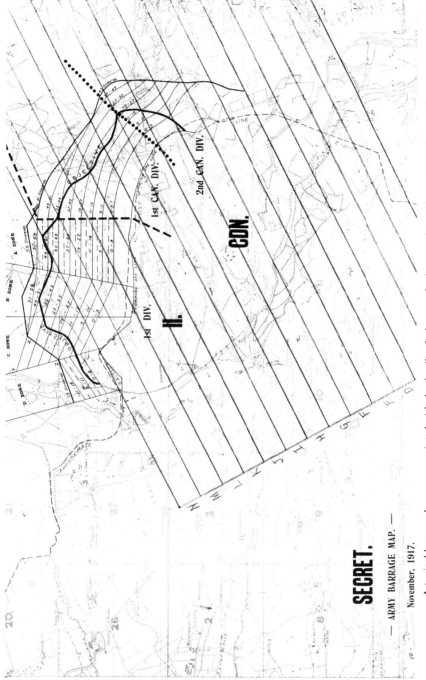

A typical large-scale map overprinted with the details of a barrage for issue to the artillery units taking part in a fire plan. Fire was brought down on the parallel lines in succession according to the timings shown; the frontage divided to batteries and individual guns; the data measured graphically; and the meteor applied. The end product was a timed programme of shooting for the Number One of each gun detachment.   (*R.A.I.*)

It was cold and dull but not raining on 13th November when the attack began. Beaumont Hamel and Beaucourt were captured but the attack on the left failed to capture Serre and the Redan ridge. Communications were difficult but the pressure was maintained. At 1220 hours on 12th November, the V Corps bombardment re-started. The barrage in front of 2nd Division had to be brought back as the infantry failed to keep up with it and this complex task was successfully accomplished. The German counter-battery work was good and their defensive fire on the attacking British infantry most effective—again the British had not paid full attention to counter-battery work and suffered because of it. It was not until 14th November, when the weather permitted aerial observation, that the British guns began to get the measure of the Germans. There were many complaints of British guns firing short at this time and, though there is never an excuse for this, there are reasons. The battle was moving, platforms were bad, guns were worn, locations of infantry were uncertain, yet fire was needed within 50 yards of them. Methods of control were poor and men were very tired. The artillery had been firing without relief or rest since 1st July and, when General Haig finally ordered operations to cease on 18th November, the Gunners in particular were almost at the end of their tether.

So ended the Somme battles of 1916. They had been very much artillery battles. They saw the start of the use of the creeping barrage, shakily in the July battles when it was not fully understood, but perfected and with confidence by October and November. They saw also the establishment of counter-battery staffs and enormous improvements in conducting the counter-battery battle. At last the vital importance of silencing the enemy guns was realised by all. Methods of controlling the fire of the guns once the attack had started were also perfected. In the area of artillery command, too, there were advances. The GOCRA at Corps HQ was shown to be all important and the Heavy Artillery Commander emerged as his subordinate—a most important step.

But there was much to do. Flash spotting and sound ranging were not yet good enough and calibration of guns was still conducted in a haphazard way while the guns were in action. There was a need for an artillery intelligence system, to pass information on targets gained from other sources to the guns by the quickest means. Meteor telegrams, too, were not as reliable or accurate as was needed. Ammunition was better but not reliable enough—there were masses of unexploded shells on the battlefield as grim testimony to manufacturing failure.

Major-General Birch, MGRA, GHQ, listed four essential artillery lessons of the Somme to be rectified during the winter. First, the highest headquarters in the battle, eg Army HQ, must lay down from the start the principles of the artillery plan; second, every available gun and period of time must be used in counter-battery work before and during an attack; third, accuracy must be improved and fourth, a more thorough artillery intelligence service was required.

Memories of the Somme in 1916 are of a long drawn out jumbled nightmare of mud, wet, death, faulty equipment, faulty ammunition, untrained reinforcements, precarious communications, constant enemy shelling, mud, mud, mud and terrible exhaustion. Nevertheless, the Somme marked another milestone; mechanical defects were to decrease, ammunition was to improve in quality and quantity and artillery tactics were advancing towards the mastering of the enemy. The mud of the Somme has become a by-word and was possibly the worst feature of the battle.

It was bad again, notably at Passchendaele in 1917.

As the Somme battles quietened down, the British line was held by Fourth Army on the right, next to the French Sixth Army, with Fifth Army in the centre and Third Army on the left.

CHAPTER 14

The Advance to the Battlefield of Arras— January to March 1917

See map 22

The cold winter months of 1916 and 1917 were devoted to holding firm to current positions and to preparing for the battles to end the war in 1917. But first the artillery organisation for command had to be put right. There were many shortcomings, as the 1916 battles had shown. In January, the War Office issued a pamphlet (Artillery Notes No.4—Artillery in Offensive Operations) which said that "there can be but one commander of the artillery of the corps, both field and heavy". This was an important step, for it meant that the position of the GOCRA at Corps HQ was now correct. At the same time the Counter Bombardment Staff Officer was established at Corps HQ, together with an orderly officer. The pamphlet also recognised the need to be able to concentrate the fire of a number of divisional artilleries to support a single division; in addition, it recognised that the requirements of the artillery must be considered at the earliest stage when planning an attack.

At the same time the roles of artillery equipments were clarified. The 18-pounders, which now had a smoke shell as well as HE and shrapnel, were to be used "primarily in barrage fire, repelling attacks in the open, raking communications, wire cutting and sometimes for neutralising guns within their reach, destroying breast-works and barriers with HE and preventing repair work on defences beyond the reach of infantry weapons". The 4.5-inch howitzers were to be used "for neutralising guns with gas shell, for bombarding weaker defences, enfilading communications trenches, for barrage work, especially at night, and for wire cutting in such places which the field guns could not reach". The 60-pounders were to be used in barrages at longer ranges, for targets in depth and for counter-battery work. The 6-inch guns were at their best in counter-battery work but "were most effective for neutralising defences and for wire cutting with fuze 106". Next, the 8-inch, 9.2-inch, 12-inch and 15-inch howitzers were best used against well protected enemy guns. Lastly, the 6-inch, 9.2-inch and 12-inch guns were for long range work against targets in depth.

This is the first mention of the important new fuze 106. It was one which burst the shell instantaneously on contact with any object, however slight. As a result, shells so fuzed burst above ground and made no crater which could form an obstacle to infantry advance. Furthermore, when used for wire cutting, it could burst the shell on contact with the wire, all the shell splinters could cut the wire and the blast could disperse it. It was in fact an effective alternative to shrapnel for wire cutting.

The alternative percussion fuze to the 106 was fuze 101, which could be provided with a delay mechanism. The object of projectiles so fuzed was to penetrate before bursting and they were used for the destruction of material.

Work was proceeding on improving artillery intelligence and methods of control. Telephone lines were buried and more use was made of exchanges, so that single observers could fire a number of batteries and not only their own. Special observing stations were established, reporting direct to HQRA at Corps, whose task was to report the progress of the infantry. A Corps Signals Officer was appointed to co-ordinate artillery communications, which became a complex trunk system far in advance of anything yet seen. It is interesting to note, however, that the alternative to line was still visual signalling. Short range (7,000 yards) radio sets were appearing but they were very bulky. Weighing 101 lbs they took four man loads to carry and it took ten minutes to erect a 10–12 foot aerial. At command posts, artillery boards (blank plotting sheets) gridded to a scale of 1 : 10,000, with provision to counter warping, replaced maps. Datum shooting was used so that guns could be checked two or three times a day. More accurate calibration drills and meteor telegrams were announced so that accuracy could be improved.

Tactically, it was stated that the role of the artillery was "to overpower the enemy's artillery, kill or shake his infantry and destroy his defences and obstacles to movement". Of this the last, in the special form of wire cutting, presented the biggest problems. The best range for 18-pounders was 1,800–2,400 yards when employed in wire cutting. Below 1,800 yards there were crest problems and fuze settings were less accurate. Calibration was recognised as vital, as was a really stable gun platform. The drill for barrages was now laid down. The aim of a barrage was "to prevent the enemy from manning his parapets and installing his machine guns in time to meet the assault". Barrages were defined as "Creeping" in support of an attack, "Standing" to cover a specific area for a length of time, possibly a phase two objective, and "Back" to cover exploitation which 'searched' and 'swept' a piece of ground in depth in order to catch troops on the move or reinforcements. It was stated that there should be one 18-pounder per 15 yards of a barrage line, and that barrage lines must be ordered by HQRA Corps after consultation with divisions. A creeping barrage should roll forward at a rate of 100 yards in three minutes but this depended on the ground and the speed of the infantry. Beyond an objective, a barrage should move out to a line 300 yards forward to allow free movement for consolidation by attacking infantry. Some guns employed on a barrage were available to divisions to be taken off the barrage, to deal with unforeseen targets, and were allotted to the barrage by the GOCRA at Corps HQ.

It was at this time, too, that an order was given that 18-pounders should never exceed four rounds per gun per minute, as the equipment would not stand more. The high rates of fire were causing "gun wear" in the barrel, which was to be a worry for the rest of the war. The use of smoke was still in its infancy but its introduction in small quantities in a barrage was recommended. Finally, on ammunition, quantities were laid down as expenditure rates for each equipment; for example, it was stated that 200 rounds per gun per day per 18-pounder was likely.

A 60-pounder at full recoil. This photograph dates from much later but gives an excellent impression of this gun in action.   *(I.W.M.)*

The drills for counter-battery work were carefully laid down. All enemy batteries and observation posts were to be plotted and registered so that they could at any time be neutralised (neutralisation was defined as giving concentrations heavy enough to prevent enemy gunners from manning their guns). Meanwhile, sound ranging sections had been formed and trained, to fix enemy guns to an accuracy of 50 yards with one observation and 25 yards with a series of observations; to give the calibre of the enemy gun firing; to indicate when it is firing and where its shells are falling and to indicate the fall of shot of British shells in relation to the enemy battery. This was a very big advance. There were, however, snags; a wind, blowing from the direction of the gun firing, deflected the sound from the microphones and a lot of guns firing together confused them. However, by March 1917, the whole front was covered by Sound Ranging Sections.

Meanwhile, the build up continued: 57th, 58th, 59th, 62nd and 66th Divisions had arrived in France by March. Each had two field artillery brigades, each of three 18-pounder batteries and one 4.5-inch howitzer battery. There was also a massive build up of heavy guns. There had been only 761 in July 1916 but by March 1917 there were over 1,500 (approximately 350 batteries).

Minor Operations—January–April 1917

There were many opportunities to put these new doctrines into practice. For example, on 10th January, after an eighteen hour preliminary bombardment, 7th Division attacked behind a creeping barrage. The attacking infantry crossed 300 yards of no-man's land in twenty minutes and raided the enemy trenches with complete success. A similar attack was made on 11th January, when the fire of 3rd, 7th and 32nd Divisional Artilleries provided a standing barrage on an objective for three battalions and a creeping barrage to get them on to it. H-Hour for attack was at 0637 hours in a thick mist and was completely successful. Again, on 3rd February, two battalions of 63rd Division attacked Puisieux on the north bank of the Ancre on a front of 1,300 yards. After a particularly effective barrage and accurate counter-battery fire, the attack was successful. Meanwhile, seven heavy artillery groups bombarded Grandcourt and completely smashed an enemy counter-attack. Grandcourt was evacuated.

However, at Miraumont on 17th and 18th February, it was another story. First came a thaw on 16th February, turning the hard ground back into deep, sticky mud; second, surprise was lost. 9, 10, 45 and 55 Heavy Artillery Groups, totalling ten 60-pounder batteries, one 4.7-inch battery, two 6-inch howitzer, two 8-inch howitzer, two 9.2-inch howitzer and two 12-inch howitzer batteries, and two 15-inch howitzers, bombarded enemy gun positions. Wire cutting was not effective and the barrage, though accurate, was not strong enough (2nd Divisional Artillery, 34 Army Brigade, 31st Divisional Artillery, 18th Divisional Artillery and 84 Army Brigade; 150 18-pounders and 42 4.5-inch howitzers, on a frontage of 3,000 yards). The infantry could not keep up with the barrage and the attack failed. Nevertheless, a strong counter-attack was "broken by exceptionally fine artillery fire, stopping the enemy just 400 yards from the British line".

The German Withdrawal to the Hindenburg Line

Field Marshal Haig (promoted in December 1916) now decided to prepare for a major British attack between Bapaume and Arras, to conform to a French attack between the Oise and Avre rivers. The British were to include in their operations an attack on Vimy Ridge. However, at this point the Germans decided to withdraw to the Hindenburg Line. This was a strong defensive zone some 6-7,000 yards in depth running from Neuville Vitasse, south east of Arras, to the Aisne and was some 70 miles in length. The positions were extremely strong and the wire exceptionally thick. Their withdrawal began on 25th February and ended on 5th April. The British followed cautiously, ever worried that the enemy would counter-attack, for he was certainly not beaten. The ground was a sea of mud—a morass—and movement at any speed was almost impossible.

However, on 26th February, 63rd Divisional Artillery and some of the Australian batteries got under way. Brigadier S.F.M. Metcalfe, CRA 18th Division, ordered wooden troughs to be tied to gun wheels so that they could slide over the mud. The Sappers laid tracks and at one point, in V Corps, even some lorries got forward loaded with ammunition. But batteries soon became bogged and strung out. In addition, the advance was opposed by strong well handled rear guards. Nevertheless, the British, most of whom were new to mobile operations, kept up the pressure.

On 11th March, II Corps attacked Grevillers with two brigades, one from 2nd and one from 18th Division. The attack, on a front of 3,300 yards, was supported by 2nd, 17th, 18th and 63rd Divisional Artilleries and three Army Field Artillery brigades, firing a barrage moving at 100 yards in four minutes.This was coupled with a machine gun barrage firing 300 yards ahead. 6-inch howitzers were used to make a series of holes on the forward slopes just short of the objective, from which Lewis gunners could cover the consolidation. The counter-battery programme was most successful, since there was virtually no German defensive fire. A most creditable performance and much credit to the Gunners involved.

Nevertheless, the advance was slow. The enemy withdrew from trench to trench, using scattered machine guns and snipers freely; he destroyed villages and all bridges and it was 18th March before the first battery could be ferried across the Peronne river. The advance guard of III Corps was formed from a cavalry force, a battalion, some sappers and two field batteries, all under command of the CRA, Brigadier H.D.O. Ward, and was known as "Ward's Force". In 32nd Division the plan was to have two brigades up and one in reserve. Each brigade had battalion and company outposts forward. One RFA brigade was forward covering the outpost lines, with the remaining two covering the two forward brigades. In this formation the division advanced 21 miles, taking all before it.

Conditions in the Fifth Army further north were very different—the ground was flatter and there were no rivers to cross. Army HQ ordered each division to push on with utmost vigour and keep contact with the withdrawing Germans, but the going was appalling, the mud thick and roads non-existent. The Chestnut Troop was moving well forward when, between Miraumont and Achiet le Petit, it became hopelessly bogged in thick ooze and then came under fire from German rear parties. Later, again under way, the guns of the Troop supported a spirited action by a squadron of the King's Dragoon Guards against 15 enemy machine guns and six field guns. As the force closed, more artillery was needed and four guns of C Battery 82 Brigade RFA joined in, a good example of control in mobile operations.

Further north again, in Fourth Army sector, XV Corps was the only one affected by the German withdrawal. News of the withdrawal made existing preparations nugatory, and guns and ammunition dumps had to be moved forward to support a series of minor operations covering the advance. Operations by 8th Division, against the villages of Heudicourt, Sorel and Fins in an area ten miles south east of Bapaume, were covered by a re-organised Divisional Artillery. Four sections of guns were deployed in each infantry brigade and the rest, including a field artillery brigade of 40th Division, were held centrally under the CRA, Brigadier H.G. Lloyd, together with a 60-pounder and a 6-inch howitzer battery. In an attack on Holnon Wood, the approach was so mobile that batteries moved across open country, giving each other cover and occupying three positions in 24 hours, all so very different from the months in the mud of the Somme. Morale was very high at this time. The operation began on 1st April with an attack on the village of Savy, four miles west of St. Quentin, by 97th Infantry Brigade supported by 161 Brigade RFA, under Lieutenant Colonel A.S. Cotton. He had in addition A, C and D Batteries of 168 Brigade RFA. Meanwhile, Lieutenant Colonel H.F. Dawson, commanding 159 Brigade RFA, using his B, C and D Batteries, put down a barrage on the right flank, while Major D.K. Tweedie controlled the fire of his battery, B of 168 Brigade, and A of 159 Brigade on to Holnon Wood, three miles north west of St Quentin. This was a particularly neat fireplan calling for quite sophisticated command and control arrangements. The attack was brilliantly successful. 159 and 168 Brigades immediately moved forward although there were some casualties from enemy defensive fire, and came into action to fire a quick barrage covering the infantry onto another successful attack on Savy Wood. During the night, the infantry pushed on to complete the encirclement of Holnon Wood and the CRA moved 161 and 167 Brigades RFA forward under cover of darkness, together with D Battery 159 Brigade. 161 had advanced at 2200 hours on 1st April, was in action at 0200 hours 2nd April, and ready to fire a barrage at 0500 hours—a remarkable feat of efficiency and training.But this sudden mobile action was a great strain on the overworked and underfed horses, hauling the guns at speed on very soft going. 167 Brigade diary records how 'many horses died of sheer fatigue'.

The fighting at Holnon Wood developed into a severe hand to hand combat. The enemy had withdrawn all his guns save one battery, which became the focal point of the action during the night of 3rd April. During the night, Major F.W. Lumsden, of the Royal Marine Artillery and now a staff officer of HQ 32nd Division, led a party of infantry and gunners of 151 Brigade RFA under heavy rifle fire to seize those guns now abandoned by the Germans. Lieutenant B.C. Trappes-Lomax followed with the teams. Meanwhile, unknown to Major Lumsden, the Germans were planning a "storm troop" to recover their guns. The British arrived there first and hooked in four guns but, as they approached the remaining two, the Germans broke onto the position and desperate hand to hand fighting took place in the darkness. Lieutenant Trappes-Lomax got four guns away, while Major Lumsden and his mixed force gradually forced the Germans back. Trappes-Lomax then managed to hook in the remaining two guns, drag them from their pits and get them away. The Gunners lost three men and two horses and Major Lumsden was awarded the Victoria Cross for this gallant action.

On 4th April, 20th Division attacked Metz-en-Couture, south of Havincourt Wood, with a complex fireplan combining a barrage and concentrations and using the guns of 20th and 8th Divisional Artilleries. The enemy were surprised and the attack was successful. On 5th April, when III Corps attacked Ronssoy, four miles south east of Heudicourt, 145 Brigade RFA arranged a fireplan but did not fire it until it was called for by the infantry. Again complete surprise was achieved, followed by success with remarkably few casualties.

9th April marked the end of the period of open warfare as the British approached the Hindenburg Line. It had been a unique period; it showed quite remarkable advances in artillery command and control. It was the day of the field batteries advancing along with their comrades of the infantry. The roads and weather were bad and these conditions prevented the heavies from keeping up. Men suffered in the open but not as much as the horses, which suffered heavily; they were unfit after months of static warfare, food was short and the task unbelievably strenuous. By mid-April, the Gunners were short of over 3,500 horses.

Preparations for the Battle of Arras—Vimy

The early weeks of April saw a difference of opinion at GHQ about the artillery policy for the forthcoming attack at Arras. In particular, General Allenby, commanding Third Army, with his GOCRA Major-General A.E.A. Holland, produced a plan for attack to be preceded by an intense 48 hour bombardment. This was not well received by Field Marshal Haig and Major General Birch, who considered that a longer bombardment policy should be adopted. At this stage, Major-General Holland was promoted to the command of I Corps and his place as GOCRA Third Army was taken by Major-General R. St. C. Lecky, who agreed with GHQ and revised the plan. However, there were throughout the Armies and Corps in France differing views on the merits of a short, intense bombardment before zero-hour as against a long, methodical bombardment.

As the two armies faced each other in April 1917, the British Artillery began a systematic counter-battery programme which was extremely successful. The German history states "even before the real British artillery preparation for the battle began, battery after battery was put out of action. By the 6th April, our *11th Division* did not possess a single battery able to develop its full fire power".

On 8th February, GOCRA First Army, Major General H.F. Mercer, issued the artillery plan for the capture of Vimy Ridge. First Army Commander, General Sir Henry Horne, was himself a Gunner and understood the problems well. The plan began by directing First Army and the Canadian Corps to divide their heavy artilleries into three counter-battery and two siege groups. The counter-battery groups were to be given no other tasks until all enemy guns were destroyed or out of action. The aim was to shoot for destruction before zero hour and for neutralisation afterwards. A flight of aircraft was allotted to each of two counter-battery groups, the third group being reserved to reinforce either. Systematic counter-battery fire began on Z minus 20 days then, at Z minus 10 days, the policy was to change to a more vigorous one of destruction of all known batteries, telephone exchanges and observation posts. The Germans had some isolated batteries but many "nests" of batteries, which were easier to locate and to neutralise. The plan foresaw the need to re-organise the artillery intelligence organisation so that information from aircraft, balloons, flash spotters, sound rangers and ground observers was quickly co-ordinated and passed to the guns. Plans were also made for the guns to move forward as the advance began.

But the main artillery attack was to be a great barrage in great depth—the greatest barrage ever seen. By now, the British Gunners were far in advance of either their adversaries or their Allies in the planning, firing and controlling of barrages. It was to be, from the initial line, a great zone of fire beaten by shrapnel, HE and smoke rolling over the enemy just in front of the attacking infantry.

The plan for the attack was for Third Army, with VI, VII and XVII Corps, to attack from Croisilles on the right to its boundary with First Army—the Arras-Lens road on the left. It was then to turn south to attack the Hindenburg Line in its flank and rear near Cambrai. The First Army was to capture Vimy Ridge and finally, Fifth Army was to attack the Hindenburg Line at Bullecourt. The area around Arras is a plateau falling to the east and cut by the river Scarpe flowing in a wide deep valley dotted with channels, marsh, small lakes and woods. The Cojeul and Sensée rivers met at Eterpigny to form the bigger Sensée river. Between the rivers are small chalk hills, providing good observation of their immediate surrounds and of the Donai plain. North of the Scarpe river is Vimy Ridge, dominating the landscape; it rises slowly in the west and drops sharply in the east. There were few woods, no hedges and few fences on the great slopes of the now famous ridge—but more of that later. Arras, astride the front line, was a communication centre of great importance.

The artillery line up for the battle was, on the British side (Third Army, Canadian Corps and that part of I Corps engaged in the attack), some 1,404 18-pounders (236 batteries); 258 60-pounders (43 batteries); 40 6-inch guns (some seven batteries); 148 9.2-inch howitzers (some 25 batteries); 450 4.5-inch howitzers (75 batteries); 364 6-inch howitzers (61 batteries); 124 8-inch howitzers (21 batteries); two 9.2-inch guns; 17 12-inch howitzers; two 12-inch guns; 8 15-inch howitzers; a total of 2,817 guns/howitzers. Against these, the Germans had 419 field guns, 240 105 mm howitzers, 118 10 cm howitzers, 148 15 cm howitzers, 15 15 cm howitzers and 74 20 cm howitzers; a total of 1,014 guns and howitzers.

One major problem for an artillery commander in such a situation, when a mass of artillery opened fire, was to identify the fall of shot of his own guns. The plan was to divide the target area into sub-areas, with a prominent target in its centre as a guide. Tasks were given to all batteries according to their equipment, ranging from wire cutting to bombardment of targets in depth and counter-battery work. Harrassing fire tasks at night were allotted and enormous quantities of ammunition were made available. Allotment for the first two days of the battle ranged from 300 rounds per gun for the 18-pounder to 60 rounds per gun for the 15-inch howitzers—massive quantities compared with availability thus far in the war.

The plan was to have a standing barrage of 4.5-inch and 6-inch howitzers fall on the German support trench at zero hour. The creeping barrage would carry the infantry to the phase one objectives (the front line trenches) and, as it met with the standing barrage, the latter would lift to the phase two objectives, leaving the creeping barrage to roll on. Meanwhile, 60-pounders were to sweep and search in depth to catch machine gunners and moving infantry; all this was quite apart from the counter-battery programme. The 18-pounders on the creeping barrage—one gun to 20 yards of front—were to fire 50% HE and 50% shrapnel. The rates were to be 100 yards in four minutes, at two rounds per gun per minute. When the infantry reached their phase two objective, known as the 'Blue Line', many of the 18-pounders were to move forward and the 60-pounders and 6-inch howitzers would move forward into their vacated positions. The 4.5-inch howitzers were also given a series of targets to engage with gas at zero minus ten hours; at zero minus one hour, they were to lift well out of the area beyond the "Black Line".

Tanks were not to be used in the initial stages, so lanes were not left in the barrage. The air situation was not good and many German fighters were about. Communications were good, cables buried, circuits were duplicated and re-duplicated; indeed, at the exchange at HQ Heavy Artillery VI Corps were 750 telephone terminals! For the first time, systematic reliefs of gun detachments were arranged to take place during the battle, so that firing would never be stopped throughout. In First Army, General Horne took personal command of all artillery allotted to him, command which, of course, he exercised through his MGRA, Major-General Mercer. This put even the 15-inch and 12-inch guns under his direct orders and was to prove a most satisfactory arrangement.

So the stage was set, the preparations complete, the plans made and orders given; all was ready for what was to be the greatest battle of the war so far; it was intended to drive through the German lines and burst out beyond. The lessons of two years of war had been learnt and, where possible, the weaknesses remedied. The greatest blow ever struck by British Arms in the history of war was about to fall, and the brunt was to be borne by the men of the Third Army, under General Sir Edmund Allenby. The most massive force of guns yet seen were all linked and co-ordinated in a way never before achieved. So, as they waited, poised, ready with high morale, let us list here for ever the artillery who would form the basis of the battle in Third Army, for without them no battle was possible, without them the infantry could not move and close with their enemy.

The Artillery of Third Army before Arras—8th April 1917:

MGRA at Army HQ   — Major General R. St. C. Lecky

GOCRA VII Corps   — Brigadier-General C.M. Ross Johnson
Commander Heavy Artillery   — Brigadier-General K.K. Knapp
  VII Corps

21st Divisional Artillery

CRA   — Brigadier General R.A.C. Wellesley

            94 Brigade RFA (A, B, C and D (Howitzer) Batteries)
            95 Brigade RFA (A, B, C and D (Howitzer) Batteries), with 58th Divisional Artillery
              in support
            290 Brigade RFA (A, B, C and D (Howitzer) Batteries)
            291 Brigade RFA (A, B, C and D (Howitzer) Batteries),
            and direct call on
            46 Heavy Artillery Group (three 6-inch howitzer batteries)

An 18-pounder in action from a painting by an unknown artist. *(R.A.I.)*

30th Divisional Artillery

CRA   —   Brigadier-General G.H.A. White

148 Brigade RFA (A, B, C and D (Howitzer) Batteries)
149 Brigade RFA (A, B, C and D (Howitzer) Batteries),
with 150 and 155 Army Field Artillery Brigades in support

56th Divisional Artillery

CRA   —   Brigadier-General R.J.G. Elkington

280 Brigade RFA (93rd, A, C and D (Howitzer) Batteries)
281 Brigade RFA (109th, A, B and D (Howitzer) Batteries),
with 293 Army Field Artillery Brigade in support

14th Divisional Artillery

CRA   —   Brigadier-General E. Harding-Newman

46 Brigade RFA (A, B, C and D (Howitzer) Batteries)
47 Brigade RFA (A, B, C and D (Howitzer) Batteries)
with 48 and 282 Army Field Artillery Brigades in support

Corps Heavy Artillery

3, 8, 35, 39, 46, 54, 58, and 85 Groups

GOCRA VI Corps   —   Brigadier-General J.G. Rotton
Commander Heavy Artillery   —   Brigadier-General H. de T. Phillips
  VI Corps

3rd Divisional Artillery

CRA   —   Brigadier-General J.S. Ollivant

40 Brigade RFA (6th, 23rd, 49th and 130th (Howitzer) Batteries)
42 Brigade RFA (29th 41st, 45th and 129th (Howitzer) Batteries), with 11th Divisional
    Artillery in support
58 Brigade RFA (A, B, C and D (Howitzer) Batteries)
59 Brigade RFA (A, B, C and D (Howitzer) Batteries)

12th Divisional Artillery

CRA   —   Brigadier-General E.H. Willis

62 Brigade RFA (A, B, C and D (Howitzer) Batteries)
63 Brigade RFA (A, B, C and D (Howitzer) Batteries), with 29th Divisional Artillery
    in support
15 Brigade RHA (B, L, 1st Warwick and 460th (Howitzer) Batteries)
17 Brigade RFA (13, 26, 92 and D (Howitzer) Batteries)

15th Divisional Artillery

CRA   —   Brigadier-General E.B. Macnaghten

70 Brigade RFA,(A, B, C and D (Howitzer) Batteries)
71 Brigade RFA (A, B, C and D (Howitzer) Batteries), with 33rd Divisional Artillery
    in support
156 Brigade RFA (A, B, C and D (Howitzer) Batteries)
162 Brigade RFA (A, B, C and D (Howitzer) Batteries)

Corps Heavy Artillery

10, 22, 32, 34, 48,   45, 72 and 81 Groups

GOCRA XVII Corps — Brigadier-General C.R. Buckle

Commander Heavy Artillery XVII Corps — Brigadier-General N.G. Barron

9th Divisional Artillery

CRA   Brigadier-General H.H. Tudor

> 50 Brigade RFA (A, B, C and D (Howitzer) Batteries)
> 51 Brigade RFA (A, B, C and D (Howitzer) Batteries), with 4th Divisional Artillery in support
> 29 Brigade RFA (12th, 126th, 127th and 128th (Howitzer) Batteries)
> 32 Brigade RFA (27th, 134th, 135th and 86th (Howitzer) Batteries), and direct call on 23 and 52 Army Field Artillery Brigades

34th Divisional Artillery

CRA   — Brigadier-General W.J.K. Rettie with 17th Divisional Artillery in support;

> 78 Brigade RFA (A, B, C and D (Howitzer) Batteries)
> 79 Brigade RFA (A, B, C and D (Howitzer) Batteries), and direct call on 86 and 311 Army Field Artillery Brigades

51st Divisional Artillery

CRA   Brigadier-General L.C.L. Oldfield

> 255 Brigade RFA (A, B, C and D (Howitzer) Batteries)
> 256 Brigade RFA (A, B, C and D (Howitzer) Batteries), with 34 84, 315 Army Field Artillery Brigades in support

Corps Heavy Artillery

> 7, 12, 16, 29, 33, 49, 55, 67, 78, 80, 83 Groups

CHAPTER 15

Arras—April to May 1917

See map 23

It is not possible here to recount in full the story of the battle of Arras but let it be said from the start that the gallantry of the infantry and the small cavalry force employed is beyond praise, their courage and devotion to duty were second to none and the final successes, as in any battle, were due to them. They suffered appalling losses but their morale and their spirit saw them through. There were successes but there were failures; the enemy was strong and resolute and he was ready, coiled like a spring, for battle; but now the Gunner story of Arras.

Let us look first at the 12th Division in VI Corps, who had a good day on 9th April 1917. Their artillery was organised into two groups for the battle, 'Right Group', under Lieutenant Colonel L.J. Hext of 63 Brigade RFA, consisted of his own Brigade and 62 Brigade RFA. They supported the attack of 37th Infantry Brigade. The 'Left Group' was commanded by Lieutenant Colonel M. Smith of 17 Brigade RFA, with 15 Brigade RHA under command; they supported 36th Infantry Brigade. These four artillery brigades employed six 18-pounder batteries on a creeping barrage (50% HE and 50% Shrapnel), with two 18-pounder and four 4.5-inch batteries in a standing barrage behind it, while one 18-pounder battery put smoke onto 'Observation Ridge'. This was crowded with German observers, who were observing for the mass of German guns in "Battery Valley" just behind them. The barrage was incredibly successful and 37th Infantry Brigade got right up onto 'Observation Ridge'; three forward observing officers (FOOs) moved forward with the leading waves of infantry reeling out cable and leaving relay posts every 400 yards as they went. Throughout the day, they not only kept communications with their guns but provided vital information on the course of the battle. As they came up to the crest, they described with amazement the sight of the enemy's batteries still in action only a few hundred yards below them. They had some wonderful shots that day.

As soon as the 'Blue Line' objective (enemy fourth line of trenches) was taken, it was planned that 63 Brigade RFA would move forward to cover 37th Infantry Brigade and 15 Brigade RHA to cover 36th Infantry Brigade. Then 62 Brigade RFA and 17 Brigade RFA would advance to within 500 yards of the German front line. When this manoeuvre was complete, 63 Brigade RFA was to be prepared to move forward to support the advance of 112th Infantry Brigade of 37th Division (Corps reserve) as it attacked Monchy. Next, 71 Brigade RFA, coming under command CRA 12th Division, was to advance to positions south of Feuchy, while 15 Brigade RHA advanced beyond the German front line and west of 'Observation Ridge'. Let us see how this complex plan worked out.

Unfortunately, there were delays in capturing the 'Blue Line' and the barrage 'got away' from the infantry, thus 62 and 15 Brigades were still in their original positions west of Arras at 1100 hours. 62 Brigade RFA went forward at 1130 hours and, incredibly, managed to be ready by 1210 hours for the attack on the 'Brown Line' objective. 17 Brigade RHA was held back but 63 Brigade RFA got forward just in time to fire the barrage in support of the attack by 35th Infantry Brigade onto the 'Brown Line' objective. It is to the great credit of these two Brigades that their barrage came down on time as ordered, but, sadly, the infantry were not ready and again the barrage 'got away' from them. Meanwhile, 17 Brigade RHA raced forward and, thundering into action at true Horse Artillery pace, got thirteen guns into action. By now Brigadier-General B. Vincent, Commander 35th Infantry Brigade, himself a gunner, and Lieutenant-Colonel Hext (who had rapidly moved from HQ 37th Infantry Brigade to HQ 35th Infantry Brigade) had reached the top of 'Observation Ridge'. Meanwhile, Commander 63 Brigade RFA and his battery commanders galloped forward right into Battery Valley among derelict German guns to look for new positions, thinking the 'Brown Line', and therefore the valley, was in British hands. Lieutenant-Colonel Hext, realising that this was not so, got an order to the guns putting them into action where they were. He then gave them a fireplan for the attack on the 'Brown Line'. By the time they were ready, it was getting dark. In the end, the attack went in at dawn on 10th April and was entirely successful, thanks to the excellence of the barrage. This episode was an excellent example of quick thinking, quick action and thorough competence on the part of the artillery commanders concerned.

But perhaps the greatest success that day fell to the men of the XVII Corps. The plan was for all three brigades of 9th Division to attack in line right up to the 'Brown Line', where 4th Division would pass through them. In spite of an order from GHQ, Brigadier-General Tudor, CRA 9th Division, favoured an HE barrage with one smoke shell in four. His argument was that the bursting HE provided better protection for the infantry and, secondly, that it avoided complex angle of sight calculations to cope with bursting shrapnel at the right height over undulating ground; thirdly, he said, it was effective at ranges beyond that of shrapnel. Brigadier Tudor had seven field brigades, 14 RHA, 5, 23, 29, 32, 52, and 57 RFA, and the trench mortars of his four divisions, 4th, 9th, 18th and 37th (some forty 2-inch and fourteen 9.5-inch mortars). Most of the batteries were in positions 1,400-2,000 yards behind the front line. The barrage was to last from zero hour to zero plus ten hours and forty seven minutes! The rate of four rounds per gun per minute for the first ten minutes, thereafter three rounds per gun per minute. It advanced for 3,500 yards in the first eight hours forty five minutes and a further 2,000 yards in the next three hours. Guns of a battery were fired three at a time, with a seven second pause before the next three fired, thus maintaining a continuous 'rain' of shells on the ground. Meanwhile, a standing barrage was fired by the 4.5-inch howitzers and 60-pounders onto the objective, and this was to lift as the creeping barrage reached it.

Since the final objective was over 7,000 yards from the guns, four artillery brigades were to advance during the battle. Although part of the barrage was fired at ranges of 7,000 yards, it was accurate and effective. The maintenance of this continuous fire was undoubtedly a feat of great endurance, especially in the conditions of cold, snow and rain that prevailed. However, the effect of the barrage was again incredible. German resistance collapsed and the infantry pushed right on to the 'Brown Line'. Indeed, they were actually held up by the standing barrage at one stage. So successful was the attack that Brigadier-General Carton de Wiart and Lieutenant-Colonel Croft were convinced that, if there was now no delay, the way was open for the cavalry to break out to total victory but, sadly, the cavalry were not to hand.

However, though the fortunes of battle varied across the front (a gap had opened between 9th and 34th Divisions which was not exploited by the enemy and in 51st Division the infantry were held up by unsubdued machine guns, which caused them to drift away from the barrage), the first day of Arras dealt a severe blow to the German defenders, though the difficulties the British experienced maintaining the advance were considerable. Great credit is due to the Engineers for the way they opened up roads and tracks across no-mans land, without which the guns could not have got forward. Communications varied and it was a feature of the battle that reports from the forward observers were often the only gauge of the progress of the battle. The few tanks that were used were not a success but their potential was clear as they rumbled forward; some did succeed in crushing machine guns and opening gaps in the wire.

The guns did well and the barrage was effective, as was the counter-battery work; where wire cutting was attempted at short range it too was successful, but at ranges of over 2,000 yards it was unreliable. But the most significant feature of all was that all the artillery, for the first time, worked to the same master-plan. This had not happened on the Somme, where each corps and division had gone its own way. Of course, there were variations but not so significant as to nullify the fire power of the greatest mass of artillery the world had yet seen co-ordinated into one battle. One such variation had been Brigadier-General Tudor's use of an HE barrage—but he did use a barrage! On the right of VII Corps, the bombardment had failed to cut the wire because it was attempted at long ranges—indeed at this point no-man's land itself was up to 2,000 yards across.

Though on the whole 9th April was a successful day, the 10th was not. The weather was bad and the mud was thick, also leadership was perhaps not all it might have been in that complex phase of battle which occurs as men struggle to consolidate after a long attack. Operations were not co-ordinated and artillery fire was not fully used. On the 9th, the counter-battery fire had all but silenced the German guns but now both they and the British guns had moved and locations were lost. Gradually, the German guns came to life. The attack on Monchy by VI Corps failed, since it was mounted without any artillery fireplan at all. The move forward of the field brigades was delayed and 15 Brigade RHA, 63 Brigade RFA and 71 Brigade RFA only reached their forward positions by 1430 hours on 10th April. For a time they were behind the heavies. In XVII Corps, the situation was similar, again the field brigades were slow in following up though some gallant efforts to keep up in the appalling conditions were made, notably in 32, 51 and 23 Brigades RFA and 14 Brigade RHA.

Meanwhile, 37th Division was ordered to capture Monchy and here came one of those events which can so easily occur in the confusion of battle. 71 Brigade RFA was in position to support 111th Infantry Brigade of 37th Division, who were to attack. Just before the attack, 71 Brigade was ordered back to its own 15th

A Battery Signaller. From a drawing by Gilbert Holiday.　(*R.A.I.*)

Division and, with almost no time left to zero hour, 14 Brigade RHA was ordered to cover the operation. Then an order to postpone the attack reached the guns but failed to reach 111th Infantry Brigade who, together with a few tanks, attacked as planned. The German artillery opened up in strength but, even though it caused heavy casualties, the gallant 111th Brigade succeeded in capturing Monchy—one of the outstanding feats of the whole battle. Immediately, the squadrons of 6th and 8th Cavalry Brigades were ordered into Monchy and came into action dismounted as the Germans mounted a counter-attack. It was at Monchy that C and G Batteries RHA galloped into action with the leading infantry. G Battery, advancing by sections, came into action in the south west outskirts of Monchy and immediately came under heavy fire and started to sustain casualties. At 1030 hours, Lieutenant-Colonel Lord Tweedmouth ordered the Battery to withdraw but, as it did so, one team was destroyed by shell fire with the result that one gun had to be abandoned until after dark. Meanwhile, C Battery brought two sections into action 700 yards south west of Monchy and opened fire on German infantry in the Bois du Sart and Bois de Vert. These four guns stuck it out under very heavy fire until ordered to withdraw by Brigadier-General Harman; the gallant C Battery had by then had three men killed and 15 wounded and had lost 27 horses killed or wounded. C and G Batteries withdrew to positions alongside K Battery and the three kept up a continual fire around Monchy for the rest of the day. Their fire was joined by that of 67 Heavy Artillery Group.

On the right of Third Army, 21st and 30th Divisions of VII Corps were struggling forward against the most difficult sector of the Hindenburg Line. The British guns were firing at long ranges and did not make a good job of wire cutting; in addition, the Germans held the dominating Hill 90. For some reason, no orders were given to concentrate the guns onto this target—and no progress was made on 11th April.

On 12th April, 17th, 29th, 33rd and 50th Divisions were made available to break through but it was too late. The Germans had filled the gaps with fresh troops and the British attacks that followed were made without proper preparation. The gunners were still not far enough forward and the liaison between the infantry and the few heavy batteries which could reach was not good. All along the line most valiant efforts were made to get the advance moving again, though action was no longer co-ordinated. A final attempt was made on 14th April by 12th and 29th Divisions but there were not enough guns forward. In addition, there were not enough heavies to conduct the counter-battery work, and 12th and 29th Divisional Artilleries suffered greatly from concentrated German counter-battery fire. On 14th April, Field Marshal Haig realised that only a well prepared attack could now break through.

The Battle of Vimy Ridge

We must now look to the fortunes of First Army, who were to attack and clear Vimy Ridge and, by so doing, to protect the northern flank of the operations of Third Army. The attack was to be carried out by the Canadian Corps, who were to seize the crest of the Ridge and Hill 120, when the British I Corps, further north, was to capture Bois en Hache.

1st, 2nd, 3rd and 4th Canadian Divisions and the British 13th Infantry Brigade were to attack on a front of four miles. The right had to go further than the left, as the Ridge lay aslant the British front line. On the left, the 3rd and 4th Divisions were given ninety-five minutes to gain the crest of Vimy Ridge—on the right, 1st Division and 13th Infantry Brigade were allowed $7\frac{1}{2}$ hours to capture their objective. There were four objectives—the Black, Red, Blue and Brown Lines.

As had been the pattern in Third Army, a forty-eight hour preliminary bombardment was arranged. The maximum use was made of observed fire by ground, balloon and airborne observers during the weeks leading up to the attack, so that all targets would be accurately fixed before the bombardment proper began. Wire cutting was left to howitzers using fuze 106. Great care was taken to avoid a pattern of fire which would advertise zero hour and great attention was also paid to accuracy, including a careful plan to check each battery against a datum point, even on the morning of the attack.

The main fireplan consisted of a creeping barrage using 18-pounders firing shrapnel and HE, with a standing barrage fired by more 18-pounders and the 4.5-inch howitzers on each objective in turn, while the heavies bombarded targets in depth. Meanwhile, a comprehensive counter-battery plan was made.

The artillery for this attack was under Major-General H.F. Mercer, MGRA First Army. Brigadier-General E.W.B. Morrison commanded the Canadian Corps artillery, with Brigadier-General M. Peake commanding the guns of I Corps. Brigadier-General R.H. Massie commanded the Canadian Heavies and Brigadier-General A. Ellershaw those of I Corps. There were a lot of Heavies. In the Canadian Corps were 1 and 2 Canadian and 13, 18, 26, 30, 44, 70 and 76 Heavy Artillery Groups and in I Corps the 63, 79, 15, 31 and 84. This amounted to 114 60-pounders, 144 6-inch howitzers, 16 6-inch guns, 40 8-inch howitzers, 56 9.2-inch howitzers, 4 12-inch and 3 15-inch howirtzers. There were many field guns also—the combined fire of the divisional artilleries of 1st, 2nd and 3rd Canadian Divisions, 5th, 31st and 63rd (RN) British Divisions, 5 and 11 Brigades RFA acting as divisional artillery for 4th Canadian Division, 5 Brigade RHA and 18, 26, 33, 72, 76, 93 and 242 Army Field Artillery Brigades; this amounted to 480 18-pounders and 138 4.5-inch howitzers. There was at Vimy Ridge one field piece per ten yards of front and one heavy per 40 yards—a greater concentration than had ever been achieved before. Six Groups of Heavies were allotted to counter-battery tasks and eight to targets in depth.

Because of the distances to be covered, particularly on the right, the field guns were carefully moved forward, many to positions only 500 yards behind the front trenches. These were cautiously registered onto enemy targets under cover of other fire but otherwise remained silent and, indeed, remained unlocated by the enemy. Dumping of ammunition was ready by the end of March and there was plenty available. Wire was buried and liaison with aircraft practised and rehearsed to a very high standard. All was silent and ready at 0530 hours on the morning of 9th April 1917 when, with a mighty crash, the most concentrated and powerful bombardment of the war thundered into the German lines on Vimy Ridge. The creeping barrage, moving at 100 yards in three minutes at three rounds per gun per minute, carried all before it, while the standing barrage only 150 yards ahead of it struck the phase one—the 'Black Line' objective—with murderous accuracy; 300 yards beyond, the massive heavy shells destroyed all life on the rear slopes of the Ridge. At the same time, some of the most accurate counter-battery fire of the war virtually silenced all response from the German guns. The artillery attack was a brilliant success. The German artillery was largely destroyed, and what was not was effectively neutralised. The powerful defences were crushed beyond recognition—only the very deep dug-outs remained—but the Canadian infantry were on top of the Germans before they could emerge and they were overwhelmed.

Vimy Ridge was a great day for the guns. The full power of concentrated artillery was demonstrated as never before—it crushed all before it. But it could not have won the day alone. The gallantry and dash of the Canadian infantry is now a legend. By supreme effort, by their courage and determination and superb fighting qualities, they exploited the bombardment as had never been done before. Their junior leaders' ability to overcome pockets of resistance and to keep their men close to the falling shells of the barrage carried the day and soon, all along the front, came messages of success as the infantry burst onto the summit of Vimy Ridge. It was infantry and artillery co-operation at its very best.

The Battle of Bullecourt

On 15th April, the Germans began a counter-thrust against Lagnicourt in an attempt to restore the precarious position they found themselves in after the fall of Vimy Ridge. This was held but, by 15th April, the Germans renewed their attacks further south in Fifth Army's area, particularly against the weary, exposed and extended Australians. The 1st Australian Division was attacked by twenty-one battalions of four German Divisions and at that moment the Australians were strung out over 13,500 yards. As the Germans burst out of the village of Lagnicourt, they overran four batteries of 1 Australian Brigade RFA and posed a threat to nine other batteries in action south west of Noreuil. At one point they were only 1,500 yards from 106th Battery RFA. The Germans claimed to have destroyed twenty-two British and Australian guns but only five were in fact destroyed and all the rest recovered. Those Australian guns had been in action only 1,000 yards from the forward trenches and the detachments did not have rifles!

Back on the Arras front near Monchy, the Germans brought up strong artillery reinforcements. They pounded the British gunners day and night, using a high proportion of gas shell. 17 Brigade RFA was heavily attacked and had two howitzers and an 18-pounder destroyed by direct hits. In 15 Brigade RHA, both L Battery and the Warwick Battery suffered direct hits on guns during the bombardments of 16th April. But the gunners stuck with their guns and gave as good as they took: they could not locate the enemy and so they pushed observers right forward ahead of the infantry in order to do so. The German bombardment continued, almost all directed upon the guns; on 18th April, it increased to a terrifying intensity. 26th Battery RFA began to suffer hits and casualties, both it and 92nd Battery were forced to move, while D Howitzer Battery of 17 Brigade had a gun overturned by blast from an exploding 5.9-inch shell. However, batteries stuck it out grimly, holding their ground and refusing to be silenced. Ammunition supply was kept up by much gallantry on behalf of the echelons; the Germans, realising what was happening, began bombarding in depth to destroy wagons and horses bringing up the vital shells. But the strain was terrible—sleep was impossible. The 17 Brigade RFA war diary says "The men are very, very tired . . . men and horses moving ammunition are about done". But, as the gunners took this terrible hammering, plans were being made to attack again, this time to renew the assault along the Scarpe.

Second Battle of The Scarpe—23rd–24th April 1917

The bombardment of enemy positions at the Scarpe began on 21st April. This was maintained for ten hours at a time, during the nights of 21st and 22nd April, and included hurricane bombardments of villages along the German line by the heavies. But counter-battery fire was not well co-ordinated and throughout the battle the German guns were never really well dominated.

At 1645 hours on 23rd April, the attack by Third Army began behind a creeping barrage lifting 100 yards every four minutes, with the guns firing two rounds per gun per minute, interspaced with short-periods of four rounds per gun per minute. Unfortunately, on 33rd Division's front, two brigades RFA fired onto the same zone, thus leaving a gap where the enemy held out and did much execution on the attacking infantry. This unfortunate error demonstrated in a tragic way the value of the barrage for, where it was applied, the attacks were successful.

On the right, 29th and 50th Divisions attacked successfully at Monchy and captured the Wancourt Tower, which deprived the enemy of his observation into the Cojeul Valley and enabled the guns of 12th and 29th Divisions to advance in spectacular form. The batteries galloped forward as soon as the success signal was observed and swung into action just west of Monchy, in full view of Wancourt Tower. It was reported by the infantry as a magnificent and inspiring sight as the advance of the guns was carried out with great dash and skill. But, at the same moment, the enemy counter-attacked the Tower and swept the infantry of 50th Division back to their start line regaining, as they did so, full observation of the British batteries coming into action in the Valley below them. Immediately, they began a heavy and relentless shelling of the exposed gunners. But heavy as the fire was, they failed to silence the gallant batteries. In spite of sustaining casualties, the detachments stuck to their guns and fired back with great ferocity, scoring many hits on the German infantry on the ridge around the Tower. Onlookers described the action of the men of B and L Batteries, in particular, as truly magnificent and in the very best tradition of the Royal Horse Artillery. But now German infantry were closing on the guns; by 1430 hours, 17 Brigade RFA were ordered to empty their limbers, hook in eight horse teams and withdraw. In 15 Brigade RHA, three guns were hit and many men and horses were dead and wounded: soon they found German infantry between the gun positions and Guemappe, and preparations were made to stand and fight around the guns. As the positions came under aimed machine gun fire, two officers of 460th Howitzer Battery were killed together and, as evening approached, the situation looked desperate. But help was to hand, the barrage was brought back and 50th Division counter-attacked and again swept the enemy from Wancourt Tower and saved the weary gunners of 12th and 29th Divisions, who had fought so gallantly all afternoon against massive enemy fire power.

But the respite was short; the positions near Monchy were well known to the enemy and he maintained a continuous rain of shells onto the cramped batteries. Headquarters 17 Brigade RFA shared a cave with Headquarters 76th Infantry Brigade, a cave described by one diarist "as like a witches' haunt of a hellish cathedral, gloomy and smoking with candles burning in various alcoves, as though before some evil shrine". But the casualties mounted, 13th Battery suffering heavily; it was reduced to two guns only.

Again during this period of bitter confused fighting it was very difficult to maintain control of operations. Mistakes were often made and casualties occurred because of them. On one occasion, 46th Infantry Brigade of 15th Division advanced as the barrage supporting them came down and they suffered losses which they could ill afford. They had not received the fireplan details and knew not of its existence! So still there were lessons to be learnt in the co-ordinated control of guns in the heat of battle.

In First Army, the attack in the north on Gavrelle was led by 63rd Division of XIII Corps but, although a massive bombardment was fired at the German wire, it was found to be poorly cut when the attacking infantry stormed the village on 23rd April. However, by sheer guts and determination, they reached their objectives and cleared what was left of the battered houses. Then the German gunners turned their full wrath onto the luckless 63rd Division, which could not move; at 1530 hours, three enemy battalions counter-attacked, moving in ten waves in full view of the gunner observer who had prepared a defensive fireplan for just this event. The leading waves were swept away by the guns and the few that were left were destroyed by machine guns and rifle fire—a perfect example of the use of guns in support of consolidation at the end of an attack. On that day, 63rd Divisional Artillery fired 78,000 rounds, and 40 Brigade RFA alone fired 15,000 rounds: it is not surprising that reports began to come through of faulty recuperators and buffers.

The Battle of Arleux

The plan on 28th April was to attack along either side of the Scarpe with VI and XVII Corps. On the right, 34th Division attacked Roeux behind a specially designed barrage, which remained on the opening line in front of the village for four minutes then made three lifts each of 100 yards, pausing on each for eight, seven and seven minutes respectively; finally, it lifted a further 100 yards which cleared the houses and remained there for four minutes. This barrage was fired by 9th and 51st Divisional Artilleries, two batteries of 160 Brigade RFA, 14 (Army) Brigade RHA and 23 (Army) Field Artillery Brigade, all under command of Brigadier-General W.J.K. Rettie, CRA 34th Division. The fire was not as effective as had been hoped and failed to cut the wire or to subdue all the enemy machine gunners. Nevertheless, the infantry fought forward and into the village when, at 0800 hours, the Germans counter-attacked. As they emerged from the woods near the village, they were mown down by the 18-pounders firing shrapnel; nevertheless, no further British progress was possible. A series of abortive attacks were then made by the British, usually hurriedly planned and with no proper fireplan and when this occurred, the attacks failed.

To the left of 34th Division, 37th Division attacked objectives only 900 yards away. The fireplan was again a creeping barrage fired by 4th and 34th Divisional Artilleries (the latter less two batteries) and 52 (Army) Field Artillery Brigade. It was under command of Brigadier-General H.H. Tudor, CRA 9th Division. The barrage successfully got the infantry onto their objectives who pressed on without proper artillery cover and consolidated in depth. A good day. Meanwhile, 2nd Division of First Army attacked Arleux under a double 18-pounder barrage. This was fired by the guns of 2nd Divisional Artillery, supported by 170 Brigade RFA of 31st Division and 34, 89 and 315 (Army) Field Artillery Brigades. The plan was made by the CRA 2nd Division, Brigadier-General G.H. Sanders, and in it he arranged for two overlapping barrages, one 200 yards ahead of the other, half the 18-pounders being allotted to each. The rear barrage was engaged with shrapnel, while the outer barrage was engaged with HE and included 4.5-inch howitzers and machine guns. There was, however, an acute deployment problem. If the guns stayed behind Vimy Ridge, they were at long range, which resulted in inaccurate shooting and a danger of being out of range as the infantry attacked. In front of the Ridge, they were in full view of the enemy's powerful artillery. In the event they did a bit of both. The artillery fire of both sides was tremendous. The double barrage worked well, but the German defensive fire was too great and no major success was scored. The Germans adopted short, sharp, concentrated deliveries of defensive fire on the attacking infantry, which proved highly successful.

The Third Battle of The Scarpe—3rd–4th May 1917

Plans were made by Third Army to attack along the Scarpe valley at dawn on 3rd May but, at the last moment, it was decided that the attack should take place at night. The result was chaotic. The confusion caused in the ranks of the attacking battalions was very great; many were heavily reinforced with new, in-experienced recruits, who had no idea of the complexity of the task ahead of them. They lost the barrage and fell victim to massive and concentrated German artillery fire brought down upon the terrified, confused young soldiers, exposed in no-man's land, with terrible accuracy and ferocity. Some said that the German artillery fire at the third Scarpe battle was the heaviest ever seen in the whole war. What was worse was the totally ineffective British counter-battery fire. The German guns kept up their massive bombardment unchecked for fifteen hours—it was too much. It was too much to ask of the young, inexperienced men of the assaulting battalions, and the German counter-attacks caught the shocked and bewildered British infantry in the open and drove them back from whence they came. Had all the lessons suddenly been forgotten? Why did such a thing happen at all? The fact was that there was still a failure in British tactics to wed artillerymen so close to the attack that they would be able to plan ahead and be ready to react quickly to the unexpected.

However, in places there were successes. The more experienced Canadian infantry kept close to its gun fire and, when a counter-attack developed, it was blasted out of existence by quick reaction defensive fire. But this was not the norm; at Cherisy, 18th Division reached its objectives but was thrown off them before defensive fire could be arranged. At the moment of consolidation on an objective, the infantry absolutely relied on their artillery, but for the artillery to react meant close liaison and much better communications. At Monchy, the

The Forward Observing Officer. From a drawing by Gilbert Holiday.   (R.A.I.)

enemy pounded the village so heavily that all the gunner observers were killed. Reserve battalions were getting over 300 casualties before being committed and the field batteries were heavily gassed. So the attack petered out and stopped. The Germans had been ready and the British had blundered, and blundered heavily.

The Second Battle of Bullecourt—3rd–17th May 1917

The last of the series of battles, which together composed the bloody, costly fighting now known as the battle of Arras, was the second battle of Bullecourt, fought by the men of Fifth Army. This battle saw trench fighting at its most horrible—fierce bombing raids and hand to hand fighting occurred, notably on the Australian sector. Rapid concentrations of artillery were also a feature, combined with the fire of Stokes mortars, machine guns and Lewis guns.

The attack began on 3rd May, and this time really effective counter-battery fire was organised. The barrage, too, was a great success—there were plenty of guns; one field piece per eleven yards and one heavy per twenty yards of front. But the tired and battered British infantry were slow and cautious, and who could blame them? They did not get far on that first day. The German infantry fought hard among the rubble which had been Bullecourt. The German guns slowly came back to life after the opening counter-battery fire—many had moved to new positions and, by 4th May, they again began to fire heavy concentrations on the attacking British infantry. However, a German counter-attack against the Australians was wiped out by the massed fire of the British guns on 6th May. The problem of distinguishing friend from foe was a major one. The British gunners were cautious of shelling their own men and any rumour that their infantry had entered a trench or village was enough to stop all guns firing there. The Germans were more ruthless and swiftly brought down their gun fire onto lost positions, even when fighting was in progress.

On 13th May, a hurriedly arranged plan with no real fireplan failed to take Bullecourt but, after a hurricane bombardment on the 17th, the Australian and British infantry finally stormed into the rubble and desolation of the village to find it piled high with German dead. The gallantry shown by the infantry of both sides had been very great but finally the British and Australians had, by sheer doggedness, become the victors, although the cost had been enormous. Meanwhile, 4th Division had at long last captured the chemical factory at Roeux, after a most carefully prepared and brilliantly executed bombardment and attack.

So operations around Arras ground to a halt. The French to the south had suffered terribly and now the British agreed to take the brunt further north around Ypres. Both infantry and gunners were exhausted; they had to rest. Guns were failing—springs and buffers urgently needed attention.

The British gunners had shown that in their preparations for attack they were masters. Methods of locating enemy guns, methods of survey and of applying meteor were all good. The failure still came once the attack had started. It was the same old story—bad communications in the confusion of battle. Once enemy guns had moved to new positions, the British were incapable of re-locating them in time to stop them interfering with the attack. The equipment just did not allow it. Even so, the gunners were still not quick enough at getting observers well forward after an attack, where they could really observe, and those who did were very vulnerable and many were killed. The problem of providing real liaison between the heavies and the infantry was considerable. A system of double grouping was tried with success, where one artillery group distributed its batteries to two others and itself set up beside the infantry purely in a command and control role. This worked quite well, providing a vital link, and soon became a generally adopted technique.

Smoke was greatly used at Arras and its value was for the first time really appreciated; it was frequently included in barrages. Gunners were concerned at the rigidity of the barrage and its timetable—many fleeting opportunities were lost. As a result, the habit of 'superimposing' some batteries onto the barrage, which could be temporarily removed without leaving gaps, was tried with success. The battle had also been a brutal training ground for the many young gunners fresh from England. They began to learn in the rough, hard school of combat how to command and control both guns and fire as the battle moved forward and backward—but many paid the supreme penalty in the learning.

Arras above all had once again demonstrated that, in this kind of battle, the British guns had to find and silence the enemy guns as a matter of priority. Once found, they then had to remain their masters during an attack—a much, much more difficult task.

So we leave Arras in May 1917. It was an enormous artillery duel and, in the duelling, the British on the whole emerged the winners, but only just. The dogged determination and gallantry of the infantry, much of it new, inexperienced and untrained, finally carried the day. By the end of the battle, and like their comrades on the guns, they were exhausted where they stood. They could do no more—for the time being.

Ready to advance into action. A field battery during the German retreat to the "Hindenburg Line" in the snow, early 1917

Snow. From a watercolour by J C Walford. *(R.A.I.)*

CHAPTER 16

The Great Victory at Messines —
7th to 14th June 1917

See map 24

0310 hours 7th June 1917 exactly, and at that moment every gun roared out in awful salvo. The flashes of the guns in the darkness were so close together and continuous that the whole western horizon seemed to be ablaze. At the same moment, nineteen landmines were exploded beneath the German lines; they rose as a vast wall of fire and destruction, lighting the night sky with red, gold and black-grey heaving earth, and the shock waves were felt in London! The battle of Messines had begun. For some weeks, the Second Army under General Plumer had been planning for this moment, and now it had arrived. Let us then look back for a moment; let us see how the artillery plan for this battle was calculated. By 1917, fireplanning was a complex art. It was based on mathematical fact; it was not just a case of banging away with all available guns. At Messines, the calculations of the requirement for heavy guns and howitzers alone went like this:

a.   The frontage of the battle was 17,000 yards.

b.   All German guns within 9,000 yards of the frontage must be neutralised. There were 169 located guns on the flanks of the line of assault; these must be dealt with by 25% of their number of British guns—42. The remaining 299 guns, closer to the German centre, must be dealt with on a one for one basis—a further 299. Thus, 341 British guns were needed for counter-battery work alone.

c.   For the bombardment to get the infantry forward, it was necessary to have one medium or heavy howitzer per 45 yards of front, or 378 guns. These to be superimposed on the divisional artilleries which were firing the barrages.

d.   Experience had shown that 5% of the total should be super heavy, so:

For counter-battery	– 341 guns/howitzers
For bombardment	– 378 guns/howitzers
Super heavy (5%)	– 38 guns/howitzers
TOTAL	– 757 guns/howitzers

In fact, 756 heavy guns/howitzers were made available and it was decided to have a timed programme throughout, with a powerful force of machine guns superimposed. The attack was to be made by II Anzac Corps on the right, IX Corps in the centre and X Corps on the left, with XIV Corps in reserve. The Artillery Order of Battle was:

184

Artillery Second Army:	MGRA	—Major-General G. McK Franks
Artillery II Anzac Corps:	BGRA	—Brigadier-General E.W.M. Powell
	BGHA	—Brigadier-General A.S. Jenour
3rd Australian Division:	CRA	—Brigadier-General H.W. Grimwade
4th Australian Division:	CRA	—Brigadier-General C. Rosenthal
New Zealand Division:	CRA	—Brigadier-General G.N. Johnston
27th Division:	CRA	—Brigadier-General W.R. Eden
Artillery IX Corps:	BGRA	—Brigadier-General G. Humphreys
	BGHA	—Brigadier-General G.B. Mackenzie
11th Division:	CRA	—Brigadier-General J.W.F. Lamont
16th Division:	CRA	—Brigadier-General C.E.C.G. Charlton
19th Division:	CRA	—Brigadier-General W.P. Monkhouse
36th Division:	CRA	—Brigadier-General H.J. Brock
Artillery X Corps:	BGRA	—Brigadier-General H.L. Reed
	BGHA	—Brigadier-General H.O. Vincent
23rd Division:	A/CRA	—Lieutenant-Colonel G. Badham-Thornhill
24th Division:	CRA	—Brigadier-General H.C. Sheppard
41st Division:	CRA	—Brigadier-General S. Lushington
47th Division:	CRA	—Brigadier-General E.N. Whitley
Artillery XIV Corps (Reserve):	BGRA	—Brigadier-General A.E. Wardrop
	BGHA	—Brigadier-General F.G. Maunsell
Guards Division:	CRA	—Brigadier-General W. Evans to 12th June 1917, then Brigadier-General F.A. Wilson
1st Division:	CRA	—Brigadier-General G.N. Cartwright
8th Division:	CRA	—Brigadier-General H.G. Lloyd
32nd Division:	CRA	—Brigadier-General J.A. Tyler

The total artillery available for the battle of Messines was 2,266 guns and howitzers; of these, as we have seen, 756 were heavies, which were organised into forty groups. The sixty-four field artillery brigades totalled 1,158 18-pounders and 352 4.5-inch howitzers, and consisted of the Divisional Artilleries listed above, plus thirty-three Army Field Artillery Brigades; the latter were allotted: ten to II Anzac corps, ten to IX Corps and thirteen to X Corps. The 756 heavy guns were made up as follows:

186	60-pounders
316	6-inch howitzers
20	6-inch guns
108	8-inch howitzers
108	9.2-inch howitzers
2	9.2-inch guns
12	12-inch howitzers
1	12-inch gun
3	15-inch howitzers

144,000 tons of ammunition were dumped in the area of Second Army for the battle. By zero day, this amounted to 1,000 rounds per gun per 18-pounder; 750 rounds per 4.5-inch howitzer and 500 rounds per heavy gun/howitzer. Much use was made of railways to move this mass of ammunition. In addition, some 120,000 rounds of gas shell and 60,000 rounds of smoke shell for the 18-pounders were made available.

During May, careful plans were made to build up this mass of guns and to dump the ammunition in secrecy. The Army Field Artillery Brigades in particular were moved into the area slowly over a long period, a battery at a time and often under the cover of local concentrations.

Each Corps organised its mass of heavy artillery differently. In II Anzac Corps there were four counter-battery groups, each with one heavy group. IX Corps had four counter-battery groups and five bombardment groups. Three of the latter were allotted as one to each attacking division, and the remaining two, which included the very heavy howitzers, remained under the BGHA to be superimposed as required. A Heavy Artillery Group Commander, a Lieutenant-Colonel, was attached to each HQRA to command the heavies once the advance began. In IX Corps, the field artillery was formed into groups and sub-groups. For example, in 19th Division each infantry brigade was supported by a group of two sub-groups, each sub-group consisted of six 18-pounder or 4.5-inch howitzer batteries. In each case, a senior major acted as liaison officer at each infantry brigade headquarters. This re-grouping meant that some field brigade head-quarters had no batteries; where this occurred, they were then briefed to be ready to replace casualties and to plan the subsequent advance of the guns.

The artillery task was not easy. The Messines—Wytschaete Ridge concealed the German second line and all his battery positions from the British OPs. This meant that much use was to be made of aerial observation and 2nd Brigade RFC produced 300 aircraft for this task alone. In addition, 2nd Kite Balloon Wing RFC produced eight captive balloons at 5,000 feet, operating from 3 to 5,000 yards behind the front line; these were to be of the greatest value. Communications linking this mass of guns and observers and the infantry was complex. The plan was based on Second Army Report Centre at Locre Chateau, four miles behind the front, and from which cables ran to Corps Report Centres, Corps Heavy Artillery HQs, HQRAs at Divisions and to the RFC, balloons, survey and radio stations. All cables were buried six feet deep. Nevertheless, the old problem of keeping contact with the foremost infantry was still there.

Major-General Franks, MGRA Second Army, co-ordinated all corps plans. These were built up between BGRAs and CRAs and in particular there was close co-ordination of counter-battery tasks for the heavy artillery. The build up of the counter-battery plan was most methodical. Each evening, the counter-battery staffs at Divisions and Corps HQs held a conference and put together all reports for the day from all sources, RFC, balloons, field survey companies, sound ranging sections and FOOs. Each Corps counter-battery area was divided into zones and each of these allotted to a heavy artillery group. Each zone was sub-allotted by Group Headquarters into map squares, which were given to batteries. Batteries had always to be able to engage targets in their allotted squares, and very quickly too. After any move of the guns, they had to report that they could still fulfill this task. Brigadier-General Humphreys, BGRA IX Corps, said after the battle "To my mind, the success of our counter-battery fire was largely due to the fact that control rested in the hands of one expert (the Counter-Battery Staff Officer) and his staff, who were free to devote their whole time, energy and brains to the one end of defeating enemy guns".

The Germans had again adopted a system of defence in depth. Each of their forward brigades had a sector 1,500 yards wide and 3,000 yards deep and this area

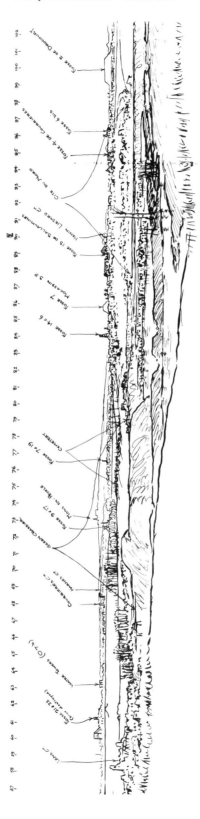

A typical panorama, drawn at an Observation Post to record the data required to engage any likely targets, preferably confirmed by ranging. This one was drawn in the neighbourhood of Lens.

was studded with machine gun nests and strong points.The forward zone extending back to the Messines ridge was thinly held. Small garrisons held the strong points with orders to hold out till the last, even if surrounded; they would then be relieved by strong counter-attacks, delivered after the British were well extended. The British were well aware of this problem and, though they reckoned that a massive fireplan would enable them to reach their objectives, they knew that they must then be able to switch artillery quickly, in the middle of the battle, onto these enemy counter-attacks. Because of the communication problems, this was the very operation that was the most difficult of all. The German strong points, circular or square with massive reinforced concrete walls, could only be destroyed by direct hits from 6 to 8-inch howitzers. Elsewhere there were small, open strong points manned by 30–40 men.

The artillery plan was not dissimilar to that used at Vimy Ridge in April 1917. About two thirds of the 18-pounders were to fire a creeping barrage ahead of the assaulting infantry, the remainder of the 18-pounder and 4.5-inch howitzers were to fire standing barrages 700 yards ahead of the creeping barrage. As the infantry reached their objectives, the creeping barrage was to become a protective barrage 150-300 yards ahead of the infantry as the consolidated. A machine gun barrage using indirect fire was to be superimposed 400 yards ahead of the creeping barrage. Meanwhile, heavy and medium artillery would bombard enemy batteries and strong points.

By now, the Germans had guessed that the British were about to attack and had massed over 200 batteries, totalling almost 700 guns, to repulse it when it came. They were confident that they could master the British artillery and sent reports to that effect in April and May. The artillery duel started in May and at times was ferocious and vicious. On 2nd May, 300 rounds fell on 197th Siege Battery between 0530 and 0700 hours, mercifully without doing too much damage; a few days later, 200 rounds fell on D Battery 235 Brigade RFA and C Battery 104 Brigade RFA, scoring twelve hits on trenches, wagons and living quarters. Again on 7th May, 600 rounds fell on 124th Heavy Battery, hitting two guns and destroying some ammunition, while the unfortunate 197th Siege Battery lost a gun on the same day. This constant day in, day out battle between the opposing artilleries was a great strain. The Gunners were constantly in action, constantly bombarded, constantly tired and repairing damage and, of course, sustaining casualties. On 12th May, 179th Siege Battery hit a German battery and destroyed it but, on the following day, 17th Heavy Battery lost one gun destroyed, two damaged and a fourth slightly damaged in a devastating attack by the Germans. C Battery 102 Brigade RFA and C Battery 103 Brigade RFA were badly hit on 12th and 13th May. On 19th May, A and C Batteries 103 Brigade were again hit, and D Battery on the same day lost its Battery Commander, a subaltern and three gunners to German medium shelling. But, on the whole, the British were getting the best of these weeks of shooting. The bombardment began on 21st May and, on 31st May, eight days of intensive bombardment began, particularly on the strong points. Using aircraft and balloons, many hits were scored and most of the German batteries were seen and engaged. By now the British superiority in numbers, 2,266 guns against 630 was beginning to tell. Between 26th May and 6th June, during the preparatory bombardment, 3,561,530 rounds were fired. On 3rd and 5th June, the barrages were rehearsed and these

Bringing up the guns. From a painting by an unknown artist.   *(R.A.I.)*

also succeeded in forcing the German batteries to retaliate and give away their positions—all went very well, the scene was set. All was now ready for zero day—7th June 1917.

When the bombardment proper started, and when the huge, terrible mines blew the German front line system to bits on that dark June morning, there was scarcely any response from the shaken German guns. They had been well and truly silenced by the massive shock and intensity of the counter-battery fire and the infantry advanced with few losses. Some shattered German infantry tried once or twice to counter-attack and the combination of the creeping and standing barrages destroyed them all. The accuracy and intensity of the British gunnery that day reached a new perfection; it was spoken of long afterwards with great admiration by the infantry who were, as a result, able to cross safely over no-man's land. The village of Messines itself had been turned into a very strong point indeed, surrounded by a deep trench system heavily wired and with five large, concrete pill boxes. But the barrage rolled over it and the heavies struck it so hard that it fell easily to a gallant assault by the Anzac Corps. The second German line had fallen by 0500 hours and the barrage, as planned, sat 300 yards ahead to protect the infantry as they consolidated and prepared for the next phase.

The story was the same on IX Corps front. Wytschaete village had been expected to be a strongly defended area so, on 3rd June, a special bombardment by siege and heavy batteries, followed by gas shelling by 4.5-inch howitzers, was arranged. On 7th June, the assaulting infantry, with a tank leading, rushed the ruins and captured the village with ease. All along the front, demoralised Germans, shattered by the bombardment, surrendered easily to the jubilant British and Anzac infantry who, by 0900 hours, were consolidating on the phase one objectives. OPs were established on the ridge and reported remarkable views over the whole of the German rear areas. Many German batteries were, however, able to get away, although some forty-eight damaged guns were captured.

The danger now was the expected enemy counter-attacks at divisional strength. The artillery had defeated all local counter-attacks, but the protective barrage now lacked depth and it was urgently necessary to move some batteries forward to achieve it. Five hours, later extended to seven because of the conditions of the ground, were allowed for the move forward of a number of heavy batteries and forty field batteries. These batteries found their way forward over appalling going in the old front line, some coming into action in prepared positions besides dumped ammunition, but the field guns moved into the old no-man's land to come into action amongst the chaos, slaughter, mud, wire and trenches of the initial battle. At 1400 hours, the Germans tried to launch their counter-attack, but this was easily smashed in its tracks by the defensive fire of the guns and the mass of machine guns now up on the ridge. At 1440 hours, a massive concentration of heavy batteries was switched to breach the wire on the phase two objective and, although this was ordered at 9,000 yards, the results were exceptionally good and the wire was no obstacle when the attack went in.

Although British counter-battery fire had neutralised most German artillery within range of the battle, they had failed to silence the guns of the *4th Bavarian Division* deployed behind the river Lys. As the 3rd Australian Division advanced onto its phase two task, these guns began to cause severe casualties. As the

Australian infantry closed on the Oosttaverne line, they became involved in fierce fighting amidst the pill-boxes with German infantry supported by the Bavarian gunners. It was some time before they were able to report success. To the left of the Australians, 19th Division attacked so hurriedly that junior commanders knew no more than to follow the barrage and keep close to it. These orders must have been about the simplest ever given for an attack. However, 57th Infantry Brigade, in particular, kept within 50 and 60 yards of the bursting shells and captured Oosttaverne, with few casualties as a result. Further left still, the two leading battalions of 17th Infantry Brigade advanced 800 yards and sustained only six casualties! Again the massive artillery attack had done its work to perfection. But a problem was slowly developing—the divisions which advanced to capture the Oosttaverne Line were controlled separately from those holding the Messines Ridge and, to make matters worse, the FOOs with each were out of contact. Then came another great lesson of modern war; artillery command and control must be separate but totally integrated with command of battle formations at all levels. This is best done by a physical link between the two.

Towards evening on 7th June, many FOOs on the Ridge, who had no knowledge of the phase two attack and unable to tell friend from foe, engaged many of the forward troops, causing casualties. At the time, neither they nor their superiors knew they were doing it, and there was no way of stopping them. Indeed, on the evening of 8th June, when one battalion of a forward brigade was withdrawn for relief, they were heavily engaged from Messines Ridge, being mistaken for an enemy counter-attack. It was not until early 9th June that this breakdown in control was rectified. But it had been a tragic lapse—a blunder which marred one of the best periods of artillery bombardment so far in the war.

Nevertheless, the results had been spectacular; 144 officers and 7,210 men were captured, with 48 guns, 218 machine guns and 60 trench mortars. But more important, the most powerfully prepared German position on the northern sector had fallen, the enemy was robbed of valuable observation and the right flank of the Ypres position was now secure. In addition, the British now had a magnificent view over the German lines south of Gheluvelt.

So ended the great victory of Messines. That it had been a huge success was beyond doubt and that the artillery plan was sound and brilliantly executed was also beyond doubt. The battle again emphasised the need for accurate counter-battery fire, forcing the enemy guns onto the defensive. It emphasised, too, that massive artillery fire in support of attacks *with limited objectives* could work, and for the first time the infantry knew the exhilaration of reaching objectives intact. A system of arranging SOS barrages, which could be called for by aerial observers, worked well. The use of protective barrages fired in depth by heavy howitzers, firing beyond the 18-pounders, had crushed almost all local counter-attacks before they could start. There was, however, one unfortunate result of the excellence of the artillery covering fire—there began a tendency for the infantry to rely on it too much—more, indeed, than on their own weapons; they began to show a reluctance to move at all without massive artillery attacks. In addition, the old problem of retaining control during the battle as assaulting infantry reached their objectives, remained as guns began to move and phase 2 operations began. This still had to be solved.

Nevertheless, never since the early battles of 1914 had the bond between Gunners and Infantrymen been so strong; at last, a weapon had been forged to win the war, a human weapon based on experience, confidence and, above all, on skill.

[*By permission of "The Gunner"*

ARRAS, 1917
BY JOHN CAMERON

The mud of Flanders. From the original by Fortunino Matania.   (*R.A.I.*)

CHAPTER 17

Third Battle of Ypres;
The Massive Bombardments at Passchendaele—
July to November 1917

See maps 25, 26, 27, 28, 29, 30 and 31

Passchendaele! What emotion that name generates, even to those who were not there! It means many things to many people, but to all it means mud, massed bombardments, bloody and cruel fighting and, above all, courage and stamina in the face of appalling conditions. Strictly speaking, Passchendaele was part of the Third Battle of Ypres, which consisted of a series of battles. First was the initial British attack on Pilckem Ridge which was launched on 31st July, and lasted until 2nd August. Then came Langemarck from 16th to 18th August, then the Battle of the Menin Road Ridge from 20th–25th September, followed by Polygon Wood from 26th September to 3rd October. Next came Broodseinde on 4th October, and Poelcappelle on 9th October. Finally, only on 12th October came First Passchendaele, followed by Second Passchendaele from 26th October to 10th November. Third Ypres was a mighty battle; it saw the mightiest bombardment so far in a war of massive bombardments. On a frontage of fifteen miles, seventeen British divisions, backed by the power of 3,106 guns firing the most massive artillery attack ever known until that time, hurled themselves onto von Ludendorf's defences. In the eighteen day preparatory bombardment alone, almost three million shells were fired onto the German forward positions. Nothing like it had ever been attempted; nothing like it had ever before been possible; it was war on the grand scale, a portent perhaps for the mobile wars of later years. It was the greatest test ever given to the Royal Regiment of Artillery—the supreme test. It was conceived by men who believed in the French doctrine that "Artillery conquers, infantry occupies". Its success had already been demonstrated in the first part of the battle of Arras at Vimy and again at Messines, where objectives were close and concentrations were heavy. It had failed at Loos, on the Somme and at the later parts of the Arras battles, where objectives were deep, concentrations were weak and techniques were shaky. What now? Had the lessons been learnt? Could the victories of Vimy and Messines be repeated on an even grander scale?

The battle was entrusted to the Fifth Army, under General Sir Hubert Gough, a cavalryman of vigour, dash and daring. The plan was for the Second Army, under General Sir Herbert Plumer, to seize the German outpost line on a front of fifteen miles, then for the Fifth Army, with the French First Army to its left, to overrun all German defences on the Gheluvelt Plateau and Pilckem Ridge. When this was done, to smash through on an axis Gheluvelt, Becelaere, Broodseinde, Thourout,

Bruges. It was an attack to lift the British out of the Ypres saucer of mud and stinking dykes of stagnant water, in which it had fought for three years, and into the green fields beyond. In doing so it would capture the U-boat bases at Ostend and Zeebrugge and finally clear the Germans out of Flanders—the main objectives for the battles. It was an attack across a number of small streams, whose names will exist forever in the annals of the regiments that fought there— the Steenbeek, the Strombeek and the Zonnebeek. The slight ridges surrounding these streams gave the Germans enormous observation over the cramped British salient below, where thousands of men wallowed in a shell torn quagmire. German observers could concentrate fire on the British batteries below them, while their own trenches and guns lay protected in reverse slope positions. The task of the British guns was to lift the attacking infantry across this desolate land—this meant defeating the German guns first. The problem was, how to concentrate sufficient guns into the salient to achieve the superiority needed and in full view of the enemy. Surprise was going to be very hard to achieve either in time or space. At Messines, the guns were assembled in secret and then they were shooting into a salient; at Ypres, they had to be assembled in full view and then they had to fire out of a salient. In the event, the Germans saw enough to warn them that something big was afoot and they were able to concentrate more artillery in the threatened sector.

General Headquarters proposed a design for battle which envisaged a succession of limited objectives but General Gough proposed to go as far as possible in the first rush; he hoped to reach a depth of 5,000 yards in eight hours. This would, however, put him beyond the range of all but his heaviest guns! Incredibly, Sir Douglas Haig supported Gough's plan; he did, however, order that the Gheluvelt Plateau and the massed German guns behind it should be a priority artillery task. It is even more incredible that, when this priority was not even mentioned in General Gough's plan, Sir Douglas Haig failed to intervene.

The German strength was growing fast. In June alone, ten new divisions reached their front at Ypres. The defences themselves were developed by Colonel von Lossberg in even greater depth than at Messines. There were three defensive zones, each 2,000-3,000 yards deep, called the 'forward', 'battle' and 'rear' zones. The rear edges of each were called the Albrecht, the Wilhelm and Flanders Lines. Forward battalions provided eight forward screens. As the attacks developed, these battalions were to mount immediate counter-attacks to destroy the first wave. As the disorganised British crossed the Albrecht Line, the forward regiments (brigades) were to attack, but out of range of the British field artillery. If this failed, reserve divisions were to counter-attack in depth. On a four mile front, there were four divisions, with six battalions in the forward zone and six more for counter-attack tasks in that zone. Behind them were a further fifteen battalions. The theme of the defence was that the British would meet increasingly strong resistance as they got further from their own guns. North of the river Lys, the Germans had twenty-five divisions supported by 1,500 guns.

Thus the problems facing the MGRA Fifth Army, Major-General H.C.C. Uniacke, were enormous. Air superiority was a basic essential, yet it had not been achieved when the artillery duel began in earnest on 12th June; indeed, it was not until the end of July that the British gained mastery of the air. The British, too, were short of guns. Many batteries were below strength. General Uniacke issued his plan on 30th June. It was based on the following principles:

a. Priority was to protect the infantry while consolidating on their objectives.
b. Enemy batteries which could provide defensive fire were to be bombarded with gas from Zero-Day minus one to Zero Day.
c. The preliminary bombardment was to last nine days.
d. Counter-battery fire was to reach a climax on Zero minus four and Zero minus one days.
e. Enemy trenches were to be destroyed by Zero minus four days.
f. Roads must not be shelled, to ease the subsequent move forward of the guns.
g. All wire cutting was to be done by mortars and howitzers to conceal the strength of the field guns.
h. The creeping barrage, which was to include shrapnel, was to start as close as possible to the British trenches and was to move at 100 yards in four minutes.There was to be one 18-pounder per fifteen yards of front and one heavy howitzer per fifty yards.
j. The protective barrage was to be placed 500 yards beyond each objective and was to search back and forward.
k. Prompt zone calls were arranged to be called for by air.
l. Field batteries were to advance beyond no-man's land and heavy batteries into it.
m. Balloons were to be established well forward.
n. Counter-battery artillery was to be organised in double groups, each with its own air flight from the Corps Squadron.

The Artillery Order of Battle of the divisional artilleries at Third Ypres was:

MGRA Fifth Army: Major-General H.C.C. Uniacke
II Corps: BGRA: Brigadier-General A.D. Kirby
BGHA: Brigadier-General D.F.H. Logan

8th Divisional Artillery CRA: Brigadier-General H.G. Lloyd
33 Brigade RFA—32nd, 33rd and 36th Field Batteries and 55th Howitzer Battery
45 Brigade RFA—1st, 3rd and 5th Field Batteries and 57th Howitzer Battery

18th Division Artillery CRA: Brigadier-General W. Evans
82 Brigade RFA—A, B and C Field and D Howitzer Batteries
83 Brigade RFA—A, B and C Field and D Howitzer Batteries

25th Division Artillery CRA: Brigadier-General K.J. Kincaid-Smith
110 Brigade RFA—A, B and C Field and D Howitzer Batteries
112 Brigade RFA—A, B and C Field and D Howitzer Batteries

30th Division Artillery CRA: Brigadier-General E.H. Stevenson
148 Brigade RFA—A, B and C Field and D Howitzer Batteries
149 Brigade RFA—A, B and C Field and D Howitzer Batteries

XIX Corps: BGRA: Brigadier-General W.B.R. Sandys
BGHA: Brigadier-General C.G. Pritchard

15th Division Artillery: CRA: Brigadier-General E.B. McNaghten
70 Brigade RFA—A, B and C Field and D Howitzer Batteries
71 Brigade RFA—A, B and C Field and D Howitzer Batteries

16th Division Artillery: CRA: Brigadier-General C.E.C.G. Charlton
177 Brigade RFA—A, B and C Field and D Howitzer Batteries
180 Brigade RFA—A, B and C Field and D Howitzer Batteries

36th Division Artillery: CRA: Brigadier-General F. Potts
123 Brigade RFA—A, B and C Field and D Howitzer Batteries
124 Brigade RFA—A, B and C Field and D Howitzer Batteries

55th Division Artillery: CRA: Brigadier-General A.M. Perreau
  275 Brigade RFA—A, B and C Field and D Howitzer Batteries
  276 Brigade RFA—A, B and C Field and D Howitzer Batteries

XVIII Corps: BGRA: Brigadier-General D.J.M. Fasson
                                      BGHA: Brigadier-General H.E.J. Brake

11th Division Artillery: CRA: Brigadier-General J.W.F. Lamont
  58 Brigade RFA—A, B and C Field and D Howitzer Batteries
  59 Brigade RFA—A, B and C Field and D Howitzer Batteries

39th Division Artillery: CRA: Brigadier-General G. Gillson
  174 Brigade RFA—A, B and C Field and D Howitzer Batteries
  186 Brigade RFA—A, B and C Field and D Howitzer Batteries

48th Division Artillery: CRA: Brigadier-General W. Strong
  240 Brigade RFA—A, B and C Field and D Howitzer Batteries
  241 Brigade RFA—A, B and C Field and D Howitzer Batteries

51st Division Artillery: CRA: Brigadier-General L.C.L. Oldfield
  255 Brigade RFA—A, B and C Field and D Howitzer Batteries
  256 Brigade RFA—A, B and C Field and D Howitzer Batteries

XIV Corps: BGRA: Brigadier-General A.E. Wardrop
                                      BGHA: Brigadier-General F.G. Maunsell

Guards Division Artillery: CRA: Brigadier-General F.A. Wilson
  74 Brigade RFA—A, B and C Field and D Howitzer Batteries
  75 Brigade RFA—A, B and C Field and D Howitzer Batteries

20th Division Artillery: CRA: Brigadier-General H.W.A. Christie
  91 Brigade RFA—A, B and C Field and D Howitzer Batteries
  92 Brigade RFA—A, B and C Field and D Howitzer Batteries

29th Division Artillery: CRA: Brigadier-General G.H.A. White
                                      then   Brigadier-General E.H. Stevenson
  15 Brigade RHA—B, L, 1st Warwick Batteries RHA and 460th Howitzer Battery
  17 Brigade RFA—13th, 26th and 92nd Field Batteries and D Howitzer Battery

38th Division Artillery: CRA: Brigadier W.A.M. Thompson
  121 Brigade RFA—A, B and C Field and D Howitzer Batteries
  122 Brigade RFA—A, B and C Field and D Howitzer Batteries

These thirty-two artillery brigades amounted to some 768 guns only! In addition, there were a further 2,400 guns, a further 400 batteries, a list too numerous to include here but consisting of the divisional artilleries not otherwise employed, Army Field Brigades and medium heavy and super heavy batteries. Such then was the enormity of the build up for battle. Those with knowledge of the difficulty that co-ordination of the fire of quite small numbers of guns caused in subsequent wars using modern means of radio, radar, computers and aircraft, will appreciate to the full the sheer marvel of the achievement of the artillery at Third Ypres. The commanders then had to rely on telephone cables, flags and heliographs, with some aircraft and only a very, very few rudimentary radios. The fact that the plans were made at all, passed to over 450 battery commanders and worked out, that guns were deployed, that ammunition was moved, dumped and checked for firing, are themselves in the realms of the miracle. As we sit back years later to think of the work of the Gunners of Third Ypres, we should appreciate the magnitude of their task and marvel at its execution.

As the day grew closer for the great attack, there were two diversions planned further south. At Lens, Second Army attacked on 28th June and, though they did distract German attention, the Germans were too convinced of the British intention to attack at Ypres to move troops away from there. It was planned that Fourth Army, under General Sir Henry Rawlinson, should also attack at Nieuport in Belgium on the 10th July, taking over from the French, using XV Corps of five divisions (1st, 32nd, 33rd, 49th and 66th). But before he could get under way, the Germans attacked between Lombartzyde and the coast, inflicting most severe casualties on the British. The Gunners alone lost some twenty-eight guns, while two battalions of 2nd Infantry Brigade were all but annihilated in that fateful battle. It did not, however, affect the preparations before Ypres.

The artillery duel, which started on 12th June, was conducted by the guns already in action. The problem now was to move this additional mass of artillery into action. Various systems were tried. For example, 110 Brigade RFA moved in on 8th July. Movement was only possible at night or in very overcast weather. All roads were constantly shelled. One officer and thirty men went forward to lay the positions and to receive ammunition (1,180 rounds per gun and 960 rounds per howitzer). Work was only possible at night, and even this work was constantly interrupted by enemy gun fire. For example, on the night 9th–10th July, nineteen men were wounded and three horses of the battery were killed. Nevertheless, the guns arrived safely on the night 13th July and registration and calibration, concealed by the fire of guns already in action, was completed on 14th July.

The plan was to attack on 25th July, but both General Gough and the French General Anthoine asked for a postponement. Sir Douglas Haig was loath to grant this because records showed that the chances of wet weather in early August were high. However, he agreed to a new zero day, on 31st July.

Meanwhile, the siege and heavy batteries, with their huge shire horses and caterpillar tractors, were moving into position. To give some idea—in II Corps area thirty-six batteries moved into the Dickebusch area; just west of Ypres stood the heavies of XIX Corps, with those of XVIII Corps around Brielen some 3,000 yards northwest of Ypres. Between Elverdinghe and Woesten were the great batteries of XIV Corps. Further forward the build up of 1,098 field guns, backed by 324 4.5-inch howitzers, was nearing completion. In II Corps area the batteries lay behind the woods, packed wheel to wheel in some cases, between Zillebeke and Verbrandenmolen. The thirty-two 18-pounder batteries of XIX Corps were crowded into the small area between Potijze and St Jean, literally lining the canal just north of Ypres. North of them was massed the field artillery of XVIII Corps just some 2,500 yards behind the forward trenches, with the guns of XIV Corps along the canal on the left. Each of the four infantry divisions of II Corps had nine extra artillery brigades in support, while the divisions of the other three corps had six. Thus, a division in II Corps had forty-four batteries or 264 field guns alone to support it.

Later records reveal that at this time the Germans had massed some 1,556 guns and howitzers which could bear on the Ypres salient and against this, by mid-July, the British had massed 2,868. Those students of history who wish to compare total figures of guns with numbers of batteries will be disappointed. They do not work out since many batteries had less than their six guns. Indeed, some were there in name only, having lost all their guns to make up losses during the opening duel.

By 16th July, this great duel of guns reached its climax. The Germans rained a merciless fire day and night on the exposed British batteries below them. They hurled every conceivable type of shell in a constant flow of devastation and swept the fire backward and forward so that none should escape. They drenched the gun areas with gas, using the dreaded mustard for the first time. The conditions in the batteries were appalling. Once located, they had to stay put—there was no room for alternative positions—and take it. They suffered terrible casualties, got no sleep or respite, and they felt upon themselves the full fury of war. Often in history the British had earned a reputation for sticking to their guns—they did it 'tween decks on men o' war, they did it in the Peninsula and at Waterloo, but never for so long under such conditions of terror as they did during those terrible days and nights of July 1917, before the Germans at Ypres. Fortunately, the German counter-battery techniques were inferior. Instead of applying a massive concentration on each battery in turn in a methodical pattern as each was located, they scattered their fire over large areas. Had they adopted this British technique, the tale might have been different. The gas was the worst. Many detachments were brought to near exhaustion by the strain of serving the guns hour after hour, day after day, night after night, while wearing gas masks. Nowhere were the conditions worse than at Zillebeke. The remains of the village made an easy target. It was occupied by several batteries which suffered terribly as the Germans bombarded it with heavy howitzers. It was here that Major Pilditch's batman had both legs blown to pulp and died quietly, saying "Oh that's alright then" when told that "the Major is alright". In the end the guns were withdrawn from the village.

At 'Hellfire Corner' outside the Menin Gate, where the Ypres-Roulers railway crossed the Menin road, some 600 yards south of Ypres, many a gallant driver died galloping full tilt past the fatal spot, his limbers bouncing behind him—to get supplies to his guns. One after another, at fifteen minute intervals, they ran the gauntlet of that terrible place, unloaded, then galloped back for another load. Such gallantry and steadiness earned great praise, for without them the guns could not have stayed in action.

Ypres in 1917 was a battle for the Gunners long before the infantry rose from their trenches on 31st July. It was truly magnificent how the batteries of the New Army, without any regulars to assist and advise, stuck to their tasks and to their guns in the truest traditions of The Regiment—The Regiment which was adding glory to its name in some of the finest hours of its long history.

But British practice and technique were telling. As a German battery was located, concentrations of four to six hundred 6, 8 and 9.2-inch shells rained upon it. Frequently this meant total destruction-it certainly meant withdrawal of the battery. It was, however, hard to achieve with Germans all concealed behind the ridge. For example, on 4th July, some 45 German batteries were neutralised in this way; again on the 8th and in bad weather a further 50 batteries were hit. On 13th July, twenty British batteries fired 3,718 shells on German positions at Zonnebeke. German prisoners subsequently said that all the batteries had been destroyed and the infantry billetted in the village had been wiped out. But, as the Gunners of each side struggled to overcome the other, success ebbed and flowed. On 16th July, 55th Battery 35 Brigade RFA had five guns hit and a week later the whole Brigade was forced to move, so fierce was the enemy attack. D Battery of 82

Brigade RFA had all its howitzers knocked out on 22nd July, suffering one officer killed, two wounded, four men killed and fourteen wounded. 83 Brigade had 130 officers and men killed or wounded on 23rd July, but somehow kept its guns in action. On 19th July, 148 Brigade fared little better. Three guns of A and two of C Battery, together with two howitzers of 465 Battery, were knocked out and more hit on 20th and 21st but, in spite of heavy gas shelling and mounting casualties, replacement guns were got into action on 29th.

Slowly, as July wore on, the British began to gain the upper hand. Often living and fighting in gas masks, rarely stopping for rest, the battle raged on. But accurate shooting and unflagging devotion to duty in conditions of hell were telling. The British system of shooting for destruction by accurate pounding beat the German system of gusts of fire and gas. On 25th July, Major-General Noel Birch was able to report a definite slackening of enemy fire. Subsequently it was learnt that, on the same day, Crown Prince Rupprecht reported that "German artillery losses of Group Wytschaete between Westhoek and the Menin Road had lost 50% of its heavy guns; 30% of its heavy howitzers; 17% of its mortars; 10% of its field guns". However, the guns behind Gheluvelt had not been mastered and this was later to affect the battle.

The Battle of Pilckem Ridge

In his diary for 30th/31st July 1917, the Master of Belhaven, commanding a battery at Ypres, records "It is now after midnight and I have just got zero hour and filled in the final details of the barrage tables. There are no fewer than 35 lifts, each involving a different range and angle for each gun. It would be simple enough if one had a room with a table and a good light to work with, but here in a mudhole with a guttering candle, it is very difficult indeed" . . . and later "Zero hour at last. We opened at 0350 hours this morning and have fired without stopping all day".

It was a dark, overcast morning on 31st July, as the infantry of Fifth Army rose from their trenches to follow the mightiest creeping barrage ever fired to that moment; never before and, indeed, never again did the British artillery fire such a fireplan. Two thirds of the field guns fired the creeping barrage, 732 guns at a rate of 4 rounds per gun per minute (24 tons of HE per minute or 1,500 tons per hour!). The other third and all the 4.5-inch howitzers fired the standing barrage on the German second line. When the creeping barrage got to within 200 yards of it, the standing barrage lifted. Back barrages behind the German second line were fired by the 6-inch howitzers and 60-pounders to break up counter-attacks and to smash machine guns firing at long ranges. At the same time, some 320 Vickers machine guns of the Machine Gun Corps, situated 500 yards behind the British forward trenches, fired just ahead of the creeping barrage.

The effects of the barrage varied. XIX Corps lost it as they dealt with strong points and pill-boxes in the assault. The Guards Division on the left of XIV Corps found it "magnificent". One snag was that, because of the weather (cloud base about 400 feet), aerial observation was impossible for British counter-battery fire. This enabled the Germans to maintain a heavy defensive barrage on Sanctuary and Château Woods, which also cut almost all cables and lines to the FOOs. Some pigeons got through, but the only news from the assault was by runners who

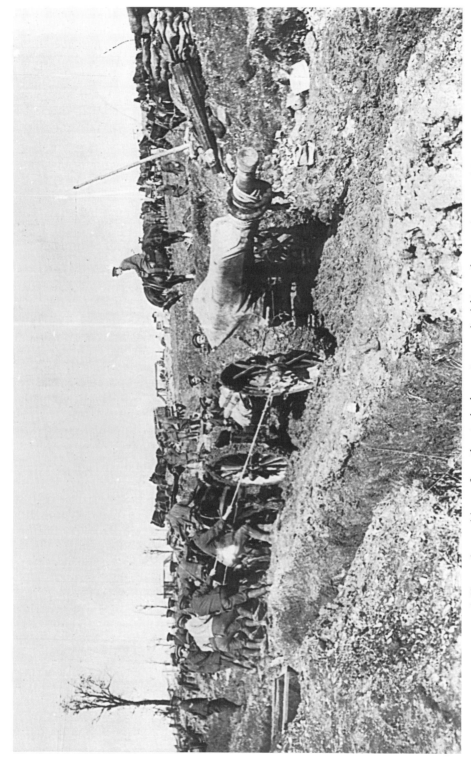

A 60-pounder requiring no fewer than twelve horses to move it; eight was the normal team. *(I.W.M.)*

sometimes took hours to get back, if indeed they ever did. In spite of its ferocity, the bombardment had failed to knock out a gigantic pill-box just north east of "Clapham Junction", on the Menin Road beyond Hooge. This held up the attack for some time. But, on balance, the fireplan was a success. By 0900 hours, the advance of the guns had started and some were in action in their new positions for the phase II fireplan. By 0930 hours, however, almost the whole ridge had fallen and at long last the German observers could no longer see the British guns. But resistance was stiff and General Gough realised that his rapid break-out would not be achieved;he must advance slowly and methodically after all. The main reason was the one feared by many artillerymen at the time. It was impossible to support an attack in great depth without moving the guns. Moving the guns over the devastation of no-man's land and maintaining communications was equally almost impossible. Before moving, and during the move, the enemy guns had to be kept silent. All this was too much for the equipment at the time, let alone because of the vastness of controlling the move of so many batteries. Communications during battle were still a problem. Virtually the only news that reached Corps headquarters from the attacking infantry came from the Gunners, and this was spasmodic. 164th Infantry Brigade reached its third objective before its divisional headquarters heard any news. The first news of the German counter-attack came from an FOO with '45th Infantry Brigade; this was at 1130 hours and reached Headquarters 15th Division at 1253 hours. By 1300 hours, drizzling rain settled in, blinding observation; the positions of forward infantry became unclear, FOOs lost touch and control of the guns became extremely difficult.

At 1400 hours, an intense German barrage fell on XVIII and XIX Corps, coming from the Zonnebeke-Gheluvelt area. It was supported by low flying aircraft bombing and machine gunning the British infantry, probably the first use of fighter ground attack aircraft operating in close co-operation with ground forces. Drenching rain began to fall, making artillery observation well nigh impossible, and the forward troops fell back. As the German counter-attack followed up, the pre-arranged protective barrage was fired by the British Gunners with such speed, accuracy and ferocity that the Germans broke and fled. Further left, as 51st Highland Division consolidated on the German second line, the Germans again counter-attacked and again the barrage smote them in the open and again they fled from the field. By evening, the rain was falling heavily—Sir Douglas Haig's misgivings were justified—slowly the field turned to thick mire, thick sucking mud—the mud of Passchendaele.

So ended the first day. A general advance of 3,000 yards had captured the enemy front and shattered nine divisions. It was not spectacular but it was a success. But the strength of the defence, and the Germans' ability to replace destroyed guns, had been underestimated. The bombardment had a terrible effect on movement, shell holes touched each other, filled with water and became almost impassable in places. But the great lesson of the first day of Third Ypres was that counter-battery fire must be continuous. Destruction of enemy guns and machine guns is probably the greatest service that can be given to the infantry after they reached their objective.

Protective barrages must be deep, the infantry must cling even closer to the creeping barrage and finally, the demands on the endurance of the gunners must not be too great. At Ypres, the labours of the artillery were as gruelling as those of the infantry and, judged by the casualties, almost as hazardous. Many detachments had almost no proper rest or relief from 16th to 31st July and were near total exhaustion at the time when they should have been most alert.

It now became clear that a second bombardment, to destroy the enemy guns yet again, was essential before operations could proceed. But the weather was bad, observation poor and most batteries were moving forward into the appalling conditions of no-man's land. Casualties mounted as the German guns pounded the exposed British guns. On 4th August they were so heavy that some brigades had to re-organise into two batteries only. Conditions at the guns were terrible, pouring rain, thick oozing mud capable of swallowing a man, a horse, or even a gun, made hopeless platforms. For shelter, a piece of corrugated iron over a water filled shell hole was all that could be done. Ammunition had to be carried forward by hand over duck-boards to the guns under constant shell and gas fire. The sheer courage and endurance shown by the exhausted, weary gunners at Third Ypres was as great as had ever been shown in the Regiment's history, for the horror of it went on and on without respite, without mercy, until death itself was merciful. Major the Master of Belhaven wrote "The mud is simply awful, worse I think than Winter. The ground is churned up to a depth of ten feet and is the consistency of porridge . . . the middle of the shell craters are so soft that one might sink out of sight . . . there must be hundreds of German dead buried here and now their own shells are re-ploughing the area and turning them up. While we were shooting last night I saw a horrid sight. A Gunner from another battery ran through my guns, he was crazed with shock and, holding a hand blown from his wrist, he ran into the darkness and mud shrieking, never to be seen again".

The Battle of Langemarck—16th to 18th August

Although Langemarck itself was captured, the battle was not a success from an artillery point of view. Since the tactics of the day demanded a thorough fireplan, it was essential to have time to prepare, and this was not given. The result was that many key points in the bombardment were not dealt with. Then, during the assault, because of the intense smoke of battle, the infantry's SOS signals could not be seen, and the bombardment of enemy counter-attacks either failed or was given too late. Surprisingly, too, although the weather and air situation were good, only one spotter aircraft was in the air. No attempt was made to use gas on the pill-boxes, and FOOs were unable to see preparations for the German counter-attacks because of the smoke. All this on XIX Corps front.

On XIV and XVIII Corps front, however, the planning was better and more thorough. Each division of XIV Corps was supported by a barrage fired by 108 18-pounders, 36 4.5-inch howitzers and four companies of machine guns. However, the ground taken was not vital to the Germans, who made no effort to recover it. The fighting for Inverness Copse was long and bitter and, though the Copse was taken, it had later to be abandoned. The problem of continuing the battle was then handed over to General Plumer and his Second Army.

The Battle of Lens: 15th to 17th August

Meanwhile near Lens, the First Army, commanded by General Horne, attacked with the Canadian Corps and conducted a brilliant attack to capture Hill 70. The battle illustrated yet again how a really well constructed fireplan, combined with the fighting elan of well trained infantry, was an unbeatable combination. The operation lasted from 15th to 17th August. FOOs moved right forward with the infantry and two seater spotter aircraft flew overhead. Some 240 calls for fire came from these aircraft and all were promptly and accurately answered.

The Canadian Corps Artillery was commanded by Brigadier-General E.W.B. Morrison, with Major A.F. Brooke (later Field Marshal Lord Alanbrooke) as his senior staff officer. Brigadier-General R.H. Massie commanded the Heavies, with Lieutenant-Colonel (later General) A.G.L. McNaughton as his counter-battery staff officer. It was a powerful team who thoroughly understood the application of artillery fire. Indeed, the preliminary bombardment of the German artillery was so systematic and thorough that 63 out of 102 German batteries were out of action at zero hour. It was significant, too, that some of the fireplan was predicted and, because of thorough calibration and the use of datum point shoots, the accuracy achieved was quite remarkable. The attack was carried out by 1st, 2nd, 3rd and 4th Canadian and 46th British Divisions and was entirely successful. The FOOs worked well forward and communications worked better than ever before during an attack. The Germans struck back with great ferocity but this massive artillery firepower shattered eighteen enemy counter-attacks with enormous losses. At the end of the day, Hill 70 was firmly held.

There then came a three week delay before General Plumer was ready to continue the offensive. There was a shortage of ammunition; vast quantities had been fired since the bombardment in June.

The Battle of Menin Road Ridge—20th to 25th September

The battle to come was to be based on the artillery plan. The Second Army plan said "success will depend primarily on the action of the Artillery". The advance was to consist of a series of methodical steps with limited objectives. Each division would advance on a front of 1,000 yards, with each objective no more than 1,500 yards away. The attack was to be carried out by both Second and Fifth Armies. Each objective was to be supported by 1,295 guns and howitzers of all sizes firing the creeping barrages. A further 1,830 guns were available for other tasks, being much of the artilleries of Third and Fourth Armies and many independent batteries. The concentration was the greatest yet, being one gun/howitzer per 5 yards of front. Not only this but, for the first time, the ratio between field and medium/heavy guns was $1:1\frac{1}{2}$, the highest proportion yet achieved. 3.5 million rounds were allotted for the first day of the assault alone, with a further 3.5 million rounds for the seven days preliminary bombardment! This time nothing was to be spared, the armies of Britain were to make one more enormous heave and burst out into the plains of Belgium to victory and it was to depend essentially on the Gunners and their power to overwhelm the German divisions opposite them.

New artillery tactics were to be tried. Massive counter-battery bombardments were directed initially, not on the guns themselves, but all around them. The guns, now located, could not move easily and, in any case, need not move, since those that were still intact were to be destroyed 24 hours before zero hour. Thus the Germans would not have time to replace destroyed batteries and have them ready

for the battle proper. The creeping barrage, too, was new in design. There would
be five lines or belts of fire. The first, line 'A' and nearest our own troops, was fired
by 18-pounders with one third of them superimposed so that they could be swung
off the barrage onto opportunity targets and leave no gap in the barrage itself.
Line 'B' was 200 yards further on and was engaged by 4.5-inch howitzers, using
Fuze 106 to give more penetration, and the rest of the 18-pounders. Then came
Line 'C', again 200 yards further on, fired entirely by machine-guns. Next, and a
further 200 yards, Line 'D' was fired by 6-inch howitzers and next again, Line 'E',
also 200 yards distant, fired by 60-pounders, 8 and 9.2-inch howitzers. This gave a
depth of 1,000 yards. 50% of the 18-pounder ammunition was to be HE, with 25%
of the fuzes set to 'delay'. The pace was to be slow, getting slower as the attack
developed and with a pause every 500 yards. Standing barrages, 2,000 yards
further on, were to be fired continuously to break up counter-attacks and to
isolate the forward enemy trenches. In addition, there were smaller barrages in
depth, to fill gaps and to thicken fire on counter-attack approaches. More were on
call as SOS tasks, to protect the infantry as they consolidated. All this called for a
massive amount of detailed work at battery positions. Guns each had dozens of
tasks which had to be calculated, plotted, recorded and prepared for use. There
must be no error, and speed in response to calls for fire was vital. The conditions
in command posts were appalling and Gun Position Officers (GPOs) worked in
conditions of wet, bad light and enemy shell and gas bombardment. At Ypres,
there were hardly any mistakes and the gun fire was more successful than ever, a
great tribute to these young, inexperienced officers who controlled and directed
the fire of the guns in such conditions.

So successful was British counter-battery fire that the Germans deployed their
guns at extreme range to avoid what they could and yet be able to fire defensive
fire tasks on the attacking British infantry. This meant that to support an attack in
any depth at all, and deal with the enemy guns, British artillery had to be deployed
well forward. General Plumer personally stressed that "continuous counter-
battery fire was of primary importance to the progress of the infantry".

But the infantry, too, were adopting new tactics. Two lines of skirmishers were
to act as advance guard right up behind the barrage. Platoon groups followed to
deal with strong points and next came "mopping up" groups to garrison the areas
cleared and finally, companies moved close behind as reserves immediately
available to local commanders. Signals to the infantry were built into barrages.
The sudden appearance of three or four rounds of smoke might give notice of a
pause or that the barrage was to roll forward and the infantry might rise again and
renew the advance. Changes in direction were similarly indicated and pauses when
all firing would cease for one or two minutes would indicate the start of the new
phase. All this took masses of ammunition. To give some idea of the numbers of
shells involved, in 1917 alone 47,992,000 18-pounder rounds were produced and
38,068,000 were fired.

Again elaborate communications plans were made, including balloons, pigeons,
deeply buried wire and some radio. Co-ordination between aerial observers, FOOs
and balloon observers was perfected; survey was carefully checked and detailed
plans to meet SOS tasks were worked out with the infantry. A careful plan was
made to hold guns ready to react immediately on any German battery which
opened fire once the assault began. For example, covering suspected enemy

battery positions behind the Gheluvelt Plateau were 222 British guns, whose sole task was to engage them as they opened fire. This happened time and again. On zero day, 20th September, the counter-battery battle had been well and truly won and German defensive fire all day was thin and disjointed. It resulted in the almost complete success of the infantry assault and the defeat of all German counter-attacks.

The barrage was described as "magnificent both in accuracy and volume". It carried the infantry forward and took the German outposts by complete surprise. The heavy shells included in it had a stunning effect on the garrisons of pill-boxes and machine gunners, many of whom were easily captured and found too dazed to fight. The infantry pushed on. As they reached their second objective, the great protective barrage rolled out 2,000 yards beyond them, then rolled back towards them, smashing two counter-attacks which it caught in the open as it did so. Crown Prince Rupprecht wrote in his diary that day that the British barrage was so dense and unbroken that it was quite impossible to launch counter-attacks through it. One tried to start at 0800 hours, but was so pounded that, when it eventually started late in the afternoon, it petered out under the rain of shells which met it.

Success was almost equal on Fifth Army front. However, the adoption of a surprise hurricane bombardment, instead of a seven day preparatory fireplan, had allowed the Germans to cause considerable damage to the British guns. By noon on 21st August, nineteen 60-pounders and forty-seven 18-pounders had been lost. Moreover, strong points were not destroyed, as these required protracted and systematic shelling to knock them out. The Eagle Trench was not hit by the guns and an attempt to deal with it by hurling blazing oil from 290 projectors, the forerunners of the flame thrower, also failed. Thus, the lesson was learnt that an attack against heavy fortifications must consist of a fireplan capable of establishing a breach and of protecting the advancing infantry.

Second Army, meanwhile, paid great attention to its fireplan and an elaborate plan was made to ensure that the Gunners knew at all times the line that our troops had reached. But it was not easy, cable was cut to pieces, radios were still too cumbersome to be used in the forward areas, but visual signalling, especially the Lucas lamp, worked well and the twelve pigeons issued to the FOOs of each divisional artillery proved most useful. General Plumer was also concerned to avoid exhaustion on the guns and insisted on arrangements being made to rest detachments, a most wise precaution. As the attack developed, the sky cleared and the sun shone and the close co-operation which had been laid down between the Gunner and the RFC paid dividends. Seven squadrons of the RFC were allotted to watch for counter-attacks, to locate targets and to control fire. Thus, as German units advanced, they were seen while still in column and were engaged by barrages from heavy and siege guns with great success. At 1902 hours, a counter-attack was clearly about to be launched by two divisions. The SOS signal of red, green and yellow launched together was clearly seen and, for nearly an hour, a massive concentration of artillery fell upon them and destroyed them until nothing was left and no further attack developed. It was the same right along the front; everywhere, the concentrated fire of the guns and machine guns broke up every attack. At 1800 hours, an attack developed in front of 58th Division. A machine gun concentration forced the enemy to spread out at 1,500 yards then, at

650 yards, rifles and Lewis guns joined in and the Germans began to drop fast, though survivors pushed on gallantly. Finally, at only 150 yards, the waiting guns were unleashed and the barrage burst among them. The effect, said an eye witness, "was beyond description and the enemy stampeded and fled the field". The German accounts of the fighting speak of the terrible artillery and machine gun fire. Some companies were wiped out and many were reduced to 30% and 40% strength.

Never had guns been used so effectively as the infantry consolidated; the German defences had been beaten and the Gunners could claim much of the credit for doing so. But the losses to the Gunners had not been light; on that day alone, 80 officers lay dead and 1,246 gunners died on their guns to ensure that no call of fire went unanswered. In addition, almost 2,000 gunners were wounded that day. But a victory it was, a magnificent victory, and morale was high in the British batteries that night. The FOOs were the heroes of the infantry trenches, for without them and their deadly fire victory would never have been possible. A word here for the signallers. For the first time at the end of an attack, the FOOs kept in touch and this was entirely due to the devotion to duty shown by the linesmen, often in the open and under shell fire, who kept on repairing the vital nerve link for victory. It was here, in the mud of Passchendaele, that the great tradition— jealously guarded by all FOOs to this day, that they are always through to the guns—was born.

The Battle of Polygon Wood—26th September to 3rd October 1917

On 20th September and in fine weather with a drying wind blowing, the guns moved forward to get well within range for the next attack on Polygon Wood. Much work was done by the Engineers and, without their plank roads, movement would not have been possible over the torn, terrible, shell-ridden ground. Fortunately, a German counter-attack then being planned was delayed until 25th September; had it come earlier many batteries would have been on the move. As it was, it was stopped. It was carried out by a single German division supported by 20 heavy and 44 field batteries, one of the heaviest artillery attacks ever given in conjunction with one division. But the British Gunners smashed the assaulting infantry and cut off all hope of reinforcement and the Germans were forced to give all ground won. They did, however, severely maul the British 33rd Division of X Corps. But again the Germans reinforced their guns so that the Gheluvelt Plateau was, by 26th September, defended by some ten divisional artilleries, probably 500 guns.

One feature of the battle was the German defended locality known as the 'Quadrilateral', south of the Menin road. It was given a special bombardment but the defences were so deep that, after it had been overrun, the Germans disgorged machine guns and infantry in such numbers that, even after bitter hand to hand fighting in which the guns could play no part, the position had to be given up. It was a new tactic and a real problem to the Gunners. But elsewhere, the attack was a success and again the anti-counter-attack barrages were successful. Gunner-infantry co-operation reached a new peak and it is interesting to note that many infantry objectives were designated solely to seize ground giving good observation for the FOOs. The result was the rapid destruction of all German counter-attacks

Heavy Artillery on the move. From the original by H Septimus Power. (*R.A.I.*)

before they could be launched, a great achievement and one which has never received the recognition it deserves. The strain was beginning to tell again in the gun lines; some barrages were maintained for over twelve hours without stopping at high rates of fire; the labour of handling the ammunition was enormous. The 18-pounders of Second and Fifth Armies alone fired 1,047,385 rounds (almost 9,000 tons) between 23rd–30th September; even the 9.2-inch howitzers managed 43,152 rounds in the same period. But casualties were high, particularly in FOOs;—119 officers and 2,292 other ranks were killed during this period. Victory is, however, infectious and, weary and worn out as the batteries were, morale was high, the break must come soon; one last effort and the way would be clear! Throughout the battle, the FOOs kept watch continuously night and day with no rest and never failed. Never had the Royal Regiment more cause to be proud of its subaltern officers, who directed its devastating fire with such success. But there was also gallantry on the guns, too much to be recorded in full, but perhaps none so much as in 134th Battery RFA when, after a devastating bombardment during the night, only Acting Lance Bombardier Fisher and Gunner Monchin remained. They were alone, except for the dead; they *were* the battery; they had inherited its traditions, its ideals, its will to win. As orders for the next barrage came down, they prepared for it and as best as two men with one gun could do, they opened fire at the appointed hour and continued to do so until more men arrived, and only then did the gallant Fisher agree to being taken away for, throughout, he was suffering acutely from gas. This story, perhaps more than any, illustrates the true nature of the Gunner and his training to fight to the end for his gun.

The Battle of Broodseinde—4th October 1917

Sir Douglas Haig now reckoned that two more mighty thrusts, first on 4th October, then on 10th October, and his cavalry would at last be able to charge a broken enemy. Reserve brigades were prepared to break out, lightly equipped and supported by two 60-pounder batteries, two 6-inch howitzer batteries and four 18-pounder brigades.

When the preparations for the battle began, the British artillery was feeling the strain of continuous fighting. Many guns had been knocked out and few replaced. In September, 350 18-pounders had been lost with a further 249 in October. Many batteries had only three or four guns and batteries were broken up to keep others up to strength. Nevertheless, some 796 heavy and siege and 1,548 field guns and howitzers were ready in Second Army. Of these, the two Anzac Corps had 985 guns for an attack frontage of 5,000 yards.

A powerful counter-attack was delivered by the Germans on 30th September, but the infantry gallantly withstood it, finally breaking it with their own weapons. For a whole day the Germans pressed their attacks, but accurate SOS fire from guns and machine guns and intense rifle fire broke their attacks so that their next attack, planned for the 3rd, had to be postponed to the 4th October, so clashing with the British assault.

The barrage opened 150 yards in front of the forming up tapes, paused for three minutes and then moved forward 100 yards every four minutes to the first objective. During the pause it searched 1,000 yards for counter-attacks, then at zero plus 130 minutes, it crept on a further 1,500 yards to the final objective. Here, there was a massive protective barrage and a deep back barrage fired by the heavies. Counter-battery fire was superimposed. It was successful beyond everyone's hopes. 4th October was a black day for the German Army. Massive numbers of enemy dead were found in the trenches, some companies losing 95% of their strength. The German artillery was severely handled; some 9,559 targets had been registered by the British, most of them enemy gun positions, and many were destroyed on 4th October.

So hopes ran high that day; the attacks were scoring successes even greater than before and German prisoners, terrified and shaken, moved back behind the lines. Yet so soon, indeed within a few hours, the whole picture changed. With a victory so great that the end of the war might be in sight—the weather broke. First a drizzle, then the clouds descended and then came the cold drenching rain which lasted for two days, producing the mud, the mud that still lives in the memories of all who were at, or who have read of, Passchendaele. However, with the prize of victory so near, Sir Douglas Haig determined to press on in spite of the weather. The conditions soon became appalling. Nowhere was it worse than in the gun lines. Guns sank and disappeared, plank roads disappeared, guns could not move. Even double platforms made of great baulks of timber sank after one or two rounds were fired. Already many guns were 6,000 yards back and valiant efforts were made to get them forward, and men and horses sank for ever into the great boiling quagmire of Passchendaele. Ammunition had to be carried forward by hand and, where possible, with pack animals; journeys normally of an hour often took sixteen to complete. Even then every shell had to be cleaned before firing. Men were wet, nowhere could they get dry, they had to remain wrapped in wet muddy blankets. A few got tin hip-baths 'to float' on the mud. Sickness spread and numbers dwindled. When 66th Division tried to advance, only 25 18-pounders were in range of the battle. Yet impossible as the task was, the effort *was* made and in a nightmare of mud and terror.

Poelcappelle—9th October 1917

In these conditions it is not surprising that, in general, when the infantry gallantly rose yet again to attack at Poelcappelle on 9th October, the barrage was erratic. HE shell buried into the mud had little effect, wire was not cut and counter-battery fire was ineffective. Even so, XIV Corps in Fifth Army reported a good barrage and did well but on XVIII Corps front the infantry, smitten by heavy machine gun fire, lost the barrage and failed to advance at all.

The First Battle of Passchendaele—12th October 1917

Conditions now became quite frightful, wounded lay unattended around the guns and pill-boxes, and trenches were full of them. Snipers did great execution on the survivors and the supply of food and ammunition became virtually impossible. New wire was discovered covering the Flanders One Line and the chance of a successful attack appeared beyond all hope in the trenches. Yet Sir Douglas Haig believed on 11th October that his troops "were practically through the enemy defences". This ignorance of the truth and of the terrible misery of the forward troops cannot really be forgiven. Reports from the front appear to have been ignored; indeed, the CRA of the New Zealand Division said he could not take part in the attack on 12th October, since it was impossible to move the batteries across the Steenbeck. The rain continued as the heavies tried to move up to take part in the attack. The Germans reported that British counter-battery fire had almost ceased and, encouraged by this, they renewed their own, particularly at night and with gas adding even more to the horrors of the mud. The enemy had been falling back onto good ground, good roads, more guns and plenty of ammunition, while the Second and Fifth Armies lay wallowing in the mire of Passchendaele before them. Except on the left where the conditions were better, the attack which went in on 12th October had little success. The barrage was poor and the gallant infantry, in conditions if anything even worse, had little chance of success. Sadly, the truth began to dawn on Sir Douglas Haig that his chance of victory had passed, yet he was determined to press on, partly to distract attention from Cambrai where preparations for battle had now started, and partly to improve the Ypres position for the winter by capturing Passchendaele and Westroosebeke.

The Second Battle of Passchendaele—26th October to 10th November 1917

The problem again was to move the guns forward to within 2,500 yards of the enemy's forward positions by 22nd October. There were six 6-inch howitzer batteries, two 60-pounder batteries and three 18-pounder brigades to move into positions near Windmill Hill. Four Anzac brigades of 18-pounders were handed over to the Canadians and these were to move to positions behind the Gravenstafel spur with 8,000 tons of ammunition. The weather did improve but the mud remained. Plank roads were made and, by a Herculean effort, all were in action by 21st October.

As the long battle ground on to its tortured end, the horrors of mustard gas and oil and a sneezing gas, which forced men to remove their masks, were added to the mud, cold and shortage of food. Gas lay in thick clouds in low areas and the battlefield took on a weird likeness to an artist's impression of hell—for such it was. But the grim, dogged courage and determination of British, Australian and Canadian persisted through conditions of horror never before experienced by men in battle.

Meanwhile, the Gunners had a new problem. The Germans had withdrawn to their next main line, Flanders Two, some 800 yards back, leaving only small outposts and patrols in front of it. A massive defensive barrage would fall in this area once the patrols had been withdrawn. The main line would be held at all costs and be re-taken by counter-attacks if lost at any point. All this meant having the guns well forward to deal with enemy artillery. However, British counter-battery fire, using a great deal of gas at zero hour on 26th October, temporarily neutralised the German batteries and spoilt their barrage. In the Canadian Corps area (they had taken over from II Anzac Corps), the infantry managed to follow their barrage so closely and consolidate so quickly that they captured all objectives on the first day with relatively light casualties. In XIV and XVIII Corps of the Fifth Army, the story was different. The infantry, advancing on lower ground, could only flounder forward in the dense mud, in some cases taking a yard a minute, and failed to reach their objectives. But, on 30th October, an excellent barrage carried the Canadians to the outskirts of Passchendaele itself; here they consolidated and beat off some five counter-attacks. Then, on 6th November, with another "splendid barrage", they swept through Passchendaele and consolidated beyond it. A German counter-attack was smothered by guns before it could develop. On 10th November, by advancing in a rain storm, the Canadians improved their position, taking a further 500 yards.

By this time some five British divisions, under General Plumer, were ordered to Italy and the preparations for the battle of Cambrai were nearing completion, so Sir Douglas Haig decided to halt the Flanders campaign. Though the great battle of Third Ypres was now over, the great roar of the guns could not stop yet. There were many more artillery fights until the end of November. In many ways, Ypres was one of the greatest battles of all time; had it occurred in isolation, in the manner of the 18th and 19th Century wars, it would have been greater and mightier than any contender. Waterloo, Austerlitz, Alamein or even Stalingrad would have been small by comparison. As it is, Ypres was one battle in a great war and as such it loses its individuality and uniqueness. But it was, nevertheless, a great battle, great in numbers, great in complexity, great in co-ordination, great in gallantry, great in the overcoming of adversity; though not the longest battle of the war—it lasted 105 days (the Somme 142, Verdun 304), it was one of the most intensive, continuous periods of fighting ever recorded.

The end came none too soon for the Gunners. The strain on the men and horses in the batteries was extreme, the constant bombardment for months on end, never out of the line in the most terrible conditions, was affecting the new inexperienced artillerymen fresh from England. Efforts were made to rest the Gunners, but little actually happened on the gun positions. There were continuous calls for fire which had to be answered day and night, week after week, as the battle moved relentlessly on and on. The fact that it was done, that with few exceptions the Gunners did all that was demanded of them, that indeed they very nearly achieved a great and mighty victory, is one of the greatest feats in the annals of The Royal Regiment. Perhaps it is right that today no battery bears the honour title "Ypres 1917", for it is an honour belonging to so many batteries in The Regiment, a jealously guarded and privileged honour enabling those who were there to say later with pride "I fought with the guns at Ypres in 1917".

The Germans admitted their "feeling of inferiority to the artillery of their opponents". In truth, the British gunnery was shown to be superior both technically and tactically. It was the use of the guns against the varying German defensive measures which did more than anything to blast through them.

But what of the lessons of this great battle? They were many and were carefully discussed by Artillery commanders. First, map or predicted shooting was not successful until the shooting was proved against a known datum point. Once this could be hit and a correction for the day, indeed the hour, established, then the fire could be swung accurately backward and forward across the battlefield without observation. Second, special observers must be detailed to deal only with enemy guns which must be neutralised during an attack. Third, barrage orders must reach batteries some twelve hours before zero hour and thereafter alterations must be minimal. Fourth, protective barrages must be ready to deal with counter-attacks from any direction once the objectives were taken. Fifth, the rate of the

Army's advance was determined by the time taken to move guns and ammunition forward. Sixth, all methods of communication must be available to FOOs and time spent perfecting visual signalling techniques paid dividends. Finally, labour must be available to help the guns forward.

Yet there is even more to Third Ypres than this. Three times the Germans were forced to re-organise their defensive tactics, each time because the British guns outwitted them. There can be no denying the extreme gallantry and courage of the infantry at Ypres and this account has not done them full justice. Without them there would have been no advance, no defeat of the enemy, but the battle was so much an artillery battle. Whether this was tactically correct or not is not the question, it was the fire of the guns which dominated all. It was notable at Ypres that, when artillery fire was absent or very bad, the infantry almost always failed; often by their sheer gallantry they recovered something when the artillery fire went wrong, but they could not get far or hold on until the guns were again ready. Indeed, Ypres proved how true co-operation between infantry and gunners could always win the day. Ypres proved also the fallacy of the French doctrine; the guns could not conquer alone nor could the infantry overrun defences unshaken by bombardment. Ypres was a siege operation on the most massive scale, and it was conducted against immensely strong concrete defences developed in great depth over three years. Surprise was not possible, the Germans could foresee every move. Yet slowly, the British gunnery tactics first drove the German guns back to extreme ranges and finally perfected ways of keeping them neutralised during the infantry assault. Barrages in great depth of many different types, each with its own mission, were successful. But the strain on the endurance of the Gunners was great. No infantry commander would allow his Gunners to rest, nor would he move without them, a great compliment indeed but, at Ypres in 1917, it came near to preventing artillery action at all, so great was the fatigue.

So near, so very near to great success, the Gunners came out well from Third Ypres; they had so nearly done it, so nearly defeated the German defences, only to be defeated in the end by the combination of the Germans *and* the weather. They could deal with either alone but combined they were too much. The Gunner at Ypres knew that his infantry comrade was bearing an equal or greater share of the horror and he would not leave him in the lurch. Whatever should happen, the men of the British regiments must hear the comforting sound of their own shells overhead. Somehow, against seemingly impossible odds, the guns must be moved forward to continue this vital task. At no time, in no battle, have Gunners fought better than did the men of those batteries at Third Ypres; their example, their courage will forever live in the annals of The Regiment, the Regiment for whose honour so many gave all they had.

Heavy Draught horse team. From the original by Lucy Kemp Welch. The larger equipments required horses such as these, smaller guns were drawn by Light Draught animals. *(R.A.I.)*

CHAPTER 18

The Guns at Cambrai —
20th to 28th November 1917

See Map 32

Although tanks had been tried in battle before, it was at Cambrai that they were first used in numbers large enough to affect the battle. Much has been written about them, and Cambrai is now remembered as the first great tank battle of all time. But there was another side to it. Even this early tank contest showed that tanks alone could not win; to do so they needed infantry and they needed guns. The story of the guns at Cambrai is fascinating on many counts. New artillery tactics were used for the first time, and co-operation with the new tanks was worked out. But strangest of all, it was a Gunner who planned the battle in the first place.

On 4th August, Brigadier-General H. Elles, commanding the new Tank Corps, and his Chief of Staff, Lieutenant-Colonel J.F.C. Fuller, submitted a plan to Third Army HQ for a surprise attack by tanks, with no artillery support. A few days later, Brigadier-General H.H. Tudor, CRA 9th Division, submitted a similar plan involving the tanks cutting lanes through the wire, and the artillery would bombard without any previous registration, and so achieve surprise. This was an entirely new proposal for the use of artillery. General Byng, Commander Third Army, approved the idea and agreed to enlarge its scope. The Tudor plan was put forward to GHQ, where it was finally approved on 13th October.

The idea was to achieve complete surprise by delivering a massive barrage onto the enemy at zero hour with no prior bombardment or registration, and to follow this up with infantry, and finally tanks, to clear up the position and to consolidate the gains. In outline, it was to be the forerunner of the battles of the Second World War and in essence it is still the basic concept in conventional (i.e. non-nuclear) operations. But in 1917 it was new and the problems were not easy to resolve. That it could even be contemplated at all illustrated the advances made in artillery techniques. First, it was necessary to 'survey-in' all guns and targets onto the same grid to ensure that all were located in precise sympathy, one with another. All barrels of all guns when laid on the same bearing must be precisely parallel; no easy task when hundreds of guns are involved. "Bearing Pickets" were established, as indeed they had been on the Somme and before, so the drills were known. This work was done by Field Survey Companies of the Royal Engineers. Next came the problem of fixing the targets. This was not so easy but, provided a good grid reference could be obtained and transferred to an accurate blank map—an artillery board—on which the guns were already located, an accurate bearing and range could be measured. We read of measures being taken to eliminate inaccuracy through warping of the artillery board covers for the first time. These drills remained standard until the artillery boards gave way to plotters in the late 1950s, thirty-three years later.

Lieutenant (later Professor) W.L Bragg completed his work on electrically controlled Sound Ranging Sections and, by mid-1917, he was fixing enemy guns to an accuracy of 90%. Lieutenant Bragg had also adapted his instruments to be able to measure the velocity of shells on discharge, thus indicating their variation from normal. The first calibration ranges were established, thus enabling guns to apply a correction to their sights before firing and ensuring that all would fire truly to the map; a big step forward. Methods of providing meteorological conditions were already in use. Thus, provided work was accurately and correctly carried out at the gun position, it should be possible for guns to hit targets without prior registration. A subsequent study of German records shows that the Germans were just beginning to get to grips with this problem in March 1918 (Die Deutsche Artillerie by Georg Bruchmüller, page 18), so they were not prepared for it in 1917. (See Annex L for Sound Ranging in France 1914–18 by Sir Lawrence Bragg).

The Gunners were worried and proposed to register some guns before zero hour, concealing the fire in the normal daily pattern of shooting, but General Byng personally forbade such action; he was determined to achieve surprise. It is to the great credit of Major B.F.E. Keeling, RE, that the necessary survey was in fact completed. Work on the northern sector was completed by 15th November, but it was a race against time in the south. By working day and night it was just done, the line being finally carried to the sights of a 9.2-inch railway gun near Metz a few minutes before the gun opened fire at zero hour on 20th November!

The plan for the battle was to break through the Hindenburg Line, seize the canal crossings at Masnières and Marcoing and to capture the Masnières-Beaurevoir line beyond. Next was the clearing of the Cambrai–St. Quentin Canal, Sensèe River and Canal du Nord position. The Third Army was to attack with sixteen divisions, with three more in reserve, together with three tank brigades and the Cavalry Corps. III Corps and part of IV Corps were to attack on a 10,000 yard front from Bonavis Ridge to the Canal du Nord. They were to seize the first objective, the Blue Line (the enemy's outpost line, including the villages of Ribecourt and Havrincourt), then the second objective, the Brown Line, which included the enemy support system and the town of Flesquières. Finally, the crossings at Masnières and Marcoing were to be captured to clear the way for IV Corps to seize the Bourlon Ridge. Bourlon itself must be captured on the first day so that the cavalry could then be passed through.

The Divisional Artilleries involved were:

III Corps   BGRA: Brigadier-General T.A. Tancred
                       BGHA: Brigadier-General A.E.J. Perkins

6th Divisional Artillery; 2 and 24 Brigades RFA
12th Divisional Artillery; 62 and 63 Brigades RFA
20th Divisional Artillery; 91 and 92 Brigades RFA
29th Divisional Artillery; 15 Brigade RHA and 17 Brigade RFA
2nd and 3rd Tank Brigades (204 tanks)

IV Corps   BGRA: Brigadier-General J.G. Geddes
                          BGHA: Brigadier-General T.E. Marshall

36th Divisional Artillery; 153 and 173 Brigades RFA
51st Divisional Artillery; 255 and 256 Brigades RFA
56th Divisional Artillery; 280 and 281 Brigades RFA
62nd Divisional Artillery; 310 and 312 Brigades RFA
1 Cavalry Division Artillery—7 Brigade RHA (H, I and Y Batteries)
1st Tank Brigade (120 tanks)

VI Corps   BGRA: Brigadier-General J.G. Rotton
                          BGHA: Brigadier-General H. de T. Phillips

3rd Divisional Artillery; 40 and 42 Brigades RFA
16th Divisional Artillery; 177 and 180 Brigades RFA
34th Divisional Artillery; 152 and 160 Brigades RFA

VII Corps   BGRA: Brigadier-General K.K. Knapp
                          BGHA: Brigadier-General F.H. Metcalfe

24th Divisional Artillery; 106 and 107 Brigades RFA
25th Divisional Artillery; 110 and 112 Brigades RFA

In Reserve. V Corps BGRA: Brigadier-General R.P. Benson
                          BGHA: Brigadier-General A.M. Tyler

Guards Divisional Artillery; 74 and 75 Brigades RFA
40th Divisional Artillery; 178 and 181 Brigades RFA
59th Divisional Artillery; 295 and 296 Brigades RFA

The Cavalry Corps

2nd Cavalry Divisional Artillery; 3 Brigade RHA (D, E and J Batteries)
3rd Cavalry Divisional Artillery; 4 Brigade RHA (C, G and K Batteries)
4th Cavalry Divisional Artillery; 16 Brigade RHA (The Chestnut Troop, Q and U Batteries)

In all, together with sixteen batteries of GHQ troops and eleven batteries from Third Army resources, a total of 1,003 guns and howitzers.

The instructions for the battle were issued in three instalments on 29th October, 10th and 14th November. The first stressed the advantages of predicted fire, stating that gun positions could be much further forward, were unlikely to be located and could therefore cover a longer advance without moving forward. A wider selection of targets would be available and the effect of the heavy and siege guns would be greater and more accurate. This instruction also went into great detail about calibration, referring to the III Corps calibration range at Quinconce and the IV Corps range at Fricourt. Guns and howitzers were to be grouped into batteries according to their muzzle velocities, thus ensuring that in one battery all guns shot together. One important policy decision was laid down, one which was later to effect the outcome of the battle. *This was that enemy guns were to be neutralised only, and no attempt was to be made to destroy them.* Intelligence sources showed that there were in any case only thirty-four German guns in range of the attack area. These were nine batteries of the *54th Division* deployed between Havrincourt and La Vacquerie. The order stated that, at zero hour, all 60-pounders were to open on the German guns with gas shell, then to switch to known reserve areas near Crevecoeur, Masnières, Marcoing, Cantaing and

Noyelles, while the 6-inch guns continued to bombard the guns. Rates of fire were laid down and again it was stressed that there was to be no pre-registration of targets. Smoke was to be used on the flanks and to blind enemy observation on the Havrincourt–Flesquières Ridge. The barrage was not to creep but to lift from one objective to the next. The 13 and 18-pounders were to fire one third shrapnel, with long corrector giving a 50% graze, one third HE and one third smoke. Delay fuzes were to be used up to 3,500 yards but no delay beyond. The proportion of smoke was to depend on weather conditions and it was arranged that at midnight before zero hour, Army HQ was to send out a signal saying "Fire full ration", "Fire half ration" or "No smoke". Meteor signals were to be sent out every two hours. Zero hour (0620 hours 20th November) and zero + 2 hours thirty minutes were to be marked by a salvo of smoke (or shrapnel, if "no smoke" had been ordered). At 1020 hours, the barrage covering the second objective was to stop to allow exploitation. If possible, smoke barrages would also be fired across the spur east of Bantouzelle, along the east edge of Havrincourt, in front of Lateau Wood and Flesquières and on the Premy Chapel spur.

For the first time, a comprehensive air defence plan was made. Twenty-eight anti-aircraft guns were deployed in a chequer-board manner, the forward edge of which covered some 3,500 yards ahead of the British front trenches. Two sections were held ready to move forward and cover the advance.

Comprehensive orders and routes were given for the subsequent move forward of guns and ammunition. It was well known that this was the weakest part of the plan. Gaps through the wire were to be cut by the Gunners where they could not follow the tanks, and some 700 fascines were issued to batteries to fill in trenches and to get the guns across.

Third Army instruction number 19 specifically laid down that a Heavy Artillery Group, consisting of one 60-pounder battery and one 6-inch battery under its own headquarters, should be allotted to each leading division. It stressed how the use of even a single 9.2-inch or 8-inch howitzer "would frequently be the quickest and always the least expensive way of expelling the enemy from a village or strong point which could not be by-passed". Accordingly, a 60-pounder battery and 6-inch battery were placed under command of Brigadier-General E.H. Stevenson, CRA 29th Division, for exploitation beyond the Hindenburg Line to support the passage of the Masnières-Marcoing line. This was to be carried out by the three brigades of the Division, each supported by a field artillery brigade. Positions for these brigades were selected from the map as follows:

15 Brigade RHA (B, L, the Warwickshire and 460th Howitzer Batteries) about 3,000 south west of Les Rues Vertes.

17 Brigade RFA (13th 26th 92nd and D Howitzer Batteries) about 1,800 yards south west of Marcoing Copse.

16 Brigade RHA (The Chestnut Troop, Q and U Batteries) about 3,300 yards south west of Nine Wood.

The Artillery problem of covering the break out by the Cavalry Corps was considerable. As soon as 29th Division had secured the Masnières-Marcoing Canal, 2nd and 5th Cavalry Divisions were to cross and push northwards, with 1st

Cavalry Division advancing through Marcoing itself to the west of the canal. The Lucknow Cavalry Brigade, with U Battery RHA, were to act independently eastwards from Masnières. The guns of 2nd and 5th Cavalry Divisions (3 Brigade RHA; D, E and J Batteries, and 17 Brigade RHA; N and X Batteries) could do little more than follow the advance until the tasks became clear for them. In 1st Cavalry Division the task was different. Here the scope for energetic cavalry action was great, but the leading brigade—2nd Brigade—was ony given one section of H Battery RHA in support. The rest of the guns were to be strung out with the other two cavalry brigades—not a good plan.

Here, indeed, was the weakness of the whole plan, easy to see in hindsight and one which has concerned commanders planning an advance from time immemorial. Field Marshal Haig was determined to push his cavalry through at the first opportunity but he could not do this until the Masnières-Marcoing canal and Bourlon had been taken. If Bourlon did not fall on the first day, more infantry would be needed quickly but more infantry could not come because the cavalry were in the way.

The salient features of the ground over which the battle was to be fought were, first, Havrincourt Wood which provided cover from the German guns; second, the depression of Grand Ravin which ran obliquely across the battle field through the villages of Ribecourt and Marcoing; third, the Havrincourt Ridge and finally, and as it turned out most importantly of all, the village of Flesquières, on a reverse slope from the line of the British advance.

All was now set; could surprise be maintained, could the complex concentration of a thousand guns be achieved unknown to the watching Germans? Could the ammunition be dumped, the survey completed, the lines laid, the observers deployed? It was the most ambitious of ambitious plans, it was a gamble of the highest order. Slowly at dusk on 7th November, the first batteries began to move into action, some to positions only 2,000 yards behind the front trenches. Silence, cover, camouflage were vital. Movements in the open by day was forbidden, leaving the hours of darkness to be a relentless period of hard work. The jingle of guns and horses increased with each day until there was a ceaseless flow of divisional artilleries, army field brigades and siege and heavy batteries down all the roads from the north, each moving according to its allotted time. All were interspersed with infantry battalions, cavalry regiments, machine gun companies and ammunition columns. The move reached its pitch on the night of 9th–10th November. That night, two Army field brigades (six batteries) and five howitzer batteries were marching through Arras, while five 6-inch howitzer batteries were entering Bapaume; further south a further five siege batteries were moving into III Corps area. Finally, on the night of 17th-18th November, the last batteries moved into action. How easy for a spy to report the build up, how easy for an enemy aircraft or even a patrol to notice the inevitable signs of preparation for battle but, incredibly, none did. A word here for the hard pressed and much criticised staff— their work had been little short of brilliant, their times and traffic control excellent—the whole move was indeed a great tribute to good staff work.

So, on the eve of 20th November, all stood ready. Five divisions of infantry, 325 tanks and 1,003 guns prepared to assault an enemy of little more than one division, the *54th Division* with some units of the *20th Landwehr Division*, supported by only 34 guns. Furthermore, the intelligence staffs estimated that no

German reserves could reach the battle area in under forty-eight hours. Spirits were high that night, even though there was apprehension; would the gunfire be accurate enough, would the tanks, to be used en masse for the first time, be a success, did the Germans know what was up? But all was not quite well. As General Byng, Commander Third Army, watched the weather and as his men made ready for battle, how could they know that, at that very moment, trains carrying a German division fresh from the Russian front were unloading their men at Cambrai Station.

The Attack on 20th November

First, the operations in the III Corps sector. The artillery standing ready to open fire at 0620 hours consisted of the division artilleries of 6th, 12th, 20th, 29th and 40th Divisions, 3 Brigade RHA (2nd Cavalry Division), 16 Brigade RHA (4th Cavalry Division), 169, 179, 282 and 276 Army Field Artillery Brigades and 21, 26, 32, 34, 50, 78, 82 and 87 Heavy Artillery Groups; some 536 guns and howitzers altogether. This mass of guns was commanded by Brigadier-General T.A. Tancred. He organised his heavies into seven groups, one to each attacking division (three), two counter-battery groups, one 60-pounder group and one super heavy group. After capture of the Blue Line, the guns of 12th and 20th Divisional artilleries were to move forward, if possible at zero plus one hour. For the assault it was assumed that tank speeds would be:

downhill in the open	50 yards per minute
level in the open	40 yards per minute
uphill in the open	30 yards per minute
through trenches	30 yards per minute

Pauses in the fireplan were arranged as follows:

The enemy front trenches	15 minutes
The Blue Line	15 minutes
Each trench to be crossed	5 minutes
La Vacquerie	30 minutes
Bonavis and Pam Pam Farms	10 minutes
Lateau Wood	10 minutes
Ribecourt	30 minutes

It was planned that the attacking troops would leave the Blue Line at zero plus two hours and thirty minutes and would reach the Brown Line at zero plus three hours and thirty minutes. At 1420 hours the guns of 40th Division were to revert to V Corps. Finally, at the end of the barrage programmes, the guns of 29th Division's Heavy Group and the super heavy group were to fire concentrations onto Marcoing until 1015 hours, Masnières and Rumilly until 1130 hours and on to Lesdain, Crèvecour and Les Rues des Vignes until 1140 hours.

It was dull and misty as the Corps stood hushed and waiting; at 0620 hours a man could just be distinguished at 200 yards. The tanks were slowly, as silently as they could, rumbling up to their start line. Suddenly, the silence was shattered by a burst of German artillery fire—was all lost? Tension gripped everyone. But the shells fell harmlessly behind the British; it was no more than the early morning hate and by 0600 hours all was again quiet. But the tension was still there; after all, the operation order had warned everyone that the barrage would not be as accurate as they had been used to. The tension was great, too, at the guns. 10,000 Gunners were poised, gun position officers looking at their watches as time crept slowly on and on to the inevitable zero hour. Then it came, a mighty roar heralding the battle; the battle of Cambrai was on. Major E.F. Norton, commanding D Battery RHA wrote "the batteries were literally flank to flank in two long lines as far as the eye could see, the rear tier firing over the front tier at 200–300 yards distance. The synchronisation was excellent and it was a most impressive sight to see the hillsides burst into a perfect sheet of flame". As the assaulting troops rose to their feet, the shells poured down in front of them with an accuracy that was unbelievable, hearts burst with relief, the pessimists were confounded, all was well, the guns—thank God, the guns—had performed the miracle and victory was certain. The Germans were stunned and dismayed, surprise was complete. Before the British tanks appeared, the enemy front trenches were overcome and when they did appear, the enemy panic was complete. Nothing could resist this powerful combination of guns, infantry and tanks. The German guns, too, were neutralised and their defensive fire all along the front was weak, scattered and ineffective. Later examination showed a 90% accuracy in fixing the enemy gun positions, a great tribute to the flash spotters and sound rangers of 3rd Field Survey Company RE; and more tribute to them for their survey work. The gun fire was incredibly accurate, thanks almost entirely to their work and devotion to duty. The Army had much to thank that small band of Sappers for at Cambrai, on 20th November 1917.

The success of the attack was immense. Objective after objective was taken, the tanks were tremendous when used together. 29th Division, with the Cavalry close behind, reached the canal and crossed it at Marcoing. Here they were checked by the Beaurevoir Line hastily manned by stragglers and the division which had so fortuitously arrived at Cambrai. But Noyelles was entered, Graincourt captured and the whole Hindenburg Line system was smashed and cleared as far north as the Cambrai–Bapaume Road. Nothing could stop the victorious British—at last, a technique for victory had been perfected. 4,000 prisoners and 100 guns were captured. How they had longed for such a victory, and the great news was flashed to London, where the bells rang in triumph. But in this mighty hour of triumph, all was not quite right. The fortunes of war are fickle, the opportunities fleeting and, unless commanders are well forward and able to make quick decisions, mighty opportunities are lost. At Cambrai, the British Commanders were not well forward. Bourlon, that vital objective, was not taken and the cavalry, on the point of break out, could not do so. German reinforcements were arriving.

Let us look carefully at what had happened, for the fortunes of war did indeed change. On the right, 12th Division was to seize the Bonavis Ridge and then to cover the right flank of the Corps. Brigadier-General H.M. Thomas commanded the artillery. He had his 62 and 63 Brigades RFA, together with 169, 179, 232 and 277 Army Artillery Brigades RFA and 21 Heavy Artillery Group of four 9.2-inch howitzers, ten 6-inch howitzers and six 60-pounders.

The barrage was fired according to plan and at 0850 hours it lifted twice to the Lateau Trench. The next lift fell to the rear of Bonavis Farm, leaving the buildings untouched while the heavies crept through Lateau Wood. Then final protective fire was put down beyond the Brown Line. Next, Bonavis Farm was shelled by a 15-inch howitzer and Lateau Wood again struck. It is interesting to note that these both fell easily to tank and infantry attacks, whereas Le Pavé, Pam Pam Farm and Le Quennet Farm all delayed the advance considerably and the guns were not called to fire onto them.

To the left of 12th Division, 20th Division had the task of capturing La Vacquerie and the trenches beyond, then to swing right to continue the defensive flank as far as Les Rues Vertes. Here Brigadier-General H.W.A. Christie commanded the guns. He had his own 91 and 92 Brigades RFA, reinforced by 178 Brigade RFA from 40th Division, 182 Army Brigade RFA, 3 Brigade RHA and 15 Brigade RHA. The surprise here had been complete. The bombardment of La Vacquerie was particularly effective and the village fell easily to a combined tank and infantry assault. Later, on their way to the Blue Line, many tanks were hit by well hidden field guns as they crossed a crest line, but the Line was taken. By 1100 hours, all was done. The infantry had secured the Brown Line without opposition, German defensive fire ceased to exist and all the British guns were in action in their forward positions. An FOO was established in the Hindenburg trenches on Welsh Ridge, with telephone communication to the CRA. The Division had carried all its objectives, capturing seventeen officers and 700 men at the cost of 31 officers and 515 men killed and wounded.

The 6th Division on the left had had the task of capturing the Hindenburg System on a front of 2,600 yards, including the village of Ribecourt, and then to form a defensive flank on the left as far as Premy Chapel. The guns were commanded by Brigadier-General E.F. Delaforce and consisted of 2 and 24 Brigades RFA, 16 Brigade RHA (less one battery) and 17 and 181 Brigades RFA. This gave him twelve 13-pounders, seventy-two 18-pounders and twenty-four 4.5-inch howitzers, which he organised into two groups, one supporting each attacking infantry brigade. In addition to the barrages on the front of the attack, a smoke screen 2,500 yards long was maintained on the Flesquières Ridge behind Ribecourt until zero plus two hours fifteen minutes, and a shorter one in front of Premy Chapel for four hours.

The assault went exceptionally well and the enemy's artillery fire was light and patchy. 2nd Durham Light Infantry carried all its objectives and captured eleven guns with the bayonet with a loss of four killed, eighteen wounded and two missing, while 14th Durham Light Infantry reached its position west of Marcoing with only seven men wounded. What a difference from the Somme.

By noon, the guns of the Division were in position inside the Hindenburg Line, some 3,000 yards behind the 18th Infantry Brigade on Premy Ridge. 16 Brigade RHA advanced at 1015 hours to a position west of Couilly Wood, not more than 2,300 yards behind 18th Infantry Brigade. Here was the first fleeting opportunity. The Division was poised and in good shape to act but it had reached its objectives and did nothing. The Divisional Commander and CRA were still three miles behind the original British front line. They were in communication with Commander 18th Infantry Brigade but he was 1,000 yards south of Ribecourt, a position fixed for him in divisional orders, from where he could see nothing and where he was 2,000 yards from his leading battalion commanders. Third Army had said that, in such conditions, commanders must have their horses ready to gallop forward and take charge, but this did not occur. Thus when vigorous action by infantry and guns might have produced great results—nothing happened.

However, it had been a good day for III Corps. The artillery had done exceptionally well. The success of the barrage, followed by the dramatic sweep of tanks through the wire and over the enemy's front line trenches, sweeping aside machine guns and spreading panic in his ranks, had achieved that surprise which had always eluded commanders in trench warfare. Nevertheless, the enemy had escaped the disaster of a complete break through by the narrowest of margins.

Meanwhile, we must now look at the fortunes of IV Corps, who attacked on about one third of the front at zero hour. Two divisions attacked, 51st Highlanders on the right and 62nd on the left. They were both to reach the line of the sunken road running from Premy Chapel, through Graincourt to Moeuvres and then to push on to Cantaing, Fontaine and Bourlon—an advance of 10,000 yards in all. In particular, 51st Division were, early on, to capture Flesquières. The GOCRA IV Corps, Brigadier-General J.G. Geddes, organised his artillery with all horses and field batteries under CRAs and the heavies, under Brigadier-General T.E. Marshall, into three counter-battery groups, three bombardment groups and one reinforcement group. He had 234 field guns, 60 4.5-inch howitzers, 35 60-pounders, 68 6-inch howitzers, 4 6-inch guns, 16 8-inch howitzers, 12 9.2-inch howitzers, 1 9.2-inch gun, 6 12-inch howitzers and 1 15-inch howitzer; 437 guns and howitzers in all. Careful orders were given for the subsequent advance of the guns. Routes were laid down but executive orders to move were to be given by CRAs.

In 51st Highland Division, the CRA, Brigadier-General L.C.L Oldfield, had his own 255 and 256 Highland Field Brigades RFA, augmented by 70 and 306 Army Brigades RFA and by 4 and 5 Brigades RHA from the Cavalry Corps. The attack was again a brilliant success as far as the crest of the ridge in front of Flesquières. Losses were remarkably light and the tanks most effective. But the Germans did show a remarkably quick recovery on this sector and the Highlanders had to fight hard to maintain the advance. But at 1000 hours, before Flesquières, the picture changed suddenly in the course of a few moments.

It just happened that the *German 54th Division*, which was holding the front between La Vacquerie and Havrincourt, was commanded by Lieutenant-General Freiherr von Watter, an artilleryman who had studied the problem of countering tanks in some detail. He had tested his theories against some French tanks in April 1917, and had specifically trained his artillery to hit moving targets with direct fire from reverse slope positions. Some of his batteries now lay waiting behind the reverse slope at Flesquières. Furthermore, the mist which had covered this part of the battlefield now lifted. Here was now to be seen the effect of neutralising guns for a short time and not destroying them, for the location of these guns was known. At 1000 hours, British tanks in line ahead moving towards Flesquières came over the crest; one by one they were hit until eleven lay stricken and the attack was called off. The tanks did, however, strike back and hit some guns. A German account of the battle describes how Under-Officer Kruger hit five tanks single-handed as they crossed his front. Major Norton of D Battery RHA reported how this gallant foe was captured and then bayonetted in cold blood by

Bringing up the ammunition, Flanders, 1917. From the work of an unknown artist. *(R.A.I.)*

an excited Highlander. The Highlanders of 152nd Infantry Brigade took the rest of the morning to close to the village, but could make no progress. Strangely, no artillery fire was called for and the reasons are not clear. The tanks had, it is known, cut most of the artillery telephone lines, so perhaps it was not possible. At 1435 hours, III Corps ordered 6th Division to attack Flesquières from the direction of Masnières, and 1st Cavalry Division to send two regiments to by-pass Premy Chapel and "to get round Flesquières from the north-east". 51st Division was to keep up pressure from the south. But these operations could not be got under way before darkness fell. How well these German field guns had acted. So few had held the advance for eight hours and now, after dark, the whole garrison slipped away, so that British dawn patrols found the village deserted.

To the left of 51st Division was 62nd Division, whose artillery was commanded by Brigadier-General A.T. Anderson. He had his own 310 and 312 Field Brigades RFA, reinforced by 77 and 93 Army Brigades RFA and 153 Field Brigade RFA from 36th Division. The Division was attacking, with 185th and 187th Infantry Brigades up, as far as the Brown Line. When this was captured, 186th Infantry Brigade was to pass through, clear the Hindenburg System, capture Graincourt and exploit to Anneux and Bourlon. The whole distance was some 10,000 yards. The artillery plan was not easy, as the initial German positions were close to the start line and considerable movement of guns was necessary to maintain the attack as far as Bourlon.

The leading brigades had to attack without tanks, which had been held up by fallen trees in Havrincourt Wood. The barrage was deadly accurate and described by the infantry as magnificent. The tanks soon caught up the victorious infantry and both objectives fell exactly as planned. At the Brown Line, the artillery was re-grouped. 131st Heavy Battery RGA (60-pounders) and 195th Siege Battery RGA (6-inch howitzers) came under command and 5 Brigade RHA was placed under command 310 Brigade RFA for the attack on Graincourt, the latter's commander being at Headquarters 186th Infantry Brigade. Great efforts were made to keep communications to the guns through, and an artillery radio link was maintained from the guns to the artillery commanders at the infantry brigade headquarters, which for the first time worked well. Again, all went well while the tanks and infantry advanced under artillery fire, but where this was not laid on or called for, the Germans quickly recovered and fought back.

186th Brigade was commanded by Brigadier-General R.B. Bradford, the youngest brigadier in the Army at 25, and an energetic and vigorous commander. He did, however, decide to dispense with a barrage and simply to bombard Graincourt. As a result, his infantry took three hours to capture the village and made it impossible for him to reach Anneux and Bourlon before dark. In the first attack, six tanks were knocked out by two German field guns and Brigadier Bradford then organised a new attack, using three more tanks but without any artillery fire. After some delay, this was successful and Graincourt fell by 1530 hours. By 1400 hours, the artillery was moving forward so that 5 Brigade RHA was in action just east of Havrincourt. 310 Brigade RFA was moving up and 77 Brigade RFA had two batteries in action in the old British front line, with two more moving up. Some prisoners were taken at Anneux but the village could not be consolidated before dark, so the Brigade withdrew to Graincourt for the night.

To the left of 62nd Division, 36th Division had deployed one infantry brigade forward, supporting it with 173 Brigade RFA, 93 Army Brigade RFA (after release from 51st Division) and 280 Brigade RFA of 56th Division. In addition, there was one 60-pounder and three 6-inch howitzer batteries. The first objective was a massive spoil heap only 250 yards from the British front trenches. A huge four minute bombardment was directed onto it and it fell with little loss to the attacking infantry, who then attacked behind their barrage to the Hindenburg Line, with great success.

So at nightfall it had been a good day. The check at Flesquières had not delayed the advance of 29th Division, although it had delayed the advance of the cavalry for a while. The guns were advancing according to plan everywhere, but FOOs were having great difficulty keeping through to the guns since the tanks—which had been so successful—were cutting all the cables. Nevertheless, the chances of a breakthrough on the morrow seemed good. Morale was high, progress was good, casualties were light and much had gone exactly according to plan.

The Exploitation

Major-General de Lisle, commanding 29th Division, was to exploit with three infantry brigades up, each with four tanks. He was to occupy the Masnières-Beaurevoir Line and Nine Wood to open the way for the cavalry. Divisional Headquarters was to remain 2,500 yards behind the original British front line, some 10,000 yards from the objective. Since this was to be a pursuit of a defeated enemy, no fireplan was made. However, his CRA, Brigadier E.H. Stevenson, planned to cover the advance as follows:

15 Brigade RHA, covering 88th Infantry Brigade, directed at Masnières from positions 3,000 yards south west of Les Rues Vertes.

17 Brigade RFA, covering 87th Infantry Brigade, directed at Marcoing from positions some 1,800 yards south west of Marcoing Copse.

16 Brigade RHA, covering 86th Infantry Brigade, directed onto Nine Wood from positions 3,300 yards south west of Nine Wood.

One 60-pounder and one 6-inch Battery joined the division as soon as the advance began. Some 600 fascines were issued to get across the trenches and the Gunners had to cut their own way through the German wire, since the tracks made by the tanks were not safe for the horses.

The advance was ordered at 1015 hours on 20th November, even though firm news of the capture of the Brown Line had not been received. The attacking brigades soon found that their task was far from a pursuit. Enemy parties were active everywhere and at 1230 hours Brigadier-General Lucas, commanding 87th Infantry Brigade, clearly saw German infantry hurrying out of Cambrai to man the Beaurevoir Line. Although the canal had been crossed, it was soon clear that the capture of the Beaurevoir Line would need an artillery attack and this had not yet been arranged. The guns were all in action as ordered by early afternoon, but still no orders came to them. Drizzling rain set in at 1500 hours, making visibility very bad, the location of our troops was not known and communications failed due to cut lines. The pre-arranged bombardment of all objectives did occur but nothing else was asked of the guns. However, a good deal had been done to open the way for the cavalry and the German position that night was extremely serious.

Third Army Orders to III and IV Corps that night were to capture the Beaurevoir Line and Bourlon as quickly as possible, and then to continue with the original plan. This involved the move forward of as many batteries as possible to be ready to cover the advance at first light. This was not easy in the mud, rain and darkness, when all trenches needed bridging to get the guns across.

Things did not go well on 21st November. At Marcoing, the fire of 15 Brigade RHA was not enough to get the infantry into the Beaurevoir Line. A later attack on Les Rue des Vignes does not appear to have included any artillery at all. German artillery reinforcements were now arriving and these were used to engage tanks at short range over open sights. It was now clear that a full bombardment was needed to get over the Beaurevoir Line. III Corps was thus told to hold, so that IV Corps could open the gap at Bourlon so desperately needed to get the cavalry going. 51st Division was ordered to clear Flesquières (the German withdrawal not yet being known) and advance to Fontaine, while 62nd Division was to attack Bourlon Wood and Bourlon village with 1st Cavalry Division close behind, ready to ride through to the open country beyond. All artillery available was to be used.

Accordingly 51st Highland Division, on finding Flesquières abandoned, bombarded the Premy Chapel-Graincourt sunken road and captured it with seventy prisoners and twelve guns at 0900 hours. A subsequent attack on Cantaing was checked. Observation was appalling and, although two 18-pounders were brought up into the firing line to fire directly, all attempts to take the village failed. Then 1st Cavalry Brigade came up to help. I Battery RHA came into action and some tanks arrived. Then tanks, cavalry, infantry and guns attacked and, after some severe fighting, the village was taken. To the left of 51st Division, the artillery of 62nd Division had great difficulty in getting forward. The only available road was so thick in mud that the guns were sinking to their axles. The battle for BourlonWood raged on for days, the fighting being conducted by infantry and dismounted cavalry. The guns struggled forward but, in the mist, rain and mud and confused fighting, could do little to help their comrades in the close quarter struggle now in progress. The story in 36th Division on 22nd November was better. 107th Infantry Brigade, with some tanks and the support of 93 Brigade RFA and 278 Siege Battery RGA, made some progress while 108th Infantry Brigade, supported by 153 and 173 Brigades RFA and three 6-inch howitzers, one 9.2-inch and one 12-inch howitzer attacking on a one hundred yard front, captured Moeuvres. However, again communications to the guns failed and the village had to be given up again in the face of a severe enemy counter-attack which could not be engaged by artillery. Of the eleven tanks that went into action that day, one was 'ditched' at the start, one lost direction and was not seen again, six were hit and only three remained at the end of the day—fifty-five men of the new Tank Corps were casualties.

By 23rd November, the Germans had strengthened their position and, realising the significance of Bourlon, had put ten battalions and a number of field guns in anti-tank positions into it. 51st Division captured Fontaine and by the end of the day, 40th Division, with a considerable artillery attack, finally succeeded in taking Bourlon Wood. 36th Division struggled on in the mud and rain and again captured Moeuvres, but again failed to beat off enemy counter-attacks and were forced to abandon it. The weather was now deteriorating rapidly, observation was very poor and 24th November dawned with high wind and heavy rain. Nevertheless, the Germans counter-attacked the six weary, wet British battalions in Bourlon Wood with eight fresh ones, supported by some fifty guns, and made some progress. The enemy was now falling back onto good ground and plentiful supplies, whereas the British were extended and had to bring everything forward over the desolation and quagmires of the battlefield. In spite of all, by super human effort and an excellent barrage, the Germans were again driven off. The Highland Light Infantry had become cut off and ran out of ammunition and, unknown to everyone else, were forced to surrender. During the night 24th–25th November, 74 and 75 Brigades RFA of the Guards Division managed to work their way forward and to join the weary batteries on the Fontaine front.

At 0600 hours 26th November, another attack on Bourlon village began with a hastily planned and not very big bombardment, but the attack was not successful. The British position was not good, as the Germans held high ground looking into their positions and stalemate had been reached. The Commander Third Army now realised that the chance of a breakthrough had been lost but was determined to improve his positions for the winter. He therefore ordered the Guards Division to capture the high ground on either side of Bourlon on 27th November. But the infantry were weary and insufficient and· there were not enough guns in range. Some tanks were hastily gathered together, but they failed to join up with the infantry they were to support. The artillery for the operation was placed under Brigadier-General F.A. Wilson, which consisted of his own 74 and 75 Brigades RFA, 70 and 306 Brigades RFA and 54 Heavy Artillery Group (one 60-pounder and one 6-inch battery). The artillery of 2nd Cavalry Division (D, E and J Batteries RHA) was ordered up to help and at dark they had a rough time of it, preparing the barrages in the open in a blizzard. They were ready by dawn but, as it broke, they found themselves on a forward slope in full view of the enemy in Cambrai and to the east of Noyelles. The enemy were in strength in La Folie Wood and Bourlon Wood so had flank positions against the Guards, who suffered greatly, and the insufficient artillery could do little to help them. They suffered fearfully but, with magnificent courage and determination, they reached their objectives. The tanks were too late to join in the attack but, at the point of the bayonet, the Guards cleared forward as far as the railway line. Some tanks worked forward and many gallant close quarter actions occurred amongst the houses of Fontaine. The situation was now desperate. The 1st Battalions Scots, Coldstream, Grenadier and Irish Guards had suffered terribly. In spite of the hurried move forward of companies of 4th Battalion Grenadier Guards, the remainder could not hold out when surrounded by violent German counter-attacks. The remnants fought their way back. Gallant as it was, the attack had failed. Three battalions had attacked the *German 119th Division* and were counter-attacked by the *221st Division* and all with inadequate artillery—how could they possibly have held? The failure was, however, mainly due to faulty intelligence and planning by a headquarters too far in the rear to understand the true position. But the guns must take some blame; their control after a long advance was still not good enough. Fire was never heavy enough or well enough co-ordinated to help the tanks and infantry at their time of greatest need.

Meanwhile, 62nd Division tried yet again to get into Bourlon. 187th Brigade attacked with fifteen tanks and a fair amount of artillery. The tanks were handled with great gallantry and some got into Bourlon, but they suffered appalling losses and only five returned, one of which was badly hit. The attack again failed. Why so much failure after so much success? With hindsight, the reasons were many. The initial plan not to destroy the enemy guns was one; the assumption that operations after the capture of the Brown Line would be in the nature of a pursuit was another; the over reliance on the tanks and the consequent failure to use the guns in sufficient force was yet another and finally, the insufficient infantry readily available was also a cause. The unfortunate arrival of an unforeseen extra German division enabled the enemy to seal a gap and strengthen the Beaurevoir Line at a critical moment and undoubtedly contributed to the failure to break out. But a major cause was the inability of the artillery to maintain its communications when operating at the end of an advance.

At the start, all had gone magnificently well. By 28th November, the Germans had lost 184 officers, 10,307 men, 142 guns, 350 machine guns and 70 mortars. Also, 10,000 yards of their invincible Hindenburg Line had been overrun. But failure to capture Bourlon made the breakout impossible and, as the fighting died down, the British were left in a dangerous salient. Orders were given by Headquarters Third Army to consolidate ground won, but the battle was not yet over.

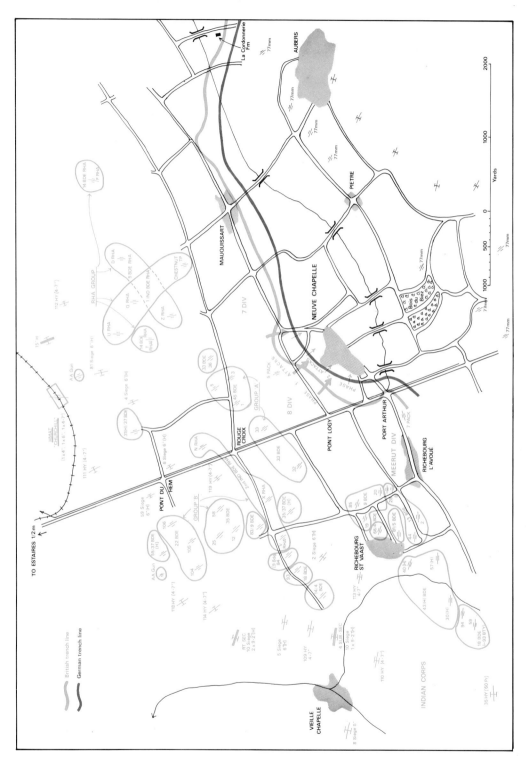

Map 16   The Battle of Neuve Chapelle—10 March 1915

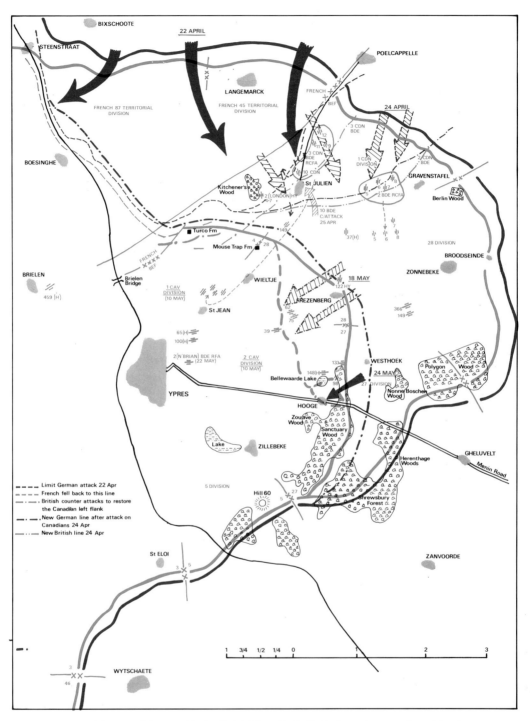

Map 17 Second Battle of Ypres, 22 April–25 May 1915 (Only batteries mentioned in the text are shown)

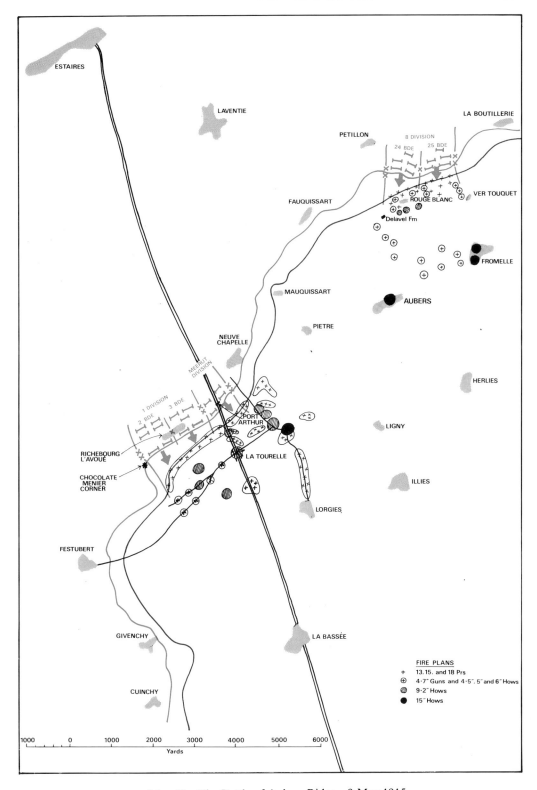

ESTAIRES

LAVENTIE

LA BOUTILLERIE

PETILLON

8 DIVISION

24 BDE   25 BDE

FAUQUISSART

ROUGE BLANC

VER TOUQUET

Delavel Fm

FROMELLE

MAUQUISSART

AUBERS

PIETRE

NEUVE
CHAPELLE

HERLIES

MEERUT
DIVISION

1 DIVISION

2 BDE   3 BDE

PORT
ARTHUR

LIGNY

RICHEBOURG
L'AVOUÉ

LA TOURELLE

CHOCOLATE
MENIER
CORNER

ILLIES

LORGIES

FESTUBERT

GIVENCHY

LA BASSÉE

FIRE PLANS
+   13, 15, and 18 Prs
⊕   4·7″ Guns and 4·5″, 5″ and 6″ Hows
◍   9·2″ Hows
●   15″ Hows

CUINCHY

1000   0   1000   2000   3000   4000   5000   6000
Yards

Map 18   The Battle of Aubers Ridge—9 May 1915

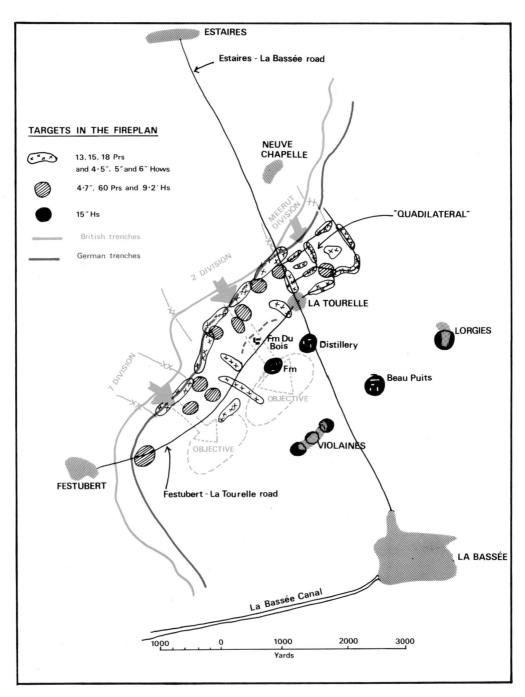

ESTAIRES

Estaires - La Bassée road

TARGETS IN THE FIREPLAN

13, 15, 18 Prs
and 4·5″, 5″ and 6″ Hows

4·7″, 60 Prs and 9·2′ Hs

15″ Hs

British trenches

German trenches

**NEUVE
CHAPELLE**

MEERUT DIVISION

"QUADILATERAL"

2 DIVISION

LA TOURELLE

LORGIES

Fm Du Bois

Distillery

7 DIVISION

Fm

Beau Puits

OBJECTIVE

OBJECTIVE

VIOLAINES

FESTUBERT

Festubert - La Tourelle road

LA BASSÉE

La Bassée Canal

1000   0   1000   2000   3000
Yards

Map 19   The Battle of Festubert—15–27 May 1915

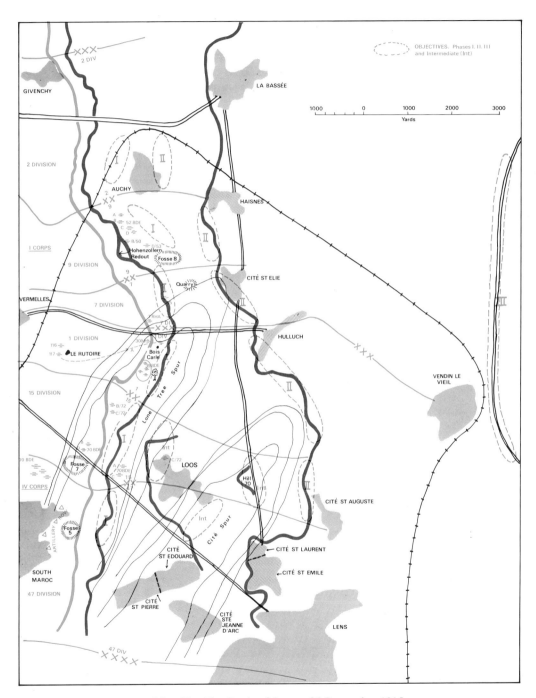

Map 20   The Battle of Loos—25 September 1915

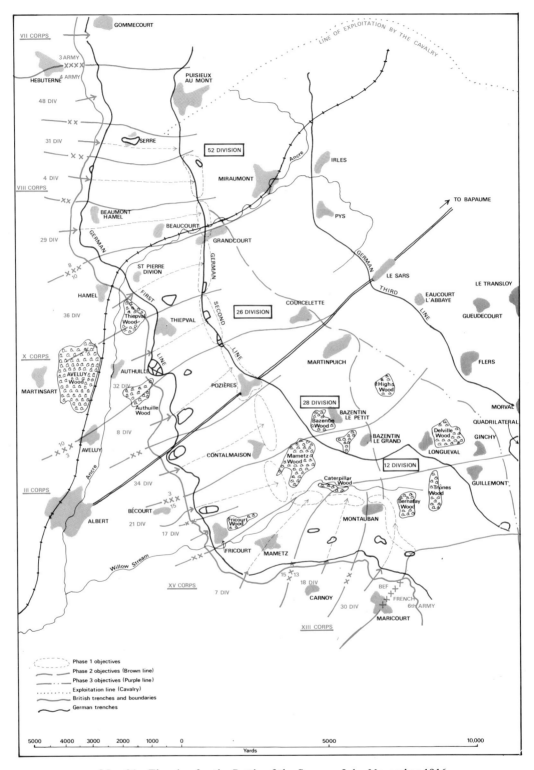

Map 21   The plan for the Battle of the Somme, July–November 1916

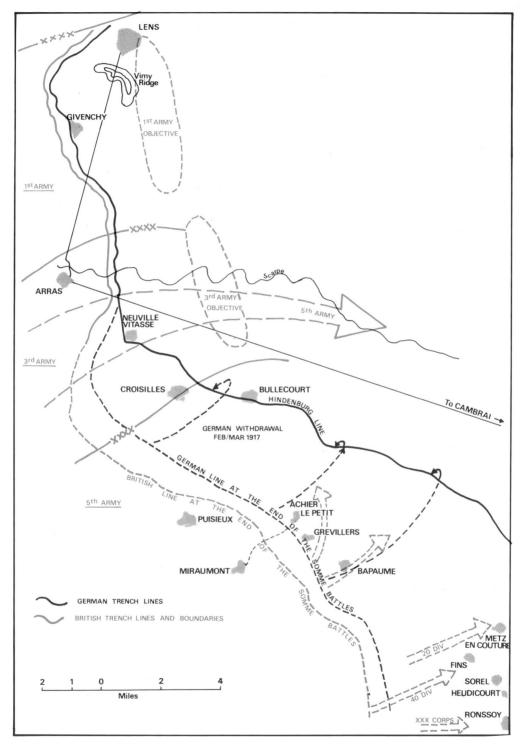

Map 22   The German withdrawal to the Hindenburg Line and the plan for the Battle of Arras—
April 1917

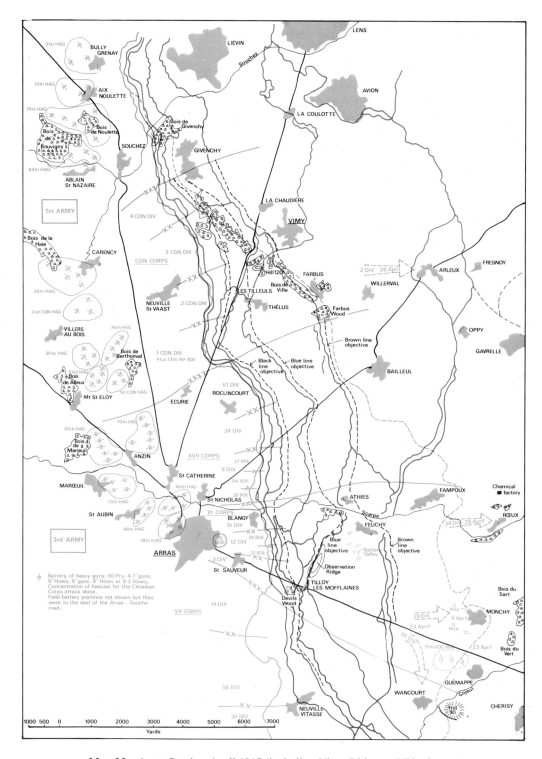

Map 23   Arras Battles, April 1917 (including Vimy Ridge and The Scarpe)

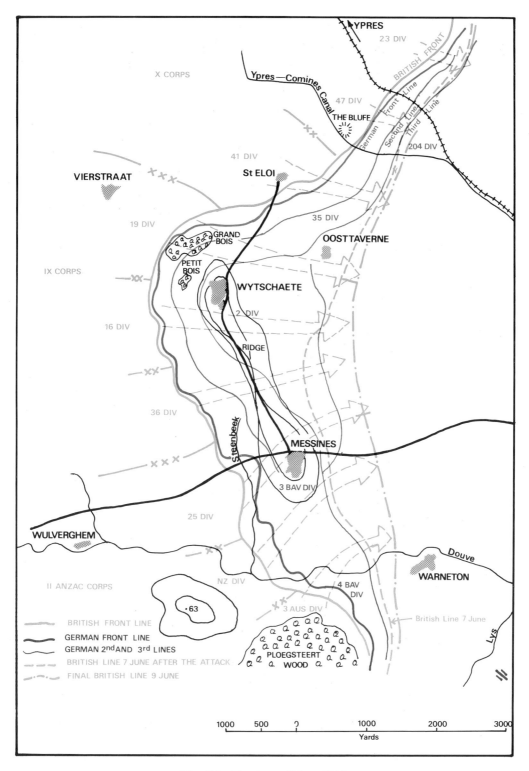

Map 24   Messines—7 June 1917

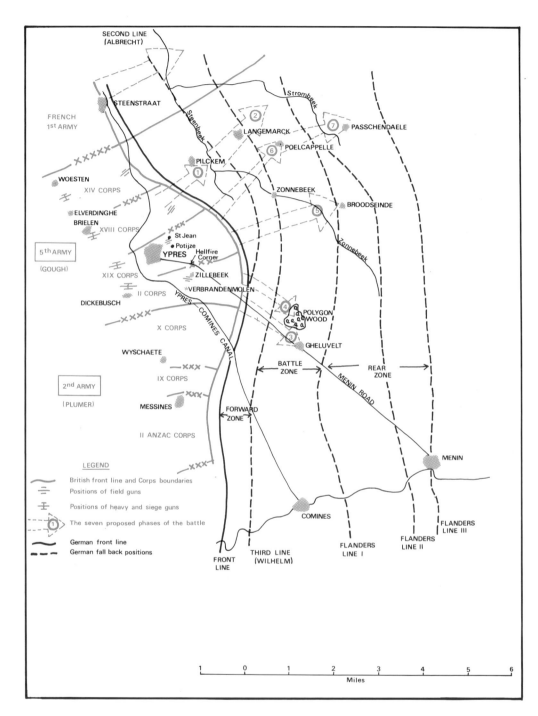

Map 25   Third Ypres—July 1917 the plan

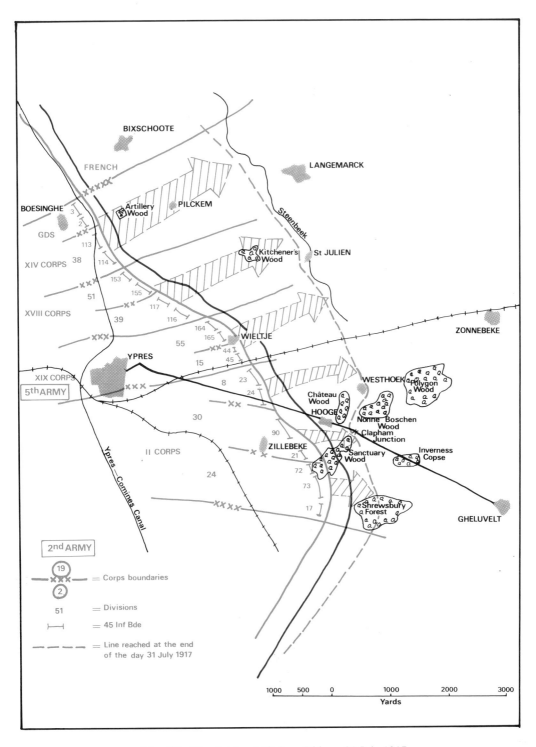

Map 26   The Battle of Pilckem Ridge—31 July 1917

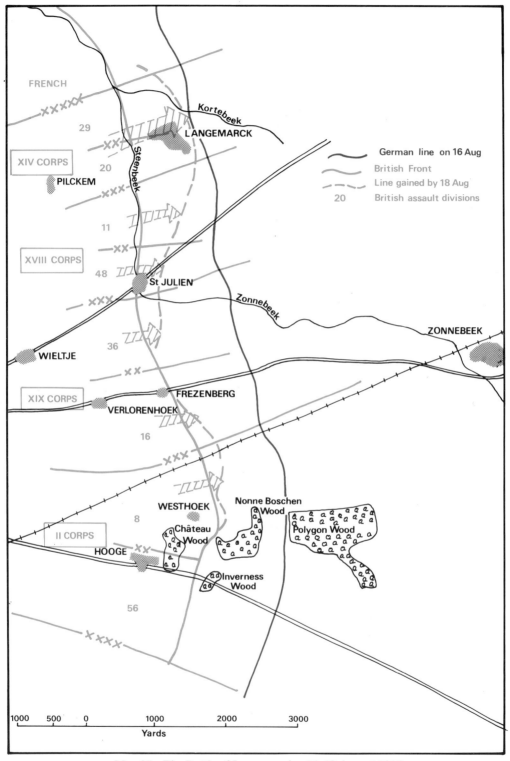

FRENCH

Kortebeek

LANGEMARCK

29

XIV CORPS

20

Steenbeek

PILCKEM

11

XVIII CORPS

48   St JULIEN

Zonnebeek

ZONNEBEEK

36

WIELTJE

XIX CORPS   FREZENBERG

VERLORENHOEK

16

Nonne Boschen
Wood

WESTHOEK   Polygon Wood

8

Château
Wood

II CORPS

HOOGE   Inverness
                                   Wood

56

German line on 16 Aug

British Front

Line gained by 18 Aug

20   British assault divisions

| 1000 | 500 | 0 | 1000 | 2000 | 3000 |

Yards

Map 27   The Battle of Langemarck—16–18 August 1917

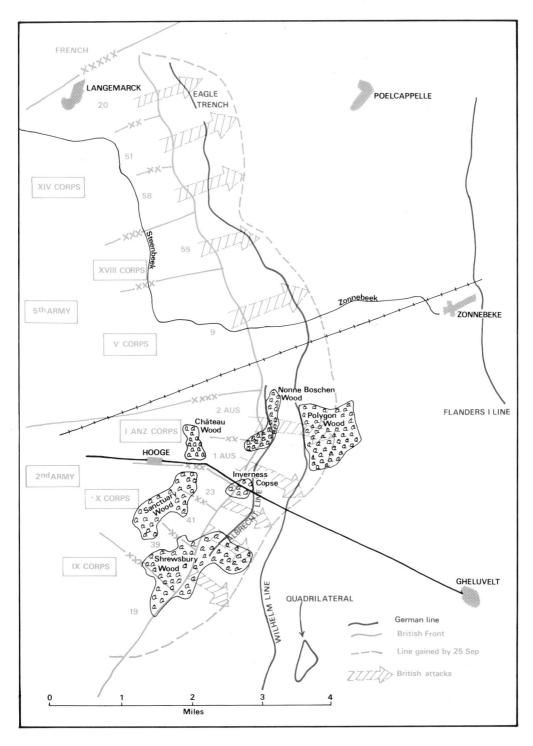

FRENCH

LANGEMARCK

20

EAGLE
TRENCH

POELCAPPELLE

XIV CORPS

51

58

Steenbeek

55

XVIII CORPS

5th ARMY

V CORPS

9

Zonnebeek

ZONNEBEKE

FLANDERS I LINE

Nonne Boschen
Wood

Polygon
Wood

2 AUS

Château
Wood

I ANZ CORPS

HOOGE

1 AUS

Inverness
Copse

2nd ARMY

X CORPS

23

Sanctuary
Wood

41

39

Shrewsbury
Wood

ALBRECHT LINE

IX CORPS

19

GHELUVELT

WILHELM LINE

QUADRILATERAL

German line

British Front

Line gained by 25 Sep

British attacks

0   1   2   3   4
Miles

Map 28   The Battle of Menin Road—20–25 September 1917

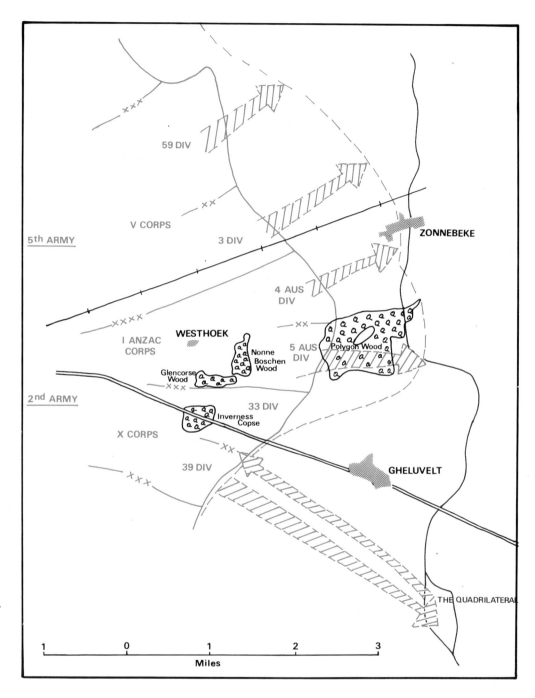

Map 29   The Battle of Polygon Wood—26 September–3 October 1917

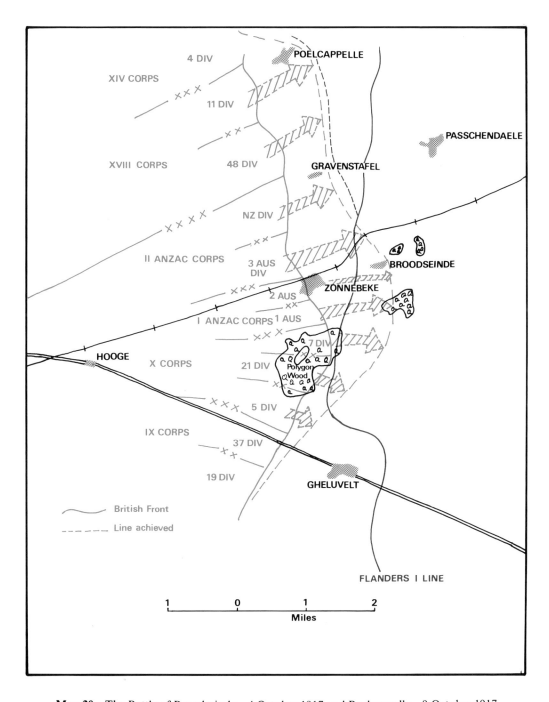

Map 30 The Battle of Broodseinde—4 October 1917 and Poelcappelle—9 October 1917

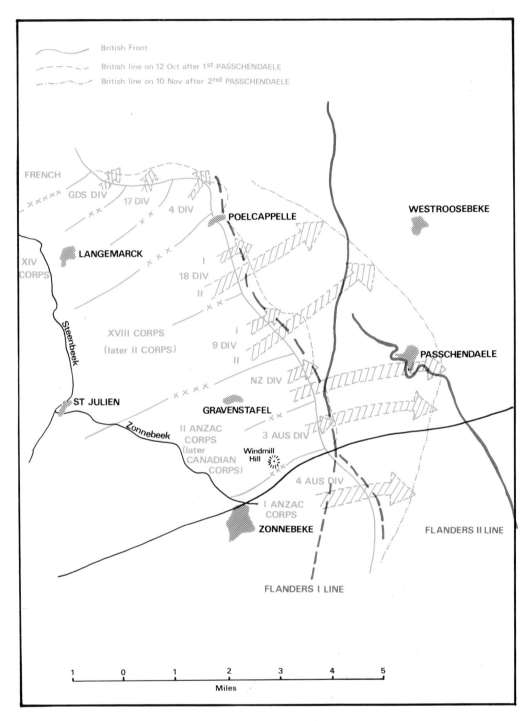

Map 31   Passchendaele—Oct/Nov 1917

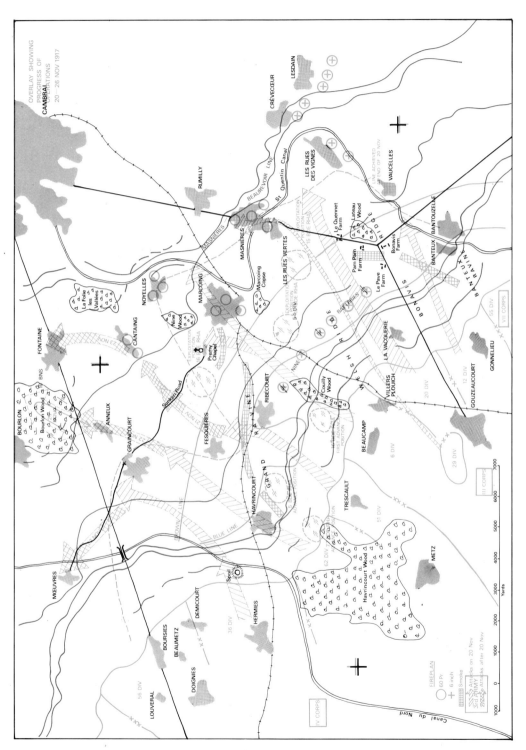

Map 32 Cambrai—20 November 1917

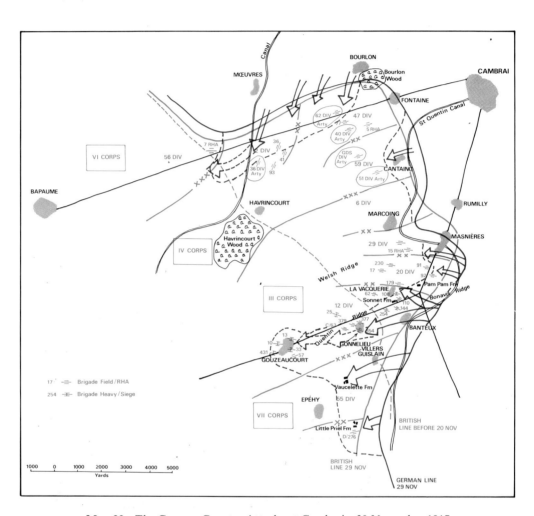

Map 33   The German Counter Attacks at Cambrai—30 November 1917

CHAPTER 19

The German Counter-Attack — 30th November to 3rd December 1917

See Map 33

The British situation was certainly precarious. The inter-Corps boundaries were drawn for the attack and were not designed to allot responsibilities for defence. The boundary between III and VII Corps ran along the Banteux Ravine, which led directly into VII Corps' left flank and into the rear areas of 12th and 20th Divisions of III Corps. The Ravine was held by 55th Division of VII Corps. The village of Villers Guislain and Vaucelette Farm, just south of Banteux, were important features in the Ravine. There were no real defences in the Ravine, except for a single trench, since no plans were made to defend it. Few guns could bear on it, as the majority faced north east, and few covered the VII Corps area. Indeed, a Corps artillery consisted of only eight 6-inch howitzers and a 60-pounder battery. On its right, 24th Division covered a front of 10,000 yards with its field brigade, less a battery. To its left, 55th Division held a front of 13,000 yards along its trenches, supported by forty-four 18-pounders and two 4.5-inch howitzers. Lieutenant-General Snow, commanding VII Corps, was convinced that the enemy would attack and was terribly concerned at his deployment and shortage of guns. He warned the Commander-in-Chief many times, but GHQ's intelligence staffs were convinced that the Germans were incapable of mounting an attack in strength, so his warnings went unheeded.

The situation in III Corps was better and it had a fair allocation of artillery. At least its divisional artilleries were intact. The difficulty was the very exposed nature of the positions on forward slopes overlooked by Germans at Rumilly and Grèvecour. The position of IV Corps was even stronger. It had ample artillery and its heavies were able to cover the whole front in enfilade from positions around Demicourt, Louveral and Beaumetz.

The Germans were not clever in concealing their preparations for attack and Lieutenant-General Snow predicted a powerful attack against VII Corps on 29th or 30th November. In fact, it came on the 30th. General Snow made what preparations he could and asked in particular for artillery support from 12th and 55th Divisional Artilleries of III Corps. Here a vital misunderstanding arose. III Corps thought that the fire was not wanted until called for and VII Corps were sure they *had* called for it. Consequently, at the vital moment no fire materialised and the Germans, on a front of 7,000 yards, swept over the British line, overrunning Villers Guislain and were only held at Vaucelette Farm. They swept up the Banteux Ravine in the rear of 12th Division, captured Quentin Ridge and Gonnelieu and were only held at La Vacquerie. It was a great success, but not as successful as the Germans had hoped.

The British had not been taken by surprise. The Gunners and infantry stood-to at 0530 hours on 30th November. The German barrage started at 0700 hours, quietly and spasmodically, swelling gradually into a roar, heralding a major attack. HE was mixed with smoke and gas and much use was made of *minenwerfers*. In addition, some guns advanced with the infantry as anti-tank guns and much use was made of aircraft in support of the attack. Up to one hundred aircraft were visible at one time, machine gunning and bombing the trenches—more aircraft than had ever been seen before in this role.

At Little Priel Farm stood a section of D Battery 276 Brigade RFA, under command of Sergeant C.E. Gourley. The two 4.5-inch howitzers were in action close to the farm, very near the front line. Soon they were firing at attacking Germans at point blank range; they were straffed by aircraft, machine guns and mortars, but the detachments stuck to their guns. The Germans could not get past. They held on and on, suffering casualties until noon. Sergeant Gourley saw the Germans preparing again, so he ran one howitzer from its pit and brought down such a devastating fire onto the attacking Germans that they gave up—the thin line had held—the guns had again been served with courage. Sergeant Gourley was later awarded the Victoria Cross for his gallantry.

But many British guns were lost that day; many were surprised and overrun before they could fire a shot. Indeed, at Villers Guislain four 6-inch howitzers, fourteen 18-pounders and four 4.5-inch howitzers of VII Corps and twenty 6-inch howitzers, four 60-pounders and twelve 18-pounders of III Corps were lost. It was the biggest single loss of British guns in one battle ever to that date. Behind Villers Guislain, 35th Infantry Brigade under Brigadier-General B. Vincent, himself a Gunner, organised a gallant defence but was eventually overrun. Brigadier Vincent gathered around him everyone he could find and formed "Vincent Force" which was to play a significant part in the battle.

The German advance pressed on at an unprecedented pace until it came to Gouzeaucourt. This was held by a pioneer company, without weapons, and five batteries, the 13th, 33rd, 57th Heavy and 100th and 431st Siege. A loaded supply train stood in the station and HQ 29th Division escaped in the nick of time. The Germans occupied the town eventually, the guns were lost firing to the last, but later many were recaptured after a spirited counter-attack by the Guards.

Meanwhile, nearby at Gonnelieu stood the remnants of 36th Infantry Brigade; three field batteries, 377th, 379th and C Battery 63 Brigade RFA, were in action on the north west of the village and five hundred yards away stood A and B Batteries 63 Brigade. 25th Heavy Battery (four 60-pounders) and 354th Siege Battery (four 6-inch howitzers) stood together inside the village. By 0730 hours, German shells were falling heavily on the village and the grey forms of attacking infantry could soon be seen in the morning mist, dust and smoke. 70th Field Company RE was rushed in front of the guns but to no avail and, after firing hard, the heavies had to be destroyed as they were overrun. 377th and 379th Batteries played havoc with those Germans who tried to come out of the village. The Germans set up machine guns to deal with the Gunners, who soon began to take casualties. The gallant Gunners stuck to their guns until they had fired their last rounds, and then had no choice but to withdraw with their breech blocks.

But it was C Battery, sitting back from the village and supported by A and B Batteries of 63 Brigade, which saved the day. Their fire checked all attempts by the

Germans to advance. The Germans reinforced, brought down artillery fire onto the gallant C Battery, then brought up machine guns. The Battery fought on until only one officer, Lieutenant S.T.D. Wallace, and twelve men were left. For two more hours this gallant few held every German effort, but by 1030 hours they were near the end. By then only two guns were left and the twelve men were reduced to five. They could only fire each gun in turn and were already firing in three directions. The enemy closed to 150 yards for the kill, but Wallace refused to give in. Almost surrounded, his ammunition all but gone, he prepared to fight by hand. But his task was done, he had held; British infantry arrived and the guns were saved. For this gallant action, which did so much to stem the German advance, Lieutenant Wallace was awarded the Victoria Cross, and the five other survivors were all awarded the Distinguished Conduct Medal.

Meanwhile, at La Vacquerie the line also held. At Sonnet Farm stood five 6-inch howitzers of 108th Siege Battery and six of 110th Siege Battery. Both batteries were overrun and lost, their detachments joining the infantry. 254th Siege Battery held until 1415 hours, when it too abandoned the guns, burying breech blocks and sights, and the same fate befell 144th Heavy Battery. But German success had cost him dear. He now met toughening resistance from the British infantry. With them were the four batteries of 62 Brigade RFA. All batteries ran their guns into the open and opened direct fire on the advancing Germans at ranges of 1,000 yards downwards. A Battery was withdrawn at noon, B at 1400 hours, using limber supply for the last half hour, with the drivers mounted beside the guns. C Battery stuck it out until 1500 hours and withdrew under intense machine gun and rifle fire. But the line, precarious and thin, had held.

Near Pam Pam Farm, British guns unfortunately shelled a trench in British hands, which was holding the Germans. A most regrettable event but, though inexcusable, it could scarcely be avoided in the confusion of mist, smoke and broken communications. But it was here, near La Vacquerie, that the gallantry of 179 Army Field Artillery Brigade RFA equalled all others. Wave after wave of enemy infantry were driven back by these guns and two machine guns. There were many casualties but the guns fought on. By 1100 hours, the infantry fell back to positions around the guns—the guns which refused to move—the guns which held on and on until nightfall. Yet again the line had held, a thin, precarious line which had prevented the Germans advancing more than 2,000 yards and had certainly prevented the breakthrough which looked so certain as the day had dawned.

Further left, the situation in 20th Division was even worse. The Division held the sweep of the canal, but could not hold it along its length and so stood back, with outposts forward. Only 91 and 92 Brigades RFA were available. The mist was very thick and the German attack at 0800 hours achieved complete surprise—the outposts fell back. 92 Brigade RFA began to answer SOS calls on the canal crossings, but German counter-battery fire was deadly. C Battery was totally destroyed, five guns hit and most of the detachments killed and the ammunition of the sixth exploded. The surviving Gunners stood by their guns with their officers trying to rally the infantry. In the end they all retired. 91 Brigade held on grimly in support of 59th Infantry Brigade. They fired continuously during the day and each Battery fired almost 4,000 rounds at ranges of less than 1,000 yards before nightfall.

A 12-inch gun on a railway mounting.   *(I.W.M.)*

Gun of a Counter-battery in action. This drawing by Fortunino Matania shows a 12-inch howitzer on a railway mounting. *(R.A.I.)*

Anti-aircraft instruments in action.   *(R.A.I.)*

Five hundred yards to the north west of 92 Brigade stood the guns of 15 Brigade RHA; B, L, the Warwickshires and 460th Howitzer Batteries. By 0900 hours, British infantry were retiring through the gun lines and by 0915 hours, no-one stood between them and the Germans. At 1040 hours, lines of German infantry could be seen crossing the Bonavis Ridge bearing down on the Horse Artillerymen. They were the leading elements of the *German 9th Division*—a reserve division—fresh for the breakthrough. The guns opened fire and began taking heavy toll of the enemy but, by 1115 hours, some had worked to within forty yards of the guns. Lieutenant-Colonel E.R. Burne, commanding 15 Brigade RHA, then ordered L Battery RHA to open rapid fire to cover the withdrawal of the detachments of the rest of the Brigade. This was done, L Battery themselves finally withdrawing. Colonel Burne now hoped that a counter-attack would enable him to recover his guns but, when he realised that this was a forlorn hope, he assembled a small mixed force of infantry and gunners which tried in vain to recover them, inflicting over one hundred and fifty casualties on the enemy in the attempt. Meanwhile, 17 Brigade RFA and 232 Army Field Artillery Brigade fired incessantly in support of the hard pressed 20th Division. The guns of 92nd Battery and D Battery, 17 Brigade RFA, were run out of their pits as the attacking waves closed in. The officers seized two Lewis guns and, together with the direct fire of the guns, halted the enemy. German guns moving forward with the infantry were destroyed one by one by these two magnificent batteries. Rapid fire was maintained until noon and a timely counter-attack by 88th Infantry Brigade relieved the pressure on the guns. During this day alone the guns of 29th Division fired 11,500 rounds of 18-pounder and 2,500 rounds of 4.5-inch ammunition. The guns had, in many cases almost unaided, stopped the enemy advance and where he tried to get on they cut him to pieces. During the night, all available guns were placed under command of Lieutenent-Colonel W.A. Murray (17 Brigade RFA), and he organised a constant bombardment of the enemy.

IV Corps fared better. Preparations were more thorough and all were poised to face the German attack. However, the High Command were not. They did not believe that the Germans could attack and ordered HQ III Corps to relieve HQ IV Corps at 1500 hours on the day of the battle. The tanks were ordered to winter quarters! The Germans attacked the three British divisions of the Corps, holding between Bourlon and the Canal du Nord, with five divisions backed by a powerful artillery.

The first assault began at 0900 hours at Cantaing, against 59th Division, but this was easily broken by the guns of the Guards and 51st Divisions. To the left was 47th Division, supported by the guns of 40th and 62nd Divisions, together with 5 Brigade RHA and 77 Army Field Artillery Brigade. Here the assaulting massed German infantry received terrible punishment. Some, however, found a gap between 47th Division and 2nd Division to its left but they were held. 2nd Division, holding a front of 4,500 yards, was covered by 36 and 41 Brigades RFA (its own), 153 and 173 Brigades RFA of 36th Division and by 93 Army Field Artillery Brigade. The guns had been well forward to cover the expected advance but, when it was clear that this would not occur, they were moved back for defensive operations. This saved them from enemy counter-battery fire, which fell harmlessly on the forward positions. At 0850 hours, masses of German infantry began advancing in great waves over the open slopes between Moeuvres and

Anti-aircraft detachments taking post. The gun is a 13-pounder 9 cwt. (*R.A.I.*)

Bourlon and the guns again began to take a terrible toll of them. Even 9.2-inch howitzers had the rare satisfaction of observing their shells falling among the Germans to great effect. But the Germans pressed on and on, taking enormous casualties and succeeded in overrunning some of 2nd Division's outposts. Their attack swung onto the tired 56th Division, whose infantry fought with extreme gallantry and finally held the advance. They were helped by the guns of 7 Brigade RHA from 1st Cavalry Division, who were well sited to fire into the enemy flanks. The defence of Bourlon was perhaps the most outstanding defensive action of the War by the British. Great courage by the infantry, backed by excellent artillery and machine gun fire, proved too much for the Germans, who themselves fought with great gallantry and courage.

So ended 30th November 1917—a day when so much gained was so nearly lost, but when so much gallantry saved the day. The night was fine but cold and dark and the tired men, desperately in need of rest, had much to do to re-organise for the morrow. Many reinforcements, hastily dispatched earlier in the day, began to arrive.

1st December 1917 was a day of fierce, confused fighting. The German plan to cut off the British salient after Cambrai had failed. The British carried out a series of small, uncoordinated counter-attacks to strengthen their positions but these were in the main unsuccessful. An attack by the Guards, supported by the guns of 70 Brigade RFA (who happened to be moving through Third Army area on 30th November!) and 235 Brigade RFA from 47th Division (who had been calibrating when the attack started) was, however, partially successful. Fierce fighting continued in 29th Division's area, but it was of a local nature. The German Army Commander admitted that "the attack had run itself out". On 2nd December, fierce fighting continued but, although it was renewed on 3rd December, that day also saw the end of the counter-attack. The main thrust was again towards La Vacquerie but by now a strong force of artillery under the CRA 2nd Division had been formed. The guns of 72, 73 Brigades RFA (12th Division), 91 Brigade RFA (20th Division), 236 Brigade RFA (47th Division) and one battery of 179 Army Field Artillery Brigade opened on Germans every time they tried to attack. Every time the attacks failed but, by last light, they got close and bombing started.

On 4th December, Sir Douglas Haig ordered a withdrawal to the Hindenburg support line. This was carried out with great skill and the Germans did not realise what was happening. They continued shelling the abandoned positions until 1500 hours on 5th December. The new British line held to the end of the year and beyond. It was tested on 30th–31st December, when the Germans attacked Welsh Ridge heavily but were repulsed with great loss by 63rd Naval Division and twenty-five field batteries.

So ended the battle of Cambrai. Brilliant success followed by wretched failure. Gallantry had again saved the day. The German counter-attack should have broken through but then, so should the British initial attacks. British artillery losses had been heavy. One hundred and three field guns and fifty-five siege places were lost on 30th November, but the British had captured one hundred and thirty-eight German guns. There can be no doubt that the initial German success on 30th November was due to the weakness of the artillery on VII Corps front—only eight 6-inch howitzers formed the Corps Heavy Artillery. It is surprising to find that, in all subsequent enquiries into the failure at Cambrai and into the success of the

German attacks, this fact is totally absent.

There were many mistakes made at Cambrai. Neither officers nor men were well trained in mobile warfare and attacks were frequently not thoroughly co-ordinated. After the undoubted initial success of map shooting, too much reliance was placed on it once things became more mobile. This was wrong. However, the battle opened a new chapter in the life of the Royal Regiment. Survey was here to stay; the Royal Regiment must now have its own surveyors. Calibration became important to everyone. The artillery doctrine born at Cambrai stayed almost unchanged until the end of the War, and lasted well into the 1939–45 conflict. Some principles remained unchanged until the arrival of the computer in the 1960s.

But there was gallantry after Cambrai, too. The defence of La Vacquerie owed much to the guns. The gallantry of Sergeant Gourley, of Lieutenant Wallace and C Battery 63 Brigade, and again of 377th and 379th Batteries, which stood up to the attacking hordes of infantry, virtually stopped the attack in its tracks.

So the thunder of battle died away. The exhausted armies turned to fight their common enemy, winter; the winter of the trenches, the fourth winter of the trenches of this most terrible of all wars.

CHAPTER 20

The Eve of the Storm — Spring 1918

See map 34

It was a grim winter, and nowhere worse than around Ypres. The mud and waterlogged ground, the incessant shelling and the lack of cover from foe or weather, made life unbearable. Great efforts had to be made to stop the guns from sinking into the vile mire and every morning was spent in repairing the damage of the night's shelling. There was no rest or respite. The Gunners did not leave the line; they stayed for the long weeks of winter, by the guns.

But much worse was going on behind the scenes. There were many problems to solve before the next campaigning season began in earnest. The 18-pounder carriages were causing grave anxiety, many were badly worn and past repair. Batteries needed Lewis guns, and plans were made to issue two per battery, though this figure was later cut by the General Staff to one. Work began on revised training manuals to gather together the lessons of the war to date. The British had decided to adopt the German system of defence by having a "Forward Zone" some 600 yards deep, a "Battle Zone" some 2,300 yards deep behind it and a "Rear Zone" some four to eight miles to the rear. This posed new problems for the artillery, who had to adopt a form of mobility within this framework to give correct coverage to each zone. This called for some study. Alternative positions became more important. Roving sections and sniping guns were to be used on special tasks and dummy positions were to be exploited. All positions within 3,000 yards of the front trenches were to be wired in and prepared for all-round defence. Battery positions were to be strong points and rallying points for the infantry "around which a stubborn defence can be organised".

Artillery headquarters were to be close by cavalry and infantry headquarters at all times, and protection and repair of artillery communications was to be a priority task for all. Great emphasis was laid on OP officers having good views and command so that all possible approaches could be covered by observed fire. All OPs were to be wired and flanked by machine gun fire. Alternative means of communication were by (but still very few) radios and lamps, flags, discs, carrier pigeons and orderlies.

Counter-battery planning received a lot of priority, as did air defence, and the training notes of this period did much to bring together the lessons of 1917 in these respects. The use of concentrated, accurate, protracted fire on known batteries was deemed better than the German method of sudden "hates" into likely areas. This philosophy proved correct. The maximum use of air observation was also deemed essential. In addition, to maintain accuracy it was laid down that guns must constantly check their performance, if necessary during a shoot, against known datum points. The technique of sound-ranging our own batteries onto distant targets was to be further developed. Artillery intelligence was to be improved. Data on enemy guns could be obtained from air photographs, reports from air observers, sound ranging sections, artillery OPs, hostile shelling reports (Shelreps, as they came to be called) and radio intelligence. So important was aerial reconnaissance of enemy artillery that one aircraft was reserved for this job alone. Balloons were also used. Flash intersections at night were used to confirm enemy positions.

Counter-battery work was divided into four tasks; the destruction of guns, the destruction of gun detachments, the destruction of ammunition or neutralisation. It was found that, to destroy a well protected gun-pit, it was necessary to expend 100 rounds of 6-inch or 8-inch howitzer ammunition or sixty rounds of 9.2-inch howitzer. The technique was to put all possible guns onto each battery in turn after checking the fire of each on a datum point. Accuracy was essential, spraying the area quite useless. When a battery had been accurately located, the technique was to fire two quick salvoes to catch the detachments before they could take cover. Persistent nightly shelling of the same batteries with gas was also used. Finally, it was laid down that counter-battery observation stations should be established, manned by an experienced officer with authority to call for extra guns for counter-battery work if the situation demanded it. The problems of counter-battery during the advance caused much worry, and the importance of radios in this connection was realised. At this time came the first reports of Gunners drawing up their own radios to be manned by Gunner operators.

The German Attack on 21st March 1918

By 17th March 1918, the Germans had 187 divisions on the Western Front and it became clear that an attack was imminent. Many indicators showed that the attack would fall on the British line where it was held by the Third and Fifth Armies. Here, the Fifth Army had taken over part of the French front, further weakening its positions. Many divisions were reduced to nine battalions.

The GOCRA of Fifth Army was Major-General H.C.C. Uniacke. His Order of Battle was:

III Corps

> *14th Divisional Artillery*
> *18th Divisional Artillery*
> *58th Divisional Artillery*
> *2nd Cavalry Divisional Artillery*
> *3rd Cavalry Divisional Artillery*

XVIII Corps

> *15th Divisional Artillery*
> *30th Divisional Artillery*
> *61st Divisional Artillery*

XIX Corps

> *8th Divisional Artillery*
> *24th Divisional Artillery*
> *1st Cavalry Divisional Artillery*

VII Corps

> *Guards Divisional Artillery*
> *3rd Divisional Artillery*
> *16th Divisional Artillery*
> *31st Divisional Artillery*
> *34th Divisional Artillery*
> *40th Divisional Artillery*
> *59th Divisional Artillery*

These divisional artilleries, plus 23 Army field brigades, gave him a total of 1,051 guns. In addition, he had 102 60-pounders; 28 6-inch guns; 59 8-inch howitzers; 4 9.2-inch guns; 61 9.2-inch howitzers; 6 12-inch howitzers and one 15-inch gun. This gave him one field gun or howitzer per seventy yards of front, not enough to sustain a heavy attack. On 10th February, Major-General Birch, still MGRA at GHQ, wrote to the Director of Artillery "The pity of it is that we ever had to take over the extra front. Our 18-pounder situation never really allowed for it, but Henry Wilson could not see it".

Third Army, holding twenty-eight miles with fourteen divisions, was better placed. Even so, it could only manage forty guns of all calibres to the mile, whereas the Germans had over eighty. In reserve were only eight divisions.

Ammunition was moved from corps dumps to divisional ARPs (Ammunition Re-supply Points), and thence to battery positions, all by light railways. Should this be out, horse transport was located to take over immediately, using alternative routes. The air defence plan was simple. Troops being attacked by aircraft from under 3,000 feet would engage using small arms, and one field gun per battery would engage at a false angle of sight on the order "Aeroplane attack". A further point of interest in the defensive planning was "that an organisation must exist whereby retiring infantry can be rallied and distributed in a manner best suited for the defence of the line of guns. Such infantry must be commanded by artillery officers, should no infantry officers be with them . . . "

The positions held by both Third and Fifth Army were not good. The "Forward Zones" were adequate but the "Battle Zones" were dangerously incomplete and it was in these zones that all the artillery stood ready. The "Rear Zones" had hardly been prepared at all. Most divisions stood in line, with few in reserve. 50th Division, in Army reserve, was 30 miles west of St. Quentin. III Corps, on the right of the Army, held 31,500 yards of front astride the valley of the Oise, thought to be an unlikely enemy approach. 58th Division, on the right of III Corps, held 16,000 yards, with 18th Division in the centre holding 10,000 yards and 14th Division on the left 5,500 yards. Next came XVIII Corps holding 16,000 yards with its three divisions, then XIX Corps holding 12,000 yards with two divisions and, on the left, VII Corps with four divisions holding 15,000 yards.

Third Army had four Corps (IV, V, VI and XVII) which were holding 15,000, 12,000, 13,000 and 10,000 yards of front respectively. Their left Corps, XVII, was not engaged on 21st March.

The German plan was to beat the British and end the war. Three Armies were to attack between the Oise and Arras. Seventeen Corps were mustered, providing seventy-four assault divisions. Forty-three divisions were to attack the fourteen of

Fifth Army and nineteen moved against six of the Third Army divisions. To support this most massive of all attacks of the war, the Germans had assembled 3,965 field guns, 2,435 heavies and 73 super heavies, a total of 6,473 guns of all calibres. In addition, 3,532 trench mortars were available; the attack frontage was fifty miles.

And so to the battle. In truth, it consisted of five great battles, whose names serve not only as memorials to some of the greatest feats of arms of the war, but also serve to show its progress. It covered almost 1,000 square miles and lasted sixteen days. Records for this period are scarce and, indeed, were they available, space would not permit more than a brief summary of each of these great battles and then only the part played in them by the artillery. More than at any time in this great story, I am conscious that this section may do less than justice to the thousands of untold acts of gallantry which occurred. Though often overwhelmed, the guns of all calibres were fought to the end, adding more laurels to the story of The Regiment.

The Battle of St. Quentin—21st–23rd March 1918

A thick, heavy mist greeted the dawn of 21st March 1918, so thick indeed that some guns reported being unable to see their aiming posts. At 0440 hours, a tremendous bombardment began, directed at forward locations, the wire and the British guns. It was deadly accurate and the guns in particular suffered heavily, but they were not crushed and they responded magnificently to desperate calls for SOS targets. But the mist enabled the Germans to crawl right up to the British wire and to complete the job of cutting it; a great advantage. Soon communications were cut and battery commanders were hard pressed to know what was happening. Light signals could not be seen in the mist. Confusion was complete and many gun batteries did not know an attack had started until the enemy were upon them. The mist also prevented all flying and, although this hampered the Germans, it hampered the British much more. Aircraft could not be used for the vital tasks of finding out what was going on or for directing fire.

Let us look at the fortunes of 18th Divisional Artillery, 82 and 83 Brigades RFA. A Battery of 82 Brigade was in action 1,000 yards west of Fort Vendeuil, under the command of Captain W. Dennes. The mist was very, very thick in the Oise Valley that morning. It was impossible to know what was going on. By noon, the mist suddenly cleared to reveal German infantry advancing 300 yards from the muzzles. The 18-pounders smote them cruelly, inflicting such casualties that every effort to rush the guns was crushed. Quick accurate gun drill took its toll and for nearly four hours the battery held its ground. Then snipers working forward began to pick off the detachments. Captain Dennes sent a runner for orders, refusing to retire when he was hit. 2nd Lieutenant R.G.M. Jones took command and fought on till 1700 hours, when the gallant A Battery was rushed and captured.

500 yards to the south, B Battery of 82 Brigade engaged the enemy over open sights until 1800 hours. It could see the death of A Battery but could do nothing. At dusk, the infantry began to retire and one section stood alone facing the enemy, with its casualties about the guns. In the end, the last men destroyed the guns and withdrew the detachments; another gallant stand.

Meanwhile, C Battery of 83 Brigade had its sections dispersed south east of Benay. Captain L. Mc G. Haybittel commanded the advanced section himself when, at 1115 hours, German infantry rushed through the mist. Seizing rifles and their breech blocks, the section fought its way back to the next section only to find German infantry closing in. Again Captain Haybittel and his men grabbed breech blocks, picked up a machine gun and withdrew to a nearby sunken road. Here they made a stand fighting as infantry and, when a line was established to the rear section, the combined small arms fire stopped every German rush, inflicting heavy casualties and knocking out each enemy machine gun. By 2000 hours, the rear section had fired 1900 rounds but one gun was irretrievably jammed. By now this gallant little force was cut off and surrounded but Captain Haybittel still managed to conduct a successful withdrawal, capturing a German machine gun and a platoon of German infantry whilst doing so. This must be a unique and rare case of a battery acting as its own infantry and then conducting a withdrawal through an encircling enemy.

D Battery of 83 Brigade had two sections well forward and one near Brigade Headquarters. This section lost all its men during the German bombardment, but new detachments were formed from the wagon lines, and men of Brigade Headquarters formed a protective screen round the guns with rifles. By noon, German infantry appeared through mist 500 yards away; they were engaged down to 200 yards, the Gunners having to duck to avoid splinters from their own shells. Throughout the afternoon the little force held out. By 1500 hours, a German battery was seen coming into action 1500 yards away. It was engaged so quickly and accurately by the section that the German teams bolted and the derelict guns never opened fire at all. By 1800 hours the last round was fired. The position was by now under close machine gun fire but the Germans, roughly handled all day, shrank from closing in before dark. The gallant section waited by its guns hoping for more ammunition, and teams to get them away, but none came and the 4.5-inch howitzers which had served so well were disabled and the Gunners fought their way back to the nearest infantry posts.

By night-fall 21st March, 82 and 83 Brigades had lost thirty-one guns and howitzers but the story of their loss is told in some detail to show that they were not given up easily.

It was not only the gun detachments which showed gallantry. We will probably never know the full details of the courage and devotion and deeds of valour carried out by the drivers in their continuous attempts to save the guns in those dark days of March 1918. Perhaps few events illustrate this more than the courage of 23015 Driver J. Terry of D Battery 150 Army Brigade RFA in XIX Corps area. During the morning of 18th March, he was ordered to take his team and limber to the battery position which was being heavily gassed. Fire could hardly be maintained on the advancing Germans, so Driver Terry picked his way through the gas and bursting shells, limbered up No. 1 gun and took it over the crest where it could continue to fire; he then repeated this feat for each of the remaining five guns. The operation took one hour, the battery maintaining its fire all the time, and its success was entirely due to the courage, skill and determination of Driver Terry.

It was not only the field artillery that was hotly engaged. 33rd Siege Battery RGA came under such heavy machine gun and rifle fire that it suffered 75%

casualties. The section commander, himself acting as Number 1 and layer, gathered the few remaining fit men around 'A' sub-section and maintained direct fire with this 8-inch howitzer for two hours. Another gun was brought into action and this section fought hard until, by 1700 hours on 22nd March, it had fired the remarkable total of 3,000 rounds; 300 tons of ammunition in 36 hours. With German infantry only 500 yards away, two caterpiller tractors managed to get the two battle-scarred guns away from their positions, standing alone in front of the British line. That night they were in action again. Such courage must never be forgotten.

Meanwhile, in XVIII Corps further north, a similar story unfolded. 30th and 61st Divisions lost many guns and 307 Brigade RFA was captured after a desperate fight, with the exception of a section which got out under heavy machine gun fire. Only fifty men got back from the eight battalions of the 'Forward Zone'.

In VII Corps, further north again, 16th Division stood around Ronssoy. 177 and 180 Brigades RFA, with 189 and 277 Army Field Artillery Brigades RFA, stood astride the main enemy thrust line. By the end of the day only four howitzers and six 18-pounders remained. D Battery of 177 Brigade, commanded by Second Lieutenant Trorey, was firing in mist in the early morning on SOS tasks when German infantry suddenly appeared through the mist on the right flank of the battery. The guns were in pits and could not be switched round, nor was there time to run them into the open. The guns of right section were disabled, the gunners gave covering fire with small arms while the left section was run out into the open and swung onto the enemy at point blank range. Lieutenant Trorey seized a Lewis gun and he himself killed many Germans. A bombardier helping him was killed at his side. By now the Germans were 100 yards away and he gave the order to disable all guns and retire, but the young Trorey was so badly wounded that he could not move. Some men who tried to help him were shot down, so he ordered them to retire to join some infantry to the rear, and this gallant young officer was captured. But the battery had held up the advance for the vital hours to co-ordinate some kind of line to the rear. Determined to save the guns, the teams thundered up straight into German machine gun fire; seven out of eighteen drivers died instantly but the rest galloped towards the guns, only to find the Germans on them in strength and they were forced to retire. Again the colours of the Regiment had been defended to the last, the battery died almost to a man in its gallant fight to stand to the guns in the hour of peril.

And so across the front on that black day, courage abounded and wherever possible the guns held the line time and time again. Records report a single 18-pounder on 21st Division's front (its battery unknown) which fired 1,000 rounds holding up an entire German brigade and then, with all ammunition gone, the subaltern in charge held off the Germans with a machine gun as a team galloped up, limbered up and thundered off into the dusk of the evening; the subaltern died. Who was he? Who were they? No one knows, but he was doing his duty, upholding the great claim of the Regiment; the guns must be fought to the end, and then they must be saved to fight again. Was he the Gunners' own Unknown Warrior?

By dusk, the gravity of the situation was reaching GHQ; reserves were ordered to stem the flow. 39th Divisional Artillery raced to assist 6th Division, and 20th Divisional Artillery came into action behind 30th and 36th Divisions, just north of where III and XVIII Corps joined. 7 (H, I and Y Batteries) and 17 (N and X Batteries) Brigades RHA of 1st Cavalry Division galloped forward to plug the line behind 24th and 66th Divisions. 50th Division was ordered to move to reinforce XIX Corps.

In Third Army area, the mist had cleared earlier and observed fire could be brought to bear. The Germans attacking 51st Division described the British artillery fire as "unbearable". By now all batteries of the Divisional Artillery were fighting furiously over open sights. 24 Brigade RFA was ordered to withdraw while covering the withdrawal of the infantry at point blank range. The withdrawal was completed as the last infantry passed the guns, without loss of a gun. It was a great feat of gunners and drivers alike. 59th Division received the heaviest of all attacks. It was a new division, just formed and rushed into the line before completion of training. By noon the German thrust up the Hirondelle Valley had destroyed four battalions and most of their guns. At 1235 hours, the last message from the Division was from an unknown artillery officer, who said the enemy were at the dug-out steps and he was destroying his papers. The battle in the valley was ferocious. Three German divisions were attacking in line. At one point, a mixed line of field guns and three 9.2-inch howitzers fired point blank at the closing enemy. Ranges got shorter and shorter and the gunners seized Lewis guns and rifles and held until the next line could be prepared. At the end of the day only two batteries of 59th Divisional Artillery escaped.

In 34th Division's area, 160 Brigade RFA greatly distinguished itself near Croissile firing over open sights at 5,000 advancing infantry and defeated three assaults in succession by the terrible accuracy and speed of its fire. Two more German divisions came up, advancing in mass, and forged forward. When only 200 yards away, the gunners fell back and fought on with the infantry until dark. The gunners crept back to the battery positions and manhandled the guns back, covered by the infantry; up came the teams and withdrew the guns, which came into action once again to cover the infantry.

In 66th Division area of XIX Corps, the Manchesters were attacked in Brosse Wood, but it was the close range fire of B Battery 330 Brigade RFA which beat off all attacks, until 1800 hours when they were at last surrounded and the few survivors captured.

So ended 21st March 1918, one of the blackest days in the history of the British Army. But all was not lost. Thanks to the gallantry of gunner and infantryman, the tenuous line had held. Ludendorf was bitterly disappointed. His casualties were far higher than he had envisaged. His losses in officers and junior leaders was so high that we now know the German Army was never able to recover. It was clear that every stubborn defence of a trench, every stand by a battery as the enemy's masses reached the muzzles of the guns, every feat of individual courage and gallantry took its toll. During the afternoon some artillery reinforcements were sent to Third Army. These were 29 and 81 (Mobile) Brigades RGA (6″ and 8″ Howitzers) and 8th Siege Battery (6″ guns). Later 92 (Mobile) and 99 (8″ Howitzer) Brigades RGA, 65th Siege Battery (12″ Howitzers) and 155 Army Brigade RFA were transferred from First to Third Army.

22nd March dawned fine but cold. The mist which formed during the night cleared by 0800 hours. The withdrawal continued and soon divisions began to get out of phase, gaps appeared, salients were cut off; indeed, it is surprising that the

Germans did not press on faster, such was the chaos. On the right, III Corps of Fifth Army held the Crozat Canal line firmly, but soon its left flank was threatened. XVIII Corps withdrew during the day to the Somme but had to abandon some fifteen heavy guns, due to the impossibility of getting tractors forward on the choked roads. In XIX Corps, 23, 68 and 76 Brigades RGA were intact, and were reinforced by 21 and 22 Brigades RGA. The Corps had 217 field guns and 112 heavies. 24th Division recovered nine guns by a spirited action of 11th Hussars and Gunners. It also had I and N Batteries RHA, A and B Batteries RCHA and 23, 106, 107 and 251 Brigades RFA, a total of 93 guns. G, H and Y Batteries RHA with 86, 250, 330 and 331 Brigades RFA galloped to save 66th Division. At 0815 hours 16th Divisional Artillery was ordered to retire.

186 Brigade RFA remained in action until the enemy were only 500 yards away and then got away successfully. 184 Brigade was less lucky. It fought on until the last infantry had passed through it. The teams could not get forward and sixteen guns were lost. 21st Divisional Artillery was ordered to withdraw at 1100 hours but the order did not reach the infantry, who were left and suffered heavily without their guns.Perhaps typical of this momentous and chaotic day is the following extract from the diary of D Battery RHA, 3 Brigade RHA (of 2nd Cavalry Division but assisting 58th Division on the right of Fifth Army):

> "*March 22nd.* Next morning found a dense mist until mid-day. We pottered about improvising camouflage and the organisation of position which was on the actual border of the wood on a carpet of wood anemones and primroses.
>
> At mid-day, as the mist showed signs of lifting, the Battery Commander and Lieutenant Haddow went up to the Observation Post—a ridge about 1,000 yards ahead of position, giving a commanding view of our front. Initial orders to check yesterday's lines of fire had been passed down telephone lines, when our attention was attracted by seeing a number of our men get up out of the long grass about 1,000 or 1,500 yards ahead and start coming back in a thin and straggling line. Simultaneously, we heard a good deal of machine gun fire and next minute out of the grass rose a German attack. They outnumbered the defenders by five to one at least and seemed to be formed in two or three waves—each wave composed of men apparently about two at yard intervals.
>
> "As you were" down the telephone. A rapid calculation on the map—"New target"—"all guns ten degrees more right"—and so on—the first two rounds burst low in the air—range exact and right in the front wave of the attack. The next orders were "five rounds gun fire". Within three minutes of their first appearance the attack had melted away—some of the enemy lying full length in the long grass—many crowded into some ruins and a garden hedge—but not one remained standing in view. Unfortunately, the grass was too high to count the bag—Captain Wright and Lieutenant R.C. Norton of "E", who happened to be standing by at the time (and whose telephone was not quite out) were hopping with excitement and filled with envy, malice and uncharitableness. "E" soon got going on our left. "J" were shooting on our right but without such good targets. No other guns were shooting, but the fire of these three batteries was sufficient to hold up the attack on their front apparently until the "cows come home"—and, until darkness, the enemy made not a yard on the front under observation".

By now the men of Third and Fifth Army were weary and confused. The situation was critical, cohesion had gone. Senior commanders, too far to the rear, had no feel for the battle which was being fought at brigade level. All along the front the guns did fine work in breaking up attacks and covering withdrawals. The German attacks in 63rd Division area on Hermies was broken by a barrage fired by 79 Brigade RFA, firing shrapnel with devastating effect. Similarly, the shells of 78 Brigade RFA smashed German attack after attack on Havrincourt, bursting

A battery of 6-inch howitzers in the open. (*I.W.M.*)

on them as they rose to assault. By 1400 hours a gap of six miles existed between Beaumetz and Mory in IV Corps area. Here, near Morchies, 256 Brigade RFA, firing over open sights, and 3rd Worcestershire Regiment foiled all enemy attempts to break through.

Large bodies of the enemy were seen around Morchies at a distance of 2,000 yards. All four batteries were run out of their pits and, for four hours over open sights (visibility being perfect), the gunners fired, plainly seeing the results of their fire. They were in action close to the divisional ammunition dump and fired over 20,600 rounds. B Battery fired 1,750 rounds per gun. Later, the Battery provided a smoke screen to cover the movement of some tanks towards Beugny. The effect of them caused the Germans to panic and 256 Brigade RFA again did great execution on them. At one stage, a German battery tried to come into action but was simply obliterated by 256 Brigade before it could fire a shot. To the north, VI Corps were in difficulty and the Germans pressed hard. The fire of 178 and 181 Brigades RFA from positions in the Ervillers Valley was so powerful that the Germans mounted a specific operation to deal with them before they could get on.

At one stage, enemy aircraft came over to locate the guns that were doing so much damage. German counter-battery fire followed and did some damage. At last, massive infantry attacks and a very heavy barrage forced an entry into the British line, but not until after dark. The diary of the Chestnut Troop records ". . . the Hun was still advancing, . . . At noon we came into action north of Bernes and fired on infantry advancing south west on Nosscourt Farm. A, C, K, Q and U Batteries were all in action together under Colonel J.G.B. Allardyce . . . we were last to pull out at 1800 hours". It was in this area that 76 Brigade RGA stood at Caulaincourt and 23 and 68 Brigades at Roise. And so to 23rd March. On this day, "Big Bertha" fired its first round onto Paris—such was the German advance. The mist did not rise till 1130 hours, III Corps withdrew and VI, XVIII and XIX had to conform. The gaps were now terrifyingly large and anyone who could be found was rushed forward to stem the tide. Lieutenant-Colonel A.C.L. Theobald, commanding O Battery RHA, was given 600 infantry just back from leave, eight Lewis guns and Number 3 Kite Balloon Company, to fill a gap near Belancourt. Co-ordinated artillery fire was now impossible and many a promising target was left untouched as it was not possible to tell if it was friend or foe. An incident in 39th Division illustrates the problem. German infantry suddenly appeared and the infantry fell back through the guns of 282 Brigade RFA, which stood its ground engaging over open sights. As the teams galloped forward, the Germans poured heavy fire onto the battery, scoring direct hits on eleven guns. But the rest, save one, escaped. This one, in a concealed flank position, waited until the German column closed to 200 yards. It then fired three rounds of shrapnel at point blank range with terrifying effect before it galloped back in triumph to safety. But many guns were lost that day.

One incident occurred to show how all were involved. The wagons of Number 2 Section appeared near the positions of Z Battery RHA as German infantry burst through the woods near the guns. There was no time to send for the teams so the wagons, acting as limbers, brought the guns to safety under heavy and close fire.

By now, forty-five German divisions had pushed an enormous hole in the British line, which was falling back everywhere. The Flesquières salient was abandoned. 17th Division was badly exposed at Hermies and paid great tribute to the magnificent performance of D Battery 74 Brigade RFA as it covered the final withdrawal at Velu Wood. It silenced all German machine guns as they came forward threatening the Foresters of 51st Infantry Brigade. Battery commanders had great difficulty locating British infantry and had to wait until the last of them had passed the guns before considering falling back. In IV Corps more cohesion was possible and all available artillery was formed into two groups under the CRAs of 6th and 51st Divisions. The infantry fighting was being co-ordinated by brigade commanders and some pattern was established. The heavies were sent back and the field brigades were ordered to fight it out over open sights. 104 Brigade RFA got away with enemy just 500 yards away, covered by a mixed party of unknown infantry under a most gallant RSM (Hopcroft of 8th Gloucesters). One battery galloped into action in the face of the German infantry and its fire was so intense that German dead "were literally piled in heaps". The German history records that, in spite of all their efforts, it was "impossible on this front to silence the British Artillery".

A final word on this tragic day from D Battery's history:

"*March 24th.* After some time, perhaps $1\frac{1}{2}$ hours, a mass of men appeared on the ridge east of Bethancourt. After careful study through glasses, the battery commander reported these as the enemy and gave orders to fire. Colonel Mellor, however, was very doubtful and by his orders "stop" was given. It was almost impossible to make sure that the grey uniforms were not those of the French—and all were puzzled by the fact that no French had retired from the crest in question. If these men were German, what had become of the French? The result of this uncertainty was the loss of many priceless minutes. Major Norton gave the order to fire two or three times, but was each time stopped by Colonel Mellor who, quitei rightly, was very apprehensive of shooting Frenchmen. Finally, the behaviour of the men settled the matter. Their advanced machine gunners could be seen rushing forward and establishing themselves in commanding posts such as the houses of Bethancourt, and almost at once the ridge we were occupying was swept by machine gun fire. The German infantry began to advance down the slope. "D" at once opened fire but, after getting a few rounds into the enemy at about 1,300 yards, began to hit the crest 200 or 300 yards to their own front. The guns were run by hand under a shower of machine gun bullets, for our flashes were evidently visible and the enemy's machine gunners concentrating on the guns. Teams were standing to close in rear of the guns under Battery Sergeant-Major Johnstone and, following his good example, were steady as rocks, several horses being hit. Sergeants Pilbeam and Woollard handled their guns with great dash and coolness. Guns were run up until just not visible from Bethancourt, but the more they were run up, the more the Germans descended the opposite slope and it was at once evident that the only chance of hitting them was to run guns well over the crest. With the concentration of machine guns opposite, this would probably have precluded the teams being able to withdraw them. The French infantry on our right and left, fresh troops who had so far not been engaged, and who had not fired a shot at the magnificent targets offered them, now rose up like one man and quietly retired through the remnants of 18th Division who were still digging.

The Battery Commander, with Colonel Mellor's approval, now gave orders to limber up and retire, with a view to taking up a position from which the line occupied and partly dug by the 18th Divisional infantry could be covered, for the guns were now the nearest troops to the enemy. It was a most difficult situation in which to make the right decision. The first alternative was to push the guns boldly over the ridge and, from a fully exposed position, engage the advancing enemy over open sights. Such a course would undoubtedly have had a great moral effect on our own exhausted infantry and, judging from the temper displayed by the enemy two days before, they would have been easy to stop on our immediate front. On the other hand, they would quickly have got round our flanks and, in addition, would almost certainly have pinned the guns to their ground by machine gun fire. The second alternative, which was to withdraw to cover 18th Division, was the one selected. It was the normal and sensible procedure; by following it, perhaps a great chance to make a brillliant name for the battery, at whatever sacrifice, was missed".

But they had been good days for the batteries. The guns had been fought to the last with great gallantry, often being the only way to hold up the enemy attacks while new positions were organised in rear. It was unfortunate that communications were not better, for nowhere do we read of heavy concentrations by whole divisional artilleries. It was just not possible. In some cases, the fire of brigades was concentrated with devastating effect; 160 Brigade and 256 Brigade are examples. The practice of batteries and sections within batteries covering each other back worked well, and resulted in many guns and infantry getting back as the rear battery engaged at point blank range. It is tragic that so much gallantry has gone unrecorded for, in sheer courage by Gunners, those were indeed great days.

CHAPTER 21

The Storm Rages—March 1918

See map 34

The battles of 24th and 25th March are now called the battle of Bapaume. The Germans, convinced that one major thrust north-westwards would drive the British into the sea, turned their fury onto the withdrawing Third Army while keeping up their pressure on the weary Fifth Army, where ammunition, food and even water were becoming short. Communications had gone, commanders had to be well forward and do the best they could by personal contact, liaison officers on horses and runners. British and French troops were very mixed on the right. The British position became a series of defended areas, which only withdrew when surrounded completely. 91 Brigade RFA formed such an island and, on withdrawal, left a battery to cover the operation. This battery soon found itself with sections firing in three directions. One section engaged Germans moving east from Villeselve in III Corps area, the others were firing north and south. As dusk fell the last round was fired and the battery limbered up, only to find its retreat cut. Seeing a gap, it galloped for Buchoire, just getting there before the enemy, and escaped. Survival now depended on initiative, mobility and quick reaction and it is to the everlasting credit of the batteries of the New Armies that they learnt these lessons so well and so quickly. At 1500 hours on 24th March, Fifth Army came under the command of General Fayolle of the French Army and all troops north of the Somme came under the command of the Third Army; so let us now turn to the story of the Third Army. As we have seen, the artillery of IV Corps was organised into two groups: Right Group, under Brigadier-General L.C.L. Oldfield, consisted of 255 and 256 Brigades RFA (51st Division), 112 Brigade (25th Division) and 235 Brigade RFA (47th Division) and 104 and 293 Army Field Artillery Brigades RFA. Left Group, under Brigadier-General A.S. Cotton, consisted of 187 and 190 Brigades RFA (41st Division) and 93 Brigade RFA (all that was left of 6th Divisional Artillery), two composite brigades each of two batteries of 25th Divisional Artillery and 236 Brigade RFA of 47th Division. A Heavy Brigade was attached to each group. Right Group retired at noon, covering the withdrawal of the infantry and bombarding the exits of Bapaume to prevent the Germans from following up.

At 1900 hours on 24th March, a general withdrawal was ordered as Right Group deployed around Ligny-Thilloy. They fell back through Achiet-le-Petit, in order to concentrate at Bucquoy, but masses of other men, horses and guns also fell back this way and soon a massive blockage occurred in that small village. Sixty guns were still there at dawn next day. But by evening on 24th March, Third Army was more secure, though every man was weary in the extreme. The danger came in the increasing gap between them and Fifth Army, made worse by a

French failure to give the British any orders to fall back on Paris. Fifth Army had a difficult time on 25th March, co-ordination failed and many batteries were left in action with no orders. The French then ordered all the British, less their artillery, to withdraw and many were the stories of confusion as British guns tried to support French infantry without knowing what was going on. But still the action of individuals saved the day. Lieutenant G.P. Chapman, of A Battery 94 Brigade RFA, was approaching Peronne with three new guns when he met German infantry. Coming swiftly into action, he opened rapid fire over open sights until his ammunition ran out; he then limbered up and galloped off to rejoin his battery, but he had held up the advance for two hours single handed.

In Third Army, the situation had again deteriorated with the dawn of 26th March; its right had to swing back further. In VII Corps, 34th Division withstood an enemy attack by five divisions by sheer dogged gallantry of the infantry—there is no record of artillery support on this occasion. In V Corps, the Germans rushed forward, believing the British to be broken, and suffered what some observers described as the heaviest losses of the March fighting. The guns of 47th Divisional Artillery did much execution and clung desperately to their positions around Contalmaison until last light. Meanwhile IV Corps, exhausted after a night on the move, was faced at dawn by fifteen German divisions. By sheer weight of numbers, this mass of infantry forced a three mile gap between the left of V Corps and the right of IV Corps. But the guns, particularly those of 47th Division, were so effective that the Germans did not follow up their advantage. In VI Corps the Germans were held almost entirely by artillery fire. So much was this so that 4th Guards Brigade complained that they were not being given a chance to use their weapons! But a withdrawal was ordered at last light in rain, hail and sleet, which tried the tired troops severely. Again the guns stayed to the last and only withdrew after the tired infantry fell back past them.

However, there was no respite for the weary, aching men of Third and Fifth Army. Again confusion reigned in Fifth Army. On 25th March, General Fayolle ordered the British to withdraw in one direction and the French, with the bulk of the British artillery, in another. General Gough put the infantry of XVIII Corps, now without guns, in the gap this move created, and so saved the situation. Thus it was that the guns of 30th, 36th and 61st Divisional Artilleries spent the day in support of the French 22nd and 62nd Divisions and ended the day around Montdidier. The situation in XIX Corps was desperate. Six weak divisions held thirteen miles of front, with a three mile gap between their right and the French, and a four mile gap between their left and Third Army. At this stage in VII and XIX Corps, 8th Division had 79 guns, 16th had 60, 24th had 53, 50th had 48 and 66th had 45, a total of 371. But as the mist cleared these guns gave good account of themselves, as the Corps fell back to close the gaps on its flanks.

The position in Third Army was better but rumour was everywhere and congestion made movement extremely difficult. VII Corps front was covered by the 21st and 35th Divisional Artilleries under Brigadier-General H.W. Newcome, CRA 21st Division. Orders were given to withdraw to the line of the River Ancre. The morning of 25th March was quiet but, at 1300 hours, a fierce attack fell on 27th Brigade; this was beaten off by combined rifle and gun fire, and artillery liaison was reported as excellent. Then suddenly a further involuntary withdrawal began and could not be stopped—there was no enemy pressure but, since orders were taking two to three hours to get through, it could not be controlled. V Corps held the line of Ancre all day and, when Germans moved into Albert at 1630 hours, the British guns blocked all exits. In IV Corps a gap of four miles existed between it and V Corps, so the GOC 19th Division sent mounted artillery patrols to discover the situation. These reported a major enemy thrust from Serre at 1000 hours, moving straight into the gap. 19th Division (only 1,800 strong) and all available guns were put into a blocking position and somehow held the advance and saved the day. A heavy attack then developed at Bucquoy, where the defence was materially assisted by one hundred machine gunners brought forward from the Machine Gun School by a Gunner destined for great fame, Lieutenant-Colonel W.E. Ironside. On the extreme right of the Corps, the New Zealand Division moved into the gap alongside 2nd Division, but came under heavy machine gun fire until the guns of 15th Battery 36 Brigade RFA systematically knocked them out one by one. At this point, a dozen Whippet tanks made their first appearance on the field of battle, and the enemy fled!

So ended the battle of Bapaume. The Third Army and Fifth Army had held when put to the test. The Germans were now as weary as the British and their morale was falling, surrenders increased, prisoners no longer showed the arrogance of the opening days of the great attack, depression had set in. On the other hand, British morale was actually rising, as the men slowly realised that their dogged determination was paying off.

But 26th March 1918 was notable in another way. For the first time, a unified command was set up in France and all the British and French Armies came under the direct command of General Foch.

Unknown to the men locked in battle, we now know that the tide had turned but, before this was clear to the weary troops, there was more hard fighting ahead. 27th and 28th March saw the battle of Avre on the British front and the battle of Rosières on the French front to the south. Records are scarce for the fighting of these two days, and this is not surprising. Men were weary, confusion reigned, the enemy was everywhere; there was no time to write records! Although the British lost some ground, somehow their line held, but part of the French gave, the enemy occupied Montdidier on 27th March and opened up a nine mile gap in the French line. Most of the British artillery supporting the French returned to their own divisions on 27th March, although the Divisional Artilleries of 2nd Cavalry, 18th and 58th Divisions and III Corps Heavy Artillery Group, with a cavalry escort from 3rd Cavalry Division, still remained in action with the French.

The main enemy attacks in this area fell on XIX Corps. Its artillery was commanded by Brigadier-General W.B.R. Sandys and its heavies by Brigadier-General C.G. Pritchard. The Artillery Order of Battle in the Corps was:

8th Divisional Artillery. CRA, Brigadier-General J.W.F. Lamont

> 16 Brigade RHA
> 23, 32 and 45 Brigade RFA
> (a total of 73 guns)

16th Divisional Artillery, CRA Brigadier-General C.E.C.G. Charlton

> 177, 180 and 277 Brigades RFA
> (a total of 60 guns)

24th Divisional Artillery, CRA, Brigadier-General E.S. Hoare-Nairne

> H and I Batteries RHA
> A and B Batteries RCHA
> 106, 107, 251 and 311 Brigades RFA
> (a total of 86 guns)

39th Divisional Artillery. CRA, Brigadier-General W.G. Thompson

> 46, 174 and 186 Brigades RFA
> One battery 282 Brigade RFA
> (a total of 53 guns)

50th Divisional Artillery. CRA, Brigadier-General A.U. Stockley

> 86 and 350 Brigades RFA
> One battery 47 Brigade RFA
> (a total of 52 guns)

66th Divisional Artillery. CRA, Brigadier-General A. Birtwhistle

> 4 Brigade RHA
> 330 and 331 Brigades RFA and 47 Brigade less one battery
> (a total of 61 guns)

The enemy attacks on 27th March were heavy and continuous, units were terribly depleted. In 50th Division, one weak brigade was trying to cling on to 4,000 yards of front. But the gallant, tired infantry hung on and did not yield. The history of XIX Corps states that it "received splendid support from the field and heavy artillery, field batteries remaining in action until the enemy were only 600 yards away".

Meanwhile, Third Army fared better. All divisional artilleries were in good gun positions, with good observation right across the front, and they did great execution. All attacks on the New Zealand Division's positions were broken by artillery fire. On 62nd Division's front "machine guns shot down the attacking waves of Germans, and the artillery barrage dropped like a blanket to finish off the survivors". In VI Corps area, the first German attacks were stopped by the artillery alone and, when two battalions were seen reforming to attack, they were destroyed by the concentrated power of the guns unleashed upon them.

It was a good day for the guns. Co-ordination was returning, communications were re-established, the tide was really turning. The value of overwhelming concentrations of artillery on men exposed in attack was being realised.

During the night 27th–28th March, the weather broke and the rain fell. 36th Divisional Artillery was still supporting the French VI Corps and 20th and 30th Divisional Artilleries were under a force commanded by the French General Mesple. XIX Corps still struggled to link British with French and was heavily attacking at 1000 hours between the Avre and the Somme. On the right the French retired and for a while the British were exposed. It was here near Warfusée that the 1st–2nd Lancashire Heavy Battery RGA had its four 60 pounders in action as the British infantry fell back at 1930 hours. They were closely pursued by

Germans, who engaged the guns with machine guns from a flank. One section withdrew but the other, under heavy fire, could not get its teams up. Lieutenant N. Roberts, the section commander, with some gunners manhandled some ammunition wagons to the threatened flank to catch the bullets. He then got his teams up and snatched his two heavies from under the very noses of the enemy, a most gallant and courageous act.

On that morning—28th March—began the battle of Arras. Twenty-nine German divisions, with sixteen in support, attacked on a thirty-three mile front from the Somme to Arleux. It was Ludendorf's final effort; the Germans attacked shoulder to shoulder with great courage, convinced the British were broken. But the British infantry and gunners were far from broken; they stood ready with rifle, machine gun and field gun. So great were the German casualties that day that no figures were published; so devastating was the British fire that the Germans halted, shot to pieces, and Ludendorf called off the action. The German artillery was ineffective and, when it opened fire, was shot to pieces by the British heavies. They tried gas on the British gunners, but to no avail. At one point, eleven divisions attacked the 3rd, 4th, 15th and 56th British Divisions in front of Arras, all veterans by now and, though sadly depleted, they threw back the attacks. By 1700 hours, the Germans were at a standstill, groping for such cover as they could find. At 1130 hours enemy were discovered forming up only one hundred yards from the Guards Division front line; the divisional artillery fell on them with a crash and they broke out and fled. Later they tried to re-form, with the same result.

It was in 56th Division that a section of 93rd Battery of 280 Brigade RFA played such a notable part. The Brigade was covering the infantry holding Gavrelle on the southern slopes of Vimy Ridge, with a section well forward near Arleux under Lieutenant G.J. Palfrey. The guns were exposed but enfiladed the German positions. In spite of the artillery fire, the forward infantry positions were overwhelmed and, after stubborn and gallant defence, they fell back. Lieutenant Palfrey was ordered to fire off all his ammunition, destroy his guns and withdraw. So he poured his fire into the attacking Germans as they closed right up to him; indeed, the British defensive barrage, creeping back, was also on him. With rounds in the muzzles and bores, the guns were shattered and the gallant Palfrey, bringing his wounded, his breech blocks and sights with him, fought his way through Germans (who by now had passed him) back to join the infantry. Seldom have orders been so rigorously obeyed. The German history says of that day that it was impossible to reach Arras "because of the great disturbance caused by the British artillery fire". British ammunition expenditure was as heavy as any in the war; the 18-pounders and 4.5-inch howitzers expended some 700 rounds per gun each and were frequently engaging at ranges of 300–600 yards.

So ended the attempt to capture Arras. But Ludendorf now determined to capture Amiens, and spent the day of 29th March reinforcing his left wing in order to do so. It was a miserable day, wet and windy, with icy water filling the rivers. The British snatched some rest, did some re-grouping, brought up the few reserves available and waited. 30th March dawned wet and miserable, with rain that was to last all day, but no major attack came. A force from XIX Corps counter-attacked, under fire from I Battery RHA and A and B Batteries RCHA. There were other events that day, including a brilliant little action by the New Zealanders which captured ground, prisoners and a large number of machine guns. By now the

Germans realised that, if they were to break through, they would have to make full preparations; this would take time, time that would allow the Allies to improve their positions. It was a dilemma but they had no choice really; they had been fought to a standstill, although neither they nor the Allies realised it. There was then a lull on 1st, 2nd and 3rd April (on 1st April 1918, the RFC was renamed the Royal Air Force). German morale dropped lower, British gun fire increased, trench warfare began again. British positions overlooked the despondent Germans as they prepared for one final effort.

So dawned 4th April 1918, and the final battle of the huge German offensive, indeed the final major offensive action by them in the War, although that was not known then. Heavy rain was falling as the German bombardment began at 0515 hours. At 0630 hours, the assault was delivered on a fifteen mile front by seventeen divisions; twelve of these attacked the French on their nine miles and five on the six mile British front. We must follow first the fortunes of the attack on the French, which was still supported by 8th, 20th, 24th and 30th Divisional Artilleries and some ten heavy batteries. Records again are scanty, but the Gunners played their part in holding the attack. By 4th April, B and C Batteries of 107 Brigade RFA could only muster five guns between them and were in action with some French dismounted cavalry at Castel. The German bombardment killed the Battery Commander of C Battery and destroyed two of its three guns, killing every man in both detachments. Captain B.G. Twycross, commanding the two guns of B Battery, took command of the remaining gun of C Battery and kept all three in action. The French cavalry retired, but Captain Twycross was determined to hold the enemy in his now isolated position, ordered his teams up and began engaging enemy infantry over open sights as they emerged from the woods to his front. He then sent two guns back to the French cavalry and remained with the third. Once again the Germans experienced the devastating effect of 18-pounder shrapnel bursting low and accurately amongst them. They stayed behind cover until Twycross fired his last round, limbered up and galloped off amidst a hail of machine gun bullets.

306 Brigade RFA also distinguished itself. As the Germans tried to storm the heights near Moreuil, they came face to face with the battery which refused to withdraw and engaged the enemy over open sights, pursuing him with shells as he fell back in disorder. The action was witnessed by the French Divisional Commander who issued an Order of the Day commending "the skilful and gallant manner in which the guns were handled".

The bulk of the attack on the British sector fell on 14th and 18th Divisions. 14th Division had its own artillery, which had arrived in the line on 1st April, together with the Divisional Artilleries of 16th and 39th Divisions. 18th Divisional Artillery was not in the line, but the Division had the fire of 50th and 66th Divisions. This part of the line was also covered by 21, 22, 23, 68 and 76 Heavy Brigades. 14th Division fell back some two miles, but the attack was stopped dead by the action of the artillery. Some say that the action of this day by the guns was one of the finest artillery stories of the whole War; it ran as follows: The guns involved, besides the heavies, were 46 Brigade (all that was left of 14th Divisional Artillery), 177 and 180 Brigades of 16th Divisional Artillery, 174 and 186 Brigades of 39th Divisional Artillery and 277 Army Brigade RFA. All batteries were heavily shelled with HE and gas during the bombardment. There was a heavy mist and OPs could see little. At 0620 hours, it was realised that the bombardment was now falling on the front trenches and batteries switched to SOS tasks. Stragglers and wounded brought back alarming stories to the guns, but it was decided not to withdraw. Soon C and D Batteries of 177 Brigade saw German infantry in the mist, caught them in enfilade and broke them up. The infantry later reported that the gunfire had completely annihilated the enemy. C Battery slowly turned with the Germans, eventually firing into their rear as they passed, and alone contributed very significantly to the destruction of the attack.

About 1100 hours, visibility cleared and the forward observers engaged the massed German infantry with shrapnel to the very greatest effect. Many of these young artillery officers were in the open and passed back such good reports that commanders knew exactly what was happening. Observation was good from the Villers Bretonneux Plateau, which was to see most of the artillery action. But, in spite of terrible losses, wave after wave of German infantry pressed forward and at last reached the ridge east of Hamel. The infantry hung on with the greatest gallantry and some cavalry were rushed into the line to help but, in spite of all efforts, they began to give. It was at this point that Brigadier-General E. Harding-Newman, CRA 14th Division, issued one of the most historic artillery orders of all time; it ran "This attack must and can be stopped by artillery fire. If any battery can no longer effectively stop the enemy from its present position, it will at once move fighting to a position on the crest, to engage the enemy over open sights. It is essential that the artillery should hold the line and they will do so".

The response was immediate, valiant and magnificent. The officers of 177 Brigade RFA established an OP in the spire of Hamel church, from which they hammered (and reported on) the enemy for the rest of the day. FOOs reports were so good and thorough that no German move occurred without it being known and heavily engaged. Concentrated fire of brigades halted attack after attack. OP lines were kept through by the greatest gallantry on the part of the signallers. Everywhere guns were being run forward to engage the enemy point blank over open sights. It was a thrilling and wonderful sight as a great new wave of determination came over the defenders in this hour of great peril for the British Army. Boldness paid off. One gun of C Battery 277 Army Field Brigade stood in the open for two hours with no pause in its firing, and lived to tell the tale. D Battery of the same Brigade smothered attack after attack with a pile of lethal gas shell which it found dumped. But not all escaped so lightly. B Battery 186 Brigade RFA came under such a withering combination of rifle, machine gun and artillery fire that it was driven back behind the crest. Meanwhile, B Battery 177 Brigade RFA, under Major D. Mackay, was hotly engaged. At 1300 hours, Major Mackay saw great masses of enemy on the high ground to the east of Hamel. Running his guns forward to the crest, he poured ninety rounds per gun into the enemy over open sights with such crushing effect that, as the smoke and dust cleared, no enemy, save their dead, could be seen on the hillside. This was a remarkable feat since only a few days before this magnificent battery had lost all but six men in the enemy attacks but, by rushing men forward from the wagon lines, it continued to fight on with such tremendous results. A Battery of 180 Brigade was accurately located in an open position and suffered heavily. On being forced to withdraw, it lost one gun when its team was annihiliated by a German shell. C Battery of the same Brigade lost its commander and two guns in a period of ferocious short range fighting.

Further south, similar great deeds of valour were being performed; responding as did the others, the guns of 41, 174 and 186 Brigades RFA were pushed boldly onto the crests or into the open to engage the enemy over open sights. The same fierce fighting followed until, slowly, the enemy were stopped and the British infantry given the respite they so badly needed.

All afternoon on that memorable day, the batteries of 14th Division fought on. The Gunners could hardly stand from fatigue, but the fire of victory was in their bellies and nothing was going to pass them. Seldom have men responded so magnificently to their orders. Although many batteries were forced to withdraw by 1500 hours, this remarkable artillery action had brought the enemy almost to a standstill on 14th Division's front. At 1530 hours, the enemy having withdrawn, the CRA ordered 'cease firing' after ten solid hours of ceaseless battle. The guns had fired over 500 rounds each. It was a magnificent climax to fifteen days of incessant combat, constant movement, hard labour, lack of sleep and heavy casualties. Many gallant officers and men of the Regiment died on their guns that day, but what if they had failed? Who knows but that those Gunners saw the actual moment which heralded the defeat of Germany. Certainly the enemy never pressed so hard again; certainly, although more attacks and battles were to follow, they never got further west; certainly, from that moment on, a great new spirit seized the Armies of the West. If this is so, then the Royal Regiment of Artillery played a major part in the event. The official history of the War does not cover the action of the artillery in any detail, but it does say "all attempts to advance made by the Germans were stopped, largely by artillery fire, the guns remaining in action although the enemy came within 1,500 yards of them; some guns of 16th Division were indeed taken forward onto the crest line and fired over open sights with great effect". This does not do justice to the real events.

At 1700 hours, the Germans attacked again as the guns were withdrawing to new positions just south of the Amiens-Villers Bretonneux road. As the Germans closed, at one point only 400 yards from the last battery to pull out, the Australians made a fine counter-attack and swept them away. So ended the great battle of the Avre on 4th April, a battle which brought great glory to the story of the Royal Regiment. Spirits were high that evening, even though it was clear that the enemy still had something up his sleeve.

The Germans renewed their attacks on 5th April, north of the Somme. By 0700 hours, their bombardment had become most irregular and the attacks themselves lacked cohesion. In V Corps area there was plenty of artillery and the enemy gained very little and only at a very high cost. In IV Corps, the enemy were met by a British attack by 37th Division, supported by a creeping barrage fired by six brigades, while four howitzer batteries laid a smokescreen and fifteen heavy batteries shelled the enemy trenches. Flanking artillery fired standing barrages on the flanks. Eleven tanks of 10th Tank Battalion were in support, though only one reached the objective. The attack, however, was completely successful. Unfortunately, the ground won could not be held, due to the enemy capture of Bucquoy. However, the enemy were now pinned down and all movements were heavily punished by artillery. The fact that such a well co-ordinated battle could be planned at all indicated the degree of robustness and recovery in the British defence.

So ended the first part of the great German offensive. They had gained much tactically, but they had not achieved their strategic aim of destroying the British and capturing Paris. Indeed, they were now firmly held on ground that was most unfavourable to them; they had sustained extremely heavy losses, particularly in leaders at all levels, and their morale was deteriorating. For the Gunners it had been a magnificent period, although many guns had been lost and casualties had been high; those that remained stuck to the guns with a tenacity which made those veterans of Mons and Le Cateau proud of young Gunners of the New Armies. The pride in battery spirit, the determination to stick it out and never to let down their cavalry and infantry comrades, had never been higher. Indeed, the magnificent way in which the gun line held along the Avre must go down in the annals of the Royal Regiment as one of their finest hours. Today these battles are forgotten because they were fought by the new batteries which have long since disappeared from the order of battle. But they must not be forgotten, for these young wartime gunners lived up to the great traditions of the Regiment in the most magnificent manner. How often on that memorable day did some weary, tired and gallant infantryman say—"The Guns! Thank God, the Guns!"

"Action" by W B Wollen.   (*R.A.I.*)

CHAPTER 22

The Second Battles of the Aisne and the Marne — Spring and Summer 1918

See maps 35, 36 and 37

On 11th April 1918, Field-Marshal Sir Douglas Haig issued his famous Order of the Day addressed to "All ranks of the British Army in France and Flanders". It is a magnificent order and one phrase in it captured the imagination of both the Nation and the Army. . . . "With our backs to the wall and believing in the justice of our cause, each one of us must fight to the end. The safety of our homes and the freedom of mankind alike depend upon the conduct of each one of us at this critical moment".

During the rest of April there was stalemate. The German positions were appalling; within their water-logged salient, every move they made was seen. The area was well known to the British and the art of harrassing fire reached a new standard of perfection. Five thousand German graves at Sailly-sur-Lys testify to the effectiveness of this fire, for nearly all were killed by shellfire during this period. The fire was directed from temporary positions, sometimes by heavies pushed right forward late in the evening, to fire a special programme while it was dark, but to be gone by dawn. German counter-battery fire almost always fell on recently abandoned positions. There is no doubt as to who had the upper hand in the artillery duels of April 1918. There was much fighting during this period, but no dramatic changes to the front.

But, on 27th May, the Germans still had fight in them. On that day they delivered new attacks on the French along the Chemin des Dames on the heights overlooking the Valley of the Aisne. The British IX Corps, under Lieutenant-General Sir A.H. Gordon, consisting of 8th, 21st, 25th and 50th Divisions, were heavily involved. In addition to the Divisional Artilleries were 41 and 77 Brigades RGA, consisting of 22 60-pounders, 22 6-inch howitzers and 5 8-inch howitzers. There were also three "Groupes" of French mediums (94 155mm guns).

General Gordon reported to the French on 22nd May that all the indications of an impending attack were present, but General Duchêne did not agree, and it was not until 26th May that he authorised even limited counter-preparation fire. The Allied line was held by 8th, 21st and 50th British and three French divisions, with 25th British and three French divisions in reserve. The position was not strong and divisional fronts were too long when, at dawn on 27th May, the Germans hurled fifteen divisions, with five supporting divisions supported by 1,036 batteries (some 6,473 guns and 3,532 mortars), at the Allied line. This is generally considered to be the heaviest bombardment of the war by either side. At the point of impact, the line held by 50th British and 22nd French Divisions, the Germans had some forty batteries per mile of front and were able to concentrate four batteries onto each located British battery. The batteries of 50th Division suffered severely, although they were not silenced. The German infantry followed their bombardment so swiftly that many guns were literally overrun as they were firing. 8th Division lost nearly all its guns in their positions in the Aisne Valley, just north of the river. In 33 Brigade RFA, 32nd Battery had one gun destroyed in the bombardment and the detachments of the rest just managed to escape with their sights and breech blocks, as enemy infantry reached the guns. 36th Battery had to abandon its guns, taking only the dial sights. 55th Howitzer Battery died firing point blank at enemy infantry. Limbers tried to get to the guns, but were driven back by rifle and machine-gun fire; only three men escaped. 1st Battery of 45 Brigade RFA, with three guns already knocked out, fought on to the end, the detachments using rifles just before they were overrun at 0700 hours on that fateful day. 3rd Battery, also of the 45 Brigade, only had one gun in action and was forced to abandon this at 0715 hours, while 5th Battery of the Brigade fought heroically to the end, with guns, rifles and Lewis guns, only to be overrun after hand to hand fighting around the guns. Only one man escaped to tell the tale of this fierce, gallant action. 5th Battery RFA was subsequently awarded the French Croix de Guerre for its magnificent stand in the defence of its guns. 57th Howitzer Battery, also with 45 Brigade, with all its guns destroyed by 1425 hours, managed to hold its positions with small arms until 1815 hours.

To the south of the Aisne, the guns of 110 Brigade of 25th Division stood about Gernicourt in a wooded area. Some French guns were there, too. This strong point held up the Germans until 1230 hours, by which time the guns were surrounded and ordered to withdraw. A Battery managed to get four guns out of action in the face of the enemy but was forced to abandon them later; C Battery abandoned its position at 1308 hours, its commander, one officer and one sergeant remaining to the last; B Battery abandoned its position at 1315 hours and D Battery was captured entirely as it tried to withdraw. But these guns had not been sold in vain; they had held twelve German battalions for more than six hours. The withdrawal of 8th Division opened the left flank of 21st Division and B Battery of 95 Brigade RFA was ordered back at 1000 hours. Unfortunately, there was a delay in passing back the orders and the battery was surrounded, only one gun escaping. The other batteries of the Brigade withdrew between 1100 and 1220 hours, losing two guns. This withdrawal was covered by good shooting from 112 Brigade of 25th Division, attached to 21st Division, in action near St. Auboeuf.

By evening, four French divisions had been swept away and the enemy had advanced some 13 miles, but the flanks of the salient held and nowhere better than in the east where stood the British 21st and 25th Divisions.

A makeshift battery of three separate sections of 110 Brigade RFA went into action near Guyencourt. These guns were highly successful in covering the weary, confused infantry and they succeeded in destroying two German batteries, which had advanced to cover their infantry forward. At 2100 hours, another makeshift battery of four guns drawn from Ordnance came into action near Montigny. These two batteries were joined during the night by two batteries of 112 Brigade RFA, and the four were organised into a composite brigade under Lieutenant-Colonel H.R. Phipps (110 Brigade RFA). 95 Brigade of 21st Divisional Artillery had to withdraw twice in the night but 94 Brigade was able to maintain its positions on the right. Further right, the heavies delayed too long. Coming under close rifle and machine gun fire, they were unable to get all their guns away. 41 Brigade RGA lost thirteen guns out of twenty four. The French "Groupe" alongside lost twenty-nine out of thirty four guns. Those that got away assembled near Jonchery by dawn on 28th May. All ammunition had been fired or lost, but a train load arrived just in time.

And so the battle raged on. In the north, the British on the Lys and not under direct attack held, but along the Aisne the French and the British IX Corps suffered heavily. The Germans pressed on but got into deeper and deeper trouble as they did so. The British IX Corps fell back south and south-east, forming the left shoulder to the German advance, until in places they were facing west. The fact that they held was significant in the German defeat. Losses were heavy and men were tired out. The artillery was all mixed up and ad hoc groups sprang up. Phipps' group already mentioned, now of twenty-two guns, was all that was left of 8th Divisional Artillery. Brigadier-General H.W. Newcome still commanded much of 21st Divisional Artillery, but only twelve guns of 25th Division remained. On 29th May, 19th Division began to arrive in IX Corps area. By the 30th, forty-eight guns of the Division, under Brigadier-General W.P. Monkhouse, were in the line, with the twenty-two of Ballard's (formerly Phipps') group and twelve of Phillips' group of the 25th Division. Twenty-nine guns of 21st Division supported the French, having been left in action when their Division was withdrawn. Two batteries of 91 Brigade RGA remained until last light on 30th May.

The last attack on the British was delivered on 6th June, but the line held and the day ended with a vicious British counter-attack which forced a German withdrawal. The British were then left in peace until they were relieved on 17th and 18th June. Seldom had the doggedness of the British soldier in defence been more strikingly displayed than on the Aisne in 1918. Five divisions had been reduced to the equivalent of seven battalions and 240 guns to 82, but morale stayed high. General Foch was so impressed that, having relieved almost all his own commanders of their commands, he asked General Gordon and his IX Corps to remain in the French area.

Although there was heavy fighting yet to come, and the French were again pushed back to the Marne, we must look at battles elsewhere before the great Allied counter-offensive of 8th August.

On 28th June, XI Corps of the First Army, using 5th Division and 31st Division of XV Corps from the Second Army, directed an operation just east of the forest of Nieppe to improve the British line. It became known as the action of La Becque. The artillery to support these two divisions was:

GOC RA, XI Corps	Brigadier-General S.F. Metcalfe
GOC, Corps Heavy Artillery	Brigadier-General R.H.F. McCulloch
CRA, 5th Division	Brigadier-General A.H. Hussey

15 Brigade RFA; 52nd, 80th, A and D (Howitzer) Batteries
27 Brigade RFA; 119th, 120th, 121st and 37 (Howitzer) Batteries

CRA, 31st Division	Brigadier-General E.P. Lambert

165 Brigade RFA; A, B, C and D (Howitzer) Batteries
170 Brigade RFA; A, B, C and D (Howitzer) Batteries
Corps Heavy Artillery; 28, 79 and 49 Brigades RGA (38 6-inch howitzers; 6 8-inch howitzers; 4 9.2-inch howitzers; 6 6-inch guns; 24 60-pounders)

From XV Corps
33 Brigade RGA and 36 (Australian) Heavy Brigade RGA (26 6-inch howitzers; 12 8-inch howitzers; 6 9.2-inch howitzers; 12 60-pounders)

The field artillery of 1st Australian Division, on the left of the attack, fired a diversionary barrage and smoke screen. Unable to stand by and see a good barrage wasted, the Australians raided the German lines, returning with fifteen prisoners, two mortars and six machine guns!

No preliminary bombardment was fired. Gas was used for counter-battery fire. The barrage started at H-hour and crept 100 yards in four minutes, with the infantry right up close to it. They were then amongst the enemy with the bayonet before he could man his trenches. The objective, 2,000 yards distant, was captured, together with 7 officers, 432 men, 4 field guns, 14-trench-mortars and 77 machine guns. Two German counter-attacks were crushed by fire as they started. It was a model operation, showing how British artillery methods were master of the field, when properly laid on.

On 4th July, the Australian Corps carried out an attack at Hamel, between Villers Bretonneux and the Somme, together with four companies of the American 33rd Division. Here again a sound artillery plan was made. The attack was to be carried out on a front of 6,000 yards to a depth of 2,500 yards. It involved the storming of Vaire Wood, Hamel Wood and Hamel village. The village and woods were strongly held, but elsewhere the defences were weak. 326 field guns and howitzers and 302 heavies were allotted to the fireplan. One 18-pounder was allotted to 25 yards of front and 11 machine guns supplemented the plan. Sixty tanks were tasked with wire cutting and smoke was used to cover them forward. The heavies were employed on counter-battery tasks, but there was again no preliminary bombardment and only minimal registration was allowed. H-hour was to be 0310 hours on 4th July, when a uniform could just be distinguished at twenty yards.

The Australians described the barrage as 'glorious' but it was marred by some short shooting, which caused a few casualties and knocked out a tank. The opening line was 60% shrapnel, 30% HE and 10% smoke and opened 200 yards ahead of the start line. 200 yards behind it was a 4.5-inch howitzer barrage, at 90% HE with impact fuzes and 10% smoke. 200 yards beyond this was the 6-inch howitzer barrage, all HE. The barrage moved at 100 yards in three minutes, this to enable the tanks to keep right up to the bursting shells with the assaulting infantry behind them. The attack was a complete success. 8th and 205th Squadrons RAF co-operated fully and strafed the enemy trenches at H-30 minutes. Counter-battery fire was so successful that there was practically no response from the German guns. By 0418 hours, 4th Australian Brigade was on its phase one objective and, at 0449 hours, 6th Brigade was also secure. The barrage was a total success. Final objectives were all taken by 0700 hours. The Australians lost 51 officers and 724 other ranks, and their American detachment 6 officers and 128 other ranks; five tanks were disabled. However, 41 officers, 1,431 other ranks, 2 field guns, 26 trench-mortars, 171 machine guns and two of the new anti-tank rifles were captured, as well as all objectives. It was a model attack and indeed it was to serve as a model for the great attacks of August, yet to come.

On 19th July, 9th (Scottish) Division attacked and captured Meteren. The division was commanded by Major-General H.H. Tudor, himself a Gunner, and the assault was made by four battalions on a front of 2,400 yards. The fireplan was carried out by seven brigades RFA and 33 and 36 Brigades RGA, together with some Australian heavies for counter-battery tasks. During the previous week the heavies flattened the remains of Meteren. Smoke was to be used in the barrage but, for the first time, the quantity was controlled as the weather and wind varied. The Germans were completely surprised; there was no counter-attack and all objectives were taken. Co-ordination between infantry and artillery was excellent and again the superiority of British artillery methods was demonstrated.

Further south, on 18th July, General Foch opened his great counter-attack to drive the Germans back from the Marne. The attack was mainly conducted by the French and Americans, but the British XII Corps (51st and 62nd Divisions) joined in on 20th July, after a long six hour approach march. The British attack went in at 0800 hours behind a barrage fired by French and Italian batteries, but this fell too far ahead, and moved too fast. Moreover, the over-sensitive French fuzes were most unsuitable in wooded country, even a twig would set them off. The British artillery was still closing up to the battle. At 1000 hours, Brigadier General A.T. Anderson got his 62nd Divisional Artillery, 310 and 312 Brigades RFA, into action. They assisted in the unsuccessful attack on Marfaux (ten miles south-east of Reims).

51st Divisional Artillery (255 and 256 Brigades RFA) covered eighty miles in three days, crossing the Marne near Epernay at 0200 hours on 20th July. After a short halt they pushed on, reaching their position of assembly near Nanteuil-La-Fosse, and were in action 500 yards south-west of Pourcy by 1000 hours. But during the day they were only involved with harrassing fire. XII Corps had no heavy artillery.

The French attacks in the western end of the great bulge were successful. On 22nd July, 15th and 34th British Divisions joined in on this sector. 15th Division relieved 1st US Division and the artillery were to relieve each other during the nights 22nd–23rd and 23rd–24th July. But, at 2235 hours on 22nd, 15th Division was ordered to attack at 0800 hours the next day; this would mean that the artillery would be half British and half American! It was therefore agreed that the Americans would stay in action to support the attack. 15th Division issued orders at midnight and the infantry relief was completed by 0300 hours. One can imagine the problems as French officers supervised the Jocks taking over from the Americans, but it worked. The trench line (there were in fact hardly any trenches) did not agree with the map so, when the American Gunners opened up their barrage at 0415 hours, it was too far ahead of the start line, and was also very thin. The weary infantry suffered in consequence, but some ground was taken.

Meanwhile, 34th Division, now separated from 15th Division by two French divisions, relieved the French 38th Division and both infantry and artillery were in action by 0300 hours on 22nd July. The French left two regiments of '75's' and a 'groupe' of twelve 155mm howitzers in action to support the British. The French Corps Commander, General Penet, discovered that the CRA of 34th British Division, Brigadier-General E.C.W.D. Walthall, spoke fluent French; he put all the Corps Artillery under his command! The Alliance was really beginning to work under the stress of battle; how different from the suspicions of earlier years. But time was too short; Brigadier-General Walthall's plan was to arrange an 18-

pounder HE barrage deepened by French 75's, with 4.5-inch howitzers and French heavies concentrating on known strong points. At this moment, all links with the assaulting infantry were lost. The infantry then lost the barrage; the issued French light signals did not fit the British rifle. The exact positions of the infantry were not known and some were hit by the Allied fireplan. The German guns sprang to life and, as there had been no time to organise counter-battery fire, the Allied attack was repulsed with considerable loss.

On the eastern flank of the enemy bulge, an attack by 62nd Division, under a fireplan fired by British and French guns, was so accurate, intense and effective that the infantry reached their objective with few casualties. 51st Division had an equal success but their attack was marred by some French guns causing casualties to the Royal Scots as they formed up. Then, on 28th July, 15th Division reported some of its toughest fighting around Soissons and Buzancy (five miles south of Soissons). Again, on 29th July, 34th Division carried out a spirited attack in the French XXX Corps area. All first objectives were taken when two nameless 18-pounder batteries charged forward to support the infantry onto their next objective. It was such an inspiring sight that the French Gunners rose and cheered them as they thundered past them. History does not record who they were, or how they fared.

The pressure on the Germans was growing, and it was certainly telling. Realising their precarious position, they withdrew on the nights 1st–2nd and 2nd–3rd August in two great bounds, until they had abandoned all that they had won in the March offensive. 34th Division was still pursuing the beaten Germans, and caught some in the act of withdrawing on 1st August, causing them great loss. During the first week of August, XII Corps (15th and 34th Division) and its artillery returned from French command to the British zone. How well and gallantly they had fought and been admired by their allies, but they too had developed a new respect for Frenchmen and Americans alike. The Alliance was getting into gear, the smell of victory was in the air. The attack techniques were working and the British Gunners knew they had the upper hand. The scene was set for the triumphs to come.

CHAPTER 23

The Turn of the Tide — The Battles of Amiens and Albert and the Fall of the Hindenburg Line — August and September 1918

See maps 38, 39 and 40

At the end of July 1918, Ludendorf wrote "Full dress attacks by the enemy are as little to be expected as a counter-attack by us". How wrong he was. On 28th July, First French Army was put under command of General Sir Douglas Haig for forthcoming offensive operations. The Germans were exhausted and morale was low; what is more, their ranks were stricken by an epidemic of influenza.

General Rawlinson was first ordered to advance east of Amiens. He proposed to make maximum use of tanks and had 400 available. Orders were produced between 31st July and 5th August. At that moment, a memorandum arrived from the War Office stating it was British policy to begin the final offensive, to end the war on 1st July 1919! Fourth Army was to consist of III Corps (12th, 18th, 47th, 58th Divisions), the Canadian Corps (1st, 2nd, 3rd and 4th Canadian Divisions and 4th, 15th, 32nd and 51st British Divisions), the Australian Corps (1st, 2nd, 3rd, 4th and 5th Australian Divisions and 17th and 32nd British Divisions, the latter only after 20th August), IX Corps (1st and 6th Division, and 32nd Division only after 11th September).

The artillery plan is interesting and illustrates how the great problems of the earlier years had been overcome. Some 1,300 field and 160 heavy guns were available. Not a vast number, but the effect was to be enhanced by co-ordination and concentration of effort. The 18-pounder barrage lifts were to be 100 yards, and the opening line 200 yards ahead of the start line. The first two lifts were to be at $H+3$ and $H+5$, thereafter at three minute intervals for eight lifts; from the eleventh lift, the interval was to be raised to four minutes. Each corps was to superimpose its own 4.5-inch barrage, and a depth barrage fired by some of the heavies was to be maintained from H hour to $H+4$ hours. Two thirds of the heavies were to open on counter-battery tasks at H hour. On capture of the first objective, specified field and howitzer batteries were to move forward on orders of infantry brigades, the foretaste of a system used to move artillery to this day.

Virtually all of the allotted artillery was in position by 4th August, the highest serviceability rate (98.5%) recorded in the war. 30,000 rounds of 18-pounder and 24,000 of 4.5-inch rounds of smoke alone, and 10,000 rounds of 18-pounder and 50,000 rounds of 6-inch gas shell, were dumped.

And so at 0420 hours on 8th August 1918, the barrage opened and the attack began. The mist had fallen during the night and was thick at H hour. No flying was possible but the Canadians and Australians soon reached their first objectives and the barrage was described as excellent. The mist made it difficult for the leading waves to keep with the barrage, and often they could not see the shells burst until they were dangerously close. But the shooting was very accurate, a great feat since no registration had been allowed. The infantry followed the sound of the barrage to keep direction right onto the first objectives. Then came the advance of the artillery; first, the field batteries galloping forward over the old trench system and coming into action, often under machine-gun fire from pockets of enemy as yet undefeated. Next came independent sections of the 60-pounders and 6-inch howitzers of the heavies and, finally, howitzer brigades. Great lines of guns surging forward, stirring the hearts of the infantry and tanks already buoyant by their success and swinging into action to continue the attack to the phase two objectives. (The advance of the artillery before Harbonnières has been painted by Septimus Power).

At 1400 hours, 471st Siege Battery RGA was honoured by a very special visitor. The battery had recently taken over two of the biggest guns ever manned by the Royal Regiment; they were 14-inch, 270 ton, railway guns firing shells, which each weighed threequarters of a ton, to a range of 20 miles. The battery had christened them HMG (His Majesty's Gun) "Boche Buster" and "Scene-Shifter" and at the appointed hour they were to be visited by the King. In his presence, one gun was fired as part of the attack on Douai; it fired some twelve rounds and subsequently it was found that the first round had been a direct hit on the railway, causing enormous destruction and preventing its use to reinforce the German front line. It became known as "The King's Shot" and was said by the Gunners to mark the turning point of the war, opening up the road to victory. Few single artillery rounds can ever have affected a battle so much both in terms of destruction and improving morale.

Even after the advance of the guns, communications were maintained, to the everlasting credit of the line parties, in itself a major feature in keeping up massive and concentrated artillery attacks. As the victorious infantry and tanks rolled on, they passed evidence of some of the most effective counter-battery fire of the war. Whole batteries were knocked out, some still with their muzzle caps on, showing how complete can be surprise when executed by accurate, concentrated artillery fire. The method was for artillery and intelligence staffs to produce a programme and systematically to attack each enemy battery, by two or even three RGA brigades, and thereafter to continue on each with a lesser harassing fire programme. So successful was this technique that the attacking infantry were not hampered by German guns. A sound ranging base and observation groups went forward on 9th August and were soon reporting new enemy gun locations. Artillery casualties on the first day of the battle of Amiens were actually nil! However, 1,030 horses were killed or hit, mostly due to the enemy bombing the great concentration of horses waiting to move the guns forward. It is interesting also to note that the majority of German casualties that day were due to shrapnel wounds, whereas only 27% of British wounds were caused by shell fire. It is possible that, on the 'eighth, eighth, eighteen', the British Artillery reached the peak of perfection. Every aspect of the artillery plan was a success. The guns lifted the assault onto its objectives, they protected the flanks, they broke up counter-attacks, they prevented the enemy from using his guns effectively, they moved

HM King George V visited HM Gun "Boche Buster", a 14-inch railway mounted gun, on 8th August 1918 at Mareuil. General Sir Henry Horne invited The King to witness the gun's firing. The first round caused immense damage at Douai railway station and became popularly known as "The King's Shot". *(I.W.M.)*

forward with the assault and repeated the process for the phase two objectives. It was a great triumph of method, skill and command, and the fruit of so much bitter trial and error for over three years.

At 0820 hours 8th August, the Canadians assaulted their phase two objectives and already their artillery had advanced and was ready, including 2, 5 and 10 Brigades RFA, and the sections of heavies already referred to. Leading the artillery was K Battery RHA of 3rd Cavalry Division, supporting 17th Lancers. At 1100 hours, this battery alone swung into action and destroyed a German counter-attack in true Horse Artillery style at Cayeux Wood. At 1500 hours, 3 Canadian Brigade CFA advanced to positions just west of Beaucourt covering its infantry forward. At 2030 hours, the Germans attempted a counter-attack eastwards from Beaucourt and ran straight into the guns of C Battery RHA, which crushed it before it started. On this sector German prisoners stated that, in almost all cases, the Canadians were on them before they could man their trenches. All guns of the *German 13th Division* were lost and only three from their *41st Division* escaped. A German commentator wrote that "The sun set on the greatest defeat which the German Army had suffered since the beginning of the war". The Canadians captured 114 officers, almost 5,000 men and 161 guns.

And the story was the same elsewhere. The attack of the Australian Corps was equally successful. The guns of 16 (Army) Brigade RHA (The Chestnut Troop, Q and U Batteries), 14, 23, 189 and 178 Brigades RFA and 5, 8, 9, 14, 21, 68, 69, 77 and 93 Brigades RGA produced a barrage so thick and accurate that all phase one objectives were secure by 0700 hours. Scarcely a German shell fell after 0540 hours. The advance continued, sometimes running into its own barrage, causing complaints of short shooting. 16 (Army) Brigade RHA pushed well forward, shooting down and clearing a valley which was holding up the infantry. The Australians attacking Cerisy were given magnificent support by 10 Australian Brigade. III Corps on the Australian left did not attack until later and the Australians suffered from German guns not yet overrun on that flank. But all objectives were taken, together with 183 officers, 7,742 men and 173 guns.

It was strange that, after such enormous initial successes, the Allies allowed the pressure to drop. True, hard fighting continued and slowly the Allied line was pushed eastwards and straightened out, but the aim of securing Amiens had been achieved and the High Command did not realise that they were on the point of breaking through the crumbling German defences. So the fighting continued.

Although the tanks at Amiens were employed in great numbers (630 British alone), and although they had great morale effect in opposite directions on both sides, they were not yet a success. The concentrated nature of the fighting prevented them being effective once close quarter fighting began. However, their potential was recognised by the British and plans were laid for a huge increase in their numbers for the expected battles of 1919.

We must now turn to the fortunes of Third Army, to the north of Fourth Army. On 21st August, it was ordered to attack and capture the line of the Albert-Arras railway. Third Army, under General Hon. Sir Julian Byng, consisted of V Corps (21st and 38th Divisions), IV Corps (37th, 42nd and the New Zealand Division) and VI Corps (the Guards, 2nd and 59th Divisions). The artillery amounted to

Field Artillery advancing at Harbonnière, 8th August 1918. From an oil painting by H Septimus Power now hanging in the Royal School of Artillery, Larkhill. *(R.A.I.)*

some 828 18-pounders and 4.5-inch howitzers and 466 heavies after eleven field and heavy brigades had been transferred from Fourth Army front.

H hour was 0455 hours on 21st August, and again there was to be no preliminary bombardment. The barrage did not creep but consisted of three overlapping standing barrages, the first between the start line and the first objective, the second on the first objective and the third on a line through Courcelles. Again there was a thick fog and the tanks lost their way up to the start line. But the attack met little resistance and VI Corps advanced to its second objective on the railway line and was ordered to halt. In IV Corps, the distances were greater and the guns of 15 and 27 Brigades RFA of 5th Division had to advance to positions near Logeast Wood after phase one. The guns were attacked from the air during the move, losing many horses and, as a result, were not forward in strength to shoot the infantry onto their final objectives, which they failed to take. Nevertheless, IV Corps advanced three miles. V Corps Artillery suffered from an acute shortage of ammunition, and some very heavy German artillery fire, and was unable to advance as had been planned.

22nd August was devoted to moving the artillery forward. The attack was renewed on 23rd August and scored success everywhere. Third Army advanced some 3 miles and, to the south in Fourth Army, the Australians and 32nd British Division swept forward. 3rd Division in VI Corps of Third Army, together with the guns of 2nd and 3rd Divisional Artilleries, 18, 34 and 76 Army Brigades RFA and 70 and 84 Brigades RGA (21 guns) were to capture Gommecourt, scene of fierce fighting in March. A creeping barrage, 75% shrapnel and 25% HE, supplemented by a fixed barrage by forty machine guns, carried the infantry over 1,000 yards of flat, open ground without difficulty. Twelve tanks helped greatly on the objective but suffered heavily. The Guards Division's attack was covered by 14 Brigade RHA, 72, 93, 155, 315 Brigades RFA and 29 and 70 Brigades RGA, and was a success. Similar fireplans carried 56th, 57th and later 40th and 52nd Divisions onto their objectives. At 1100 hours, 2nd Division attacked through 3rd Division with the assistance of Whippet tanks, and Ervillers was captured. The artillery then moved right forward.

Stories of success came from IV and V Corps of Third Army. Everywhere the attacking infantry stayed close behind the barrages and everywhere objectives were taken, together with over 5,000 prisoners. During the night of 23rd–24th August, the hot, dry weather gave way to drizzle and cloud but, at 0100 hours, the advance continued behind further creeping barrages. The night attacks went quite well and pushed forward to Pozières, which was quickly counter-attacked. 50th Infantry Brigade reported how a single 18-pounder repulsed this attack over open sights. IV Corps decided to attack without a barrage and suffered heavily on 24th August. The deterioration of the German Army was not yet so great that artillery could be dispensed with.

General Rawlinson now directed that artillery, including heavies, must be pushed right forward. The heavies were to bombard the enemy's communications in depth, particularly the bridges over the Somme; 12 and 14-inch guns were to bombard Péronne (15 miles south east of Albert) until further orders. Subsequent German records show how these tactics caused great disorganisation and demoralisation. So, during the last days of August, the advance continued, but always under the cover of the guns. Where this was ignored, success was costly and often illusive. The Gunners were becoming expert in the quick barrage and in leap-frogging guns forward to guarantee continuous fire. Surprise was important and registration was often forbidden in order to achieve it. Counter-battery fire was top priority, sometimes taking 70% of all available guns. Heavies and super-heavies were reserved to destroy villages and strong points, and gas and smoke were used freely.

Success now followed fast. On 29th August, Bapaume fell and in Fourth Army the old trench systems of the 1916 battles were reached. At this time, great strides were made in the mobility of heavy artillery. 6 and 8-inch guns and howitzers did great work, often in the forefront of the battle. Liaison between infantry and Gunners was never better or closer. A good example was the attack by the Irish Guards on Mory Copse on 27th August with 72 Army Brigade RFA, commanded by Lieutenant-Colonel F.W. Richey. The Guards were held up only 100 yards from their start line by heavy fire and Colonel Richey sent his orderly officer, Lieutenant Fowler, to ask the Guards what could be done. He discovered that the enemy were on a reverse slope which A Battery could just hit, whereas B and C Batteries could not clear the crest. Lieutenant Fowler had established a line to A Battery, when both signallers were hit, one seriously. With the other he carried on and then registered D (Howitzer) Battery some 200 yards beyond the objective. When the Guards were ready, he ordered five minutes of 'gun-fire'. So accurate was the shooting that 150 Germans surrendered and the Guards walked over to the enemy trench without opposition. A perfect little fireplan, perfectly executed with complete success, and a pattern for such fireplans to the present day.

As the signs of Autumn began to show themselves, the Germans fell back towards the Hindenburg Line; the fighting remained of an open nature and the young officers and men of the new batteries learned how to operate a mobile war, not easy after years of trench warfare. They learned how barrages were neither necessary nor effective against a retreating enemy but they saw that, as soon as the pursuing infantry were checked, the quicker a barrage was arranged the better. Often the mere firing of such a barrage was enough to induce the shattered, tired Germans to retreat. Experience also showed the value of artillery well forward, often single guns right in the van. It soon became practice for infantry brigadiers to organise their own fireplans with their own artillery brigade commanders, the CRA co-ordinating, stiffening and confirming them. It was soon found that, in such mobile operations, the ever vital counter-battery work was hard to arrange and often brigades RGA were found well forward with commanders at infantry brigade headquarters. The need for gunner reconnaissance parties to be well forward, working very quickly, and the layout of local defence of battery positions when right forward had to be learned again. It must not be forgotten that the officers and men involved had not faced these problems before and it is to their eternal credit that they performed so well. But the flush of success stimulates the brain and works wonders as a result. As always, the logistic problems of keeping the ammunition flowing forward as the advance continued became more difficult. Fatigue again became a problem, with batteries constantly in action or on the move.

On the heels of the enemy. Batteries advancing through the Forêt de Marchiennes under cover of mist. From a drawing by Gilbert Holiday. (*R.A.I.*)

As the offensive gathered momentum in First, Third and Fourth Army areas, so the Second and Fifth Armies in the north around Ypres and Hazebrouck became involved. The action by 9th and 29th Divisions on 18th August, to capture Outtersteene Ridge, was an example. The barrage supporting 9th Division was arranged by Brigadier-General A.R. Wainewright and was fired by his own 50 and 51 Brigades RFA and 113, 119 and 186 Army Brigade RFA. It consisted of a first line entirely of smoke and thereafter 25% smoke, moving at 50 yards per minute and then halting as a protective barrage 200 yards beyond the first objective.

To assist Brigadier-General Wainewright he had 15 Brigade RHA and 17 Brigade RFA from 29th Division, and 64 and 174 Army Brigades RFA. He also had 1, 10, 33, 36, 45 and 64 Brigades RGA under Brigadier-General C.W. Collingwood, Commander Heavy Artillery, XV Corps. The heavies bombarded special targets and then put down a final protective barrage. The barrage opened at H + 1 minute. The infantry were ordered to count ten from the first shells seen to fall and follow it. The attack was a great success, achieving complete surprise. All objectives were taken by noon. Further advances followed on 19th August, and pressure was maintained to the end of the month. On 30th August, Bailleul was found abandoned and, on 31st, Kemmel Hill and Vierstraat were occupied. 1st September saw XV Corps in Steenwerck and Neuve Eglise, but the enemy clung to Messines Ridge and Armentières and resistance stiffened.

Now back to Fourth Army. On 1st September, the Australian Corps captured Péronne and Mont St. Quentin, advancing almost ten miles by 11th September. Barrages were not used for these attacks, but a series of predicted concentrations fired at H hour. This unnerved the Germans, who were growing used to the barrage technique. In addition, sections and sometimes single guns were pushed right forward to deal with machine guns at point blank range. It was this remarkable flexibility in artillery tactics in September 1918 that did so much to keep the enemy guessing and to achieve the ever vital element of surprise. But successful barrages were fired, and Morval and Sailly Saillisel were captured by 38th Division in a night attack on 1st September, which achieved complete surprise. Frequently, attacking divisions were supported by artillery from other divisions, such was the flexibility achieved. Infantry commanders were urged to keep their Gunners informed of the positions of their leading troops and it was stressed how vital it was in battle that infantry and artillery commanders should command from the same spot.

The German High Command now ordered their armies to occupy the Hindenburg Line, where a stand was to be made throughout the winter. By 2nd September, the British were up to the Drocourt Queant portion of the line and determined to attack as soon as possible. Yet again artillery tactics had to change; here was a heavily fortified line in depth with thick belts of wire and concrete dug-outs. The Canadians of First Army attacked at 0530 hours on 2nd September, but the standing barrage was ragged and not as effective against machine guns as a creeping barrage would have been. However, those magnificent infantry scored considerable success. At the same time, III Corps attacked Moslains (3 miles north-east of Mont St. Quentin) with 18th, 47th and 74th Divisions. The latter had just arrived from Palestine and ran into difficulty, having first to fight for its start line! The Germans had pushed machine guns right forward to escape the barrage and these held up the gallant 74th Division, who lost their barrage. Nevertheless, by sheer hard, tough fighting this fine division reached the Canal du Nord.

The attack by First Army hinged on operations of the Canadian Corps. The artillery was commanded by Brigadier-General E.W.B. Morrison and consisted of twenty field and eleven heavy brigades. The latter were used to engage bridges over the Canal du Nord and the Sensée River, and for counter-battery work. This seems to have been effective, for enemy artillery fire was light and the Canadians captured all objectives. The Canadians soon got beyond the range of the guns but kept up the pressure, capturing Cagnicourt with ease. By 0800 hours, when phase two began, the attacking brigades only had the support of one battery each plus mortars. This was insufficient and no more progress could be made. However, the British 4th Division attacked under a fireplan by five brigades RFA, four heavy batteries and nine tanks, and successfully captured all objectives. The Drocourt-Queant line had fallen; Ludendorf was so shaken that he ordered an immediate retreat. First and Third Armies were now on the Canal du Nord. Fourth Army lay along the Somme and was well east of it at Peronne. On the British right, the French had advanced in places up to twenty miles.

During this great surge forward, so much was due to the gallantry and dogged fighting qualities of the infantry of the Empire, but it was they who said that they could not have done it without the guns. Almost always where operations were attempted without them, they failed. Ammunition expenditure was enormous. The 18-pounders of Fourth Army alone fired 1,532,545 rounds during August and, between the 21st August and 3rd September, the field artillery of VI Corps of Third Army alone fired 804,929 rounds.

The Germans were now back on the positions from which they had launched their great offensive on 21st March, and it was clear they were going to stand and fight. The British began to plan a major attack for the end of September, but first they determined to mount a series of preliminary operations around Havrincourt and Epéhy. It was necessary to clear both these places and, on 12th September, the New Zealand 37th and 62nd Divisions attacked Havrincourt, under a fireplan consisting of a series of heavy concentrations fired by eighteen field and nine heavy brigades. It was a great success and, when the Germans counter-attacked with a fresh division that evening, it was defeated almost entirely by the guns alone. But the fighting had been hard and this convinced Sir Douglas Haig that only a major operation would break through the Hindenburg Line.

Accordingly, on 18th September, some 1,500 guns and howitzers were assembled to attack Epehy with the Australian Corps, III and IX British Corps. Only twenty tanks were available. There was to be no preliminary bombardment and the artillery was to achieve maximum surprise. So it happened but, astonishingly at this stage of the war, very few guns were allotted to counter-battery tasks.

The first objectives were taken behind a barrage described as 'splendid' all along the front. In 1st Division area, however, one of those tragic misunderstandings occurred, as can so easily in battle. Before H hour the assaulting infantry of the centre advanced 600 yards forward of their start line. Then the flank battalions were withdrawn to avoid being hit by the flank division's barrage. Orders were given to hold 1st Division's barrage to allow these battalions to catch up and it came down heavily on the centre battalions. How vital is the crucial link between a commander and his gunner in battle!

The Australian Corps had a wonderful day, taking all objectives by 2300 hours and capturing 4,243 prisoners, 76 guns and over 300 machine guns. III Corps had more difficulty. 18th Division attacked under a barrage fired by 82, 110, 290 and 291 Brigades RFA, but failed to reach its second objective. 12th Division attacked with 35th and 36th Infantry Brigades, the former supported by 62 Brigade and 92 Brigade RFA and the latter by 83 Brigade RFA, 231 Brigade RFA and 139 Heavy Battery (60-pounders) were under the CRA, Brigadier-General H.M. Thomas. 35th Infantry Brigade captured Epehy with five battalions, wresting it from twelve battalions of the crack Alpine Corps. The bombardment had been particularly effective and was described as follows: "Sections of trench were flattened out in minutes, dug-outs blown in, wall collapsed, machine guns and mortars were covered by earth and rubbish, and ammunition dumps exploded".

Meanwhile, 58th Division attacked Peiziére with 174th Infantry Brigade, supported by 63 and 108 (Army) Brigades RFA and 85 Heavy Brigade RGA (12 60-pounders and 12 6-inch howitzers). The village was taken.

To the left of Third Army, the men of V Corps rose from their trenches to hurl back the Germans onto the Hindenburg Line. The guns which fought that day were:

21st Divisional Artillery under Brigadier-General H.W. Newcome
94 and 95 Brigades RFA
2 (NZ), 72 and 315 Army Brigades RFA
35 Brigade RGA
(Some 144 guns)

17th Divisional Artillery under Brigadier-General P. Wheatley
122, 156 and 162 Brigades RFA
18 and 34 Army Brigades RFA
22 Brigade RGA
(Also some 144 guns)

38th Divisional Artillery under Brigadier-General T.E. Topping
79, 121 and 78 Brigades RFA.
93 and 155 Army Brigades RFA
17 Brigade RGA
(144 guns)

Further heavy batteries were allotted to counter-battery tasks.

From H hour to H+30 minutes, the 4.5-inch howitzers put down a smoke screen right across the whole Corps front, a sight to gladden the eye of any professional Gunner; it blinded Villers Guislain and Gonnelieu. It was supported by a creeping barrage of 18-pounders and 6-inch howitzers, and a hurricane bombardment of selected points. 21st Division was completely successful and 17th Division secured all its objectives, although it did suffer casualties from German artillery. By sheer dogged fighting by the infantry, the final objective and some 1,000 prisoners were taken that day. 38th Division also took all objectives. It was again a great and exhilarating day for the guns. At long, long last, and after years of toil, sweat and blood,they watched this enormous artillery machine lift the infantry forward onto their objectives with the minimum loss. By evening 18th September 1918, the way was almost clear for the final assault on the Hindenburg Line, and then would the great break-out to the east, a break-out to end the war, come at last?

Hard, continuous fighting now occurred day after day, and night after night. Much of it was bitter, close combat with little quarter given. Bombing attacks and clearing derelict farms and battered trenches followed assaults across open ground, under close gun fire. By 26th September, all was ready and, at 1030 hours on that day, the great preparatory bombardment of the guns of Fourth Army for the attack on the Hindenburg Line began. It had never before been seriously bombarded or attacked and was, for the most part, intact. It was extremely strong, with massive wire, concrete machine gun positions and great trenches and earthworks. In front of it lay the Canal du Nord, itself a formidable obstacle. Destruction of such a series of defences was a major problem, but captured maps gave the British great detail about their task. The guns blazed away furiously until the day for the attack—the 29th—dawned. 1,050 field guns and howitzers and 584 heavies were assembled to cover the infantry forward that day. Their plan of attack is interesting and terrifying in its proportions:

> a. From 2200 hours 26th September to 0600 hours 27th September, a mustard gas barrage was fired onto all known trenches and gun positions along the whole front. 32,000 rounds of the new BB gas shell were fired.
> b. From 0600 hours 27th September to H hour on 29th September, a bombardment of selected points was carried out. At the same time, a massive and varied harassing fire programme was fired, so that the enemy were never free from falling shells from front to rear.
> c. Wire-cutting began by huge 4.5-inch and 6-inch howitzer programmes and vigorous counter-battery programmes were fired.
> d. Finally, a programme of long range fire was directed at headquarters, railways, roads and dumps, many of which were accurately pinpointed.

The effect on the already demoralised Germans was enormous. The gas caused widespread casualties and drove the rest deep into their shelters, so demoralising them that many failed to emerge as the attacking divisions fell on them. Large numbers of guns were unable to fire, so great were the casualties to the gun detachments. The wire cutting programme was highly successful and the gaps cut enabled the infantry, whose morale was skyhigh, to race for their objectives. The German artillery had been defeated, casualties from them were low and some guns were captured before they could open fire. The Germans had suffered cruelly at the hands of our guns. At Usigny one hundred dead were counted, all killed by shell fire. The objectives fell—the great Hindenburg Line had fallen. The guns were ordered forward, no easy matter with so few bridges over the Canal, with so much wire and the deep trenches. The Germans began to fall back along the whole front, from Lens to Armentières. The longed-for breakthrough, the breakthrough for which the Allies had waited for four years, had occurred and more easily than even the optimists had hoped. The gallant, tough, victorious infantry of the

Empire surged forward, determined to finish the job, but the Empire's Gunners had also played a mighty part—they had conquered their adversaries in the greatest artillery duel in history and they had enough to spare to lift the infantry forward. It was a magnificent achievement but, now that they had perfected their techniques, nothing could stop them and nothing could save the Germans from the deadly fire of the guns.

A Battery "in mobile reserve" moving up into action. From a drawing by W B Wollen.   *(R.A.I.)*

CHAPTER 24

The Glorious March to Victory — September 1918

See map 40

It began on 27th September 1918. The German Armies started to fall back along the whole front from Lens to Armentières, and the British Fifth Army began the advance that was to end the war. By 8th October, Third and Fourth Armies had attacked and captured Cambrai and, on 14th October in the north, the British Second Army and Belgians together attacked from Comines to Dixmude. Thorout fell on 15th October, Ostend and Donoir on 17th and the victorious Fifth Army entered Lille on 18th October. But let us pause and see how these final battles were fought.

Artillery techniques had to change to support the advance. Much had to be kept mobile. More gas was used, aircraft were used for counter-battery work in particular and heavy artillery had observers well forward. Enemy guns were smothered as soon as they opened fire and some guns were always ready to move forward rapidly during the battle to keep within range of the German guns.

Training Notes No. 24, issued on 6th November, emphasised that it was the infantry who were responsible for calculating the pace of the barrage and the duration of pauses on objectives. It stressed the time needed to construct a successful barrage and the importance of avoiding last minute changes. It stated clearly that the Artillery Commander at Corps Headquarters was finally responsible for the co-ordination of its barrages. When these were issued, no changes were permitted unless the attack plan itself was changed. Finally, it spelt out the amount of work necessary to prepare a barrage, including calculation of each gun's firing data and preparation of ammunition. This was all a big step forward, since it finally acknowledged artillery command (not only advice) at Corps HQ and put a stop to infantry commanders demanding instant barrages and then changing them just before H hour.

The Battle of the Beaurevoir Line—3rd–5th October

On 3rd October, Fourth Army began the battle that was to drive the Germans finally from the mighty Hindenburg Line. The attack began at 0605 hours, with IX Corps and the Australian Corps attacking together. On their left, XIII Corps attacked to protect the flank. Here, the attack by 46th Division of IX Corps, supported by nine horse and field artillery brigades, was entirely successful. Tanks were used in close support of the infantry, while the heavies shelled Sequehart, Ramicourt and Montbrehain. To their right, 32nd Division attacked and rolled up the German trenches before Sequehart. The Australian Corps attacked under a massive fireplan, blocking their entire left flank by the concentrated fire of XIII Corps Heavy Artillery. The barrage lifted the infantry onto their phase one objective, the front trench of the Beaurevoir Line. They captured all but 500 yards of it, but all attempts to bomb their way along it failed. They decided to call in the guns, no easy task in the middle of a battle with no radio, but the FOOs were ready and quickly bombarded the trenches for 30 minutes; the enemy surrendered, some 200 of them with 18 machine guns. Meanwhile, 7th Australian Brigade suddenly came under heavy flank fire and was threatened by a counter-attack. Again they called in the guns, whose concentrated fire so held their flank that they were able to advance almost to Beaurevoir itself. But the day had not been easy; 1,000 men died for a few yards of ground, 1,192 prisoners, 163 machine guns and 11 field guns.

XIII Corps attacked with 50th Division in the lead, and supported it by thirteen brigades of guns, 312 guns in all. After heavy fighting they captured Gouy, Le Catelet and Prospect Hill.

On 4th October, the task of capturing Beaurevoir itself was given to XIII Corps. The divisional artilleries of 1st, 6th, 18th, 25th, 32nd, 46th, 50th and 60th Divisions, together with those of the 1st, 2nd, 3rd, 4th and 5th Australian Divisions, 15 Army field brigades, 21 heavy brigades and 14 siege batteries. This mass of artillery pounded the village and it was taken after heavy fighting. General Rawlinson, commanding Fourth Army, was now determined to push on. On 5th October, he ordered all artillery as far forward as possible. By the end of 5th October, the British line was beyond Beaurevoir and Montbrehain.

By 8th October, Fourth Army was ready to attack again. A massive barrage was arranged in detail to begin at H hour, with the field batteries firing 200 yards ahead of the assaulting infantry and tanks, and the 4.5-inch howitzers 200 yards beyond this. Lifts were to be of 100 yards and at three minute intervals. A protective barrage was to be laid on the objective. Mobile batteries were to follow the assault to provide immediate cover as the advance continued. Corps HQ was to handle all heavy artillery directly. It was a hard day's fighting and the absence of a really well co-ordinated counter-battery programme caused many casualties from enemy guns, but this mass of guns forced the passage and, by nightfall, all objectives were taken. It was on this day that 30th American Division was supported by the guns of the Australian Corps and took all objectives before it, with 1,500 prisoners and 30 guns. XIII Corps also attacked on that day and after hard fighting reached Serain. Attempts to push cavalry through were not successful, although two troops of 19th Hussars got among some field guns with the sword. It was not possible to push ahead until the artillery could be got forward in force.

Just south of Cambrai, Third Army started an attack at night on 8th October. Here a brilliant little action, conducted by the battery commander of C Battery 122 Brigade RFA, enabled guns and tanks to work well together to carry the infantry triumphantly into Villers Outreaux. Meanwhile, 21st Division of V Corps attacked Walincourt, supported by three brigades of field artillery under Brigadier-General H.W. Newcome, with 17 and 34 Heavy Brigades RGA. V Corps overran its section of the Beaurevoir Line and advanced 5,000 yards, capturing almost 1,000 prisoners. IV Corps attacked to the left of V Corps, its attack being carried out by 37th Division and the New Zealand Division. 56 and 90 Heavy Brigades RGA were affiliated to them respectively, while 57 and 92 Brigades RGA (60-pounders) were allotted for counter-battery tasks. 37th

Division attacked under a barrage fired by four field brigades, under Brigadier-General F. Potts. It was a complex barrage which, at one point, swung right along the Beaurevoir Line, but it was highly successful. Although at one time the infantry lost it, the tanks kept with it and the second objective was captured. Alongside them the New Zealanders had a wonderful day. They attacked under a barrage fired by six field brigades under Brigadier-General G.N. Johnston, CRA the New Zealand Division. All objectives were taken by 0800 hours 8th October and by 0930 hours they took Esnes, in spite of tough resistance by a *German Jager division*. So much for IV and V Corps operations on that day.

To their left, VI Corps did not have such a good day and it was not until 2nd and 3rd Divisions paused and mounted a properly organised attack at 1800 hours, under a properly organised barrage, that they were able to advance at all. Meanwhile XVII Corps had the complicated task of encircling Cambrai from the south. It had nine field brigades and four heavy brigades for this task, all under Brigadier-General C.H. de Rougemont. Six field brigades were ordered to fire the barrage and one complete brigade to put down a smoke screen to cover the left flank of 63rd Division. The remaining two brigades were allotted to the destruction of machine gun emplacements in front of 57th Division. The attack went well and the fireplan was a great success. A German counter-attack, led by four captured British tanks, was broken. A British tank carrying an FOO knocked out one enemy tank and went on to capture some field guns, another tank was knocked out by the infantry using a captured German anti-tank rifle. All objectives were taken and, during the night 8th-9th October, Cambrai was evacuated. The break-in battle was over, the German withdrawal had now begun. The Beaurevoir Line battles were the last tough struggles of the war, although this was not realised at the time. The tanks were now paying off, and were accepted as essential to any attack. The combination of massed artillery fire, plus the direct fire of the tanks, was a war-winning combination. At last, the infantry could be carried onto their objectives to finish the job. Command and control of artillery had reached a peak. Fireplans were massive, but good drills now allowed them to be carried out quickly. Movement of guns was always a part of the plan, and mobile guns earmarked to engage "on call" targets became a feature also. The power and flexibility of massed artillery was being demonstrated as never before and never before had it been so successful. The long years of trial and struggle had paid off at last. The month of October 1918 must have been one of the most triumphant in the annals of the Royal Regiment.Everywhere the power of the guns was victorious, nothing could survive when the guns swung onto a target; artillery used in this way in attack became a pre-requisite to success then as now. It did not in itself finish the job, but it enabled tanks and infantry to do so.

So, just before first light on the morning of 9th October 1918, the pursuit to the line of the River Selle began. Attacks started all along the line, but both cavalry and infantry, impatient to get on, underestimated the strength of isolated pockets of enemy and, in many cases, casualties were unnecessarily high. Attacks into the unknown, such as these, needed artillery and, where it was used, casualties were less and success was quicker. Lord Strathcona's Horse of the Canadian Cavalry Brigade mounted an attack covered by three batteries RCHA, capturing 230 men, a 5.9-inch howitzer and forty machine guns. Later, another attack by the Royals and 3rd Dragoon Guards covered by C Battery RHA had a similar success. The time for the cavalry and the Horse Artillery was at hand, the time for the break out into the land beyond the trenches, dreamed of for four years.

V Corps advanced without a barrage, but with its field batteries advancing in magnificent array right behind the infantry. On that day, 33rd Division advanced seven miles and 17th Division, five. Pursuit was new to the Army and new to the Gunners, and operations between 9th-12th October saw many novel ways of handling artillery. Let us look at some examples. In XVII Corps, the advance guard consisted of an infantry brigade, a troop of cavalry, 56 and 181 Brigades RFA, two sections of Royal Engineers and two machine gun companies. The force advanced by bounds and captured its objectives after arranging a rapid barrage. The Canadians kept their artillery concentrated, bringing down the barrage on the least resistance and advancing under its umbrella. Near Cambrai, when the enemy had withdrawn, they did not fire the barrage, but they still advanced under the cover of the guns, ready at an instant to open fire.

So the Germans fell back all along the front. The British First, Third and Fourth Armies surged forward and, to the north, Second, Fifth and Belgian Armies prepared to advance. The Germans planned to fall back onto the Hermann Position which ran (on paper only) from the canal west of Ghent along the Schelde Canal to Condé, Valenciennes, Solesmes, Le Cateau (on the Selle) and Bohain, then turned eastwards (to become the Brunhild Position) to Rethel, Dun and to the Meuse, 20 miles south of Verdun.

On 10th October the Fourth Army continued the pursuit. IX Corps advanced with patrols and FOOs leading, engaging any copse, house or sunken road with artillery in case it should be defended, the true fireplan in support of the pursuit. XIII Corps advanced with all infantry brigades up, each closely followed by a field artillery brigade. The village of St. Benin was taken after a vicious attack and barrage, but it soon became clear that the enemy was going to hold the line of Selle River in force. The infantry of V Corps advanced down a forward slope onto the Selle and came under heavy fire and were pinned down in the open. Only the gallant action of 156 Brigade RFA in Third Army area, which galloped forward to an exposed position just east of Troisvilles and engaged four German batteries which were in action on the forward eastern slopes of the Selles Valley, saved the situation. But thanks to some gallant work by the Engineers during the night,bridges were erected over the river near Caudry and some troops of the New Zealand Division got across.

Meanwhile, First Army pressed forward, the Canadian Corps moving ahead under barrage after barrage, fired by ten field brigades. By nightfall on 10th October, VIII and XXII Corps were in positions before the Drocourt-Queant Line.

By now logistic problems began to show themselves. Supplies of ammunition and food were running low and it was decided to pause and plan a major assault on the Selle on 17th October. Minor attacks were tried all along the line, but the enemy's position was strong and his concentrated machine gun fire made all daylight movement west of the river impossible. 37th Division of IV Corps did, however, manage to cross under some very good artillery fire. Bursts of ten rounds per gun on machine gun nests in turn were most effective and caused the German machine gunners to abandon their weapons and flee.

On 11th October, in First Army, 2nd Canadian Division attacked across the river supported by five field artillery brigades from 4th and 49th Divisions and 147 Army Brigade RFA, all under Brigadier-General A.B. Forman, CRA 49th Division. It was not far from there that, four years previously, when commanding E Battery RHA, he had fired the first round of the War. The attack went well until a powerful German counter-attack with tanks and infantry forced the Canadians back some 2,000 yards. Brigadier-General Forman galloped three field batteries to the threatened area. These swung round into action, opening direct fire onto the tanks, which at once retired carrying the German infantry with them.

On 12th October, First Army closed around the Drocourt-Queant Position and cleared it, sweeping on to Fressies which fell after a short, sharp bombardment. By evening, the approaches to the Schelde were reached, advances being conducted by firing concentrations onto defended areas combined with enveloping tactics. But resistance was stiffening and 12th Division were held by heavy artillery fire from positions east of the Sensée Canal.

On 12th October, the first armistice feelers were put out, but Ludendorf was determined to hold the line of the Selle. On that day, he ordered his artillery to prevent the Allies crossing the river at all costs.

Let us look quickly back to the Flanders front where, on 14th October, the British Second Army, with Belgian and French contingents, was fighting for Courtrai. As the attacks developed there came to light a problem on the inter British-Belgian boundary. The Belgians wanted their barrage to move at 100 yards in three minutes, whereas the British wanted theirs at 100 yards in two minutes. Furthermore, the Belgian infantry would not keep as close to the barrage as did the British, thus gaps soon appeared as the two Armies got out of phase. The solution was to send a special detachment of British infantry and machine guns to move astride the boundary to try to keep the two Armies in contact. 30th Division of X Corps reached its objectives, but 34th Division had more opposition from defended farms and had to bring guns right forward to destroy each in turn over open sights. By evening it, too, was on its objectives. 35th Division had a more difficult task, with objectives oblique to the line of advance and some 8,000 yards away. Guns fired thermite shells to help the infantry keep direction and others advanced right behind the infantry to enable the barrage to cover the whole advance. By last light, it reached the Lys and prepared to capture Gulleghem next morning. 9th Division, in contact with the Belgians, had a section of 18-pounders with each attacking battalion and, with its barrage lifting only 50 yards per minute, made good progress. The attack went well and, after some stiff fighting by the "boundary force", the Belgians ended the day in line with the British.

By 15th October, the victorious Second Army had crossed the Lys and found Comines abandoned. II Corps pressed on hard beyond Gulleghem, the infantry moving so well and so fast that they almost ran into their own barrage. Smoke was used extensively and soon the infantry were on the Courtrai-Roulers railway. Here guns came forward silencing enemy opposition and the infantry pushed on, mostly at the double, until they reached Harlebeke. The French in the north were not doing so well, having only covered a mile and a half to the British seven miles. Marshal Foch ordered them forward at all costs. The Germans reported their failures as being due to masses of British tanks using direct fire, but none were present on this sector. There is no doubt that they were referring to the accurate direct artillery fire from the guns. The guns kept right up with the lead attacks throughout these exhilarating and memorable days. Guns in pursuit must be handled boldly and right forward to blast away anything which might hold the advance as a whole, and that is exactly how they were handled.

So, from the hell of the years of the trenches had at last come the advance; the surge to victory. It was not over yet, but the magic spirit of victory was in the air and all knew that it was now only a matter of time. But the pressure must be kept up, none could relax, least of all the guns. The enemy must be given no respite; he must never be free from the guns; he must now be destroyed. The ammunition trains and echelons worked frantically to keep the hungry guns fed with their murderous food. The work was round the clock, the distances were great, but all depended on them. As always they responded, and at no time do we read of anything but the most minor restrictions on ammunition.

Fireplanning for the pursuit had reached its peak, commanders understood the guns and artillery commanders were quick to respond. The barrage was still used but the rapid "on call" fireplan, such a feature of later wars, became a new, vital and well developed drill.

And so on to the last phase of this gigantic struggle.

CHAPTER 25

Breakout at Last
The Battle of the Selle — October 1918

See map 40

Preparations for the crossing of the Selle began on 11th October. A massive fireplan was prepared and it is notable how the heavy batteries were right forward to shell the German lines of retreat across the Sambre. The attack was to be carried out by Fourth Army and the artillery allotment was as follows:

IX Corps. BGRA—Brigadier-General G. Humphreys

6th Divisional Artillery. CRA—Brigadier-General E.F. Delaforce
1st, 6th and 32nd Divisional artilleries
Two Army Brigades RFA
(Total 10 brigades)

46th Divisional Artillery. CRA—Brigadier-General Sir H. Child
46th Divisional Artillery
Two Brigades RHA
Two Army Brigades RFA
(Total 6 brigades)

Heavy Artillery. BGHA—Brigadier-General G.B. Mackenzie
12, 14, 40, 69, 89, 83 and 98 Brigades RGA
50th and 498th Siege Batteries RGA
80th, 499th and 1st RMA Siege Batteries in reserve

The American II Corps. CRA—Brigadier-General K.K. Knapp (of the British VII Corps)
2nd, 3rd, 4th and 5th Australian Divisional Artilleries
Two Australian Army Brigades RFA

Heavy Artillery. BGHA—Brigadier-General E.H. Metcalfe
9, 18, 21, 41, 68, 71, 72, and 75 Brigades RGA
222nd, 312th, 449th and 504th Siege Batteries RGA

XIII Corps. CRA—Brigadier-General R.A.C. Wellesley
18th and 25th Divisional Artilleries
Five Army Brigades RFA

Heavy Artillery. BGHA—Brigadier-General J.D. Sherer
23 (less one 9.2-inch Howitzer Battery) 27, 47 (each less one 8-inch Howitzer Battery), 76 and 89
Brigades RGA
189th, 312th and 545th Siege Batteries RGA

15th and 16th October were wet and misty, which prevented flying, counter-battery shooting was affected and the German artillery remained effective throughout the battle. IX Corps attacked on 17th October to the south-east, with

46th Division on the right. It was supported by two great belts of fire, which leapfrogged forward. The fire was very concentrated and intense and lifted the infantry onto their objectives. A German counter-attack from the area of Regnicourt was hit by every gun within range, in a fury of concentrated fire, and it was reported that only one solitary German emerged on the British side of the bombardment! To the left 6th Division lost the barrage and, as a result, its direction, and was brought to a halt. 1st Division, moving close behind, was ordered to pass through and gain the intermediate objective. On its left were found German machine guns in great strength, determined to hold their ground. The barrage was far ahead and it was time to move the guns forward. Accordingly, the advance ground to a halt, as movement was impossible without the fire of the guns. By 1715 hours, an attack was organised with a barrage, but the fire was ragged. However, the infantry gallantly struggled on until they were finally stopped, overlooking the Selle Valley, by the unsubdued German guns.

To the left again, the American Corps attacked with 27th and 30th U.S. Divisions, supported by ten Australian field artillery brigades. They found the Selle to be no great obstacle and made good progress. They did, however, take more time than planned in mopping up Molain and in doing so they lost the barrage. But by evening they were between their intermediate and first objectives and dominating the Selle Valley.

The attack in the XIII Corps sector was made by 50th Division on the right and 66th Division on the left. The engineers constructed floating bridges over the river within a few minutes of H hour, working just behind the opening line of the barrage. They displayed great gallantry in doing so and their action was fundamental to the success of the day's battle. Brigadier-General K.J. Kincaid-Smith organised the barrage to be fired by three field brigades (12 batteries; 72 guns) and 96 machine guns. The opening line fell just on the enemy side of the river, paused for three minutes and then lifted to the railway and beyond. There was a thick mist at H hour and this hampered the move up of the tanks. Fighting soon became very heavy indeed; the Germans counter-attacked but were held. Meanwhile, plans were made to attack Le Cateau railway station and the heavies bombarded the objective for thirty minutes from 1500 hours. At the same time the Germans counter-attacked again. By now, the 50th Division area was hopelessly mixed up and brigade commanders were given the task of sorting it out, while the divisional commanders planned to press on with the attack. By this measure, relentless pressure was maintained on the exhausted Germans and the intermediate objectives were carried by last light.

To the left of 50th Division, 66th Division, using the South African Brigade, was to attack south-eastwards and capture Le Cateau. As a deception measure, a "Chinese Barrage" was fired to the left of the assault axis (a "Chinese Barrage" was a barrage fired in order to mislead the enemy into thinking that an attack was coming in its direction when none was planned). It was fired from 0520 hours until 0538 hours on 17th October by the guns of 38th and 66th Divisions. At 0732 hours, the real barrage was fired but it was not strong enough to cope with the formidable German defences. The wire was not well cut and the railway cutting and a sunken road, both heavily wired and defended by machine guns, were tough obstacles. The infantry fought hard and 198th Infantry Brigade captured Le Cateau by 1800 hours. It was a fine feat of arms.

So, by the end of 17th October, Fourth Army was across the Selle and firmly established between it and the Sambre. The German Hermann Stellung I position had been well penetrated.

On 17th October, President Wilson offered surrender terms to the Germans. Ludendorf was insistent that there was still plenty of fight left in the German Army and that, if only he could obtain reinforcements, he could still hold the Allies in check. The Chancellor, Prince Max of Baden, however, wrote in his diary "a reversal of fortune in our favour is inconceivable".

So the Allies pressed on relentlessly. They advanced up to five miles and almost reached the line of the Sambre Canal by the evening of 19th October. An attack by 1st Division on 18th October, with H hour of 1130 hours, achieved complete surprise, so much so that many German officers were captured seated round mess tables, many guns were captured (in one case, a complete battery of 4.2-inch howitzers by 75th Brigade of 50th Division).

German resistance was now visibly weakening, as losses had been very great. Few divisions could muster more than 3,000 men, almost half the guns were without horses and ammunition was critically short. Morale was low and men began to surrender easily and in large numbers. The Geman High Command was fast losing its nerve and began to realise that there was little it could do to stop the Allies now.

On 20th October at 0200 hours, Third and First Armies resumed their attacks. Their orders were to seize the area west of the River Selle, which was to become the start line for the next offensive. No preliminary barrage was to be fired, to achieve surprise under a full moon.

The Artillery of Third Army for this attack was to be:

V Corps Artillery—GOCRA Brigadier-General R.R. Benson
    38th Divisional Artillery under Brigadier-General T.E. Topping
    17th Divisional Artillery under Brigadier-General P. Wheatley
    12, 13, 17, 54 and 58 Heavy Brigades
    Plus the guns of 21st and 33rd Divisional Artilleries

IV Corps Artillery -GOCRA Brigadier-General J.G. Geddes
    5th and 37th Divisional Artilleries under Brigadier-General A.H. Hussey
    42nd and 63rd Divisional Artilleries under Brigadier-General F.W.H. Walshe
    1 and 3 Brigades RNZA
    56, 57, 90 and 92 Brigades RGA under Brigadier-General T.E. Marshall

VI Corps Artillery—GOCRA Brigadier-General J.G. Rotton
    3rd and 62nd Divisional Artilleries under Brigadier-General A.T. Anderson
    2nd and Guards Divisional Artilleries under Brigadier-General F.A. Wilson
    14 Brigade RHA
    86 Army Brigade RFA
    32, 39, 58, 60, 84 and 88 Brigades RGA under Brigadier-General A. Ellershaw

XVII Corps Artillery—GOCRA Brigadier-General E.H. Willis
    19th, 24th and 61st Divisional Artilleries under Brigadier-General E.J.R. Peel
    93 and 315 Army Brigades RFA
    2 Brigade RNZA
    35, 62 and 71 Brigades RGA under Brigadier-General N.G. Barron

Solesmes was full of French civilians, which complicated the barrage plans. It was decided to fire shrapnel and machine guns at the town, relying on cellars to shelter the population, with the main barrage creeping around the town. The attack there was carried out by 62nd Division and was most successful. Final objectives were reached by 1000 hours on 20th October and a German counter-attack was beaten off at 1600 hours.

In XVII Corps, 19th Division met tough opposition, but reached its final objective by 0700 hours on 21st October. During the night, sections of 18-pounders crossed the Selle on trestle bridges and by dawn, three field brigades were across, no mean feat.

So much for Third Army. In First Army, 4th Division of XXII Corps attacked at 0200 hours on 20th October; it soon found the enemy retreating. One battalion was quickly passed through the leading brigades under cover of a fireplan provided by five field brigades (120 guns). This battalion then took the divisional objective alone. It was an excellent example of quick thinking, quick reaction and pressing home an advantage. The Canadian Corps met stiffer resistance especially at Wavrechain. There, at 1430 hours they called for a special bombardment of the village, followed by another at 1800 hours. That was enough—the Germans withdrew.

On 21st October, wet weather made further advances difficult. Ammunition was running low and time was needed to get it forward, supply was not easy. Accordingly, the advance was not resumed until 23rd October. First and Third Armies were to get across the Sambre Canal and to reach Valenciennes. Fourth Army was to form a protective flank facing east to protect the right flank. A creeping barrage was to be fired at H hour, and advance some 200 yards ahead of the attack. Heavies were superimposed on sunken roads, farms, strongpoints and likely enemy positions. The barrage was to slow down wherever it crossed a wood. Field artillery brigades were to advance close behind the assault as far as the second objective.

At 1510 hours on 16th October, Ludendorf had ordered the Northern Group of Armies, under Crown Prince Rupprecht, "to retire according to plan to the Hermann Position, running from Ghent through Tournai and Condé, east of Le Cateau to join the Hunding-Brunhilde Line". This operation was, however, badly upset by the attacks on 17th October, when the British Fourth Army broke into the Hermann Line. Accordingly, Prince Rupprecht ordered a general retreat on 18th October. Thus, on 23rd October, 8th and 12th Divisions of VII Corps in First Army, advanced across the Haute Deule Canal without opposition. Douai was found evacuated. By the 19th, First Army was also reporting only minor opposition and this was confined mostly to long range shelling. Soon First Army were in line with Third Army on the Selle.

V Corps fired a barrage at H hour with eight field brigades and two heavy brigades (230 guns). The night was wet and misty and the light from the moon weak, but the attack went well and all objectives were taken. In IV Corps, the attacks were equally successful. In VI Corps, conditions were more difficult, the Selle had first to be crossed and all bridges had been blown. In the Guards Division, sections of 18-pounders accompanied the attacking infantry crossing the Selle on precarious trestle bridges, and saved the day by point blank fire as the enemy counter-attacked onto the objectives. By 0500 hours, 19th Division advanced across the plateau between the Rivers Selle and Harpies with success everywhere. Morale was high as the men of the batteries realised that the enemy was offering little resistance.

During the September and October operations, much had been learnt about the handling of artillery in an advance. The advantage of ordering sections of 18-pounders to move right forward with the attacking battalions was proven. Battalions learned how vital it was to keep their artillery commander fully informed of future plans and of the locations of forward troops. Battalion Headquarters realised the value of locating themselves near to Gunner observation posts. The value of enfilade fire was learned, as was the use of field guns as anti-tank guns, as protection when the inevitable counter-attack came in. The value of single guns run forward to engage machine guns was realised. Such guns needed infantry protection and, where this was provided, success usually followed. But the German artillery was not yet finished. They were concentrating on counter-battery work and were just learning a lesson learnt by the British many years before.

A feature of the October fighting was the problem of dealing with forested areas such as the Forêt de Mormal. There were a number of Gunner solutions. One was to fire a creeping barrage of shrapnel immediately ahead of the infantry, with a slight increase in angle of sight to bring the shell bursts level with the tree tops. Beyond this barrage 4.5-inch and 6-inch howitzers fired 400 and 600 yards ahead of the 18-pounders. Meanwhile, the 60-pounders searched roads, tracks and clearings. At other times 4.5-inch howitzers, firing fuze 101 non-instantaneous only 300 yards ahead of the infantry, were used with success. Block barrages were used on smaller woods. Sometimes a barrage would be made to creep up to a wood, then dwell on it as the infantry closed up and then, when they were ready, it lifted on to escape routes. By this time in the war, the British artillery was supreme. Fire could be moved about the battlefield in large quantities and in varying natures, HE, shrapnel or smoke, wherever it was needed. Command being well forward and artillery commanders being at each level of command, flexibility was complete. It is possible that, in terms of sheer numbers of guns and weight of fire, the Royal Regiment has never known a more technically proficient period in its history.

23rd October saw the start of the combined attacks of First, Third and Fourth Armies. The aim now was to close up and break through Hermann Position II, which followed the Sambre Canal to Ors and then northwards to the Schelde at Trith, a little south-west of Valenciennes. Fourth Army, which was to face east to protect the right flank of First and Third Armies, consisted of IX and XIII Corps.

So the long awaited day arrived. At long, long last the British Army would be beyond the mud and horror of the trenches and into the rolling downland east of the Selle. Here were more slopes, high hedges and large areas of woodland. There were no continuous trench systems but the Germans had organised villages, woods and features into a defensive zone of great depth.

H hour for Fourth Army was 0120 hours for IX Corps and 0200 hours for XIII Corps. First objectives were to be taken by 0340 hours, second by 0520 hours, third by 0800 hours and fourth by 1012 hours. IX Corps attacked with 1st and 6th Divisions up. CRA 1st Division, Brigadier-General H.F.E. Lewin, had 1st, 32nd and 46th Divisional Artilleries, 5 Army Brigade, RFA, 16 Brigade RHA and 83

Brigade RGA—some 204 guns. Alongside him was CRA 5th Division, Brigadier-General E.F. Delaforce, with another 114 guns, those of 3rd, 4th and 5th Australian Divisions, 14 Army Brigade RAA and 41 Brigade RGA. But behind this powerful force was a Corps reserve of guns under Brigadier-General G. Humphreys, the GOCRA and co-ordinator of the artillery battle. He had 2nd and 6th Australian Divisional Artilleries, 5 Brigade RHA, 23 Army Brigade RFA, 6 and 13 Brigades RAA and a mass of heavy artillery under Brigadier-General G.B. Mackenzie: 9, 12, 14, 18, 21, 51, 68, 69, 71, 79, 93 and 97 Brigades RGA, plus 50th and 498th Siege Batteries—a further 252 guns, making 570 guns to support two divisions!

Meanwhile, XIII Corps attacked, with 18th and 25th Divisions in the lead and 50th and 66th Divisions in reserve. The artillery was commanded by the GOCRA, Brigadier-General R.A.C. Wellesley. CRA 25th Division, Brigadier-General K.J. Kincaid-Smith, had his own Divisional Artillery (110 and 112 Brigades RFA), 86, 104 and 150 Army Brigades RFA (102 guns) while Brigadier-General T.O. Seagram, CRA 18th Division, had his own Divisional Artillery (82 and 83 Brigades RFA), 50th Divisional Artillery (250 and 251 Brigades RFA), 65 and 84 Army Brigades RFA, a total of 132 guns. Finally, backing up this powerful force was the Corps Heavy Artillery under Brigadier-General J.D. Sherer, consisting of 23, 47, 73, 85 Brigades RGA and 449th and 504th Siege Batteries, making a total of 306 guns—1,076 guns for the four attacking divisions of the two Corps.

Unfortunately, bad weather from 19th–22nd October limited air operations and this adversely affected location of enemy guns and consequent counter-battery attacks. The German artillery produced an intense defensive fireplan which caught the right brigade of 1st Division at H hour. How vital it is to have a really effective counter-battery plan. There was a thick mist on the morning of 23rd October, which reduced visibility to 30–40 yards. Though on balance this helped the attacking British infantry, it did cause confusion and some loss of direction. Nevertheless, with the help of a few tanks the objectives were taken. The artillery was deadly accurate. 25th Division reported that 1/8th Worcesters had only four killed and forty-three wounded for the whole operation, while they captured fifteen officers and 371 other ranks.

The batteries supporting 18th Division had some difficulty finding gun positions, so much so that half the front of one leading brigade could not be covered by the 18-pounders. The flexibility of the barrage was demonstrated as the division crossed the Richemon stream. The barrage crossed the stream and swung right, its right remaining stationary for 32 minutes, while its left wheeled round slowly at a rate of 100 yards in ten minutes, carrying the tanks and infantry with it and onto their objectives.

It was, however, 2000 hours before most of Fourth Army's objectives were taken. Casualties were light, except in tanks. Only nine of the twenty engaged rallied that evening. The guns of Fourth Army demonstrated, on 23rd October, the crushing effect of well co-ordinated, massed artillery. They simply swept away the opposition and, though stiff fighting was reported in places, it was not on a large scale.

H hour for Third Army (IV, V, VI and XVII Corps) was 0200 hours. The left Corps, XVII, had some 1,500 yards to go, whereas the right, V Corps, had some 9,500 yards, taking five objectives and there was an ammunition shortage. Again the German guns caused considerable casualties to the infantry as they began to assemble. As a result, the infantry in V Corps got behind the barrage. Nevertheless, 21st Division took its third objective under a barrage fired by 94 Brigade RFA. It went on to capture its fourth but could get no further. IV Corps had a good day, but it took them until 0230 hours on 24th October to capture all objectives. One classic action was an attack by a New Zealand brigade under a highly successful and very quickly laid on barrage by five field brigades. It was entirely successful. VI Corps was next in line. It attacked with 2nd and 3rd Divisions, each supported by five field brigades. The enemy was surprised and the attack went well. By 1430 hours, all objectives were taken. So successful was the operation that GOC 3rd Division ordered the Oxfordshire Hussars, with a field brigade, to pass through the fifth objective and exploit eastwards. It was a gallant effort and a correct decision, but it failed due to stiff resistance on the River Ecaillon which the cavalry could not force. It had been a good day. The advance in strong moonlight behind excellent and powerful barrages had been relatively easy; the situation became more difficult in daylight and poor weather still hampered air support.

First Army made no major move on 23rd October, but it did manage to consolidate its line forward towards the Schelde.

The fighting on 24th and 25th October marked the end of the battle of the Selle, although XIII Corps, Fourth Army, still had to achieve its 4th and 5th objectives. It was ordered to do so. These lay beyond the Hermann Position II with its thick belts of wire. So, at 0400 hours, 25th Division attacked in the moonlight under a creeping barrage. This smothered the enemy and, by 1000 hours, the fourth objective was secured at the point of the bayonet. By 1800 hours so was the fifth. 18th Division had a tougher time and was involved in a great deal of hand-to-hand fighting before clearing the fourth objective, but it could not achieve the fifth. Accordingly, at 0900 hours 25th October, a final attack was made. 54th Infantry Brigade of 18th Division lost the barrage and its locations were unknown. It is tragic to relate that it suffered some casualties from our own guns. Command and control in mobile operations is always complex and here it failed with tragic consequences. There is, of course, no excuse, but it is a lesson always to be learnt.

Fourth Army had done well. It had completed its task and with four divisions it had defeated eight German divisions, capturing 1,240 prisoners and 66 guns.

Meanwhile, Third Army planned to exploit to the northwest and rather vague orders were given. 33rd Division attacked in front of Le Quesnoy under a barrage fired by the four field brigades of 33rd and 38th Divisional Artilleries. They failed to capture Englefontaine. 21st Division attacked but only used the fire of one field brigade. It was not enough. It was not until a full barrage was ordered at 1600 hours that the objectives were all taken at 1800 hours. In IV Corps the story was similar. A barrage was cancelled during its attack, which became bogged down until the barrage re-started. However, the Corps advanced some five miles and took 633 prisoners.

By now First Army was lagging behind and it was ordered to push forward XXII Corps on the right to conform with Third Army. 4th and 51st Divisions were given the task. CRA 4th Division, Brigadier-General C.A. Sykes, had his own and 49th Divisional Artilleries (29, 32, 245 and 246 Brigades RFA) and 17,

26, 52, 175 and 282 Army Brigades RFA. Brigadier-General L.C.L. Oldfield, CRA 51st Division, had his own and 39th Divisional Artilleries (174, 186, 255 and 256 Brigades RFA) and 77, 147 and 189 Army Brigades RFA. All the heavies were under Brigadier-General L.J. Chapman. He had 7, 8, 34, 42, 48, 53, 78 and 81 Brigades RGA.

The attack went well, even though in places the infantry lost the barrage. The Germans were now badly shaken and exhausted. They had also used up all their reserves and this meant that they could no longer replace their enormous losses.

In the battle of the Selle, the British had captured some 20,000 prisoners and 475 guns. But the British too had problems—they were again running ahead of their supplies, so a pause was essential before the next thrust to capture Valenciennes and the Sambre river line.

The battles of October had shown how the lessons of war had been learned. The British artillery was now a well-oiled machine; it knew what it had to do, it had the equipment and the command structure was right. Massive artillery concentrations were hurled about the battlefield, primarily because artillery commanders were well forward and were able to order alterations in time to be effective and in concert with the infantry and tanks.

CHAPTER 26

Victory!
Valenciennes and the Sambre — November 1918

See maps 40 and 41

By the end of October 1918, the German Army was nearer to defeat than the Allies knew. The spirit had gone—some, especially machine gunners, fought hard but the infantry was poor and unreliable. Co-operation with artillery was very poor; there were acute shortages and the effect of constant defeat after defeat resulted in low morale. Meanwhile, just the same factors were extremely good and improving in the Allied Armies. The operations of early November 1918 were concerned with the passage of the Schelde. In the last two weeks of October, Fifth Army had crossed the Haute Deule Canal and captured Lille. It was some 10–12 miles west of the Schelde around Tournai and the passage of the Lys had seen some tough fighting.

Let us just look at the October fighting before the Schelde. On 17th October, Second Army crossed the Lys; it immediately ordered a pursuit with only light artillery in support. But the Germans had not retreated; they had prepared a strong switch line between the Lys and the Hermann Line. This was not crushed until a full fireplan was arranged. Hasty attacks without proper fireplans were organised by 41st Division and these met nothing but misfortune. In II Corps, 29th Division had only three field brigades. It came suddenly upon a strongly organised German position and suffered heavily. There were no heavies in range; they were west of the Lys and considered that a fireplan was unnecessary. The German artillery had not yet been broken along the Schelde sector—it was still too strong. But Second Army was not slow in learning and, when the next main attack was launched on 31st October, all the artillery was brought to bear, under Brigadier-General W.B.R. Sandys, GOCRA XIX Corps, and Brigadier-General A.D. Kirby, GOCRA II Corps. The attack was a great success and the Army reached the Schelde in one huge surge forward. However, it was not all easy going and German machine guns offered a great deal of opposition. It had become customary to keep one section of 18-pounders right forward during an advance to deal with machine guns at point blank range. An example of this procedure had occurred a few weeks earlier at Ledeghem on 1st October, when Lieutenant R.V. Gorle was engaged in this manner with the Royal Scots. He had one gun of A Battery 50 Brigade RFA and he brought it into action four times in line with the leading infantry against German machine guns, and each time he knocked them out by firing over open sights under direct machine gun fire, at close range. Later, seeing that the infantry were being driven back by intense hostile fire, he, without hesitation, galloped his gun in front of the leading infantry and, coming into action completely isolated and in the open, knocked out two more enemy machine guns which were causing trouble. For his disregard of personal safety, for his dash and for the magnificent example he set to a wavering line, which rallied and re-took the village, Lieutenant R.V. Gorle was awarded the Victoria Cross. This was an action in the very best traditions of the Regiment and acknowledged the bravery of many such Gunners operating in this manner.

General Plumer now laid down the artillery policy for the forthcoming offensive over the Schelde. He laid great stress on counter-battery fire. He said that every possible piece of artillery was to be got into action to cover the crossing and the subsequent break out to the east. Field batteries were therefore to be right up to the western bank of the river, and even the heavies were to be within 2,000 yards of it. The crossing was planned for 11th November, unless the enemy withdrew first. Meanwhile, Valenciennes was to be captured by 3rd November. The town was full of civilians and refugees and therefore could not be shelled, except for the houses overlooking the Schelde Canal. This canal, greatly swollen by flooding, protected the town to the west, and its eastern bank was well wired and covered by machine guns. However, XXII Corps of First Army was already across the canal south of the town, so General Horne decided to attack it from the south. The enemy had six divisions available and two more close by, so this was not going to be an easy operation.

During the night 31st October/1st November, the Germans fired a great deal of HE and gas and their defensive fire fell promptly when the attack developed. But the British Gunners were ready and gradually located the enemy batteries and dealt with them one by one. 61st Division of XVII Corps, Third Army, was on the right covered by nine brigades RFA and four heavy brigades, all under GOCRA XVII Corps, Brigadier-General E.H. Willis. The field brigades were those of 19th, 24th and 61st Divisions, together with 315 (Army) Brigade and 41 and 42 Brigades RFA. H hour was 0515 hours. The village of Préseau was smoked off. For the first forty-five minutes, every available gun was employed on counter-battery tasks; thereafter they swung onto a timed programme, bombarding strong points and approaches. The artillery fire was deadly accurate and the attack was successful everywhere by 0830 hours. Then suddenly at 0930 hours, a powerful German counter-attack by a division (*fresh 28th Reserve Division*), led by four captured British tanks, struck the left of 61st Division, but the 4th and 49th Divisions forced them back. Two sections of 107 Brigade RFA had crossed the river at 0830 hours and immediately came into action, quickly knocking out two of the tanks. The line steadied and held until 1930 hours. 4th Division, attacking under the fire of the guns of 4th and 11th Divisional Artilleries, together with 18, 26, 52, 175 and 182 (Army) Field Brigades RFA and 7 Brigade RGA, had just reached its objective when the attack came. 49th and 51st Divisions were doing well when they too were struck by the attack. All possible guns were brought to bear, commanded by Brigadier-General A.B. Forman, and this sudden threat was held.

The way in which the use of a quick, creeping barrage had developed is well illustrated by the attack on the German position near Famars (three miles south of Valenciennes), as part of the general attack on Valenciennes on 1st November 1918. The attack was to be carried out by 6th Duke of Wellington's Regiment of 49th Division. Its 245 and 246 Brigades RFA were reinforced by seven more. Two artillery groups were formed, the Right Group (five brigades) supporting the Dukes was commanded by Lieutenant-Colonel K. Duncan, of 246 Brigade RGA.

He had eighty 18-pounders at 500 rounds per gun and twenty-four 4.5-inch howitzers at 325 rounds per gun. Two sections of 18-pounders were to move forward with the attack, to engage targets over open sights and to act as anti-tank guns. In addition, 34 Brigade RGA with three 6-inch howitzer batteries and one 60-pounder battery was made available. Sixteen Vickers machine-guns of 102nd Battalion of the Machine Gun Corps were to fire a seventy-minute barrage.

The Dukes were to attack in two waves, A Company (Major H. Farrar) followed by B Company (Lieutenant S.E.G Bilham). They carried 20-foot duck-boards to cross the Rhonelle stream during the attack.

At 0515 hours on 1st November, the barrage opened on a six mile front. Right Group's fire came down with superb accuracy just 200 yards in front of A and B Companies' start line. The Dukes had three minutes to run forward and form up just 50 yards behind the exploding HE shells. It then led them forward at a rate of 100 yards per minute, giving them twenty-one minutes to reach the Rhonelle stream. On the way, all B Company's officers were hit in dealing with some machine guns but, as they crossed the stream, the barrage halted on the far side and was joined by a smoke-screen fired by the 4.5-inch howitzers. By 0700 hours the two companies were on their objectives, with 100 German prisoners.

It was now the turn of C and D Companies. It was a fine, dry day but surprise had gone. The barrage moved off but at the slower rate of 100 yards in five minutes, going slightly uphill. The Germans still had machine guns well dug in and began to cause casualties. The barrage stopped as the companies got to the objective, and the danger of counter-attack was in everyone's mind. The position was reinforced before this came in at 1600 hours. It was easily defeated by an SOS concentration, so powerful that under its fire the Dukes managed to capture even more ground. The Dukes had lost 2 officers and 27 ORs killed and 12 ORs missing, but the enemy lost 300 dead and almost 650 prisoners as a result of this action alone.

The Dukes' war diary states that "the concentrated, powerful and accurate artillery support which 1/6th Dukes received played a very important part in the almost total success of the attack".

The concentration was one gun per 12 yards of front. The tasks of the guns were to:

a. Open a creeping barrage at H hour, 200 yards ahead of the infantry.

b. A second barrage was to be fired 200 yards in front of this barrage.

The rate of fire was rapid from zero to 28 minutes (4 rounds per minute) up to the stream, then normal to the end of the barrage at 180 minutes (0815 hours). The length of the barrage was 2 miles. The 4.5s had special superimposed targets, particularly on known positions east of the stream, then were to lift to targets on the Aulnoy-Préseau road, remaining there till plus 60, then creep forward to plus 105, keeping 300 yards ahead of the 18-pounder barrage, then lift to the final objective.

Further to the left, the Canadian Corps attacked with 4th Canadian Division, covered by the guns of 2nd and 4th Canadian Divisions and 39th Division. The enemy guns caused some trouble, but Valenciennes was entered and cleared on the morning of 2nd November. The Germans suffered heavily and began to withdraw all around the city. New orders were given to First Army to begin the pursuit as soon as possible, but the situation in front of Third and Fourth Armies was not so easy, as the Germans there were still fighting hard. The First French Army was to co-operate on the right to give a total frontage of forty miles for this final heave to victory. Inside this area running from the Guise to Condé, four armies of nineteen divisions were to attack. An infantry division in those days consisted of 16,035 all ranks when at full strength. It had 48 guns and 400 machine guns (64 Vickers and 336 Lewis), 36 mortars and 822 carts and vehicles. So something like a quarter of a million men and almost 2,000 guns had now to be given new orders, orders of pursuit, orders to final victory. We today must never underestimate the enormities of such problems.

The Sambre Canal was a considerable obstacle, being 70 feet wide from bank to bank and 40 feet at water-level. It was 6 feet deep with a muddy bottom. In addition, there were many swollen streams, some up to 15 feet wide, and, of course, the great Forêt de Mormal itself, astride the junction of Third and Fourth Armies.

Fourth Army's task was to force the passage of the Sambre/Oise Canal and secure a footing in the Forêt de Mormal. IX Corps was to force the Canal. Catillon, some six miles south-east of Le Cateau, was still in German hands. The plan was for 1st and 32nd Divisions to attack across the Canal and establish bridgeheads. Each division was to be covered by nine field brigades under their CRAs, Brigadier-Generals H.F.E. Lewin and J.A. Tyler respectively. The Corps heavy artillery, under Brigadier-General G.B. Mackenzie, consisted of fourteen heavy brigades and three siege batteries, all in all 278 guns. The artillery plan was a creeping barrage moving at 100 yards in six minutes right up to and over the canal, with all heavies on counter-battery work. It went wonderfully well and, although the fighting was tough in places and 1st Division had some five hundred casualties, the bridgeheads were established. German artillery fire faltered and became ragged and, by 0800 hours on 5th November, their guns could be seen moving back. They were clearly losing heart. When a cavalry patrol reported enemy in Vieville and the guns were turned onto it, the enemy fled. 32nd Division found so little opposition as it continued the advance that it did not call for a barrage.

XIII Corps had the Forêt de Mormal to its front with the Canal running between Landrecies and Maubeuge—how familiar are the place names—the points of first contact in the early battles of 1914—revenge was sweet in those great days. 18th, 25th and 50th Divisions were to attack in line with H hour at 0615 hours on 4th November. Thirteen field brigades were to fire the barrages. 25th Division on the right advanced in thick mist and closed up to the canal after some stiff fighting, but took 800 prisoners and 27 guns. 150th Brigade of 50th Division attacked through the Forêt de Mormal, using an 18-pounder shrapnel barrage adjusted to burst the shells at tree top height, and a 4.5-inch and 6-inch barrage, 400 and 600 yards respectively beyond it. 60-pounders pounded roads, tracks and clearings. The barrage moved relentlessly on, to pause for one hour on the Canal. The Germans fought hard in the forest, but their morale, already low, flagged heavily under the terror of the barrage and, with their flanks gone, they pulled back to the line of the canal where they stood firmly. 50th Division dug in facing them. 18th Division attacked the village on the left of the 25th. They cleared the village of Preux Aux Bois almost entirely with the barrage and swept on to the forest, clearing all before them until they too were on the canal. It was a great success, a bridgehead 15 miles long and $2\frac{1}{2}$ miles deep had been achieved in the south and, in the north, the great forest was dominated. 4,000 prisoners and 80 guns were taken that day.

H hour for Third Army, to the left of Fourth Army, was 0530 hours on 4th November, except for V Corps which attacked at 0615 hours to conform with Fourth Army. The artillery of V Corps, under Brigadier R.P. Benson, consisted of ten field and five heavy brigades. One field brigade was attached to each leading infantry for close support. Sections of 18-pounders were attached to leading battalions. These guns were to cover the infantry forward and to engage any opposition by direct fire. 17th and 38th Divisions led with great success, achieving all objectives and in places even more. It is interesting to note that by last light the infantry adjusted their positions to a given line, so that the barrage for next day could be calculated from it—a great step forward in artillery–infantry co-operation. IV Corps attacked with 37th and New Zealand Divisions up. They were covered by twelve field and five heavy brigades, all under Brigadier-General F. Potts. Their first objective was Le Quesnoy, still to the west of the Forêt de Mormal. They attacked through more open country so that their barrage could move at 100 yards in eight minutes. Le Quesnoy was to be encircled, but the New Zealanders had to attack the bastions surrounding it. The fighting here was severe but by noon the attack had passed Le Quesnoy, which surrendered later that afternoon after considerable bombardments of the bastions.

VI Corps attacked with the Guards and 62nd Divisions, with 2nd and 3rd Divisions following. The artillery, under Brigadier-General J.G. Rotton, was nine field and five heavy brigades. The country was not easy and the Germans fought hard, so that the final objectives were not reached, though 1,500 prisoners and 24 guns were taken.   19th and 24th Divisions of XVII Corps did, however, achieve complete success. The artillery of 20th and 61st Divisions was also available, as were 35, 62, 66 and 86 Brigades RGA. So by evening, Third Army had achieved almost all objectives and in some places more so. This superbly well-oiled machine moved relentlessly on—artillery and infantry co-operation reaching a peak hitherto never achieved in the history of war. The battle of the Sambre was a great British victory, a victory which finally broke the enemy's will to fight. Had it occurred outside the context of a great war, it would still be heralded as an example of what can be achieved in military terms by well led, well trained troops of high morale.

Meanwhile, all was not well in Germany. The Navy had mutinied in Kiel and troops sent to deal with them fraternised with them. The spirit of revolt was spreading. Ludendorf was removed and General Gröner, his successor, told the German Chancellor that it was now urgent to obtain terms, as he could not guarantee to hold the Army together. Meanwhile, on 6th November, as the victorious British Army began the pursuit beyond the Sambre, the Armistice Commissions were being assembled in Marshal Foch's railway coach. The scene was set for the final act. The pursuit continued energetically, Maubeuge was reached and taken—the place where the gallant BEF had assembled four and a quarter years before—Mons was entered, the scene of the BEF's baptism of fire—and so on 10th November came the order to halt all operations at 1100 hours on

11th November. Everywhere the people turned out, screaming at the tops of their voices "Vive l'Angleterre"; everyone was cheering, coffee, beer and wine were produced, women kissed the exhilarated but weary troops, many wept, bells were ringing, everyone wanted to shake hands. Sometimes, one lone person stood by a house shouting again and again "Vive l'Angleterre". It was a great and memorable day, this the last of the war—it was a day filled with emotion.

Let us read how Lieutenant-Colonel W.A. Murray, commanding 15 Brigade RHA, recorded the last day. "We had just completed a bridge over the Dendre and got a battery across when "Cease Fire" was given. I had gone on in the hope of seeing some fun, but was too late. Freyberg galloped over the bridge at Lessines, shooting the German who was left to blow it up and, with the cavalry, rounded up 200 Boches. He got a bullet through his saddle, and then the clock struck and he had to return. Some of the prisoners were taken after 11 a.m. and demanded to be released. But the civilians were tearing them to pieces, so they asked for protection. It was refused unless they laid down their arms. This, in aggressive Prussian manner, they declined to do, so they were left to their own devices and had to get away as best they could, stoned and torn by the civilians. The whole countryside gave itself up to wild excitement. Bands of released civilian prisoners came over with some of our own men and received a great welcome.

I had ridden 15 miles and had to go back, so I returned to my batteries and we billeted in Arc-Annieres".

So, at the eleventh hour of the eleventh day of the eleventh month, the "Cease Fire" was sounded. It was over; until then the greatest feat of arms of all times, the mightiest armies ever assembled, the heaviest sacrifice in loss of life and in numbers wounded and maimed. Never had soldiers of any nation been asked to endure so much, for so long. Conditions were borne with a fortitude and courage which make the softer men of today wonder. How did they do it? How did they keep going? How did they bear the long years of defeat? Why did they not give in when the horrors of death, the trenches and the winter weather smote upon them? If one talks to them now, the survivors of those great days of British history, they are modest men, but they are proven men, for they know they did not give in, they know that they did succeed, they know that they could overcome adversity. They are a special breed of men who achieved what no other generation is likely to be asked to achieve. They remember their battles, their comrades, their conditions with fierce pride, they still hold their heads that much higher than the rest of us for, when put to the test, they did not fail.

And the Gunners of this victorious Army, what of them? Let it be said by their Commander-in-Chief, Field-Marshal Sir Douglas Haig:

"No period of history has witnessed a more tremendous development in the power and importance of artillery than that steady growth in numbers, weight of metal and intensity of fire which was so marked a characteristic of the Great War. In no war has the lot of the artillerymen been harder, more dangerous or more exacting. At no time has the efficient discharge of his duties demanded greater application and skill from officer, non-commissioned officer or man.

It is with a profound sense of the extraordinary success with which all ranks of the Artillery—whether Regular, Territorial or New Army—rose to the demands made upon them, and of the unfailing gallantry they displayed in so doing, that I write this brief foreword to their Memorial Book. Yet the record of their actions is

''Cease Firing'', the 11th hour of the 11th day of the 11th month. From a drawing by Gilbert Holiday.   *(R.A.I.)*

their best memorial and I am confident that, judged by the supreme test, the reputation of the Royal Regiment of Artillery has never stood higher than it does today".

Now, as the years go by, we Gunners assemble each year in front of our Memorial at Hyde Park Corner; we assemble separately under our Master Gunner at the same time as the rest of the Nation assembles to remember. We must never forget them, the young men of our Nation and Empire who stood by their guns that we might live as free men. 3,507 officers and 45,442 men died in the service of the guns. They died in the greatest artillery duel ever fought; they died alongside the cavalrymen and infantrymen who were their comrades. Men who, to this day, when they think back to the great battles, have cause to say:

"The Guns! Thank God, the Guns!"

The Royal Artillery War Memorial at Hyde Park Corner, London. The equipment represented is a 9.2-inch BL howitzer and the fine bronze figures were the work of C S Jagger.   *(R.A.I.)*

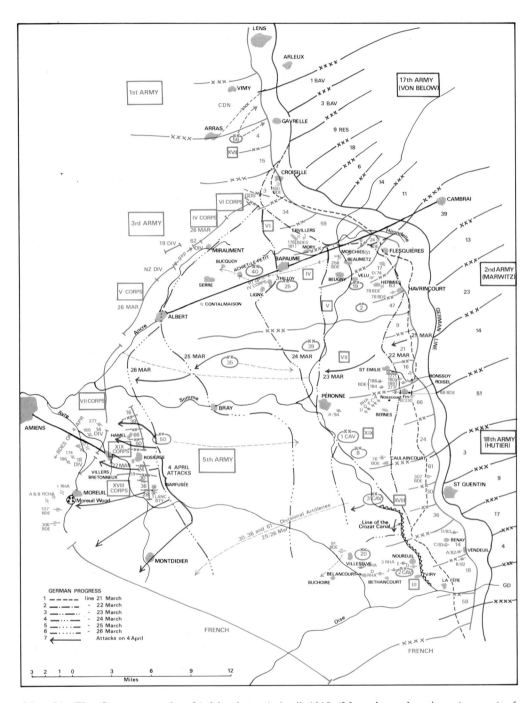

Map 34 The German attacks—21 March to 4 April 1918 (Map shows locations (approx) of batteries and events in the text only) (Chapters 20 and 21)

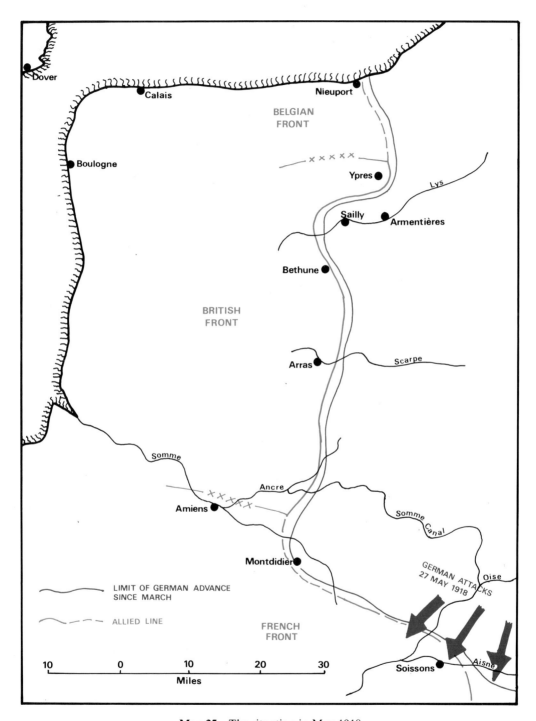

Map 35   The situation in May 1918

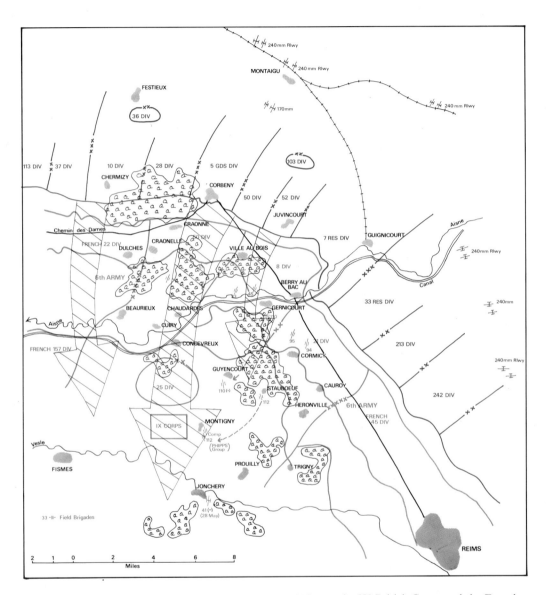

Map 36   The German attack on the Aisne—27 May 1918—on the IX British Corps and the French 6th Army

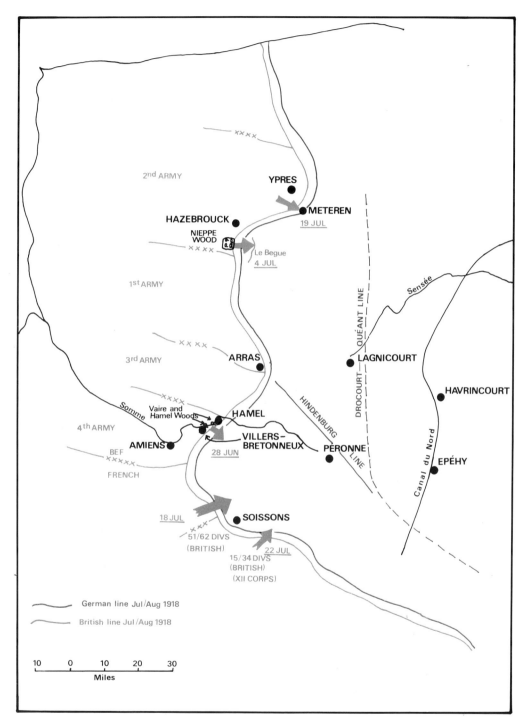

Map 37   Actions in June/July 1918

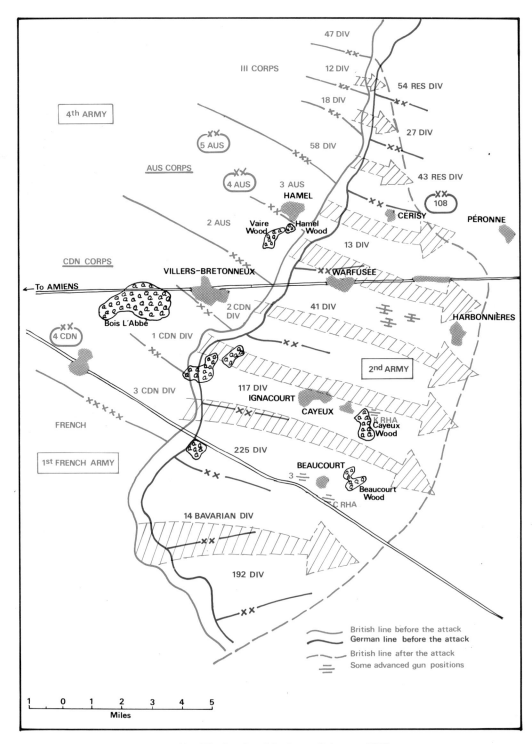

Map 38   The Battle of Amiens—8 August 1918

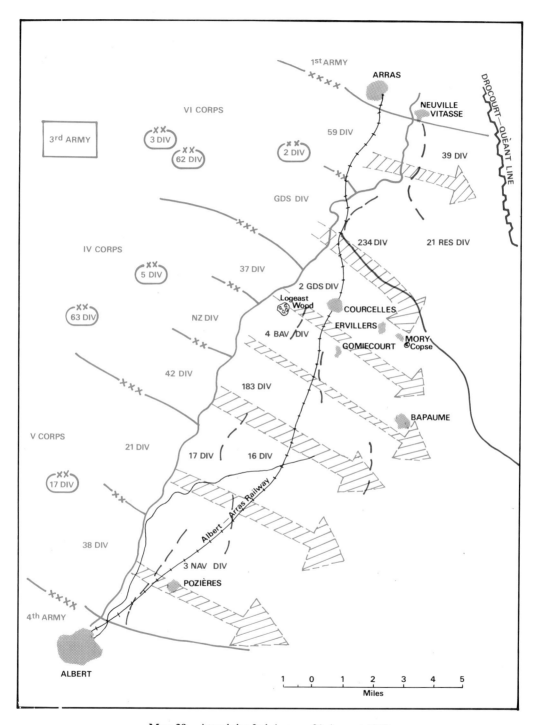

Map 39   Attack by 3rd Army—21 August 1918

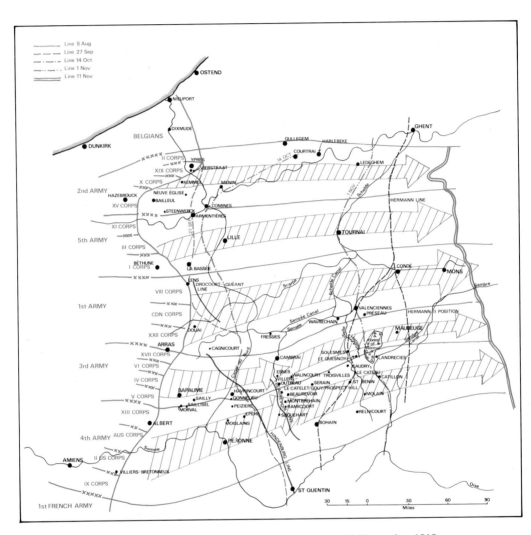

Map 40   The Advance to Victory—8 August–11 November 1918

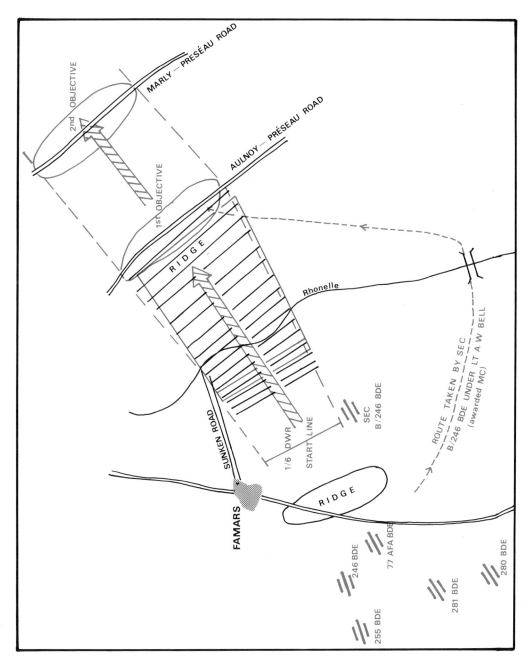

Map 41   Attack on German positions near Famars—1 November 1918

The Epilogue

It is now (1986) 68 years since the Great War ended. Since then, another great war has occurred which was of a different nature but, in parts, particularly in Russia, North-West Europe and Burma, was of almost equal proportions. Since then, too, several minor wars have been fought in Palestine, Korea, Malaya, Cyprus, Borneo, South Arabia and the Falkland Islands, all of which have seen guns and gunners in action, but none with such a prolonged and concentrated period of siege warfare as the Great War. In a sense, that war was fought with 20th Century weapons using 19th Century tactics. Massed cavalry and massed infantry were no match for QF field guns firing shrapnel, machine guns or tanks. The gun became the real Queen of the battlefield. It could not win battles alone but, where it was properly used, the cavalry and infantry could win—where it was not, they could not. Guns were the catalysts that made success possible.

At the beginning of the war, the guns were used much as they had been used in South Africa. They were an integral part of the defence system, firing normally over open sights and were used and fought as batteries or sections. It was not easy to concentrate the fire of even two batteries in 1914. But 'covered' positions were used. Tactics were on the turn. Artillery commanders knew that they could help their infantry or cavalry comrades best if the guns were not exposed to the same direct fire as they were. Rudimentary systems of doing this were in vogue in 1914 but not to any large degree.

The Great War produced for the British the principles of handling artillery which have stood the test of time. It produced the branches or categories of artillery so vital for success in battle. All things are relative but the great German attack in March 1918, when 74 German divisions and 6,473 guns attacked 3rd and 5th British Armies, produced problems facing the men of the day not dissimilar to the problems facing commanders in NATO today. The principles of using artillery which emerged survived those battles and became the principles upon which the Second World War and all other campaigns have been fought. They are therefore proven and tested and need recording, and he is a brave man who tampers with them.

What then were the lessons of war? These became clear year by year and artillery men worked hard to learn them but in those early days of the century the technology did not exist to solve many of the problems.

The Lessons of 1914

    a.   *The failure of open or semi-open positions.* It soon became clear that the guns must not be subject to the same direct fire as the cavalry or infantry they were fighting with, otherwise both could be neutralised together. This demanded forward observers to work with the infantry and cavalry and communications for them.

    b.   *The success of bursting shrapnel low.* Infantry cannot advance through a wall of low airburst shells when on their feet.

    c.   *The need for better communications between the CRA (Commander Royal Artillery) and his brigades.* This was required to enable him to concentrate the fire of more batteries onto the same target.

d. *The need for fireplans in attack and defence.* Guns must not sit and wait for something to happen; they must themselves seize the initiative and at greater range than other Arms.

e. *The need for cover from aerial observation.* A new and lasting requirement in modern war.

f. *The need for air defence artillery.* Another new and lasting requirement in modern war.

g. *Very high rates of fire occur—much higher than expected.* In battle, artillery provides the quickest possible response to enemy action. Ammunition expenditure is always higher than expected, since the unexpected always occurs. Furthermore, an efficient and high speed system of ammunition resupply is essential.

h. *The need for Divisional operation orders.* Up to 1914, artillery was neither grouped, controlled nor commanded higher than brigade level (equivalent to regimental or battalion level in modern armies). This soon proved to be unsatisfactory.

j. *The vital need to destroy enemy guns.* This became a prime requirement, and is still vital. If enemy guns are not destroyed, they are free to destroy our own operations. It is, however, easier said than done, since they first have to be located.

So, even by the end of 1914, the test of war demanded a whole range of new techniques; notably, an artillery command and control system which would allow guns to be hidden from direct fire and aerial observation and yet be fully integrated into the fighting. Also needed were air defence artillery, a system of locating enemy guns and then engaging them and, finally, a logistic system which could keep up with high rates of ammunition expenditure. Some of these were not fully met until much later in the war.

The Lessons of 1915

In some ways, 1915 was the turning point in artillery tactics, for it was during that year that the foundations were laid and the requirements set out. Some were further developments of the lessons of 1914. They were:

a. *The need for drills to concentrate maximum fire.* This was now pressing but, with rudimentary survey and no radios, it could only be done by early allocation of tasks to batteries and then waiting for them to report "ready".

b. *Artillery must be co-ordinated at Corps level.* The principle of flexibility was being learned, yet it was difficult to achieve, although 1915 saw the first allocation of resources at Corps level.

c. *Artillery must have accurate information.* This not only applied to information about the enemy but also about our own troops. Gunners needed to know the tactical plan in great detail and a great deal about the ground, the enemy layout and his defences.

d. *The ratio of medium/heavy guns to field guns should be 1:2.* Field guns were essential to attack targets close to our own troops and to play their part in the tactical plan. Medium and heavy guns were, however, essential to destroy defences and for counter battery work.

e. *Counter battery fire must be controlled by the HQ controlling the battle.* Only that HQ could lay down and, later, alter priorities. Unless it occurs, a separate artillery battle will begin and this is dangerous.

f. *The need for an air defence fire control system.* The air defence battle was rising in importance but needed proper co-ordination.

g. *The need for mortars.* In trench warfare, mortars were essential. A move to form a separate mortar corps was resisted. In the end, all but the small Stokes mortar (manned by the infantry) were manned by special trench mortar batteries of the Royal Artillery.

h. *Communication must be guaranteed and must be able to withstand bombardment.* As the war went on, this became of increasing importance and was only solved with the arrival of radio. Radio was now essential for communications with aircraft which were proving their worth for air observation, particularly for counter battery tasks.

j. *The need for a repair system in the field, due to excessive wear on the guns after excessive firing.* Special RAOC workshops were established for the guns. The lesson of war is that excessive firing puts great strain on equipments and they must, wherever possible, be repaired *in situ.*

k.   *More guarantee of ammunition supply.* The 'A' and 'B' echelon system was invented, on the grounds that commanders must have a reserve of ammunition under their own command in war.

So in 1915 the stage was set—the demands were clear—most revolved around command and control and logistics. In 1916 came a totally new requirement. To achieve the illusive principle of surprise, artillery must not announce its intention by ranging (adjusting) onto targets. This brought new demands.

The Lessons of 1916

a.   *The need for a comprehensive flash spotting and sound ranging system.* The vital need to locate and destroy enemy guns was still there. New equipment was invented and was beginning to show results.

b.   *Calibration must be improved to ensure that guns could fire accurately from the map.* The system of converting muzzle velocity differences into range corrections, as a result of datum shooting, began.

c.   *The need for exclusive artillery intelligence.* Normal intelligence was not accurate enough, nor fast enough in transit, for the guns. To be effective, it had to be turned into specific accurate firing data and had to be handled by Gunners.

d.   *Meteor telegrams had to improve.* For predicted fire, range and bearing corrections for the prevailing weather conditions had to be available on a regular basis.

e.   *Ammunition had to be reliable.* Ammunition had to perform consistently, demanding a much higher standard of manufacture, particularly in fuze performance.

f.   *Army HQ must lay down artillery objectives.* If this was not done, great variations could occur in different parts of the same battle. In essence, this meant allocation of priorities and resources at above divisional artillery level.

g.   *Maximum effort must be given to counter battery fire.* The same principle again, allocation of priorities and resources must be made at above divisional level.

The Lessons of 1917

The lessons of 1917 were of a quite different nature. The year saw the solution of many of the previous problems and the emergence of artillery doctrine and tactics. For example:

a.   *There can only be one artillery commander at each level and he must command all artillery of all types allotted.*This fundamental principle needs no elaboration.

b.   *Speed in concentrating fire is a battle winning factor.*

c.   *The roles of artillery are to destroy (in order of priority):*
    (1)   Enemy guns.
    (2)   Attacking infantry.
    (3)   Defences.
    (4)   Obstacles to movement (wire in particular).

d.   *The aim of a barrage is to stop the enemy infantry manning his parapets and machine guns during an attack.*

e.   *Sound ranging can be used to direct our own shells on to counter battery targets.*

f.   *In fireplans, some batteries should be superimposed.* This is so that their removal for sudden requests for fire does not leave a gap in the original fireplan.

g.   *Guns deployed in the anti-tank role are best deployed in depth, in pairs, in defilade, using reverse slopes.*

h.   *Quick, accurate survey is essential.*

j.   *Co-location of artillery commanders with tactical commanders at all levels is essential.*

k.   *Aircraft must be allotted for the exclusive use of artillery.*

Even a cursory examination of these lessons will show how tactical principles born on the battlefields in France in 1917 have become the principles still in use today. Cambrai has, quite rightly, become famous as the first real tank battle, but in one way it had an even greater effect on war than the introduction of the tank to battle. It heralded the predicted bombardment on a massive scale.

Never before had artillery alone created such powerful surprise, by suddenly and without the slightest warning opening fire at H hour, with an accuracy so great that the assaulting infantry reached their objectives almost unopposed. It was a great triumph for artillery command, survey, calibration, intelligence, sound ranging, logistics and gunnery. It marked the start of the new era; no artillery battle was quite the same after Cambrai.

The Lessons of 1918

Apart from perfecting the lessons of three years of war, 1918 brought yet another range of problems, this time associated with mobility.

> a. *Artillery command and control must be directly linked to the tactical plan.* In other words, all plans consist of fire and movement, with the artillery providing the 'fire' part of the equation.
> b. *Operations without a fireplan fail.* This is a lesson so fundamental that it is hard to realise that the Israelis forgot it in 1973 and had to relearn it in battle.
> c. *Artillery command must be well forward.* Artillery will never be handled correctly unless its eyes are on the enemy. Remote control will never work, since an enemy is quite unpredictable once he is being fired on. Only in this way can advantage be taken of enemy tactical errors.
> d. *Command must be retained during mobile operations.* This lesson was well learned throughout the war but was never really solved. Time and time again the battle went well until the whole artillery machine, guns, observers, surveyors, transport, had to move and start again. When this happened, control was nearly always lost. The equipment and, in particular, the communications were simply not up to it. So many battles, Cambrai included, started so well only to fail as the fighting outstripped the range of the guns which could not move and regain communications before the enemy counter-attacked. Even in the Second World War, this problem still existed.

So, the Great War provided the pattern for artillery operations for the future. No other part of the Army can meet the severe demands of the principles of war as successfully as can the Gunners. Whether it be the persistent *maintenance of the aim,* day or night, in any weather or on any ground; the *maintenance of morale* by the constant demonstration of destructive power against the enemy; the pursuit of *offensive action,* which is the hallmark of all artillery operations; *surprise*—no Arm can produce surprise as can the Gunners; nothing is more surprising than the sudden, unexpected arrival of tons of high explosive on an unsuspecting target; no Arm can *concentrate force* as rapidly at one point on the battlefield, without the movement of its units, as can a divisional artillery correctly handled; a fundamental facet of the *security* of any position is an effective defensive fireplan; *economy of effort* cannot be better demonstrated, when needed, provided all guns are in range of the target; *flexibility* must be one of the most powerful characteristics of artillery, whether in method of attack, timing of attack or place of attack; no Arm relies so much on *cooperation* to achieve its aim. Alone it is effective but limited—with its comrades in the cavalry and infantry in full concert it is unbeatable; however, finally, without effective *administration* and, in particular, the provision of the weapon itself—the shell—it is useless.

But this is not all. Artillery command, control and communications must be second to none or all is lost. Battery commanders and forward observers without communications are useless. Guns out of contact with the battle are little more than mobile road blocks. In any operational plan the fireplan is paramount, for what is war but a gigantic fireplan? Artillery is flexible but is never unlinked to the main manoeuvre battle. It has never made, and must never make, the mistake of air-power which is totally flexible and, in the pursuit of flexibility, has disconnected itself from the operations of ground troops. Artillery must be kept clear of the manoeuvre battle but must remain an integral part of it.

When things go wrong, guns can be used in the direct fire role, as they were in March 1918 and later in the Western Desert in 1941–43, and they should be. In those battles also, the guns provided a firm base around which others could rally and concentrate, a major factor when disaster was at hand. Artillery alone does not win wars but, correctly handled, it enables wars to be won.

All this came from the story of the guns in the Great War. The great battles which ranged across France and Belgium from 1914–1918 proved these principles. They were developed and proved again in later wars. Even in this modern age, the evidence of war is that they are still true today.

The following works will be of assistance in looking at the period 1914–1918 in both a more general and/more technical way:

Arthur Banks and Alan Palmer, *A Military Atlas of the First World War,* Heinemann Educational Books Ltd., London, 1975.
I V Hogg and L F Thurston, *British Artillery Weapons and Ammunition,* 1914–1918, Ian Allan, London, 1972.

Senior Artillery Commanders
1914–1918

1. GENERAL LORD HORNE, GCB, KCMG

   (a) August 1914   — BGRA I Corps, France
   (b) January 1915   — Commander 2nd Division, France
   (c) January 1916   — Commander XV Corps, Dardanelles
   (d) September 1916   — Commander First Army, France

2. GENERAL SIR GEORGE MILNE, GCMG, KCB, DSO

   (a) August 1914   — CRA 4th Division, France
   (b) July 1915   — Commander 27th Division
   (c) May 1916   — Commander XVI Corps, Salonika
   (d) December 1918   — C-in-C Army of the Black Sea

3. LIEUTENANT GENERAL SIR JOHN DU CANE, KCB

   (a) January 1915   — BGGS III Corps
   (b) September 1916   — Commander XV Corps
   (c) April 1918   — Senior British Representative Allied Armies

4. LIEUTENANT GENERAL SIR NOEL BIRCH, KCMG, CB

   (a) August 1914   — Commander 7 Brigade, RHA
   (b) July 1915   — GOCRA I Corps
   (c) March 1916   — MGRA Fourth Army
   (d) May 1916   — MGRA QHQ

5. LIEUTENANT GENERAL SIR ARTHUR HOLLAND, KCB, KCMG, DSO, MVO

   (a) September 1914   — CRA, 8th Division
   (b) July 1915   — BGRA, VII Corps
   (c) June 1916   — MGRA, Third Army
   (d) February 1917   — Commander, First Army

6. MAJOR GENERAL F. D. V. WING, CB

   (a) August 1914   — CRA 3rd Division
   (b) November 1914   — Commander 12th Division
   (c) October 2nd, 1915   — Killed in action near Loos

7. MAJOR GENERAL SIR ARCHIBALD MONTGOMERY, KCMG, CB

   (a) August 1914   — GSO 24th Division
   (b) November 1914   — GSO 14th Division
   (c) February 1915   — BGGS IV Corps
   (d) February 1916   — Chief of Staff Fourth Army

8. **MAJOR GENERAL SIR HERBERT UNIACKE, KCMG, CB**

    (a) August 1914   — Commander 5 Brigade RHA
    (b) April 1915   — MGRA V and then III Corps
    (c) July 1916   — GOCRA Fifth Army
    (d) July 1918   — Deputy Inspector of Training British Armies in France

9. **MAJOR GENERAL SIR GEORGE MACMUNN, KCB, KCSI, DSO**

    (a) June 1915   — AQMG Dardanelles
    (b) April 1916   — MG Lines of Communication, Mesopotamia

10. **MAJOR GENERAL SIR WEBB GILLMAN, KCMG, CB, DSO**

    In August 1914 he was Commander 114th Battery RA, later GSO 1 13th Division; BGRA IX Corps; BGGS HQ MELF; Commander 17th Indian Division.

Artillery Commanders in the Field 1914–1918

(The first holder of each appointment in 1914 only is shown).
The date shown is when the formation first deployed for action.

GHQ
1.	MGRA	5th August 1914	Major-General W. F. L. Lindsay

First Army
| 2. | MGRA | 16th February 1915 | Major-General H. F. Mercer |

Second Army
| 3. | MGRA | 25th February 1915 | Major-General J. E. W. Headlam |

Third Army
| 4. | MGRA | 19th July 1915 | Major-General R. A. K. Montgomery |

Fourth Army
| 5. | MGRA | 5th February 1916 | Major-General J. F. N. Birch |

Fifth Army
| 6. | MGRA | 22nd May 1916 | Brigadier-General W. Strong |

Corps—BGRAs

7.	The Cavalry Corps	14th October 1914	Brigadier-General B. F. Drake
8.	I Corps	5th August 1914	Brigadier-General H. S. Horne
9.	II Corps	5th August 1914	Brigadier-General A. H. Short
10.	III Corps	5th August 1914	Brigadier-General E. J. Phipps-Hornby
11.	IV Corps	5th October 1914	Brigadier-General A. H. Hussey
12.	V Corps	8th January 1914	Brigadier-General S. D. Browne
13.	VI Corps	27th May 1915	Brigadier-General W. L. H. Paget

14. VII Corps	19th July 1915	Brigadier-General A. E. A. Holland
15. VIII Corps	24th May 1915	Brigadier-General H. A. D. Simpson-Baikie
16. IX Corps	16th June 1915	Brigadier-General S. C. U. Smith
17. X Corps	19th July 1915	Brigadier-General F. E. Johnson
18. XI Corps	12th September 1915	Brigadier-General G. G. S. Carey
19. XII Corps	19th September 1915	Brigadier-General W. H. Onslow
20. XIII Corps	13th November 1915	Brigadier-General R. St. C. Lecky
21. XIV Corps	5th January 1916	Brigadier-General H. K. Jackson
22. XV Corps	22nd April 1916	Brigadier-General E. W. Alexander
23. XVI Corps	18th January 1916	Brigadier-General A. W. Gay
24. XVII Corps	9th December 1915	Brigadier-General C. G. Henshaw
25. XVIII Corps	15th January 1917	Brigadier-General D. J. M. Fasson
26. XIX Corps	4th February 1917	Brigadier-General W. B. R. Sandys
27. XX Corps	2nd August 1917	Brigadier-General A. H. Short
28. XXI Corps	12th August 1917	Brigadier-General H. A. D. Simpson-Baikie
29. XXII Corps	24th July 1916	Brigadier-General E. W. M. Powell
30. XXIII Corps	17th February 1918	Brigadier-General G. H. W. Nicholson

Corps Heavy Artiller Reserve Groups—Commanders

31. No 1 HAR Group	28th February 1915	Brigadier-General G. McK. Franks
32. No 2 HAR Group	28th February 1915	Brigadier-General H. C. C. Uniacke
33. No 3 HAR Group	26th June 1915	Brigadier-General A. C. Currie
34. No 4 HAR Group	25th July 1915	Brigadier-General W. St. C. Bland
35. No 5 HAR Group	18th August 1915	Brigadier-General T. A. Tancred
36. No 6 HAR Group	7th March 1916	Brigadier-General C. R. Buckle

Divisions—CRAs

37. 1st Cavalry Division	August 1914	Brigadier-General B. F. Drake
38. 2nd Cavalry Division	August 1914	Lieutenant-Colonel R. W. Breeks RHA
39. 3rd Cavalry Division	September 1914	Lieutenant-Colonel C. H. de Rougemont RHA
40. Guards Division	August 1915	Brigadier-General C. E. Goulburn
41. 1st Division	August 1914	Brigadier-General N. D. Findlay
42. 2nd Division	August 1914	Brigadier-General E. M. Perceval
43. 3rd Division	August 1914	Brigadier-General F. D. V. Wing
44. 4th Division	August 1914	Brigadier-General G. F. Milne
45. 5th Division	August 1914	Brigadier-General J. E. W. Headlam
46. 6th Division	August 1914	Brigadier-General W. L. H. Paget
47. 7th Division	August 1914	Brigadier-General H. K. Jackson
48. 8th Division	September 1914	Brigadier-General A. E. A. Holland
49. 9th Division	September 1914	Brigadier-General E. H. Armitage
50. 10th Division	October 1914	Brigadier-General A. J. Abdy
51. 11th Division	October 1914	Brigadier-General R. D. Gubbins
52. 12th Division	October 1914	Brigadier-General S. E. G. Lawless
53. 13th Division	October 1914	Brigadier-General A. B. Helyar
54. 14th Division	October 1914	Brigadier-General D. G. Prinsep
55. 15th Division	October 1914	Brigadier-General E. A. Lambart
56. 16th Division	October 1914	Brigadier-General C. E. Goulburn
57. 17th Division	October 1914	Brigadier-General A. B. Purvis
58. 18th Division	October 1914	Brigadier-General F. G. Stone
59. 19th Division	October 1914	Brigadier-General W. H. Stuart
60. 20th Division	November 1914	Brigadier-General J. Hotham
61. 21st Division	November 1914	Brigadier-General C. H. Alexander
62. 22nd Division	October 1914	Brigadier-General J. W. Hawkins

63. 23rd Division	November 1914	Brigadier-General F. B. Elmsie
64. 24th Division	November 1914	Brigadier-General Sir G. V. Thomas
65. 25th Division	November 1914	Brigadier-General H. A. Bethell
66. 26th Division	November 1914	Brigadier-General E. M. Flint
67. 27th Division	November 1914	Brigadier-General A. Stokes
68. 28th Division	December 1914	Lieutenant-Colonel A. L. Walker
69. 29th Division	February 1915	Brigadier-General R. W. Breeks
70. 30th Division	February 1915	Brigadier-General A. J. Abdy
71. 31st Division	May 1915	Brigadier-General S. E. G. Lawless
72. 32nd Division	June 1915	Brigadier-General H. H. Butler
73. 33rd Division	July 1915	Lieutenant-Colonel A. Symons
74. 34th Division	July 1915	Brigadier-General F. B. Elmsie
75. 35th Division	June 1915	Brigadier-General A. B. Purvis
76. 36th Division	June 1915	Brigadier-General J. W. Hawkins
77. 37th Division	April 1915	Brigadier-General S. Lushington
78. 38th Division	July 1915	Brigadier-General W. A. M. Thompson
79. 39th Division	September 1915	Brigadier-General C. E. Goulburn
80. 40th Division	September 1915	Brigadier-General F. G. Stone
81. 41st Division	November 1915	Brigadier-General S. Lushington
82. 42nd Division	August 1914	Brigadier-General A. D'A. King
83. 43rd Division	September 1914	Brigadier-General J. J. MacMahon
84. 44th Division	October 1913	Brigadier-General C. T. Caulfeild
85. 46th Division	August 1914	Brigadier-General H. M. Campbell
86. 47th Division	August 1914	Brigadier-General J. C. Wray
87. 48th Division	August 1914	Brigadier-General H. H. Butler
88. 49th Division	August 1914	Brigadier-General S. D. Browne
89. 50th Division	August 1914	Brigadier-General A. H. Hussey
90. 51st Division	August 1914	Brigadier-General H. A. Brendon
91. 52nd Division	August 1914	Brigadier-General F. B. Johnstone
92. 53rd Division	August 1914	Brigadier-General W. K. McLeod
93. 54th Division	August 1914	Brigadier-General G. W. Biddulph
94. 55th Division	August 1914	Brigadier-General A. W. Gay
95. 56th Division	August 1914	Brigadier-General G. S. Duffus
96. 57th Division	January 1915	Brigadier-General G. Kyffin-Taylor
97. 58th division	August 1915	Brigadier-General G. S. Duffus
98. 59th Division	February 1915	Brigadier-General A. H. C. Philpotts
99. 60th Division	January 1915	Brigadier-General H. G. Weir
100. 61st Division	January 1915	Colonel W. Hanna
101. 62nd Division	January 1915	Colonel J. H. Balguy
102. 63rd Division	February 1915	Colonel E. Gunner
103. 64th Division	January 1915	Colonel D. E. Dewar
104. 65th Division	January 1915	Colonel H. C. Dunlop
105. 66th Division	November 1914	Lieutenant-Colonel J. Magnus
106. 67th Division	November 1914	Brigadier-General C. T. Caulfeild
107. 68th Division	January 1915	Colonel R. A. G. Harrison
108. 69th Division	January 1915	Colonel A. C. Bailward
109. 71st Division	November 1916	Brigadier-General C. T. Caulfeild
110. 72nd Division	November 1916	Brigadier-General F. B. Johnstone
111. 73rd Division	November 1916	Brigadier-General J. J. McMahon
112. 74th Division	July 1917	Brigadier-General L. J. Hext
113. 75th Division	July 1917	Brigadier-General H. A. Boyce

ANNEX B

Growth of Artillery
1914–1918

Production of Guns

1. In 1914   91 guns and howitzers were produced
2. In 1915   3,226 guns and howitzers were produced
3. In 1916   4,551 guns and howitzers were produced
4. In 1917   6,483 guns and howitzers were produced
5. In 1918   10,680 guns and howitzers were produced

6. Total produced   25,031

Strengths

7. The strength of the Royal Artillery in August 1914 was:

    4,083   Officers   88,837   ORs

8. The strength of the Royal Artillery in November 1918 was:

    29,990   Officers   518,790   ORs

Batteries

9. In August 1914 there were 554 Batteries of all types in the British and Indian Armies. By 1918 there were 1,796 Batteries in the Army. This expansion is shown in the following table:

| | Number of Batteries in all Theatres in India and at Home | | | |
| | On 4th August 1914 | | On 11th November 1918 | |
	Reg	Territorial	Regular and Special Service	Territorial
RHA	26	14	28	22
RFA	153	151	609	267
RGA:				
Companies	87	76	42	—
Heavy Batteries	12	20	87	30
Siege Batteries	3	—	400	1
Mountain Batteries	9	3	17	4
Anti-Aircraft Batteries	—	—	289	—
	290	264	1472	324

341

11.   Approximate Expenditure of Ammunition in France and Belgium during the war 1914-1918:

13-pr 6 cwt gun	1,520,155
13-pr 9 cwt gun (A.A)	2,794,081
18-pr gun	99,397,670
4.5-inch howitzer	25,326,276
60-pr gun	10,125,321
6-inch gun	1,022,581
9.2-inch gun	45,104
12-inch gun	5,263
14-inch gun	235
6-inch howitzer	22,387,363
8-inch howitzer	4,189,165
9.2-inch howitzer	3,119,158
12-inch howitzer	226,493
15-inch howitzer	25,332
3-inch gun (A.A)	201,098
TOTAL	170,385,295

The above compares with the expenditure during the Siege of Sebastopol (1854–55): 252,872 rounds from 401 guns and mortars.

Guns

12.   When the Armistice was signed there were 6,437 guns and howitzers in battery service in France alone. These were made up as follows:

   a.   *Guns*

13-pounders	56
75 mm	24
18-pounders	3,162
60-pounders	456
6-inch	152
9.2-inch	16
12-inch	5
14-inch	4
	3,875 guns

   b.   *Howitzers*

4.5-inch	984
6-inch	1042
8-inch	240
9.2-inch	224
12-inch	66
15-inch	6
	2562 Howitzers
Total Guns and Howitzers	6437

   c.   In addition, there were 24 light and 6 medium trench mortars per division. In France, at the end of the war, there were 71×9.45-inch, 812×6-inch and 1,636 Stokes mortars. There were 168×13-pounder 9 cwt; 56×3-inch 20 cwt and 10×12-pounder 12 cwt anti-aircraft guns. Two 4-inch MK4 AA equipments arrived for trials in July 1918.

Command and Control of Artillery in France 1914–1918

Artillery Command at General Headquarters

In 1914 there were no artillery commanders above division. At General Headquarters and Corps there were artillery advisers only, without any staff at all. When First and Second Army Headquarters were formed in January 1915, "Artillery Advisers" in the rank of Major General were established, together with a Brigade Major and a Staff Captain. Their duties were described as "not a commander nor a staff officer". This was highly unsatisfactory and caused endless confusion. The term adviser fell into disuse during 1915 and at Army Headquarters the artillery advisers began to sign themselves "Major-General RA". Nevertheless, it soon became clear that the relationship between the artillery and General Staffs was wrong. The latter often dealt exclusively with detailed artillery matters, often without references even to the 'advisers'. In September 1915, Artillery Advisers were formally authorised to deal with:

a. Questions of design of artillery equipments and ammunition.
b. Defective ammunition.
c. Accidents to guns, howitzers and trench mortars.
d. User problems relating to equipment and ammunition.

Much credit is due to Major-General J.F.N. Birch and his able staff officer, Major S.W.H. Rawlins, at General Headquarters for rectifying this state of affairs. General Birch quickly made his view felt on all artillery matters, including organisation and tactics, and gradually his great experience, patience, determination and charm bore fruit. In April 1917, the term Army Artillery Adviser was dropped and the title Major-General Royal Artillery (MGRA) was introduced. But the misunderstandings continued until the War Office issued a memorandum laying down the responsibilities of all staff branches in artillery matters. This important document is reproduced in full at Appendix 1.

In May 1918, General Headquarters stated that the MGRA should supervise the gunnery of the Tank Corps, dealing direct with GOCs on these matters. In June 1918, it was similarly ordered that the MGRA should deal with chemical warfare, both offensive and defensive. This finally established the position of the MGRA at General Headquarters.

Artillery Command at Army and Corps Headquarters

In December 1916, the title of MGRA at Army Headquarters was altered to GOCRA, thus recognising him as a commander in his own right. In April 1915, a staff had been provided for the MGRA at Army Headquarters, consisting of a captain, a clerk, two batmen, two horses and a car. In July 1915, General Birch (then a brigadier) wrote to Major-General Du Cane, MGRA at General Headquarters. He forecast that the war would bring large concentrations of artillery and that in this the artillery of reserve divisions must be used. He recommended, therefore, artillery commanders at Corps and Army Headquarters. They must be "the very best men available, with adequate staffs, and be vested with the power to co-ordinate the action of the artillery in certain areas". On 6th August, the General Staff asked Army Commanders for their views. The replies varied. First and Third Armies approved the idea but said that additional staff should only be provided for specific operations at Corps level. Second Army opposed the proposal. The MGRA, Major-General J.E.W. Headlam, wrote "Taking all such matters into consideration it seems probable that there will not be many occasions on which artillery advisers at Corps will be called upon to assume the position of artillery commanders . . ." While this was being written, Brigadier-General Birch was in fact busy setting up a Corps Artillery Headquarters in I Corps from his own HQRA, out of sheer operational demand. Moreover, the planning for the battle of Loos had started and this showed that one MGRA at Army Headquarters could not possibly co-ordinate all the artillery direct to CRAs at divisions for an attack of 12,000 yards.

General Du Cane wrote "The introduction of Artillery Advisers has brought into our system an element of friction and discord. If they are energetic and pushful, they are apt to infringe on the prerogatives of subordinate commanders and staffs. If they are the reverse, they rapidly become the fifth wheel of the coach and their advice is either not sought or, if tendered, ignored". He went on to say that, even so, there is no place for an artillery commander "unless he is required to command artillery in action and is responsible for its tactical distribution". The problem was compounded by the rapid increase in heavy artillery outside the divisions. This, said General Du Cane, demanded a Brigadier-General to command Army Heavy Artillery Groups, and Colonels to command Corps Heavy Artillery Groups. Experience had already shown how vital it was for one commander to co-ordinate all guns within a corps.

Accordingly on 23rd August 1915, a letter was sent from General Headquarters to First Army which said "If and when a corps artillery is formed in a corps, it will be necessary to substitute , for the officer now holding the appointment of Artillery Adviser, an officer of the rank of Brigadier-General who would be appointed to command the Artillery of the Corps. The Corps Artillery would be under the command of this officer for all purposes—no change, however, would be made to the command of the divisional artillery—a suitable staff would be provided—the commander of the Corps heavy artillery would be a Colonel".

Thus on 7th October 1915, General Du Cane recommended that the commander of all the artillery in a Corps be titled GOCRA and that his staff should be a Brigade Major and an ADC. This was accepted and all seemed well. But, as the increase in heavy artillery continued, it soon became clear that there was a need for a heavy artillery commander of more senior rank. Then, incredibly, the War Office, on 1st March 1916, ordered the abolition of Brigades RGA and ordered the establishment of "Lieutenant Colonel's Groups", on a scale of two per Army and two per Corps. This was strongly opposed in France and in 1917 there was a return to the Brigade organisation. Then, again incredibly, General Headquarters ordained on 7th May 1916, that the GOCRA at Corps should become the Brigadier-General RA (BGRA). This clearly degraded him and removed from him the clean cut control of the heavy artillery, now also commanded by a Brigadier-General. This was clearly unworkable and proved itself so on the Somme during the same year. Accordingly, on 5th December 1916, General Headquarters issued a new memorandum restoring the title of GOCRA at Corps and gave a similar title to the MGRA at Army Headquarters. It solved the problems of high command for the rest of the war. An important memorandum setting out the duties of principal staff officers as regards Artillery in France is at Appendix 1.

Artillery Staff Officers

The status of artillery staff officers was argued throughout the war. There was great opposition to granting them General Staff status, since most came from within the Regiment and not from the Staff College. This was understandable, as there were large numbers of officers involved. By November 1918, there were 480 artillery staff officers in France. Without staff training these officers had created new appointments and battle procedures for handling masses of artillery. That they were successful was greatly to their credit; most of this was because they came from the batteries in action and knew exactly what was required.

In July 1916, all artillery staff officers were re-graded to DAAG. No real reason for this was given and it was an anomaly, as nearly all the work carried out by the artillery staffs was operational, indeed, it was laid down that it should be. By the middle of 1917, it was argued that the status of gunner staff officer needed rationalising. There was a problem arising, in that artillery officers were essential for artillery work but the General Staff expected to draw on the Regiment for General Staff officers as well. Since the best had to remain for artillery work, less good officers joined the General Staff and gained by the process. On 28th August 1917, the War Office agreed that henceforth the artillery staff officers would be graded exactly as General Staff officers, under a 'G', 'A' or 'Q' title.

The Artillery Staff at General Headquarters

Early in 1915, there were three artillery staff officers at General Headquarters, a Brigade Major and "two experts in artillery material". By the end of 1915, this was reduced to two, a GSOI RA and a

DAQMG RA. In November 1916, a Staff Captain RA was added. But, during 1916, the tremendous growth of artillery produced masses of technical work and evaluations. Accordingly, in October of that year, an officer of the rank of Colonel known as "Assistant Director of Artillery" was appointed.

By 1917, the artillery staff at General Headquarters were becoming involved in operations co-ordinating the artillery of adjoining armies and making large scale artillery appreciations. Intelligence became vital and, on 10th May, a "Staff Lieutenant 1st Class" was appointed "to assess artillery information". By 1917 also, anti-aircraft artillery had expanded enormously and a major—a DAAG(AA)—was appointed "to visit AA units in the field and to maintain touch with developments at Home". Later, a GSOI Liaison was appointed to co-ordinate artillery with flanking armies. He also looked after artillery staff appointments and artillery training. Then, in June 1917, a major was appointed "Deputy Assistant Director of Artillery" (DADA) to look after the increasing technical work resulting from the enormous expansion of the artillery.

Finally, a Brigadier-General Royal Artillery (BGRA) was established to co-ordinate the expansion and development of the heavy artillery—the RGA.

The Artillery Staff at Army Headquarters

Apart from some changes in title, there were very few changes in the artillery staff at Army Headquarters throughout the war:

a. *1915.* A Brigade Major and Staff Captain.
b. *1915.* Re-graded as GS02 RA and a Staff Captain.
c. *July 1916.* Re-graded DAAG and Staff Captain.
d. *August 1917.* Re-graded GS01 RA and DAA&QMG RA.
e. *September 1918.* GS01 RA, DAA&QMG RA and Staff Captain.

The Artillery Staff at Corps Headquarters

When the GOCRA at Corps Headquarters was appointed in 1915, so was a DAAG (Major) and an ADC (Captain), who later became Reconnaissance Officer. In December 1916, a Staff Captain was added to cope with the extra work involving the newly formed Army Brigades RFA. At the same time, as a result of the Somme battles, a GSO1 CB was appointed, together with an 'orderly officer'. In October 1917, a Staff Captain CB was also agreed.

The Artillery Staff at Corps Heavy Artillery Headquarters

When Heavy Artillery Reserve Groups were formed in 1915, each group Headquarters had a BMRA, a Staff Captain and an ADC. In March 1916, when Group Headquarters became Corps Heavy Artillery Headquarters, the same staff, less an ADC, was approved. This remained the case for two years. In May 1918, a 'Staff Lieutenant 1st Class' was added to each Headquarters for 'ammunition duties'.

The Artillery Staff at Divisional Headquarters

This remained unchanged throughout the war as a BMRA and a Staff Captain, apart from an ADC being added in 1916 to act as Reconnaissance Officer.

Appendix 1

O.B. 549 20th December 1917

Memorandum

(1)   Subject to the instructions of the Commander-in-Chief, the responsibility of the principal Staff Officers as regards all questions connected with Artillery in France is as follows:

    (a) CGS.   Employment, distribution, policy and organisation.

    (b) QMG.   Inspection, maintenance and provision of all artillery equipment, material and ammunition.

    (c) AG.   Provision and maintenance of personnel. Discipline.

(2)   The MGRA acts as Adviser to the principal Staff Officers on all artillery matters. On matters pertaining to the functions of artillery and on questions of experiment and research, not affecting (a), (b) and (c) above, he is authorised to correspond direct with D of A and GMD up to the point where action requires to be taken by GHQ, when he will submit his recommendations to the principal Staff Officer concerned.

All matters that require reference to the War Office will, in every case, emanate from the office of the principal Staff Officer concerned.

(3)   Subject to the above general ruling, the MGRA will be responsible for submitting:

To the General Staff:

    (i)   Estimates of artillery requirements as regards:

        (a)   Types and numbers of guns and howitzers and their carriages.

        (b)   Heavy and medium trench mortars; and

        (c)   Artillery and heavy and medium trench mortar ammunition.

    (ii)   Recommendation as regards:

        (a)   Allocation of guns, howitzers and medium trench mortars and their ammunition, in accordance with the plan of operations for the General Staff.

        (b)   The adoption of new designs or new equipments; and

        (c)   Any change in artillery policy or organisation affecting the British Armies in France.

To the Quartermaster General:

    (iii)   Recommendations as regards alterations in approved design or defects in artillery equipments and ammunition, from the point of view of the user of the gun.

(4) To enable the above recommendations and estimates to be submitted, the MGRA is authorised to correspond direct on the subjects enumerated below with Armies and the DOS:

    (i)   Questions of pattern or designs of artillery equipment, including ammunition;

    (ii)   Defective ammunition or components of ammunition;

    (iii)   Accidents to guns and howitzers and to trench mortars used by RA.

    (iv)   General questions affecting artillery equipment from the point of view of the user of the gun.

(5)   In order to avoid duplication of work in the respective offices, the following procedure will be adhered to:

    (i)   In framing estimates for the requirements of guns and ammunition, the MGRA will consult the QMG in order that the necessary quantities to cover difficulties of distribution may be taken into account. The estimated requirements will be forwarded by the MGRA to the QMG through the General Staff, on whom the responsibility for the adequacy of the demands will rest. All demands for supply will be forwarded Home by the QMG, who will be responsible for the provision to meet requirements as estimated above.

    (ii)   Demands for artillery stores and for spare parts for maintenance will be prepared and submitted by the DOS in the usual manner.

(iii)   The DOS is authorised to correspond direct with the Director of Artillery on routine questions of provision and maintenance of guns and ammunition, including spare parts, and with the Director of Artillery of the DGMD as regards mechanical details not suggesting any alteration of main design. Copies of all letters dealing with maintenance of guns and ammunition or mechanical details will be sent to the QMG and MGRA as at present. Recommendations regarding mechanical alterations in design or defects in artillery equipments and ammunition affecting the engineering point of view may be submitted by DOS to QMG direct, who will, if necessary, refer to MGRA in accordance with para 5(v).

(iv)   If the MGRA considers that any steps are necessary to increase demands for maintenance or to hasten supply, he will inform the QMG.

(v)   Except as above, in every case where artillery questions are affected, letters and reports drafted by the DOS will be signed by the QMG, who will pass the drafts to the MGRA for his remarks before despatch, in accordance with the ordinary office procedure.

(vi)   (a)   Inspection reports of CIs OM or IOOs of Armies will be passed by the DDOS direct to the DOS, a copy at the same time being sent to the MGRA through Army Headquarters.

    (b)   Reports or suggestions submitted by Armies to GHQ on questions of pattern or design of artillery equipment will be passed to the MGRA and a copy will be sent to the QMG.

In both the above cases the responsibility will rest with the MGRA of at once informing the QMG and the DOS respectively, whether or not he proposes to take action in his office in accordance with para 2 or para 3(iii), in order to avoid letters on the same subject being drafted in two offices at the same time.

In the case of (vi) (a) the DOS will inform the QMG and MGRA if he takes action in accordance with 5 (iii), but in any case of doubt he will refer to the MGRA before taking such action. Whichever office takes action as above, will send a copy to the other office.

Field Artillery Organisation in France
1914–1918

General

There were four major changes in field artillery organisation during the war:

a. The variety of organisations when the war started.
b. The New Army 4 gun batteries, which later reverted to 6 guns.
c. The creation of Army Brigades RFA.
d. The abolition of Ammunition Columns.

Initial Organisations

The first six divisions that went to France were organised as described in Chapter 1. But there were no 4.5-inch howitzers or 60-pounders available for 7th and 8th Divisions. These two divisions were each given one RHA brigade of two 6 gun batteries (12 × 13-pounders) and two brigades each of three 6 gun batteries (36 × 18-pounders) and two 4.7-inch (4 gun) batteries. When 3rd Lahore and 7th Meerut Indian Divisions arrived, they both had three brigades of 18-pounders (54 guns). 27th and 28th Divisions, made up from regular troops from overseas, arrived with 54 × 18-pounders each, but 28th Division also had 6 × 4.5-inch howitzers.

The New Army Divisions

The Territorial divisions still had 15-pounders and 5-inch howitzers and it was agreed in 1915 that this made them so weak in battle that regular artillery had to support them as well, thus putting great strain on regular batteries. It was agreed that they should have an establishment of four brigades, each of three batteries each of 4 × 18-pounders, making 48 guns. In principle, one 18-pounder battery was taken from each division in France and used to reform two batteries. This caused a revision of thought of the organisation of divisional artilleries and the mix of 18-pounders and howitzers. Those in action favoured mixed brigades of two 18-pounder batteries and one 4.5-inch battery, all of 6 guns/howitzers. There was no doubt the 6 gun batteries were superior to 4 gun batteries like those of the French. However, it would take some time before there were enough guns and howitzers to ensure a uniform organisation throughout.

Divisional Ammunition Columns

In May 1916, General Headquarters proposed the abolition of Brigade Ammunition Columns and the re-organisation of Divisional Ammunition Columns into an 'A' and a 'B' Echelon. 'A' Echelon was to accompany the division at all times, but 'B' Echelon would only arrive when needed and would spend much of its time under Corps control. The effect of this would be to reduce the total rounds carried for the artillery to:

		'A' Echelon	'B' Echelon	Total	Old BAC
a.	18-pounders	76	27	103	202
b.	4.5-inch howitzers	48	66	114	92

(figures in rounds per gun)

These measures saved 60 officers, 255 other ranks and 310 horses per division but the War Office insisted that the full total of artillery ammunition be carried. This was met by giving each artillery brigade its own section of the new A Echelon. This system stood up to all demands made on it throughout the war.

Army Field Artillery (AFA) Brigades

After the battle of the Somme, the strain on the Gunners was acute. It had become practice to withdraw a tired infantry division from the line to rest, but to leave its artillery in action. There is no doubt that the infantry when in combat became very tired quickly but, between bouts of combat, they could get some rest. But the Gunners could never really rest, day or night answering calls for fire incessantly. Soon confusion arose, since a division, withdrawn for rest, would be hurriedly sent back to the line somewhere else without its artillery and would have to take on someone else's. This broke the vital team spirit between Gunner and Infantryman. But Gunners were relieved from time to time. A staff check at General Headquarters in 1916 showed that, right across the front, at any one time, as many as eighty batteries were on the move for one reason or another—seven divisional artilleries! This loss of gun power, extra strain on men, horses and equipment, cutting up the ground and extra labour to relay cables became serious. General Headquarters realised that the Commander-in-Chief urgently needed a reserve of field artillery with which to reinforce sectors of the front without breaking up the divisional structure.

A meeting held at Advanced General Headquarters on 10th November 1916 decided that:

a. A divisional artillery should henceforth consist of two brigades each of three batteries of 18-pounders (36 guns) and one battery of 4.5-inch howitzers (12 howitzers).
b. Units saved from this reduction, basically two brigades per division, were to be formed into AFA Brigades, each organised in the same way as a divisional brigade.
c. Empire Divisions would be requested to do the same.
d. That part of the Divisional 'A' Echelon allotted to the Gunners would be split in two, and half given to each AFA Brigade as a Brigade Ammunition Column.

Unfortunately, the savings from divisional artilleries were not quite enough and, on 13th November, General Headquarters asked the War Office for a further thirty four 6 gun 18-pounder batteries to make up the artillery reserve required. The plan was received with enthusiasm in the whole Army, as it responded exactly to the demand from the men in battle. On 30th November, General Headquarters forwarded their plan for carrying out this r-organisation with resources then in France, including 3rd Australian, 4th and 5th Canadian Divisions and a New Zealand Artillery Brigade. It was possible to provide:

a. 47 British and 11 Empire divisional artilleries (58) on the new organisation.
b. 32 British, 3 Australian, 3 Canadian and 1 New Zealand (39) AFA Brigades.

This would result in 2,784 guns and howitzers in divisions and 934 in the AFA Brigades—a total of 3,718 field guns and howitzers in France. But the Commander-in-Chief still needed his extra 34 batteries of 18-pounders—a further 204 guns—making a total of 1,138 in the Army Field Brigades.

On 13th December 1916, the plan was approved by the War Office. On 21st December, the Army was ordered to re-organise, but the War Office said that it would be at least June 1917 before all guns and howitzers would be available for both the plan and to meet battle casualties. Even so, the new batteries (the 34) would arrive initially with only four guns each. In practice, the last AFA Brigade (18-pounder)—96—did not arrive in France until 17th March 1918 and the last 4.5-inch howitzer battery—49—until mid-April 1918!

In March 1917, an Army Brigade RHA was formed from the Chestnut Troop, Q and U Batteries, all from the Indian Cavalry Corps and then a second, 5 Army Brigade RHA, consisting of G, N, O and Z Batteries.

At the end of the war, General Headquarters recommended that, in peacetime, a divisional artillery should consist of four mixed (3 × 18-pounder and 1 × 4.5-inch batteries) brigades. In war two can, if necessary be removed to form AFA brigades.

The Order of Battle of the Divisional Artilleries and AFA Brigades in France on 11th November 1918 was:

Divisional Artilleries	Batteries	13-Prs	18-Prs	4.5" Hows
a. 3 × Cavalry	$9\frac{1}{3}$	54	—	—
b. 51 × Infantry	306	—	1836	—
	102	—	—	612
c. 4 × Canadian Infantry	24	—	144	—
	8	—	—	48
d. 5 × Australian Infantry	30	—	180	—
	10	—	—	60
e. 1 × New Zealand Infantry	6	—	36	—
	2	—	—	12
Army Field (Artillery) Brigades				
f. 33 × British,	99	—	594	—
full establishment	33	—	—	198
g. 8 × British	32	—	192	—
(4 × 18-Pr btys)				
h. 3 × British	9	—	54	—
(3 × 18-Pr btys)				
j. 3 × Canadian	9	—	54	—
	3	—	—	18
k. 3 × Australian	9	—	54	—
	3	—	—	18
l. 1 × New Zealand	3	—	18	—
	1	—	—	6
Totals	$698\frac{1}{3}$	54	3162	972 Guns/Hows

These batteries were (sub-paragraph letters correspond to those above):

a.   *Divisional Artilleries of:*

1st Cavalry Division (18 × 13 Prs)	7 Brigade RHA—H, I and Y Batteries RHA
2nd Cavalry Division (18 × 13 Prs)	3 Brigade RHA—D, E and J Batteries RHA
3rd Cavalry Division (20 × 13 Prs)	4 Brigade RHA—C and K Batteries RHA and the RCHA Brigade

b.   *Divisional Artilleries of:*

Guards Division	74 Brigade—A, B, C and D(H) Batteries 75 Brigade—A, B, C and D(H) Batteries
1st Division	25 Brigade—113, 114, 115 and 40(H) Batteries 39 Brigade—46, 51, 54 and 30(H) Batteries
2nd Division	36 Brigade—15, 48, 71 and D(H) Batteries 41 Brigade—9, 16, 17 and 47(H) Batteries
3rd Division	40 Brigade—6, 23, 49 and 130(H) Batteries 13 Brigade—29, 41, 45 and 129(H) Batteries
4th Division	29 Brigade—125, 126, 127 and 128(H) Batteries 32 Brigade—27, 134, 135 and 136(H) Batteries
5th Division	15 Brigade—52, 80, A and D(H) Batteries 27 Brigade—119, 120, 121 and 37(H) Batteries
6th Division	2 Brigade—21, 42, 53 and 87(H) Batteries 24 Brigade—110, 111, 112 and 43(H) Batteries
8th Division	33 Brigade—32, 33, 36 and 55(H) Batteries 45 Brigade—1, 3, 5 and 57(H) Batteries

9th Division	50 Brigade—A, B, C and D(H) Batteries
	51 Brigade—A, B, C and D(H) Batteries
11th Division	58 Brigade—A, B, C and D(H) Batteries
	59 Brigade—A, B, C and D(H) Batteries
12th Division	62 Brigade—A, B, C and D(H) Batteries
	63 Brigade—A, B, C and D(H) Batteries
14th Division	46 Brigade—A, B, C and D(H) Batteries
	47 Brigade—A, B, C and D(H) Batteries
15th Division	70 Brigade—A, B, C and D(H) Batteries
	71 Brigade—A, B, C and D(H) Batteries
16th Division	177 Brigade—A, B, C and D(H) Batteries
	180 Brigade—A, B, C and D(H) Batteries
17th Division	78 Brigade—A, B, C and D(H) Batteries
	79 Brigade—A, B, C and D(H) Batteries
18th Division	82 Brigade—A, B, C and D(H) Batteries
	83 Brigade—A, B, C and D(H) Batteries
19th Division	87 Brigade—A, B, C and D(H) Batteries
	88 Brigade—A, B, C and D(H) Batteries
20th Division	91 Brigade—A, B, C and D(H) Batteries
	92 Brigade—A, B, C and D(H) Batteries
21st Division	94 Brigade—A, B, C and D(H) Batteries
	95 Brigade—A, B, C and D(H) Batteries
24th Division	106 Brigade—A, B, C and D(H) Batteries
	107 Brigade—A, B, C and D(H) Batteries
25th Division	110 Brigade—A, B, C and D(H) Batteries
	112 Brigade—A, B, C and D(H) Batteries
29th Division	15 Brigade RHA—B, L, 1st Warwick Batteries RHA and 460(H) Battery RFA
	17 Brigade RFA—13, 26, 92 and D(H) Batteries
30th Division	148 Brigade—A, B, C and D(H) Batteries
	149 Brigade—A, B, C and D(H) Batteries
31st Division	165 Brigade—A, B, C and D(H) Batteries
	170 Brigade—A, B, C and D(H) Batteries
32nd Division	161 Brigade—A, B, C and D(H) Batteries
	168 Brigade—A, B, C and D(H) Batteries
33rd Division	156 Brigade—A, B, C and D(H) Batteries
	162 Brigade—A, B, C and D(H) Batteries
34th Division	152 Brigade—A, B, C and D(H) Batteries
	160 Brigade—A, B, C and D(H) Batteries
35th Division	157 Brigade—A, B, C and D(H) Batteries
	159 Brigade—A, B, C and D(H) Batteries
36th Division	153 Brigade—A, B, C and D(H) Batteries
	173 Brigade—A, B, C and D(H) Batteries
37th Division	123 Brigade—A, B, C and D(H) Batteries
	124 Brigade—A, B, C and D(H) Batteries
38th Division	121 Brigade—A, B, C and D(H) Batteries
	122 Brigade—A, B, C and D(H) Batteries
39th Division	174 Brigade—A, B, C and D(H) Batteries
	186 Brigade—A, B, C and D(H) Batteries
40th Division	178 Brigade—A, B, C and D(H) Batteries
	181 Brigade—A, B, C and D(H) Batteries
41st Division	187 Brigade—A, B, C and D(H) Batteries
	190 Brigade—A, B, C and D(H) Batteries
42nd Division	210 Brigade—A, B, C and D(H) Batteries
	211 Brigade—A, B, C and D(H) Batteries
46th Division	230 Brigade—A, B, C and D(H) Batteries
	231 Brigade—A, B, C and D(H) Batteries

47th Division	235 Brigade—A, B, C and D(H) Batteries
	236 Brigade—A, B, C and D(H) Batteries
49th Division	245 Brigade—A, B, C and D(H) Batteries
	246 Brigade—A, B, C and D(H) Batteries
50th Division	250 Brigade—A, B, C and D(H) Batteries
	251 Brigade—A, B, C and D(H) Batteries
51st Division	255 Brigade—A, B, C and D(H) Batteries
	256 Brigade—A, B, C and D(H) Batteries
52nd Division	9 Brigade—19, 20, 28 and D/69th(H) Batteries
	56 Brigade—A, B, C and 527th (H) Batteries
55th Division	278 Brigade—A, B, C and D(H) Batteries
	276 Brigade—A, B, C and D(H) Batteries
56th Division	**280 Brigade—93, A, C and D(H) Batteries**
	281 Brigade—109, A, B and D(H) Batteries
57th Division	285 Brigade—A, B, C and D(H) Batteries
	286 Brigade—A, B, C and D(H) Batteries
58th Division	290 Brigade—A, B, C and D(H) Batteries
	291 Brigade—A, B, C and D(H) Batteries
59th Division	295 Brigade—A, B, C and D(H) Batteries
	296 Brigade—A, B, C and D(H) Batteries
61st Division	306 Brigade—A, B, C and D(H) Batteries
	307 Brigade—A, B, C and D(H) Batteries
62nd Division	310 Brigade—A, B, C and D(H) Batteries
	312 Brigade—A, B, C and D(H) Batteries
63rd Division (RN)	223 Brigade—A, B, C and D(H) Batteries
	317 Brigade—A, B, C and D(H) Batteries
66th Division	330 Brigade—A, B, C and D(H) Batteries
	331 Brigade—A, B, C and D(H) Batteries
74th Division	44 Brigade—340, 382, 425 and D(H) Batteries
	117 Brigade—366, A, B and D(H) Batteries

c.   *Divisional Artilleries of:*

1st Canadian Division	1 Canadian Brigade—1, 3, 4 and 2(H) Batteries
	2 Canadian Brigade—5, 6, 7 and 48(H) Batteries
2nd Canadian Division	5 Canadian Brigade—17, 18, 28 and D/23(H) Batteries
	6 Canadian Brigade—15, 16, 25 and D/25(H) Batteries
3rd Canadian Division	9 Canadian Brigade—31, 33, 45 and D/36(H) Batteries
	10 Canadian Brigade—38, 39, 40 and D/35(H) Batteries
4th Canadian Division	3 Canadian Brigade—10, 11, 12 and 9(H) Batteries
	4 Canadian Brigade—13, 19, 27 and D/21(H) Batteries
5th Canadian Division	13 Canadian Brigade—52, 53, 55 and 51(H) Batteries
	14 Canadian Brigade—60, 61, 66 and 58(H) Batteries

d.   *Divisional Artilleries of:*

1st Australian Division
2nd Australian Division
3rd Australian Division
4th Australian Division
5th Australian Division

e.   *Divisional Artillery of:*

The New Zealand Division

f. *British Army Field Artillery Brigades each organised as 3×6 gun 18 pr and 1×6 how 4.5" Howitzer batteries.*

> 14 RHA—F, T, 400 and 401 Batteries
> 5 Brigade—64, 73, 81 and D(H) Batteries
> 11 Brigade—83, 84, 85 and D(H) Batteries
> 18 Brigade—A, 59, 91 and D(H) Batteries
> 28 Brigade—A, 123, 124 and 65 (H) Batteries
> 33 Brigade—107, 108, C and D(H) Batteries
> 34 Brigade—50, 70, C, and 56 (H) Batteries
> 38 Brigade—A, B, C and D(H) Batteries
> 48 Brigade—A, B, C and D(H) Batteries
> 52 Brigade—A, 122, C and D(H) Batteries
> 64 Brigade—A, B, C and D(H) Batteries
> 72 Brigade—A, B, C and D(H) Batteries
> 76 Brigade—A, B, C and D(H) Batteries
> 77 Brigade—A, B, C and D(H) Batteries
> 84 Brigade—A, B, C and D(H) Batteries
> 86 Brigade—A, B, C and D(H) Batteries
> 104 Brigade—A, B, C and D(H) Batteries
> 108 Brigade—A, B, C and D(H) Batteries
> 113 Brigade—A, B, C and D(H) Batteries
> 119 Brigade—A, B, C and D(H) Batteries
> 126 RHA—A, 2/1 HAC, 2/1 Warwicks and 411 (H) Batteries
> 147 Brigade—A, 10, 97, D/147 (H) Batteries
> 150 Brigade—A, B, C and D(H) Batteries
> 155 Brigade—A, B, C and D(H) Batteries
> 175 Brigade—A, B, C and D(H) Batteries
> 189 Brigade—A, B, C and D(H) Batteries
> 232 Brigade—A, B, C and D(H) Batteries
> 242 Brigade—A, B, C and D(H) Batteries
> 277 Brigade—A, B, C and D(H) Batteries
> 282 Brigade—A, B, C and D(H) Batteries
> 293 Brigade—A, B, C and D(H) Batteries
> 298 Brigade—2/1 Hants, 2/1 Essex C and D(H) Batteries
> 311 Brigade—A, B, C and D(H) Batteries
> 315 Brigade—A, B, C and D(H) Batteries

g. *British Army Field Artillery Brigade each organised as 4×6-gun 18 pr batteries:*

> 5 RHA—G, N, O and Z Batteries
> 14 Brigade—A, 68, 88 and 402 Batteries
> 65 Brigade—465, 466, 504 and 505 Batteries
> 96 Brigade—407, 408, 409 and 410 Batteries
> 126 Brigade—2/A, 2/B, HAC, 2nd/1st Warwick (RHA) and 411 Batteries
> 158 Brigade—A, B, C and D Batteries
> 169 Brigade—376, 377, 378 and 379 Batteries
> 179 Brigade—383, 462, 463 and 464 Batteries

h. *British Army Field Artillery Brigades each organised as 3×6-gun 18 pr batteries:*

> 16 RHA—The Chestnut Troop, Q and U Batteries
> 26 Brigade—116, 117 and A/26 Batteries
> 93 Brigade—A, B and C Batteries

j.   *Canadian Army Field Artillery Brigades each organised as 3 × 6-gun 18 pr and 1 × 6-how 4.5″ How batteries:*

8 Brigade RCA
13 Brigade RCA
14 Brigade RCA

k.   *Australian Army Field Artillery Brigades each organised as 3 × 6-gun 18 pr and 1 × 6-how 4.5″ How batteries:*

3 Brigade RAA
6 Brigade RAA
12 Brigade RAA

l.   *New Zealand Army Field Artillery Brigade organised as 3 × 6-gun 18 pr and 1 × 6-how 4.5″ batteries:*

2 Brigade RNZA

Artillery Communications—Field Artillery

By the end of 1916, it was clear that the Divisional Signals Company could no longer cope with the increasing demands of the artillery. On 3rd March 1917, an artillery detachment of Signal Servicemen, of 5 officers and 22 other ranks, was attached to the Divisional Signal Company to provide communications between the CRA and his brigades. At the same time, a detachment of one officer and five other ranks was attached to each brigade to provide communications from brigade headquarters to batteries. Battery signallers remained gunners.

Horses

By 10th June 1918, there was a great shortage of horses and General Headquarters ordered that all first line wagon teams of Divisional Echelons and AFA Brigades be reduced to four horses. When more mobile warfare occured later in the summer, the MGRA reported much reduced mobility as a result—but the matter remained unresolved at the Armistice.

ANNEX E

Heavy Artillery Organisation in France 1914–1918

In 1914, the BEF went to war with 1×4 gun 60-pounder battery per division. These were joined later by 6×4 gun 6-inch howitzer batteries. 7th and 8th Lahore and Meerut divisions, when they arrived in France, were each provided with 2×4 gun 4.7-inch gun batteries. 7th and 8th Siege Batteries RGA were formed from coast defence gunners and were armed with 6-inch guns on mobile mountings. 7th Siege Battery also had a 9.2-inch howitzer—"Mother"—and was sent at first to Antwerp. The formation of 9th, 10th, 11th and 12th Siege Batteries exhausted the supply of regulars available and 13th Siege Battery became the first 'New Army' Siege Battery to be formed.

During the winter 1914–1915, all "heavies" were withdrawn from divisions and formed into Army artillery under the command of the MGRA. He normally sub-allotted them back to divisions but he and his staff were responsible for them. Then, early in 1915, heavy tractor drawn 8-inch howitzers began to arrive in France. These were at first formed into "Reserve Heavy Artillery Groups" and were allotted to Corps Command so that they could influence the battle. The abbreviation for these groups—RHA—was confusing and it was accordingly changed to Heavy Artillery Reserve—HAR. In the spring of 1915, the 60-pounders and 4.7-inch batteries were added to the HAR Groups and became responsible for counter-battery work. However, the battles of Festubert and Loos proved that artillery groups not directly controlled by Corps Headquarters, nor with any liaison with the infantry, were not a success.

On 25th June 1915, Sir John French reported to the War Office on artillery strengths. He estimated the German strength on 18th May 1915 as 7,150 field guns and howitzers and 3,350 heavy guns and howitzers of 5.9-inch calibre and over. At the same time, the British had 1,080 field and 407 heavy guns of calibres over 4.5-inch. He proposed that he needed immediately:

a. The replacement of all 4.7-inch guns by 60-pounders.
b. Every new division must arrive in France with a 60-pounder battery.
c. Every division should also have a 6-inch howitzer battery.
d. Every corps of three divisions must have a brigade of two batteries of 8-inch or 9.2-inch howitzers.
e. Every Army of three corps must have one 12-inch or 15-inch howitzer battery.
f. During the winter 1915-1916 these figures to be doubled!

Thus, by the spring of 1916, if 50 divisions were deployed by then as expected, he would have 400×60-pounders; 400×6-inch howitzers; 250×8-inch or 9.2-inch howitzers and 40×12-inch or 15-inch howitzers—a total of 1,090 heavy guns and howitzers. By June 1916, this programme ambition was nearing completion. The resultant force of heavies was divided into three rather arbitrary groups:

a. Corps Heavy Artillery
b. Army Heavy Artillery
c. Heavy Artillery Reserve

On 26th January 1916, Major-General Headlam reported that this division caused confusion. He advised that the whole of this force should be called "The Heavy Artillery". It should be allotted to Armies, and by them to Corps, and a 'Commander Heavy Artillery' should be appointed to each Corps. At this stage, the General Staff insisted that heavy artillery should drop its brigade organisation and be organised into "Lieutenant-Colonel's Groups". The Gunners protested strongly,

saying that the system would prove unworkable in practice. They were right and the heavies returned
to brigades in 1917! However, the plan proposed to the War Office on 16th March 1916 was:

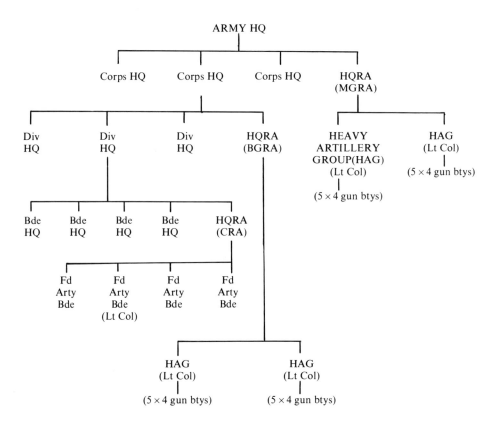

The failure of the group system of controlling artillery was that batteries had no permanent
command system and they always suffered administratively. However, one ASC company and one
workshop was provided for each Heavy Artillery Group at Army and Corps. These proposals were
approved by the War Office on 30th June 1916, and they added that 60-pounder batteries should
forthwith be increased from four to six guns.

When Major General Birch arrived at General Headquarters as MGRA, he studied the whole
problem of artillery support. He reported over the signature of General Haig to the War Office on
24th June 1916 and this is a letter of great importance to the Royal Artillery. It is reproduced in full
at Appendix 1.

These proposals were approved by the War Office on 30th June 1916, and they added that 60-
pounder batteries should forthwith be increased from four to six guns.

It is interesting here to note that steps to remove the Corps Heavy Artillery Commander from
Corps Headquarters itself were successfully resisted in 1916, and he remained where he should be,
with the MGRA and therefore alongside the Corps commander.

By December 1916, the War Office agreed that all Corps Artillery batteries, including 8-inch and
9.2-inch batteries, should be organised on a six gun basis. This was not done by choice but as the
only way to increase gun-power with the minimum increase of men, horses and vehicles.

By June 1917, the regimental disadvantages of the Group System were apparent. Batteries were, as
had been forecast, moved from group to group and sometimes Group Headquarters were moved
without their batteries. It was all most unsatisfactory. The General Staff were, however, not
sympathetic but, by August, Major-General Birch reported that administration, discipline and
training, and therefore fighting efficiency, were suffering and that urgent action was needed to return
to the brigade system. he proposed five types of Heavy Artillery Brigade, excluding railway guns.

Still the General Staff opposed the idea, although they gave no real reason for doing so, other than that it would alter a ruling which they had previously given against artillery advice. However, Army Commanders were approached and were unanimously in favour of doing away with the awful, unwieldy groups. As a result, the MGRA proposed:

			Total
a.	Mobile Brigades	— 2 × 60-pounder batteries	
		— 2 × 6-inch howitzer batteries	20
b.	Howitzer Brigades	— 3 × 6-inch howitzer batteries	
		— 1 × 8-inch or 9.2-inch howitzer battery	40
c.	Mixed Brigades	— 2 × 60-pounder batteries	
		— 2 × 6-inch howitzer batteries	
		— 1 × 8-inch howitzer battery	20
		— 1 × 9.2-inch howitzer battery	

This organisation exactly matched the number of guns and howitzers asked for by the MGRA in his letter of 24th June 1916 — scale B. There remained the 6-inch guns, the super heavies and 10 available HA Group Headquarters. A plan was made after Vimy Ridge to produce extra Group Headquarters to control groups of guns, so great had the concentrations become. The idea was often carried out in practice with success but formal approval was not achieved before the Armistice.

Meanwhile, three brigades of Canadian Heavy Artillery were formed.

On 3rd December 1917, an order was sent out by General Headquarters to revert to the brigade system, and the amount of work involved can be imagined. Most of it would have been unnecessary if only the War Office had listened to the experience of men fighting the battle. After six months of hard work, all was complete, including nomenclature. The new brigades would be known as "——th Brigade RGA" followed by its description in brackets afterwards eg (mixed), (mobile) or (howitzer). The remaining ten Group Headquarters were re-styled "Army Brigades RGA" in July 1918, to take command of the 6-inch gun batteries and the 12-inch and 15-inch railway guns.

In August 1918, the Canadians re-organised into three brigades; one of 2 × 60-pounder batteries; one of 2 × 6-inch howitzer batteries and one of 1 × 8-inch howitzer battery. At this time, too, South Africa raised two SA Brigades RGA, which contained 6 × 6-inch howitzer batteries and 2 × 8-inch howitzer batteries.

In September 1918, the final re-organisation of Heavy Artillery was proposed because of the changed, more mobile, nature of the war and the success of the mobile RGA brigades. Even the 8-inch howitzer had proved to be more mobile than was thought possible. The 9.2-inch howitzer remained much less mobile and would 'hold back' any mobile brigade. The existing mixed brigades, with six batteries, were unwieldy.

Therefore, it was proposed to form:

a. 40 × Mixed Brigades RGA each; 2 × 60-pounder batteries
(including 2 × Canadian) 2 × 6-inch howitzer batteries
1 × 8-inch howitzer battery

b. 28 × Howitzer Brigades RGA each of 3 × 6-inch howitzer batteries
1 × 9.2-inch howitzer batteries
1 × 6-inch gun battery

This would result in one 'Mixed Brigade RGA' per division and the howitzer brigades would form the Army and Corps reserve.

However, these recommendations were never effected by the time of the Armistice in 1918.

Letter from the MGRA, General Headquarters,
to the War Office of 24th June 1916

O.B./796/G.   Secret.   24 June 1916.

Sir,

    I understand that the scale of provision
of heavy guns and howitzers submitted in   O.A.2/118D. of 9.7.15.
the General Headquarters letters noted in   O.B./376 of 11.8.15.
the margin is nearing completion. I have   O.B./19 of 28.2.16.
now the honour, therefore, to submit my
further recommendations as regards:–

  (i)   the policy of provision for the future, and
  (ii) improvements in design of existing armament.

    2. As regards policy of provision for the future, I consider that sufficient experience has now been gained to enable a policy to be framed both as regards the natures of guns and howitzers for which provision should be made, and their number and distribution. This policy must be directed towards simplicity and uniformity; the great variety in natures which exists at present is a very serious drawback to efficiency, movement and ammunition supply.

Guns and howitzers may be considered under three principal categories:–

  (i)   *The Divisional Artillery*—to consist of the mobile field artillery, i.e. such guns and howitzers as can normally be allotted permanently to, and move with, a division.

  (ii) *The Corps Artillery*—to consist of medium artillery, i.e. the next heavier natures of guns and howitzers, including those specially suitable for counter-battery work, which are of greater power than field artillery but which are sufficiently mobile to take part in a movement of troops.

  (iii) *The Army Artillery*—to consist of the heaviest artillery, i.e. those guns and howitzers which are more in the nature of siege artillery and require special arrangements for their transit and for coming into action.

As regards (i), I do not recommend any change in the Divisional Artillery. This should consist, as heretofore, of 18-pdr guns and 4.5-inch howitzers. The total number will be forty-eight 18-pdrs and **sixteen 4.5-inch howitzers in all divisions. I presume that the question of completing all divisions to** this scale of howitzers still has its place in the programme of provision.

As regards (ii), I consider that the Corps Artillery should consist of not more than two classes of guns and two classes of howitzers, i.e., 60-pdr and 6-inch guns, the 6-inch howitzer, and one heavier mobile howitzer of the type of the present 8-inch howitzer, but with increased range. The number of these to be, per Corps of three divisions:–

60-pounder guns	24
6-inch howitzers	60
6-inch guns	8
Heavy howitzers	24
	116 *Vide* attached Table A.

As regards (iii), the Army Artillery should include all guns on railway mountings, and should consist eventually of one type only of heavier howitzer and one type of heavy gun of a calibre of 9.2-inch or over. The howitzers should be both tractor-drawn and on railway mountings, the proportion of the latter being dependant on the railway facilities in theatre of war. The number of these to be, per Army:–

Howitzers	16	(probably 50% tractor-drawn)	20
Guns	4	(all on railway mountings)	

(iv)   The question of anti-aircraft guns is dealt with separately in paragraph 5.

3.   In the above paragraph I have outlined the general policy recommended and the result to be attained. I am, however, fully aware that, except for the 4.7-inch guns, it is not practicable to eliminate at present any existing types, and that circumstances governing the manufacture of guns, howitzers and ammunition will probably necessitate the present variety of types remaining in use for this war. Also the necessity for a large force of artillery is at present too great to admit of the reduction or withdrawal of any existing types until such time as the total number of guns in France shall have reached the figures recommended in the above stated policy.

4.   The attached Table shows the total number of guns and howitzers, independant of Divisional Artillery, for which I consider provision should be made now, and the distribution of the same by natures. Priority of construction should be given to the guns and howitzers detailed in paragraph 2 (ii) above, i.e., Corps Artillery. I have taken into consideration the guns and howitzers which are already in France and for which, from the information at my disposal, I understand provision has already been made (see paragraph 3).

No mention is made of the 4.7-inch gun, as I understand that this gun will be gradually eliminated and replaced by the 60-pdr. I should like definite information on this point.

It will be noticed that the number of guns and howitzers given in this Table represents a considerable increase on the original recommendations contained in the three letters quoted in paragraph 1. I have arrived at the recommendations now presented, both as regards numbers and types, after a careful consideration of the tasks which now devolve upon heavy artillery.

As regards numbers, the importance of being able to develop a superiority of heavy artillery fire when and where required, without having to resort to the laborious and often dangerous process of transferring large numbers of guns from other parts of the battlefront, cannot be over-rated.

From available information it may be assumed that the Germans are working up to a scale of 84 heavy guns and howitzers per Corps of three division. I now recommend that the total of heavy guns and howitzers with the Armies in France be increased to an average of 76 per Corps (Scale A) and eventually to 121, including Army Artillery (Scale B), as shown in the attached Table.

As regards types, although the 6-inch howitzer, the counterpart of the German 5.9-inch, is recognized as our most generally useful weapon, it is not sufficiently powerful against the modern gun emplacements. Experience shows that, given time and material, there is no difficulty in constructing an emplacement which is proof against the howitzer. The range also of the 6-inch howitzer is limited. For these reasons a considerable increase in the number of heavier howitzers (of **approximately the type of the 8-inch howitzer**) with the Corps Artillery is especially necessary.

In submitting this recommendation, the question of grouping and command has been considered and will form the subject of a separate communication.

5.   *Anti-Aircraft guns.*

In letters No. O.B./478 of the 31st July and 20th August 1915, the scale of anti-aircraft guns to be provided was fixed at one section per division in the front line, plus 15 sections for posts on the Lines of Communication.

This scale should, I consider, be increased, and I recommend anti-aircraft guns being provided in future on the following scale:–

(a)   For use in the front line:–
    Five sections per Corps of which four sections (two batteries) should consist of 13-pdr 9-cwt. guns and one section of 3-inch 20-cwt. guns.

(b)   For use on the Lines of Communication:–
    Thirty sections, either 3-inch 20-cwt. or 12-pdr 12-cwt.

6.   As regards improvements in design of existing armament, I submit the following suggestions:–

HEAVY GUNS AND HOWITZERS

60-pdr.   Improvement to the carriage in the direction of mobility. This to be considered with a view to the introduction of an improved carriage, and when this can be done without interfering with the output.

6-inch Guns.   If possible, an increase of range; in addition, modern tractor-drawn mounting to be provided giving internal traverse. The present mounting for this gun is not considered suitable and should eventually be eliminated.

8-inch Howitzers.   An increase of range, provided that mobility at least equal to that of the Mk. VI Howitzer will be assured.

9.2-inch Howitzers.   An increase of range up to about 15,000 yards, even if an increase in the weight of the equipment is entailed.

9.2-inch Gun.   The provision of railway mountings to allow of an elevation giving the maximum range and as much traverse as possible.

12-inch and 15-inch Howitzers.   An increase of range if possible up to about 15,000 yards; the weight of the projectile being reduced, if necessary, in order to obtain this increase.

Ammunition.   For all heavy guns, a projectile giving extra range with a long-burning time fuze.

ANTI-AIRCRAFT GUNS

13-pdr 9-cwt. Mark I Guns.

   (a)   Increased range and a longer burning fuze.
   (b)   An improved design of buffer. The present short recoil system is unsatisfactory.
   (c)   The Cosine sight to be fitted to all guns, if possible.

3-inch 20-cwt. Guns.   An increase in the power of these by improvements, similar to (a) above, would be advantageous.

I have the honour to be,

Sir,

Your obedient servant,

(Sd.) D. HAIG, General,

Commanding-in-Chief, British Armies in France,

TABLE ATTACHED TO LETTER O.B./796/G, d/24TH JUNE 1916.

	Number of Guns to be maintained in action	
	Scale "A" per Corps	*Scale "B" per Corps*
(a) Corps Artillery.		
60-pdr. No change in previous scale	16	24
6-inch howitzers. Previous scale to be increased to 20 per division. All old 30-cwt howitzers to be replaced by the new 26-cwt	40	60
6-inch guns. Previous scale to be increased to 8 per Corps	4	8
8-inch and 9.2-inch howitzers. Scale to be increased to 24 howitzers per Corps. all new howitzers to have a range of 15,000 yards. The extra howitzers may be either 8-inch or 9.2-inch, though the 8-inch howitzer is preferred on account of its mobility. The present 8-inch howitzer to be replaced throughout by the new pattern howitzer	16	24
	76	116
(b) Army Artillery.		
12-inch howitzers		
15-inch howitzers On a total scale		
9.2-inch guns of 20 per Army*		5
12-inch guns or 5 per Corps		
Total—Army and Corps Artillery, per Corps	76	121

*NOTE.   The total number of pieces required for a force of 5 Armies of 4 Corps each will be 100, made up as follows:–

12-inch howitzers + 15-inch howitzers	80	(50% tractor-drawn)
9.2-inch guns + 12-inch guns	20	
Total	100	

+ No more 15-inch howitzers or 12-inch guns to be provided on the completion of the present programme of construction.

[A corollary of the demand for more heavy artillery was a revision of the numbers of Group Headquarters needed. A letter dealing with this subject accompanied that quoted above. It was based on the assumption that a Corps H.A. Commander could deal with four or five groups; that the limit in size of a group was five batteries; and that a 6-gun organization would eventually be necessary to absorb the total number of guns required. The letter is of sufficient importance to warrant its quotation here in full.]

O.B. 446.   General Headquarters,
                                                          British Armies in France,
                                                                24th June 1916.

Sir,
     With reference to previous correspondence, I have the honour to submit the following remarks regarding the scale of allotment of H.A. Group Headquarters, together with certain recommendations for the provision of these headquarters in future.
2.   In my letter No. O.B. 446 of 11th March, I recommended an allotment of heavy Artillery Groups on a scale of two Groups to each Army and two Groups to each Corps.
     This scale was arrived at as follows: from information then available it was anticipated that there would be approximately 195 heavy and siege batteries in France by July next. Allowing 5 batteries to each Group the number of Groups required worked out to 39. Forty Groups were accordingly asked for, in order that the scale mentioned abouve might be completed for the number of Armies and Corps in France at that time. To allow for any increase in the number of guns sent to France, a further request was made for a Group Headquarters to be sent out with every consignment of 16 guns.
3.   Subsequently, owing to thc cxpansion of the Army and to the increased number of heavy guns in France, and in anticipation of further consignments, the need of more Group Headquarters was felt, and four more were asked for on 17th and 26th May.
4.   I have recently submitted certain recommendations as to the scales on which heavy guns and howitzers should be provided in future. It will not be possible or advisable to obtain the number of Group Headquarters which will eventually be required to control these guns if the existing scale for the provision of Group headquarters is adhered to. I consider, therefore, that the scale formerly submitted needs revision, and that the future requirements should be calculated on a somewhat different basis.
5.   It is considered:–

   (a)   That the Commander of the Heavy Artillery Corps can deal with from 4 to 5 Groups.
   (b)   That the limit of command capacity of a Group Commander is 5 batteries.
   (c)   That to absorb the number of guns required it will be necessary eventually to increase the number of guns from 4 to 6 in batteries of certain natures.

6.   Based on the above considerations, I recommend the following policy:–

   (i)   The provision of:–
         (a)   2 Group Headquarters per Army.
         (b)   4 Group Headquarters per Corps.
   (ii)   Each Group should consist of 5 batteries.

In my letter No. O.B./796/G dated 24th June, I recommended a scale of:–

Per Army, 20 guns and howitzers.
Per Corps, 76 guns and howitzers, rising to 116.

     The policy recommended above provides sufficient Group Headquarters to control the Army guns and the 76 guns per Corps. As soon as the total number of guns in France reaches this total, I recommend all additional 60-pounders, 6-inch howitzers and 8-inch and 9.2-inch howitzers being added to existing batteries and the establishment of batteries of these natures being raised from 4 to 6 guns each. This will absorb the difference between the 76 guns already provided for and the 116 guns eventually to be provided.

7.   The attached Table* shows the Army and Corps Artillery in an Army when the establishment of guns, howitzers and Groups is complete.

8.   In conclusion, I have the honour to request that two more Group Headquarters may be sent out to France as soon as they can be prepared. These, I realize, are in excess of the normal number of Group Headquarters which should be in France, based on the number of guns now in this country. They are, however, required for a special purpose, in anticipation of the arrival of more batteries, and will eventually be absorbed.

I have the honour to be,

Sir,

Your obedient servant,

(Sd.) D. HAIG, General

Commanding-in-Chief, British Armies in France

To the Secretary,
    War Office,
        London.

* Not included in the text.

Anti-aircraft Artillery Organisation in France 1914–1918

In September 1914, in early recognition of the air threat then developing during the retreat to the Marne, the first anti-aircraft guns were issued to divisions in France—the '1-pounder Pom-poms', firing solid shells. The chances of achieving a hit were very remote! By December 1914, three sections of 13-pounder AA guns (MT) and one single 18-pounder (horse drawn) were in France. Sir John French then needed one AA section per division and 15 sections for his L of C. by August 1915, there were 13 sections in France. In July 1915, two AA Searchlight Sections RE, each with 3 × 60 cm light projectors, arrived to cover General Headquarters at St. Omer, which had been twice bombed at night!

In October 1915, all AA sections were grouped into four gun batteries under the MGRA at Army Headquarters. In November 1915, the first AA staff officers were attached to HQRA at Army headquarters.

Between March and May 1916, 50th Field Searchlight Company RE arrived in France with both 90 and 60 cm lights. These, together with 5 more AA gun sections, were deployed around General Headquarters and the L of C. Improvements to guns were now in hand and, by boring out and re-lining an 18-pounder to a calibre of 3 inches, a gun known as the 13-pounder 9 cwt was produced, capable of shooting to a height of 19,000 feet. By July 1916, 70 of the 113 AA guns in France were of this type.

By November 1916, a new organisation for air defence was agreed. The idea of batteries was dropped and some 3–4 sections were agreed per Corps, with an AA Group Headquarters at Army Headquarters to command all AA defences in the Army.

The first major night attack came during the night 20th/21st June 1916, when the ammunition depot at Andruicq (NW of St. Omer) was attacked by several planes effectively. Then night bombing attacks occurred during the battle of the Somme. In November 1916, the first 3-inch 20 cwt transportable guns arrived and an AA Artillery Group Headquarters was established at each Army Headquarters, with one for the L of C. Each Group was commanded by a lieutenant-colonel. New style 'lettered' batteries were formed, with a varying number of sections in them. The Signal Service was made responsible for laying line to these sections. By the end of 1916, there were 91 AA sections (including two Canadian) in France; ten had the new 3-inch 20 cwt gun. There were also 22 AA Searchlight Sections RE.

Although more men were needed to make the sections effective, rudimentary height finders were arriving and fuze indicators were improvised. One AA Section now consisted of:–

Officers	—	2	
Detachments, each 12	—	24	(including 2 × ASC drivers)
Telephonists	—	2	
Linesman	—	1	
Height Finders	—	4	
Welson Dalby Director	—	4	
Height and Fuze indicator	—	2	
Setter for order board	—	1	
Lookout man	—	1	
Cook	—	1	
Orderly	—	1	
Total		43	all ranks

To achieve this, it was necessary to disestablish one trumpeter per field battery and to disband two General Headquarters Ammunition Parks and redistribute the manpower cover to AA batteries.

It was now realised that air defence involved AA artillery, machine guns, searchlights and aircraft, and the whole needed co-ordination. A committee was formed to decide on the future of AA. It recommended that:

a.   AA defence was the responsibility of the General Staff, with RA responsible for technical direction.

b.   An Anti-Aircraft Defence Commander, with a staff, must be appointed per Army and four for the L of C.

c.   Each Army should appoint a number of AA Area Commanders.

d.   A directorate should be established at General Headquarters to co-ordinate AA defence.

The MGRA strongly disagreed with those recommendations, saying that AA defence must be under overall artillery control. AA defence could not be independent of the main battle; it was and would always be essentially an artillery problem. But in spite of General Birch's strong words, the General Staff accepted the recommendations on 21st December 1917. Their subsequent memorandum laid down that all commanders would be responsible for low flying aircraft, below 3,000 feet. This would be co-ordinated by Corps Headquarters, who themselves would be responsible for all aircraft above 3,000 feet and for the point defence at important targets at all levels, headquarters, railheads etc.

The first Assistant Director (AA) at General Headquarters was Lieutenant-Colonel N.W. Webber, a Sapper but, on 30th March 1918, such was the expansion of AA that a Gunner, Brigadier C. Evans, became the first Brigadier-General Director AA. He was followed on 18th July 1918 by Colonel V. M. C. Napier. At Army Headquarters, the Army Anti-Aircraft Defence Commander controlled the Anti-Aircraft Area Commanders, who were the Anti-Aircraft Battery Commanders. They also controlled searchlights and any machine guns allotted. However, Corps Commanders could not directly command AA defences in their areas.

However the demand was outstretching available resources and both manpower and guns were very short. Lower calibre men would have to be accepted and, indeed, they were.

In January 1918, the Commander-in-Chief re-organised the AA defence of the L of C. He nominated an "Anti-Aircraft Defence Commander (AADC)" in command of all AA units, searchlights and machine guns. These were controlled under the AADC by four Battery Headquarters, each with seven or eight sections under command. At the front, too, policies changed. A chain of "Front Line AA Areas" was established and a battery of five sections allotted to each. A line of guns 4,000 yards apart was deployed in the First Line and a similar line 6,000 yards apart in the Second Line. First Line sections were about 3 miles behind the front trenches and the Second Line was about 4 miles behind the first. Some searchlights were added to the Second Line. By 1918, two Balloon Barrages were introduced to stop low flying aircraft; these were linked to the gun lines which could engage aircraft restricted by balloons.

Success rates were hard to determine. During the week ending 27th April 1918, 5 aircraft were damaged and 10 destroyed out of 2,039 machines engaged but, to be fair, of all these aircraft, only 658 had crossed to the British side of the front line trenches, so perhaps there was a major deterrent effect showing itself.

Early in 1918, it was decided that the AA organisation should also become responsible for reporting the movement of all enemy aircraft; this called for a further 27 officers, which were approved. The effect of this measure was to clog all communications with hostile aircraft reports and it showed that the air defence system would need its own separate communications. This became essential when it was decided to link the AA Defence reporting system in France to the Home Air Defence System so as to give early warning of the approach of bombers to Great Britain.

But all was not well. AA was a Cinderella Service; there was little interest in it, except during actual raids, and units suffered from having no affiliation with the formations they protected. The MGRA urged again, in June 1918, that the command of all AA Units should be restored to GOCs RA of Armies and policy should be directed by the MGRA at General Headquarters. "Experience has shown" he said, "that in all artillery matters, the tactical and the technical cannot be divorced, except at the cost of delay and duplication of labour, if not of actual mistakes". Finally, he remarked that AA batteries should have six guns and the guns should be lighter and more mobile. However, the Armistice came before these decisions were faced.

Nevertheless, in December 1918, the Inter Allied AA Conference stated "so technical has AA Defence become that all members feel that the Service must not be allowed to become subsidiary to any other branch of the Armed Forces. The whole of AA defence guns, searchlights, machine-guns, balloons and other devices should form a separate Corps".

Trench Mortar Organisation in France
1914–1918

There were no mortars in service in the British Army in August 1914, although a few of very old design did see service before the end of the year. The requirement was established first on the Aisne in September and later in Flanders, when trench warfare started in earnest. In February 1915, the Artillery Adviser at General Headquarters, Major-General Du Cane, said that mortars were not artillery weapons and they should be manned by the infantry or even Sappers!

In March, however, $1\frac{1}{2}$-inch, 2-inch and 4-inch mortars were designed, the former firing "stick bombs" with the bomb outside the bore and a rod inserted into it. They were heavy, clumsy weapons and it was soon clear that the artillery would have to man them. In April 1915, batteries of four mortars with very meagre establishments were authorised. Mortars were regarded as trench weapons only and, in the rare need to move them, ad hoc arrangements would have to be made. By August 1915, batteries were allotted on a divisional basis and a Trench Mortar School was established in France. But men were short and many detachments were made up of 50% artillerymen and 50% infantry. It was still not clear whether the weapon was truly an artillery or infantry weapon; Second Army proposed the former and First Army, the latter.

On 16th December 1915 a decision was made. Trench mortars were classified as light, medium and heavy. The infantry were to man the light and medium batteries, and the Gunners the heavy. There were to be two light and one medium battery per brigade and one heavy per division. Early in 1916, the 3-inch Stokes mortar—simplicity itself—appeared and became the main infantry mortar. They were organised into 2×4 mortar batteries per brigade, they were numbered and a Divisional Trench Mortar Officer, a DMTO, was appointed. Training began on the French 240mm heavy mortar, which became the artillery weapon, and one battery of four such mortars was made an integral part of each divisional artillery. At the end of May 1916, the idea of forming a separate Trench Mortar Corps, on the lines of the Machine Gun Corps, was rejected. The French mortars were not satisfactory and, in June 1916, 30 new British mortars firing a 150 pound bomb were issued, followed by a further 200 in December. They soon became known as the "flying pigs".

In June 1917 came the first issue of the 6-inch Newton mortars. In December, General Headquarters proposed major changes. First, the number of heavy batteries was reduced to one per Corps. The men released were to form medium batteries of $6 \times$ Newton mortars on a scale of two per division. Next, the heavy batteries were re-styled "— Mortar Battery RGA" and the medium batteries "— Mortar Battery RHA/RFA". In July 1918, it was ordered that all officers and men for heavy and medium batteries were to come from the Royal Artillery.

In July 1918, a plan was drawn up to make the Newton mortar mobile. This would need more men if it was achieved and the plan included the abolition of the remaining heavy batteries, which had never been a real success, to provide them. The plan was just ready when the war ended.

The Development of Artillery Intelligence in France 1914–1918

The requirement for specific artillery intelligence grew up in the war. At first, there was confusion between specific artillery intelligence and General Staff intelligence.

At "First Ypres" in 1914, CRAs did their best to locate enemy batteries. When Heavy Artillery Reserve Groups were formed in 1915, they took on this task. When GOCs RA at Corps Headquarters were established, they in turn took it on, using the ADC for the task. By 1915, much more information was coming in about enemy guns from the RFC, and the Observation Sections RE (balloons). In April 1916, Second Army requested an artillery officer to be added to their staff "to collect, collate and distribute all information as to hostile batteries". But confusion resulted from an 'intelligence' officer being appointed who owed allegiance to the Director of Intelligence at General Headquarters who tasked him, and to artillery commanders and staffs. These officers were established by the time the battle of the Somme began in July 1916. Fourth Army Commander reported, on 13th October 1916, that the "Intelligence Corps Officers had not been satisfactory, through no fault of their own, but because of their ignorance of artillery, and he urged strongly that they should be replaced by artillerymen". By January 1917, the following posts were approved by the War Office "to carry out special artillery reconnaissance, to study and collate the information derived from aeroplane photographs and maps so far as it affects the artillery, and to keep in close touch with the Royal Flying Corps":

a. *Army Headquarters.*   A Staff Captain on the staff of the GOCRA.
b. *Corps Headquarters.*   A Staff Captain (vice ADC) on the staff of the GOCRA.
c. *Corps Heavy Artillery Headquarters.*   A Staff Lieutenant 1st Class.
d. *Division Headquarters.*   A Staff Lieutenant 1st Class (vice ADC) on the staff of the GOCRA.

These officers were called reconnaissance officers deliberately to avoid confusion over the word intelligence. In May 1917, a Staff Lieutenant 1st Class was added to the staff of the MGRA at General Headquarters as reconnaissance officer.

The introduction of these staffs greatly improved counter-battery work, but as yet there was no common system of collating results. Also flash spotting and sound ranging were added to other sources and much more information was available. Accordingly, on 23rd January 1918, the MGRA ordered all Armies to render to him a daily list of all hostile batteries reported active in the previous 24 hours. These returns revealed glaring inconsistencies and a conference was called at General Headquarters in February to discuss the problem. The result was a letter dated 10th February 1918, which finally laid down a policy for artillery intelligence. It is repeated in full at Appendix 1.

A month later, General Headquarters sent out a further memorandum instructing Artillery Reconnaissance Officers (AROs) and ASO3 Intelligence Officers at Division to work more closely together and to establish and visit divisional OPs. All such officers were to report on the effects of bombardments, enemy positions, wire, trenches, harrassing fire and fall of shot. The ARO at Corps Headquarters gathered together all evidence and data and passed it to Army Headquarters, who rendered a report right across the front, as at 1500 hours daily. So, after three years of trial, a system was perfected which worked—it was entirely run by artillery officers and none were properly graded Staff Officers. But, by the summer and autumn of 1918, the British counter-battery work was supreme and a major factor in winning the war.

Appendix 1

Orders from General Headquarters to Army Headquarters on Artillery Intelligence

O.A. 127. Secret. First, Third, Fourth, Fifth Armies.

. . . the following instructions, based on the recommendations of the Conference held at G.H.Q. on 4th February 1918, are issued as regards the collection of intelligence regarding hostile artillery:

1. Close co-operation between G.S. "I" and R.A. Staffs in relation to artillery intelligence requires to be developed in all formations. Duplication of work and independent reports and estimates are to be avoided.

In principle G.S. "I" Staffs will be responsible for all documentary evidence concerning hostile artillery, R.A. Staffs for location and activity. All estimates of the hostile artillery strength must represent the combined work of the two Staffs.

2. A hostile battery map will be prepared by Armies, in normal periods twice a month, namely on the 15th and last day of each month. This map will serve all purposes; 3 copies of it will be submitted to G.H.Q. During operations the map will be required at shorter intervals.

(a) The map will be compiled in the office of the G.O.C.R.A. of the Army.
(b) It will show all hostile gun positions *believed to be occupied* on the day of compilation.
(c) On the copies submitted to G.H.Q., positions believed to be occupied will be stamped with the G.H.Q. conventional sign, namely:

    (i)   A blocked-in RED CIRCLE for Field Artillery (77 mm guns and 10.5 cm howitzers).
    (ii) A blocked-in RED TRIANGLE for Heavy Artillery.
    (iii) GREEN CIRCLES or triangles will be stamped over new positions occupied since the issue of the previous map.
    (iv) An OPEN GREEN CIRCLE will be stamped over any newly-constructed positions or positions in course of construction revealed by air photographs since the issue of the previous map, but regarded as not yet occupied.

3. A report as to our own and the enemy's artillery activity for the period will accompany the fortnightly map. It will include an estimate of the strength of the hostile artillery in the line, by groups, together with an estimate of the strength of the hostile artillery in reserve opposite the Army front. The report will be prepared on the lines laid down in para. 1 of this Memorandum, i.e. the estimates of the strengths will represent the joint work of the G.S. "I" and R.A. Staffs. Three copies of the report will be sent to G.H.Q. and a *précis* of it will appear in the Army Summary.

4. Weekly hostile artillery activity reports will no longer be made out.

5. Daily artillery activity reports will be prepared, as heretofore, by Armies. One copy of the report will be forwarded by the G.O.C.R.A. of each Army direct to M.G.R.A., G.H.Q. and a *précis* of the report will be included in the Army Summary.

6. (This paragraph referred to an Intelligence Staff paper on the method of estimating enemy strengths which is of small historical interest. Previous instructions were then cancelled).

Artillery Training in France
1914–1918

During 1915, it became clear that the new officers and men arriving hurriedly in France would need some training, both before and during periods of active service. Each Army was authorised to withdraw one battery to establish a school in its area. Initial courses lasted 12 days for 20 officers at a time. The syllabus was co-ordinated by General Headquarters. About this time, too, Trench Mortar Schools were established separately.

By September 1916, the demand had grown so big that Army Artillery Schools were running courses for 60 officers and 60 NCOs respectively, and the Trench Mortar Schools for 8 officers and 100 other ranks. By March 1917, the training organisation in the United Kingdom was filled to capacity and the Commander-in-Chief agreed to accept half trained officers and men and to complete their training in Army Schools.

Many schools had to close during the German attack in March 1918 to avoid being overrun or to help fill gaps in the line. There was an idea in May 1918 to form one large school under General Headquarters, but this was rejected as being too impersonal for the small resultant savings. Slowly, the schools re-opened in April and May, but the MGRA was not satisfied with them all and on 18th August 1918 he directed that:

a. The syllabus should be revised with more emphasis on battery tactics in open warfare.
b. The Commandant should be an officer who had commanded a brigade at the front. He should serve for 18 months.
c. The instructors, both officers and NCOs, should have battle experience and hold their jobs for at least 12 months.
d. At least three instructors should be majors.
e. Officer students should have three months experience in the line.
f. Brigade and battery commanders should visit their schools and Commandants should visit commanders. Instructors should be exchanged between France and England.

By the end of 1918, only First and Third Army Artillery and First Army Trench Mortar Schools remained, students from other Armies being allotted to them.

The Chapperton Down Artillery School (Salisbury Plain)

One of the lessons of the Somme was that some of the officers of the New Army did not really understand their gunnery. So, on 30th September 1916, it was decided to establish a School of Gunnery in England, where commanders and seconds-in-command of batteries in France could, during the winter months, undergo a course in technical gunnery and practice. The instructors must all come from France.

The first course opened on 1st November 1916 and a series of two-week courses was planned to run until 10th March 1917. There would be 60 officers per course. This would train 600 officers. The first week was devoted to theory and the second to practice. Instruction included co-operation between artillery and aircraft, and meteorological work. In summer, the school was used to try out new equipment and ammunition.The programme was a great success. It was decided to repeat it in winter 1917/1918, but to change the location to Larkhill to give a bigger impact area. The MGRA urged that training was now necessary under three headings:

370

a.   The higher training of some 250–300 lieutenant colonels and majors in field artillery tactics and technical gunnery.
b.   The training of 150 battery commanders.
c.   The training of anti-aircraft officers and men.

The scope of the school at Chapperton Down was expanded to include balloon observation, field survey and camouflage. Senior officers and officers of other Arms were encouraged to attend and to try their hands at shooting. Special training was also arranged for senior officers, especially in tactics for mobile warfare and in the tactical handling of heavy and siege artillery.

On 17th October 1918, the Inspector-General of Training, Home Forces, attended a conference with the MGRA at General Headquarters. The result was the suggestion that the Artillery Schools at Lydd, Winchester and Chapperton Down should be combined into one Central Artillery School. But the Armistice, which followed three weeks later, put an end to the idea for the time being.

Development of Meteor in France
1914–1918

At a meeting held at the Royal Artillery Institution in 1913, an idea proposed by Captain J. E. W. Headlam, that allowance should be made when firing artillery for variations in meteorological conditions, was laughed at.

On 30th June 1915, Lieutenant-Colonel R. Brooke-Popham, Staff Officer to the Major-General, RFC, wrote to Major-General Du Cane, Artillery Adviser at General Headquarters, asking whether details of the velocity of the wind taken every morning at 1000 hours would be of any value to the Heavy Artillery. The MGRA replied "we cannot make any use of this information".

Meanwhile, Major E. Gold, RE, was studying the effect of wind on projectiles at various altitudes. In March 1916, he produced some notes on the subject which were so conclusive that, on 12th April 1916, General Headquarters issued a directive that in future, twice daily at 0900 and 1500 hours, a report for artillery would be issued giving the wind speed and direction at 2,000 and 4,000 feet. On a foggy or cloudy morning, the report would give figures for 3,000 feet only!

Example:

> "X Corps A × .50. 10th AAA two thousand 33 at 100, AAA
> four thousand 45 at 110. AAA meteor 9am".

Meaning:

> "At 2,000 feet 33 feet per second at 100° (bearing)
> At 4,000 feet 45 feet per second at 110° (bearing)".

On 12th June 1916, it was decided to send an additional report at 0700 hours and to add the values for 200 and 500 feet for the field guns.

In August, the air temperature at the specified heights was included. In January 1917, the telegram despatch times were altered to 0530, 1000 and 1530 hours and the time of flight was introduced instead of the height in feet. The times of flight used were 50″, 40″, 30″, 20″, 10″ and 7″. The appropriate temperature to be used for these times of flight was also included. The information was now passed in groups of figures, e.g. "5056 41267, etc". These figures were "50 seconds time of flight, an air temperature of 56°F, a wind speed of 41 feet per second from a direction of 267°.

From 2nd March 1917, telegrams were issued six times daily, with specific instructions about the use of the contents:

> "0300 Telegrams X1. Information to be used between 0400–0800
> 0700 Telegrams X2. Information to be used between 0900–1200
> 1100 Telegrams X3. Information to be used between 1200–1500
> 1400 Telegrams X4. Information to be used between 1500–1700
> 1800 Telegrams X5. Information to be used between 1900–2300
> 2200 Telegrams X6. Information to be used between 2300–0400"

At the same time, a pamphlet "Notes on Meteorological Telegrams to the Artillery" was issued.

In January 1918, the 60 second time of flight was issued. In March 1918, the barometer readings at mean sea level (MSL) were added to the nearest 1/100th of an inch, forecasting a rising or falling barometer. Batteries were warned of the need to correct the MSL value to that at battery height, using the formula:

$$\frac{\text{Ht of Bty in metres}}{3} = \text{Number of 1/100ths of an inch to subtract from MSL value to give the value at the battery.}$$

Finally, on 23rd August 1918, a further telegram was issued daily at Dawn minus two hours, to be applied for the four hours starting Dawn minus one hour. This was to ensure the most accurate shooting possible when engaging targets at dawn.

Sound Ranging in France 1914–1918

by
Sir Lawrence Bragg

It is very tempting to reminisce about people and incidents in such an account as this, because memories of them are so vivid and interesting to those of us who served in the First World War, but I think this temptation must be sternly resisted, because they cannot have the same interest for a later generation. I shall instead concentrate on the technical development of sound ranging. It must be hard for those who only know World War II to realize how little science of any kind was involved in World War I. The thermionic valve had been invented, and its use for radio communication was just starting; in addition, it was used in trench listening sets to pick up enemy messages sent over a circuit with an earth return. Meteorological conditions were forecast. Survey and mapping had already established their expert position. But apart from this I cannot recall any organisation in the Army which specifically enlisted scientists in its service. When I was seeking recruits for sound ranging, I had only to ask for a parade at the depot and say "Bachelors of science, one step forward" to get a generous response of eager aspirants to some job in which their knowledge could be used. There was an almost impassable barrier between the military and the scientific minds. The military thought us scientists far too visionary and gadgety to be of any help in the field; the scientists could not understand why their brain waves, which seemed to them such war-winners, made no appeal to the military mind.

It was into this rather unfriendly world that British sound ranging was born. It had been started in both the French and the German Armies. The principle is simple. A series of listening posts or microphones are situated in known positions along a base behind the front line. The time differences between the arrival of the report at the posts are measured. Suppose the sound to reach post 1 first at time T_1, post 2 at time T_2 and so forth. Then, if one draws a circle on the map around post T_2 with radius $V(T_2 - T_1)$, when V is the velocity of sound, and similar circles for the other posts, a great circle which passes through T_1 and touches the other circles represents the form of the report wave, with the gun at its centre.

The French experiments were viewed with great interest by some of our Sappers, Colonel Winterbotham in particular, and he pressed for a similar organisation in the British Army. The Gunners would have nothing to do with it, but Winterbotham was a persistent man. I saw the files after the war, when I was writing a sound ranging manual, and one letter said in so many words that the R.A. could see no possible advantage in sound ranging but that, if an officer were detailed to experiment with it who was of no use for anything else, they supposed there was no harm in giving it a try. As a result, 2nd Lieutenant W. L. Bragg was summoned to the presence of Colonel Hedley in M15, and told that he was to proceed to France, collect a sound-ranging outfit in Paris, and experiment with it at the front. I was at that time in a Territorial Horse Artillery battery, very much out of my element, as my knowledge of horses was not at all extensive, and my fellow officers and men were Leicestershire hunting enthusiasts. Returning from my interview down Whitehall, I realized what is meant by "walking on air", having a scientific job in the war thrilled me so greatly.

The French had tried several systems. In the simplest, the arrival of the sound was registered by observers who pressed keys. There is always, of course, a small lag of about 1/5th to 1/10th second in the response to the sound. An attempt was made to assess the typical delay for each observer, so as to allow for it. This system has the advantages of great simplicity and also that of discrimination by the observer, who only pressed his key for the gun report and ignored other sounds. It was a possible though approximate method when guns were very close to the observer. It broke down completely for guns at longer ranges because the determination of position was meaningless with such large errors in timing.

In the method which was finally adopted as standard by the French Army, currents from the microphones at the posts actuated "pens", whose movements were recorded on smoked paper at the headquarters behind the base, to which the microphones were connected.

Yet a third system employed a recorder which had been designed by Lucien Bull, of the Institut Marey in Paris. This was the most elegant and accurate of the recorders, but it was complex and required photographic development. Bull employed a six-string Einthoven galvanometer, in which the currents were recorded by the displacement of fine wires in a strong magnetic field. The wires were strongly illuminated and their shadows were thrown by six small totally reflecting prisms, into juxtaposition across a slit. A cine film ran behind the slit and a toothed time wheel governed by a tuning fork interrupted the light 100 times a second, so ruling time markings across the film. The apparatus was switched on and off by one or more forward observers in front of the base, who heard the sound before it reached the microphones. When the apparatus ceased running, the operator at headquarters cut off the portion of film which had run, developed and fixed it, and passed it to the reader who measured the time intervals and deduced the position of the gun.

Lucien Bull has kindly given me an account of the way in which he and Charles Nordmann, of the Paris Observatory, started their experiments on sound ranging together. It is so interesting that I must quote it in full:

> "In the middle of October 1914, I was working at the Marey Institute, on Electro-cardiography and recording heart-sounds, when a knock came at the door of my laboratory. "Come in", and appeared a non-commissioned officer (brigadier) in full uniform. Introduced himself as Charles Nordmann, astronomer at the Paris Observatory called up for military service in the artillery. Asked me, with a more or less air of mystery, if I could give him some information concerning the registration of "faint" sounds of low frequency?" Replied I thought I could, guessing without the slightest difficulty the sounds he meant. On my saying so, he abandoned his mysterious airs and exposed his whole object.

> He had conceived, as a mathematician, the idea that it should be possible to locate on the front the position of the enemy's guns by measuring the time-interval between the arrival of the sound at different points of a measured base. He was lucky enough to have had his immediate superiors sufficiently intelligent to allow him to make some experiments!

> These were made with three human observers with well-regulated stop watches who noted the time they heard the sound of the detonation. His crude experiments, in spite of their lack of precision, showed the possibility of doing better and Nordmann obtained permission to return to Paris and work out his idea.

> Having no personal knowledge of how this could be done, he went to the Sorbonne to inquire and met Professor Dastre, Professor of Physiology, who knew me well and my work on registering heart beats, and who directed him to the Marey Institute. That is how, by mere chance, Nordmann and I met and commenced work together.

> I proposed at once the use of the Einthoven string galvanometer and our first experiments were carried out with our big physiological instrument weighing over 150 lb. Thanks to our clever mechanic G. Kelsen, without whose remarkable skill I don't know if we could have ever completed so well, and certainly never so rapidly, our instrumentation. He managed to lodge, in the narrow magnetic field of our huge instrument, three strings instead of one. This enabled us to record the signals from three microphones placed a kilometer apart on our experimental base. With these we succeeded, in the middle of November, in demonstrating the excellence of the method before a jury of French generals, by locating the position of a gun fired in the woods of St. Cloud, 4 or 5 kilometers away, with an error of only 5 metres in azimuth and 25 meters "en portée" (don't know the English term for this). This convinced the military authorities and we received the order to construct three sets of apparatus for use on the front.

> And this set me working for a portable set, constructing a small galvanometer for 5 (later 6) strings, a device for bringing the enlarged and consequently widely separated images (a prism bench) on to a 35mm film and a timing device (phonic wheel). All this was completed towards the middle of December and, in the beginning of February 1915, the first set came into service on the French front.

> There is one date that I dont remember, that is when Captain Leroy was sent over to France by the War Office to investigate on the front the different methods of sound ranging used by the French; as you know there were at least three: the T.M. (Telegraphic militaire) system with mechanical recording pens, the Cotton-Weiss method, photographic like ours".

I am also not sure of the precise time when Leroy investigated the methods, but it probably was in the summer of 1915. It was in October of that year that I went to Paris to take over the Bull equipment, which had been housed in a specially built lorry by our transport depot.

The Bull system was chosen for the British experiments, and it was very fortunate that this choice was made, though I am not sure that its potential advantages were all appreciated at the time. As the war went on, and the ranges at which guns fired became increasingly great, the timing had to be very accurate indeed if the results were to be significant. The arrival of the report had to be recorded with an error less than 1/100th second. The Bull recorder amply met this demand. Indeed, at a later stage of the war, it was used to record the time interval between the passage of a shell through two screens about 100 ft apart, and so to calibrate guns, by speeding up the film. The simpler fool-proof systems, of some service in the first stages of the war, were incapable of an improvement which would meet this demand for accuracy. A prejudice against the Bull system, because it involved photographic equipment, showed a false sense of values. The importance of locating an enemy battery infinitely outweighed the bother of a dark-room and its equipment.

So in the autumn of 1915, I was ordered to report to Colonel Jack, head of Maps General Headquarters, which was then at St. Omer, with a view to my starting sound ranging at the front with the Bull equipment. I was to find a fellow-officer in England who had a scientific training to accompany me, and the choice fell on H. Robinson, afterwards Professor of Physics in London University and its Vice-Chancellor. He was also serving in a battery in England.

We went first to the Vosges where a Bull section was installed in a ski-lodge, under a Captain Schultz. He was to instruct us in running the apparatus. It was so quiet a sector of the front that, if I remember rightly, not a single enemy battery fired during our fortnight's training. A French battery near us, with whose officers we messed, used to spread its washing on the gun emplacements, hastily taking it in if there was a rumour of an enemy plane. Then, when we returned to General Headquarters, Robinson remained at St. Omer to arrange about the siting of the experimental section, while I went to Paris to collect the set. We set up our gear with a headquarters at a village called La Clytte just south of Ypres (it was moved later to Kemmel Hill). The section consisted of Robinson and myself, the driver and mate of the lorry who also operated the set, the two drivers of two small Singer cars for our personal use, one linesman and one N.C.O. It was a very small show compared to the establishment of 50 or so which sections were subsequently allotted. Neither Robinson or I had any experience at the front, and our only official contact was Colonel Jack at General Headquarters. We were two "innocents abroad" with a vengeance.

All the first sound ranging systems suffered from a defect which made them useless for placing guns, though they could, under ideal conditions, place howitzers. The microphones were sensitive to high-frequency noises, and quite insensitive to low-frequency noises, which is just wrong for gun-recording. The Bull system used carbon granule microphones of the "Paris-Rome" type. They were excellent at recording traffic noises, rifle fire, people talking near them, dogs barking and, in fact, everything but the muffled low "boom" of a gun going off. In particular, they were very sensitive to the "shell-wave" made by a gun with a muzzle velocity greater than the velocity of sound. When a high-velocity gun is firing towards an observer, he hears a very loud crack coming from a point in mid-trajectory, followed by a far fainter boom, which is the true gun report. It is, of course, the latter which must be recorded in order to calculate the position of the gun. The microphones were so disturbed by the shell wave that they failed to give any record of the gun report.

The French tried to get round this difficulty in a typically ingenious way. They constructed curves of the forms assumed by the shell wave for each type of gun, such as the 88mm field gun firing at a series of ranges. One tried to find a shell-wave which fitted the observation. But this did not really work. Not only did every type of gun require a different set of curves, but also they varied with range and direction of fire. It was all too complicated. For the first year, from October 1915 onwards, sound ranging was really a wash-out, though we tried to pretend it was not. Clearly we had to find a selective microphone which responded to the right kind of noise if sound ranging were to be any good.

The solution came in stages. First, it was clear in a number of ways that, although the gun report produced very little impression on the ear, it was associated with large pressure changes. It rattled windows. In our billet at La Clytte, of the usual Belgian farmhouse type, the lavatory opened out of the kitchen and, as all windows were hermetically closed, one sat on the only aperture to the outer air. The deafening shell-wave of a six-inch gun which fired over us left one's posture undisturbed, whereas the faint gun report had a marked lifting effect. A phenomenon which led nearer to the solution was our noting in winter, in the tarred-paper hut in which we were quartered, the jet of bitterly cold air which came through each of the many rents in the wall when a gun report arrived.

The final touch was added by Tucker. Corporal Tucker came to our section on Kemmel Hill from a post in the Physics Department of Imperial College. He had been making experiments on the cooling of very fine hot platinum wires, known as Wollaston wires, by air currents. Somehow we arrived at the brilliant idea of using the jet of air coming through an aperture in the wall of an enclosure to cool a Wollaston wire, heated by an electrical current, and so to alter its resistance. What we hoped was that high frequency sounds, with their very rapid oscillations, would not drag away the film of warm air round the wire, but that the slow but large air movement, due to low frequency sounds, would do so. We got some fine wire from England, placed it across a hole we drilled in an ammunition box, and made it one arm of a Wheatstone Bridge which we balanced, with our galvanometer in the usual circuit. I remember vividly the night we rigged it up. A German field battery obligingly fired towards us, and when the film was developed there was a small sharp "break" for the shell wave, followed by a quite characteristic and definite large break made by the gun report, which could be read with accuracy. It was a wonderful moment, the answer to prayer. It converted sound ranging from a very doubtful proposition to a powerful practical method.

The passage of air into or out of the container cooled the wire. Hence the displacement of the galvanometer string was always in the one direction, as if the lower sections of a sine wave had been reversed upwards. The characteristic frequency of a field gun report was about 25, that of a large piece about 10, though this was only a rough guide to calibre. The great advantage of sound ranging was that it recorded shell-bursts as well, so that one could determine the type of gun or howitzer from the time of flight or by recovering fuzes from the shell holes. A typical report gave the calibre, number of guns, and target on which the battery had registered.

The Tucker microphone satisfied another condition which was important, in that the record it gave was a faithful transcript of the actual pressure variations. This faithfulness enabled the reader to become expert in recognising sounds of various kinds. We were fortunate in choosing an ammunition box as a vessel, because it was heavily damped and so did not impose its own characteristics. Later, when the microphones were made in England, a tidy-minded instrument designer supplied metal containers, but these were far inferior because they were resonant and imposed their own character on all the sounds.

It was a tricky business keeping the Wheatstone Bridges in balance. The current was fed to the microphones from the headquarters battery, and any variations of resistance of the lines disturbed the balance. They had to be of good quality and hence batteries and infantry found it hard to resist the temptation of pinching sections of attractive cable which apparently led nowhere. Lines on posts were obvious loot. Buried lines were run over by transport and tanks and developed leaks to earth. Line maintenance was a great problem.

A special difficulty which had to be overcome with the Tucker microphone was interference by wind. It is not the noise of the wind but the fluctuations in pressure, due to turbulence, which causes the trouble. Putting a solid wall around the microphone to shelter it from the wind current only makes matters worse, because the wall increases the turbulence. We found that anything in the nature of a thick hedge, or of multiple sheets of camouflage netting, was the answer. The gusty wind stream is converted into a steady flow, an effect like that of holding a piece of gauze across a tap. After the war Hemming and I had an opportunity to study the German reports on British apparatus which had been captured. It was interesting to see that they could not understand how we avoided the wind trouble, which seems to have defeated them completely when they tried out our method. In the Second World War, this same device was useful to the Observer Corps. They listened for enemy aeroplanes from the tops of towers, and found the buffeting by turbulent wind very baffling. A horizontal shelf projecting about six feet round the top of the tower, made of something like hop-netting, much reduced the disturbance.

Two inventions greatly increased the efficiency of sound ranging. The first was originally proposed, I think, by Lloyd Owen at Armentieres. I confess I thought it an over-elaboration at first and quite failed to see its usefulness. He proposed putting the microphones at exactly equal distances in a straight line. The consequence is that the six "breaks" on the film due to any one sound fall on a smooth curve and, with experience, it is easy to spot a set of breaks which belong together, even when there are many noises. One can also see at a glance roughly where the gun is, and neglect the sets of breaks due to our own batteries or to anti-aircraft fire. It enabled location to be made when quite a strafe was going on. The straight base was later abandoned for an arc of a circle, with its centre roughly in the most interesting area behind the enemy lines. Plotting boards were printed for a few standard-sets of radii and distances between microphones, and it was always possible to shuffle a standard layout so that the six microphones fell in convenient places. The surveyors fixed three places correct to a metre.

The next great scheme was the "wind-section". In this J. A. Gray made a main contribution. Wind and temperature corrections were always troublesome if one tried to deduce them from meteor data, because both varied so much with height and local contours. On the other hand, upper winds and temperatures were much the same along the whole front. The "wind section" was a sound ranging section behind the lines which recorded reports from a known position. A pound or so of explosive was set off at intervals of a few hours, and the sound was recorded by a series of microphones in two or three areas, at about the same range as enemy guns. Since the position of the explosion was known, one could measure the extent to which the wind and temperature had affected the readings, and so circulate to the sound ranging sections the required corrections.

All those schemes were developed at the front, and I think this was the main reason why sound ranging got going so quickly, after the first wasted year when we lacked an effective microphone. Each section (there were, if I remember rightly, about 40 in all) had a mechanic with a kit of tools, a watchmaker's lathe, and a chest of assorted bits and pieces of wood and metal, so each could try out its own schemes. At intervals of two months or so, we had a meeting at some central point such as Doullens, to which each section sent an expert. They swopped stories, schemes, and boasts of their achievements and I am sure emulation made everything go much faster. The meeting generally ended with a binge of heroic magnitude. If the experiments had been done in England with (a) the inevitable lessening of a sense of urgency (b) less touch with the actual problems and (c) delay in communicating and testing ideas, sound ranging would have taken two or three times as long to develop. An experimental section was later established on Salisbury Plain and did very good work, but by this time the problems were well defined.

An interesting side issue of the Bull recorder was its use for calibrating our field guns, a tribute to its extreme accuracy. Bob Chapman was responsible for setting it up. It was thus possible to record with sufficient accuracy the time between breaking wires on screens through which the shell was fired. Chapman had a special section on the coast near Dunkirk where the field guns fired out to sea.

Towards the end of the war, we had an apparatus (horribly messy) which developed and fixed the film as it issued from the camera. I doubt if it was really worthwhile, as it easily went wrong and one lost precious records. By using strong solutions, the developing and fixing were done in a matter of seconds. It is true that the photographic recording was a complex process but, if one bears in mind the great value of a location (something for which an aeroplane was commonly risked), this fuss about the photography is seen to be utterly meaningless.

The Germans had a great respect for our sound ranging. It was a great day when a captured German order was circulated to the sound ranging section which read:

"All Field Survey Companies.

The following extract from a German Order is forwarded for your information:–

Group Order. "In consequence of an excellent sound ranging of the English, I forbid any battery to fire alone when the whole section is quiet, especially in east wind. Should there be occasion to fire, the adjoining battery must always be called on, either directly or through the Group, to fire a few rounds".

Maps, G.H.Q.	E.M.J
23 June 1917.	Lieutenant-Colonel,
	General Staff. "

We were particularly pleased because, with our Tucker microphones and regular bases, we could record almost any number of guns firing at once, the more the merrier. It is interesting that the scientific Germans never developed a refined method. Right towards the end of the war they had a system which depended on the binaural effect. An observer had two horns at the end of a rod, each connected to an ear and, by estimating the direction of the sound with reference to direction posts, he deduced its bearing. Intersections from three or more stations gave a location. I cannot believe they were of any value. I think they were committed too early to a simpler but crude system, and it was too late to change it when ranges increased and greater accuracy was essential. We were extremely fortunate in having started with the Bull recorder.

The one thing which was never developed was the "radio link". It would hardly have been possible to develop it in World War I when radio was so very crude. I find it extraordinary, however, that it was never established in the years between the two World Wars, when it was such an obvious goal. In fact, when World War II threatened and I was asked to give my view on the sound ranging apparatus as it had been developed in the interim, I was appalled. It was like the World War I set which had grown the most complex whiskers. I much doubted the usefulness of most of the gadgets, possibly because I was so keen on the "stripped down" unit we were using at the end of World War

I. I regret greatly now that I was tactless in expressing my doubts; I would have made my influence felt far more usefully if I had been wiser, and not put up so many backs. But, as the war progressed, the frills mostly disappeared and the set came back to very much the one we had been using in World War I. It was fascinating to see that sound ranging was once more of great use. Much doubt had been expressed on this point because it was thought it would take too long to survey and install a base, and so sound ranging would never get into action in a war of movement. This, however, was a wrong assessment. When there is a hold up of any kind, guns must be got into position and surveyed, and sound ranging can be installed as quickly as can the batteries. We had reports that sound ranging was often the only way, particularly in country where maps were inadequate, of getting information about enemy batteries.

The great drawback of sound ranging is that it fails when the wind is blowing away from our lines towards the enemy lines. In these conditions, not only is the sound faint but also it has an irregular beginning. One does not know what point to read on the film. The wind gradient is responsible for this effect. Since the wind velocity is less nearer the ground, the sound is refracted upwards. On the other hand, with the wind blowing towards the base, the sound is crisp and its time of arrival can be read to 1/100th second. Unfortunately, on the Western front the prevailing wind was westerly, and sound ranging sections were often cursed for their ineffectiveness when it was really as impossible to work as it is to use visual observation in a thick mist. On the other hand, in easterly winds, and particularly in foggy weather when wind was light and temperature uniform, sound ranging worked perfectly.

Whether it will ever be used again is hard to guess when so much is uncertain. The story of sound ranging in World War I is perhaps of special interest, however, as an example of the very rapid development of a scientific technique right in the front line.

Order of Battle

Royal Artillery

France and Flanders

11th November 1918

GHQ TROOPS

Major General RA—Major General J F N Birch

AA Artillery

AA School of Gunnery
No 14 AA Section (2 × 13 pdr guns)
No 75 AA Section (2 × 3 inch guns)

ARMY TROOPS

FIRST ARMY   GOC   RA   —Major General E W Alexander

Army Brigades RFA

Bde		18 pdr Btys		4.5 How Bty
18	A	59	91	D
26	A	116	117	
52	A	122	C	D
77	A	B	C	D
126	A	2/1 HAC	2/1 Warwickshire	411
147	A	10	97	D
175	A	B	C	D
189	34	B	C	D
242	A	B	C	D
277	A	B	C	D
282	A	B	C	D
293	1/1 Shropshire	1/1 Glamorgan	C	D
311	A	B	C	D

Brigade RGA

Bde	Heavy Btys 60 pdr gun		Siege Btys 6″ How Btys			8″ How Bty	9.2″ How Bty
1 (Mobile)	16	21	49	254			
7 (Mixed)	115	125	27	28		193	158
8 (How 9.2″)			16	235	290		90
16 (Mobile)	23	146	204	280			
19 (How 9.2″)			288	297	231		46
29 (Mobile)	12	121	195	303			
30 (How 8″)			23	241	308	39	
34 (How 9.2″)			112	142	278		48
40 (How 8″)			40	186	196	256	
45 (How 9.2″)			32	38	208		62
48 (Mobile)	108	1/1 Lancs	4	5			
50 (SA)(How 8″)			72(SA)	74(SA)	75(SA)	275	
53 (Mixed)	136	1/1 Welsh	251	252		249	188
67 (Mixed)	17	110	149	162		234	79
78 (How 8″)			87	108	139	36	
81 (Mixed)	31	1/1 Lowland	163	179		239	184
91 (How 9.2″)			140	326	337		96

Note: 1. **Brigades RGA**
(mobile)—two 60pr btys and two 6 inch how btys
(mixed)—six btys of all natures of guns
(How 9.2″)—three 6 inch how btys and one 9.2 inch how bty
(How 8″)—three 6 inch how btys and one 8 inch how bty

2. SA = South Africa

Army Brigades RGA

Nos 26 and 31

Unbrigaded Siege Btys RGA

4 × 6″ guns—60, 192, 393, 450, 488, 520, 527
2 × 9.2″ guns on railway mountings—366, 461, 523
12″ gun on railway mountings—92*, 543*
2 × 14″ guns on railway mountings—471*, 515
2 × 12″ How   —65, 493
2 × 12″ How on railway mountings—52, 86, 444, 514*

* one gun only

Anti Aircraft Artillery

HQ First Army AA Defence Commander—Lt Col D H Gill

AA Bty	Sections 13 pdr						3″
C	20	69		143	158		202
K	9	25	230	134	168		226
Y	7	49	79	133	156	162	
E(Cdn)	1	2	3	4	5		

SECOND ARMY   GOC RA—Maj Gen C R Buckle

Army Brigades RFA

Bde		18 pdr Btys			4.5″ How Bty
11	83	84	85		D
23	107	108	C		D
28	A	123	124		65
38	50	70	C		56
64	A	B	C		D
96	407	408	409	410	
113	A	B	C		D
119	A	B	C		D

Brigades RGA

Bde	Heavy Btys 60 pdr gun		Siege Btys 6″ How Bty		8″ How Bty	9.2″ How Bty
2 (How 9.2″)			177	250	352	66
3 (Mixed)	48	112	88	268		152	21
4 (Mixed)	131	2/1 N Midland	223	301		261	129
6 (Mixed)	109	114	111	245		227	42
10 (Mobile)	150	159	113	226		
33 (How 8″)			31	279	298	221
36 (Mixed)	140	151	155	353		1 (Aus)	2 (Aus)
43 (How 9.2″)			147	190	351	154
59 (IIow 8″)			37	335	350	30
64 (How 8″)			100	101	102	61
65 (How 9.2″)			115	202	212	118
70 (How 9.2″)			15	157	217	12
77 (Mixed)	9	26	116	119		286	191
86 (Mobile)	141	1/1 Wessex	203	324		
87 (Mobile)	154	156	194	219		
70 (How 8″)			282	285	405	151

Army Brigades RGA

Nos 25, 72

Unbrigaded Siege Btys RGA

$4 \times 6″$ gun—7, 29, 187, 198, 479, 526, 528, 546
$2 \times 9.2″$ gun on railway mountings—45, 53*
$2 \times 12″$ How—85, 375
$2 \times 12″$ How on railway mountings—22, 63, 82, 104, 359, 381

* one gun only

Anti Aircraft Artillery

HQ Second Army AA Defence Commander — Lt Col H W Hill

AA Bty	13 pdr			Sections		3″	
H	8	17	116	144	159		
J	19	88	111			53	214
R	42	54	115	145		232	
T	35	43	56	78		76	216
U	21	34	81			217	
—	171	177					

THIRD ARMY   GOC RA—Maj Gen A E Wardrop

Army Brigades RHA

Bde	18 pdr Btys				4.5″ How Bty
14 RHA	F	T	400		401
16 RHA	A	Q	U		

Army Brigades RFA

34	50	70	C		56
72	A	B	C		D
76	A	B	C		D
93	A	B	C		
155	A	B	C		D
169	376	377	378	379	
232	A	B	C		D
315	A	B	C		D

Brigades RGA

	Heavy Btys		Siege Btys				
					6″ How	8″ How	9.2″ How
Bde		60 pdr gun			Btys	Btys	Bty
5 (How 8″)			160	200	295	47	
13 (Mobile)	22	1/2 London	201	379			
17 (Mixed)	135	2/1 Lancs	51	248		56	13
22 (How 9.2″)			182	253	287		265
35 (Mobile)	111	145	170	267			
39 (How 9.2″)			206	266	281		133
54 (How 8″)			173	199	207	262	
56 (How 9.2″)			106	144	220		175
60 (How 9.2″)			183	305	342		136
62 (Mixed)	122	126	224	274		67	76
63 (Mobile)	38	119	420	443			
66 (How 8″)			122	306	325	120	
84 (Mixed)	24	152	276	336		77	34
88 (How 8″)			123	258	328	78	
90 (How 9.2″)			244	277	299		95
92 (Mobile)	14	127					
	129	1/1 Kent					

Army Brigades RGA

Nos 32, 57, 58

Unbrigaded Siege Btys RGA

4 × 6″ gun—8, 26, 35, 58, 409, 434, 484, 5υ0, 503, 525 500, 503, 525
2 × 9.2″ gun on railway mountings—363, 442
12″ gun on railway mountings—92*
2 × 12″ How—431, 495
2 × 12″ How on railway mountings—83, 89, 333, 343

* one gun only

Anti Aircraft Artillery

HQ Third Army AA Defence Commander— Lt Col W Lewis

AA Bty			Sections				3″
			13 pdr				
L	16	39	41	66			
M	40	65	84	87	129	155	
N	11	48	50	62	64		
O	58	86	104	107			225

FOURTH ARMY GOC RA—Maj Gen C E D Budworth

Army Brigade RHA

Bde	**18 pdr Btys**			
5	G	N	O	Z

Army Brigade RFA

	18 pdr Btys				4.5″ How Bty
5	64	73	81		D
14	Λ	68	88	402	
48	A	B	C		D
65	465	466	504	505	
84	A	B	C		D
86	A	B	C		D
104	A	B	C		D
298	2/1 Hants	2/1 Essex	C		D

Brigades RGA

	Heavy Btys		Siege Btys				
				6″ How Bty		8″ How Bty	9.2″ How Bty
		60 pdr					
9 (Mobile)	128	130	153	260			
12 (How 8″)			242	263	319	70	
14 (How 8″)			11	150	296	214	
21 (Mobile)	71	1/2 Lancs	24	354			
23 (How 9.2″)			41	327	355		94
27 (Mixed)	25	144	110	216		33	143
41 (Mobile)	1/1 Northumbrian	1/1 N Midland	1	6			
47 (How 8″)			109	146	309	156	
51 (Mixed)	137	138	255	283		169	161
68 (How 8″)			114	168	211	25	
69 (How 9.2″)			238	291	331		93
71 (How 8″)			9	17	332	126	
76 (Mixed)	113	132	228	233		19	91
79 (Mixed)	142	1/1 Essex	14	174		145	185
83 (Mixed)	116	1/1 Highland	230	284		135	69
85 (Mobile)	120	139	2	3			
93 (Mixed)	35	2/1 Lowland	231	232		215	124
98 (How 9.2″)			210	270	294		121

Army Brigades RGA

73

Unbrigaded Siege Btys RGA

$4 \times 6''$ gun — 50, 189, 222, 312, 449, 498, 499, 504, 545
$12''$ gun on railway mounting — 543*
$2 \times 12''$ How — 80, 243, 494
$2 \times 12''$ How on railway mountings — 374

*one gun only

Anti Aircraft Artillery

HQ Fourth Army AA Defence Commander — Lt Col R B Hay

AA Bty	Sections					
	13 pdr Gun				3″ Gun	
F	6	44	57	110		
G	31	46	82	137		
P	12	52	128	146		
Q	15	67	71	109	236	
Z	37	127	148		205	227

FIFTH ARMY

GOC RA — Maj Gen C C Van Straubenzee

Army Brigades RFA

Bde	18 pdr Btys				4.5″ How Bty
108	A	B	C		D
150	A	B	C		D
158	A	B	C	D	
179	383	462	463	464	

Brigades RGA

Bde	Heavy Btys			Siege Btys				
	60 pdr				6″ How Bty		8″ How Bty	9.2″ How Bty
18 (How 9.2″)			180	218	236			117
28 (Mixed)	117	1/1 West Riding	141	329			213	148
42 (Mobile)	124	1/1 London	237	323				
44 (SA)(How 8″)			71SA	73SA	125SA	20		
46 (Mobile)	108	1/1 Lancs	4	5				
49 (How 8″)			99	166	346			
52 (How 9.2″)			164	259	264			10
89 (How 8″)			68	178	225	57		

Army Brigades RGA

11, 55

Unbrigaded Siege Btys RGA

4 × 6″ gun — 330, 481, 521, 544
2 × 9.2″ gun on railway mountings — 53*, 456
14″ gun on railway mountings — 471*
2 × 12″ How — 349
2 × 12″ How on railway mountings — 18, 44, 64, 128, 514*, 524

* one gun/how only

Anti Aircraft Artillery
HQ Fifth Army AA Defence Commander—Lt Col G P R MacMahon

AA Bty			Sections				
			13 pdr				3″
A	22	26	77	100	165		219
B	33	70	101	142	164	174	220
D	18	61	89	132	166		218

CORPS TROOPS

I Army Corps

HQ Corps Artillery   Brig Gen H C Sheppard
HQ Corps Heavy Artillery   Brig Gen F G Maunsell
V/I Heavy Trench Mortar Bty RGA

II Army Corps

HQ Corps Artillery   Brig Gen A D Kirby
HQ Corps Heavy Artillery   Brig Gen D F H Logan
V/II Heavy Trench Mortar Bty RGA

III Army Corps

HQ Corps Artillery   Brig Gen C M Ross-Johnson
HQ Corps Heavy Artillery   Brig Gen A E J Perkins
V/III Heavy Trench Mortar Bty RGA

IV Army Corps

HQ Corps Artillery   Brig Gen J G Geddes
HQ Corps Heavy Artillery   Brig Gen T E Marshall
V/IV Heavy Trench Mortar Bty RGA

V Army Corps

HQ Corps Artillery   Brig Gen R P Benson
HQ Corps Heavy Artillery   Brig Gen A M Tyler
V/V Heavy Trench Mortar Bty RGA

VI Army Corps

HQ Corps Artillery   Brig Gen J G Rotton
HQ Corps Heavy Artillery   Brig Gen A Ellershaw
V/VI Heavy Trench Mortar Bty RGA

VII Army Corps

HQ Corps Artillery	Brig Gen K K Knapp
HQ Corps Heavy Artillery	Brig Gen F H Metcalfe
V/VII Heavy Trench Mortar Bty RGA	

VIII Army Corps

HQ Corps Artillery	Brig Gen H D O Ward
HQ Corps Heavy Artillery	Brig Gen L J Chapman
V/VIII Heavy Trench Mortar Bty RGA	

IX Army Corps

HQ Corps Artillery	Brig Gen G Humphreys
HQ Corps Heavy Artillery	Brig Gen G B Mackenzie
V/IX Heavy Trench Mortar Bty RGA	

X Army Corps

HQ Corps Artillery	Brig Gen W P Monkhouse
HQ Corps Heavy Artillery	Brig Gen A H Ollivant
V/X Heavy Trench Mortar Bty RGA	

XI Army Corps

HQ Corps Artillery	Brig Gen S F Metcalfe
HQ Corps Heavy Artillery	Brig Gen F A Twiss
V/XI Heavy Trench Mortar Bty RGA	

XIII Army Corps

HQ Corps Artillery	Brig Gen R A C Wellesley
HQ Corps Heavy Artillery	Brig Gen J D Sherer
V/XIII Heavy Trench Mortar Bty RGA	

XV Army Corps

HQ Corps Artillery	Brig Gen B R Kirwan
HQ Corps Heavy Artillery	Brig Gen C W Collingwood
V/XV Heavy Trench Mortar Bty RGA	

XVII Army Corps

HQ Corps Artillery	Brig Gen E H Willis
HQ Corps Heavy Artillery	Brig Gen N G Barron
V/XVII Heavy Trench Mortar Bty RGA	

XIX Army Corps

HQ Corps Artillery	Brig Gen W B R Sandys
HQ Corps Heavy Artillery	Brig Gen F A Wynter
V/XIX Heavy Trench Mortar Bty RGA	

XXII Army Corps

HQ Corps Artillery	Brig Gen E W M Powell
HQ Corps Heavy Artillery	Brig Gen A S Jenour
V/XXII Heavy Trench Mortar Bty RGA	

DIVISIONAL TROOPS

1st Cavalry Division
7 Bde RHA　　　　　H　I　Y　Btys (each 6 × 13 pdr guns)

2nd Cavalry Division
3 Bde RHA　　　　　D　E　J　Btys (each 6 × 13 pdr guns)

3rd Cavalry Division
4 Bde RHA　　　　　C　K　Btys (each 6 × 13 pdr guns)

Guards Division
HQ Divisional Artillery—CRA　　　　　Brig Gen F A Wilson
74 Bde RFA　　　　A　B　C　Btys (18 pdr)　D Bty (4.5″ How)
75 Bde RFA　　　　A　B　C　Btys (18 pdr)　D Bty (4.5″ How)
X/Guards Medium Trench Mortar Bty
Y/Guards Medium Trench Mortar Bty
Guards Divisional Ammunition Column

1st Division
HQ Divisional Artillery—CRA　　　　　Brig Gen H F E Lewin
25 Bde RFA　　　113 114 115 Btys (18 pdr)　　40 Bty (4.5″ How)
39 Bde RFA　　　　46　51　54 Btys (18 pdr)　　30 Bty (4.5″ How)
X/1 Medium Trench Mortar Bty
Y/1 Medium Trench Mortar Bty
1st Divisional Ammunition Column

2nd Division
HQ Divisional Artillery—CRA　　　　　Brig Gen G H Sanders
36 Bde RFA　　　　15　48　71 Btys (18 pdr)　　D Bty (4.5″ How)
41 Bde RFA　　　　9　16　17 Btys (18 pdr)　　47 Bty (4.5″ How)
X/2 Medium Trench Mortar Bty
Y/2 Medium Trench Mortar Bty
2nd Divisional Ammunition Column

3rd Division
HQ Divisional Artillery—CRA　　　　　Brig Gen J S Ollivant
40 Bde RFA　　　　6　23　49 Btys (18 pdr)　　130 Bty (4.5″ How)
42 Bde RFA　　　　29　41　45 Btys (18 pdr)　　129 Bty (4.5″ How)
X/3 Medium Trench Mortar Bty
Y/3 Medium Trench Mortar Bty
3rd Divisional Ammunition Column

4th Division
HQ Divisional Artillery—CRA　　　　　Brig Gen C A Sykes
29 Bde RFA　　　125 126 127 Btys (18 pdr)　　128 Bty (4.5″ How)
32 Bde RFA　　　　27 134 135 Btys (18 pdr)　　136 Bty (4.5″ How)
X/4 Medium Trench Mortar Bty
Y/4 Medium Trench Mortar Bty
4th Divisional Ammunition Column

5th Division

HQ Divisional Artillery—CRA   Brig Gen A H Hussey
15 Bde RFA   A 52 80 Btys (18 pdr)   D Bty (4.5″ How)
27 Bde RFA   119 120 121 Btys (18 pdr)   37 Bty (4.5″ How)
X/5 Medium Trench Mortar Bty
Y/5 Medium Trench Mortar Bty
5th Divisional Ammunition Column

6th Division

HQ Divisional Artillery—CRA   Brig Gen E F Delaforce
 2 Bde RFA   21 42 53 Btys (18 pdr)   87 Bty (4.5″ How)
24 Bde RFA   110 111 112 Btys (18 pdr)   43 Bty (4.5″ How)
X/6 Medium Trench Mortar Bty
Y/6 Medium Trench Mortar Bty
6th Divisional Ammunition Column

8th Division

HQ Divisional Artillery—CRA   Brig Gen J W F Lamont
33 Bde RFA   32 33 36 Btys (18 pdr)   55 Bty (4.5″ How)
45 Bde RFA   1   3   5 Btys (18 pdr)   57 (4.5″ How)
X/8 Medium Trench Mortar Bty
Y/8 Medium Trench Mortar Bty
8th Divisional Ammunition Column

9th (Scottish) Division

HQ Divisional Artillery—CRA   Brig Gen A R Wainewright
50 Bde RFA   A B C Btys (18 pdr)   D Bty (4.5″ How)
51 Bde RFA   A B C Btys (18 pdr)   D Bty (4.5″ How)
X/9 Medium Trench Mortar Bty
Y/9 Medium Trench Mortar Bty
9th Divisional Ammunition Column

11th (Northern) Division

HQ Divisional Artillery—CRA   Brig Gen O de l'Epee Winter
58 Bde RFA   A B C Btys (18 pdr)   D Bty (4.5″ How)
59 Bde RFA   A B C Btys (18 pdr)   D Bty (4.5″ How)
X/11 Medium Trench Mortar Bty
Y/11 Medium Trench Mortar Bty
11th Divisional Ammunition Column

12th (Eastern) Division

HQ Divisional Artillery—CRA   Brig Gen H M Thomas
62 Bde RFA   A B C Btys (18 pdr)   D Bty (4.5″ How)
63 Bde RFA   A B C Btys (18 pdr)   D Bty (4.5″ How)
X/12 Medium Trench Mortar Bty
Y/12 Medium Trench Mortar Bty
12th Divisional Ammunition Column

14th (Light) Division

HQ Divisional Artillery—CRA   Brig Gen E Harding Newman
46 Bde RFA   A B C Btys (18 pdr)   D Bty (4.5″ How)
47 Bde RFA   A B C Btys (18 pdr)   D Bty (4.5″ How)
X/14 Medium Trench Mortar Bty
Y/14 Medium Trench Mortar Bty
14th Divisional Ammunition Column

15th (Scottish) Division

HQ Divisional Artillery—CRA   Brig Gen E B Macnaghten
70 Bde RFA   A   B   C   Btys (18 pdr)   D Bty (4.5″ How)
71 Bde RFA   A   B   C   Btys (18 pdr)   D Bty (4.5″ How)
X/15 Medium Trench Mortar Bty
Y/15 Medium Trench Mortar Bty
15th Divisional Ammunition Column

16th (Irish) Division

HQ Divisional Artillery—CRA   Brig Gen C E C G Charlton
177 Bde RFA   A   B   C   Btys (18 pdr)   D Bty (4.5″ How)
180 Bde RFA   A   B   C   Btys (18 pdr)   D Bty (4.5″ How)
X/16 Medium Trench Mortar Bty
Y/16 Medium Trench Mortar Bty
16th Divisional Ammunition Column

17th (Northern) Division

HQ Divisional Artillery—CRA   Brig Gen P Wheatley
78 Bde RFA   A   B   C   Btys (18 pdr)   D Bty (4.5″ How)
79 Bde RFA   A   B   C   Btys (18 pdr)   D Bty (4.5″ How)
X/17 Medium Trench Mortar Bty
Y/17 Medium Trench Mortar Bty
17th Divisional Ammunition Column

18th (Eastern) Division

HQ Divisional Artillery—CRA   Brig Gen T O Seagram
82 Bde RFA   A   B   C   Btys (18 pdr)   D Bty (4.5″ How)
83 Bde RFA   A   B   C   Btys (18 pdr)   D Bty (4.5″ How)
X/18 Medium Trench Mortar Bty
Y/18 Medium Trench Mortar Bty
18th Divisional Ammunition Column

19th (Western) Division

HQ Divisional Artillery—CRA   Brig Gen E J R Peel
87 Bde RFA   A   B   C   Btys (18 pdr)   D Bty (4.5″ How)
88 Bde RFA   A   B   C   Btys (18 pdr)   D Bty (4.5″ How)
X/19 Medium Trench Mortar Bty
Y/19 Medium Trench Mortar Bty
19th Divisional Ammunition Column

20th (Light) Division

HQ Divisional Artillery—CRA   Brig Gen H W A Christie
91 Bde RFA   A   B   C   Btys (18 pdr)   D Bty (4.5″ How)
92 Bde RFA   A   B   C   Btys (18 pdr)   D Bty (4.5″ How)
X/20 Medium Trench Mortar Bty
Y/20 Medium Trench Mortar Bty
20th Divisional Ammunition Column

21st Division

HQ Divisional Artillery—CRA   Brig Gen H W Newcome
94 Bde RFA   A   B   C   Btys (18 pdr)   D Bty (4.5″ How)
95 Bde RFA   A   B   C   Btys (18 pdr)   D Bty (4.5″ How)
X/21 Medium Trench Mortar Bty
Y/21 Medium Trench Mortar Bty
21st Divisional Ammunition Column

24th Division

HQ Divisional Artillery—CRA				Brig Gen E S Hoare Nairne	
106 Bde RFA	A	B	C	Btys (18 pdr)	D Bty (4.5″ How)
107 Bde RFA	A	B	C	Btys (18 pdr)	D Bty (4.5″ How)

X/24 Medium Trench Mortar Bty
Y/24 Medium Trench Mortar Bty
24th Divisional Ammunition Column

25th Division

HQ Divisional Artillery—CRA				Brig Gen K J Kincaid Smith	
110 Bde RFA	A	B	C	Btys (18 pdr)	D Bty (4.5″ How)
112 Bde RFA	A	B	C	Btys (18 pdr)	D Bty (4.5″ How)

X/25 Medium Trench Mortar Bty
Y/25 Medium Trench Mortar Bty
25th Divisional Ammunition Column

29th Division

HQ Divisional Artillery—CRA   Brig Gen R M Johnson
15 Bde RHA   B   L   1/1 Warwickshire Btys (18 pdr)   460 Bty RFA (4.5″ How)
17 Bde RFA   13   26   92   Btys (18 pdr)   D Bty (4.5″ How)
X/29 Medium Trench Mortar Bty
Y/29 Medium Trench Mortar Bty
29th Divisional Ammunition Column

30th Division

HQ Divisional Artillery—CRA				Brig Gen F F Lambarde	
148 Bde RFA	A	B	C	Btys (18 pdr)	D Bty (4.5″ How)
149 Bde RFA	A	B	C	Btys (18 pdr)	D Bty (4.5″ How)

ʹX/30 Medium Trench Mortar Bty
Y/30 Medium Trench Mortar Bty
30th Divisional Ammunition Column

31st Division

HQ Divisional Artillery—CRA				Brig Gen E P Lambert	
165 Bde RFA	A	B	C	Btys (18 pdr)	D Bty (4.5″ How)
170 Bde RFA	A	B	C	Btys (18 pdr)	D Bty (4.5″ How)

X/31 Medium Trench Mortar Bty
Y/31 Medium Trench Mortar Bty
31st Divisional Ammunition Column

32nd Division

HQ Divisional Artillery—CRA				Brig Gen J A Tyler	
161 Bde RFA	A	B	C	Btys (18 pdr)	D Bty (4.5″ How)
168 Bde RFA	A	B	C	Btys (18 pdr)	D Bty (4.5″ How)

X/32 Medium Trench Mortar Bty
Y/32 Medium Trench Mortar Bty
32nd Divisional Ammunition Column

33rd Division

HQ Divisional Artillery—CRA				Brig Gen G H W Nicholson	
156 Bde RFA	A	B	C	Btys (18 pdr)	D Bty (4.5″ How)
162 Bde RFA	A	B	C	Btys (18 pdr)	D Bty (4.5″ How)

X/33 Medium Trench Mortar Bty
Y/33 Medium Trench Mortar Bty
33rd Divisional Ammunition Column

34th Division

HQ Divisional Artillery—CRA   Brig Gen E C W D Walthall
152 Bde RFA   A   B   C   Btys (18 pdr)   D Bty (4.5″ How)
160 Bde RFA   A   B   C   Btys (18 pdr)   D Bty (4.5″ How)
X/34 Medium Trench Mortar Bty
Y/34 Medium Trench Mortar Bty
34th Divisional Ammunition Column

35th Division

HQ Divisional Artillery—CRA   Brig Gen W R N Madocks
157 Bde RFA   A   B   C   Btys (18 pdr)   D Bty (4.5″ How)
159 Bde RFA   A   B   C   Btys (18 pdr)   D Bty (4.5″ How)
X/35 Medium Trench Mortar Bty
Y/35 Medium Trench Mortar Bty
35th Divisional Ammunition Column

36th (Ulster) Division

HQ Divisional Artillery—CRA   Brig Gen C St L G Hawkes
153 Bde RFA   A   B   C   Btys (18 pdr)   D Bty (4.5″ How)
173 Bde RFA   A   B   C   Btys (18 pdr)   D Bty (4.5″ How)
X/36 Medium Trench Mortar Bty
Y/36 Medium Trench Mortar Bty
36th Divisional Ammunition Column

37th Division

HQ Divisional Artillery—CRA   Brig Gen F Potts
123 Bde RFA   A   B   C   Btys (18 pdr)   D Bty (4.5″ How)
124 Bde RFA   A   B   C   Btys (18 pdr)   D Bty (4.5″ How)
X/37 Medium Trench Mortar Bty
Y/37 Medium Trench Mortar Bty
37th Divisional Ammunition Column

38th (Welsh) Division

HQ Divisional Artillery—CRA   Brig Gen T E Topping
121 Bde RFA   A   B   C   Btys (18 pdr)   D Bty (4.5″ How)
122 Bde RFA   A   B   C   Btys (18 pdr)   D Bty (4.5″ How)
X/38 Medium Trench Mortar Bty
Y/38 Medium Trench Mortar Bty
38th Divisional Ammunition Column

39th Division

HQ Divisional Artillery—CRA   Brig Gen W G Thompson
174 Bde RFA   A   B   C   Btys (18 pdr)   D Bty (4.5″ How)
186 Bde RFA   A   B   C   Btys (18 pdr)   D Bty (4.5″ How)
X/39 Medium Trench Mortar Bty
Y/39 Medium Trench Mortar Bty
39th Divisional Ammunition Column

40th Division

HQ Divisional Artillery—CRA   Brig Gen C E Palmer
178 Bde RFA   A   B   C   Btys (18 pdr)   D Bty (4.5″ How)
181 Bde RFA   A   B   C   Btys (18 pdr)   D Bty (4.5″ How)
X/40 Medium Trench Mortar Bty
Y/40 Medium Trench Mortar Bty
40th Divisional Ammunition Column

41st Division

HQ Divisional Artillery—CRA   Brig Gen A S Cotton
187 Bde RFA   A   B   C   Btys (18 pdr)   D Bty (4.5″ How)
190 Bde RFA   A   B   C   Btys (18 pdr)   D Bty (4.5″ How)
X/41 Medium Trench Mortar Bty
Y/41 Medium Trench Mortar Bty
41st Divisional Ammunition Column

42nd Division

HQ Divisional Artillery—CRA   Brig Gen F W H Walshe
210 Bde RFA   A   B   C   Btys (18 pdr)   D Bty (4.5″ How)
211 Bde RFA   A   B   C   Btys (18 pdr)   D Bty (4.5″ How)
X/42 Medium Trench Mortar Bty
Y/42 Medium Trench Mortar Bty
42nd Divisional Ammunition Column

46th (North Midland) Division

HQ Divisional Artillery—CRA   Brig Gen Sir S H Child Bart
230 Bde RFA   A   B   C   Btys (18 pdr)   D Bty (4.5″ How)
231 Bde RFA   A   B   C   Btys (18 pdr)   D Bty (4.5″ How)
X/46 Medium Trench Mortar Bty
Y/46 Medium Trench Mortar Bty
46th Divisional Ammunition Column

47th (London) Division

HQ Divisional Artillery—CRA   Brig Gen E N Whitley
235 Bde RFA   A   B   C   Btys (18 pdr)   D Bty (4.5″ How)
236 Bde RFA   A   B   C   Btys (18 pdr)   D Bty (4.5″ How)
X/47 Medium Trench Mortar Bty
Y/47 Medium Trench Mortar Bty
47th Divisional Ammunition Column

49th (West Riding) Division

HQ Divisional Artillery—CRA   Brig Gen A B Forman
245 Bde RFA   A   B   C   Btys (18 pdr)   D Bty (4.5″ How)
246 Bde RFA   A   B   C   Btys (18 pdr)   D Bty (4.5″ How)
X/49 Medium Trench Mortar Bty
Y/49 Medium Trench Mortar Bty
49th Divisional Ammunition Column

50th (Northumbrian) Division

HQ Divisional Artillery—CRA   Brig Gen W Stirling
250 Bde RFA   A   B   C   Btys (18 pdr)   D Bty (4.5″ How)
251 Bde RFA   A   B   C   Btys (18 pdr)   D Bty (4.5″ How)
X/50 Medium Trench Mortar Bty
Y/50 Medium Trench Mortar Bty
50th Divisional Ammunition Column

51st (Highland) Division

HQ Divisional Artillery—CRA   Brig Gen L C L Oldfield
255 Bde RFA   A   B   C   Btys (18 pdr)   D Bty (4.5″ How)
256 Bde RFA   A   B   C   Btys (18 pdr)   D Bty (4.5″ How)
X/51 Medium Trench Mortar Bty
Y/51 Medium Trench Mortar Bty
51st Divisional Ammunition Column

52nd (Lowland) Division

HQ Divisional Artillery—CRA   Brig Gen A D Musgrave
 9 Bde RFA   19   20   29   Btys (18 pdr)   D/69 Bty (4.5″ How)
56 Bde RFA   A   B   C   Btys (18 pdr)   527 Bty (4.5″ How)
X/52 Medium Trench Mortar Bty
Y/52 Medium Trench Mortar Bty
52nd Divisional Ammunition Column

55th (West Lancashire) Division

HQ Divisional Artillery—CRA   Brig Gen A M Perreau
275 Bde RFA   A   B   C   Btys (18 pdr)   D Bty (4.5″ How)
276 Bde RFA   A   B   C   Btys (18 pdr)   D Bty (4.5″ How)
X/55 Medium Trench Mortar Bty
Y/55 Medium Trench Mortar Bty
55th Divisional Ammunition Column

56th Division

HQ Divisional Artillery—CRA   Brig Gen R J G Elkington
280 Bde RFA   A   93   C   Btys (18 pdr)   D   Bty (4.5″ How)
281 Bde RFA   A   B   109 Btys (18 pdr)   D   Bty (4.5″ How)
X/56 Medium Trench Mortar Bty
Y/56 Medium Trench Mortar Bty
56th Divisional Ammunition Column

57th Division

HQ Divisional Artillery—CRA   Brig Gen W C E Rudkin
285 Bde RFA   A   B   C   Btys (18 pdr)   D Bty (4.5″ How)
286 Bde RFA   A   B   C   Btys (18 pdr)   D Bty (4.5″ How)
X/57 Medium Trench Mortar Bty
Y/57 Medium Trench Mortar Bty
57th Divisional Ammunition Column

58th Division

HQ Divisional Artillery—CRA   Brig Gen J McC Maxwell
290 Bde RFA   A   B   C   Btys (18 pdr)   D Bty (4.5″ How)
291 Bde RFA   A   B   C   Btys (18 pdr)   D Bty (4.5″ How)
X/58 Medium Trench Mortar Bty
Y/58 Medium Trench Mortar Bty
58th Divisional Ammunition Column

59th Division

HQ Divisional Artillery—CRA   Brig Gen J F Laycock
295 Bde RFA   A   B   C   Btys (18 pdr)   D Bty (4.5″ How)
296 Bde RFA   A   B   C   Btys (18 pdr)   D Bty (4.5″ How)
X/59 Medium Trench Mortar Bty
Y/59 Medium Trench Mortar Bty
59th Divisional Ammunition Column

61st (South Midland) Division

HQ Divisional Artillery—CRA   Brig Gen R G Ouseley
306 Bde RFA   A   B   C   Btys (18 pdr)   D Bty (4.5″ How)
307 Bde RFA   A   B   C   Btys (18 pdr)   D Bty (4.5″ How)
X/61 Medium Trench Mortar Bty
Y/61 Medium Trench Mortar Bty
61st Divisional Ammunition Column

62nd (West Riding) Division

HQ Divisional Artillery—CRA   Brig Gen A T Anderson
310 Bde RFA   A   B   C   Btys (18 pdr)   D Bty (4.5″ How)
312 Bde RFA   A   B   C   Btys (18 pdr)   D Bty (4.5″ How)
X/62 Medium Trench Mortar Bty
Y/62 Medium Trench Mortar Bty
62nd Divisional Ammunition Column

63rd (Royal Naval) Division

HQ Divisional Artillery—CRA   Brig Gen C H de Rougemont
223 Bde RFA   A   B   C   Btys (18 pdr)   D Bty (4.5″ How)
317 Bde RFA   A   B   C   Btys (18 pdr)   D Bty (4.5″ How)
X/63 Medium Trench Mortar Bty
Y/63 Medium Trench Mortar Bty
63rd Divisional Ammunition Column

66th Division

HQ Divisional Artillery—CRA   Brig Gen A Birtwistle
330 Bde RFA   A   B   C   Btys (18 pdr)   D Bty (4.5″ How)
331 Bde RFA   A   B   C   Btys (18 pdr)   D Bty (4.5″ How)
X/66 Medium Trench Mortar Bty
Y/66 Medium Trench Mortar Bty
66th Divisional Ammunition Column

74th (Yeomanry) Division

HQ Divisional Artillery—CRA   Brig Gen L J Hext
 44 Bde RFA   340   382   425 Btys (18 pdr) D Bty (4.5″ How)
117 Bde RFA   A   B   366 Btys   (18 pdr) D Bty (4.5″ How)
X/74 Medium Trench Mortar Bty
Y/74 Medium Trench Mortar Bty
74th Divisional Ammunition Column

LINE OF COMMUNICATION TROOPS

Unbrigaded Siege Btys RGA

103 Siege Bty — 2 × 12″ How on railway mountings
529 Siege Bty — 1 × 12″ gun on railway mountings

Anti Aircraft Artillery

HQ L of C AA Defence Commander   Lt Col R R Curling

AA Bty			Sections						
			13 pdr				3″		
—	175	176							
Northern Group AA Area	68	113	147	163		201	203	204	207
						212	224	237	240
						241	243	244	
Central Group AA Area	1	27	29	114	161	209	210	234	235
Southern Group AA Area	2	3	10	36		28	213	215	229
	47	160				231	233	238	
Base Ports	4	5	45	83	105	13	221	223	239

AA Bty			**Sections**					
			13 pdr			**3″**		
AA Area	149	150	157	169	170	242	245	246
Base Ports								

AA Defence Command, Independent Force (RAF)

AA Bty			**Sections**					
			13 pdr			**3″**		
W	108	112	167	206				
X						51	211	222	228
	172	173						

Depots

RH and RFA Base Depot
RGA Base Depot

Some of the terms, inseparable from a work of this nature, may not be familiar to all readers. A brief glossary is provided, therefore, which employs outline definitions appropriate to the First World War. Later developments have led to changes in some cases and, on occasion, to changes in the terms themselves.

BARRAGE
A curtain of shell bursts created by continuous fire. It can be static or may move forward and back or at any angle required. The purpose is to ensure that all unsuspected or unlocated enemy weapons on the frontage of attack are dealt with by fire during the approach.

BL
BREECH LOADING. All guns employed by the Royal Artillery in France and Flanders were breech-loaders but the initials used here referred to the use of bagged *charges* as opposed to those contained in metal cartridge cases. The number of bags could be varied to increase or reduce the explosive power of the *charge* and the breech of the BL *gun* or *howitzer* was self sealing but often slower in operation than that of the *QF*, e.g. 6-inch 26 cwt BL howitzer.

BLC
BREECH LOADING CONVERTED. Some earlier *BL*s were modernised by the fitting of a faster operating breech. Bagged *charges* were still used, e.g. 6-inch BLC siege gun.

CB
COUNTER-BATTERY. The employment of any *gun* or *howitzer*, but usually the medium and heavy *equipments*, to neutralise or destroy enemy gun positions and thus afford long range protection for troops being supported.

CHARGE
The propelling explosive contained either in a brass case or in a cloth bag, usually silk. The initiating explosive within the charge or in the breech of a *BL* may be included.

c.r.h.
CALIBRE RADIUS HEAD. The precise description, by formula, of the shape of the nose of a shell; rounded, sharply pointed etc. The shape plays an important part in determining the way in which a shell behaves in flight and on the target.

DIAL SIGHT
A form of periscope, horizontally movable over a scale of 360 degrees and thus capable of reading an angle to an aiming mark by reference to which a gun or guns may be accurately aimed.

EQUIPMENT
Any *gun* or *howitzer* complete with all that is necessary for it to be employed save for the ammunition itself. In other words the term means the barrel, breech, carriage or mounting, and limber which, if supplied, would contain the ammunition. A limber, or wheeled ammunition box, was supplied for the lighter equipments such as the 18-pounder.

FIRE PLAN
The more or less precise ascertaining of the position and type of a target and, consequently, how it is to be engaged. In support of an infantry assault it was vital to know what the guns had to do and when. The *barrage* was a more complicated and extensive version of this.

GUN
A weapon which fires at high velocity using a *charge* giving a relatively flat trajectory (i.e. a low angle above the horizontal). A gun would only very rarely fire at an angle of greater than 20 degrees, e.g. the 18-pounder QF gun.

    The term can also refer to the barrel and breech assembly excluding the carriage or mounting. It can also be used generically to mean any piece of artillery, gun or *howitzer;* "The Guns! thank God, the Guns!"

HOWITZER	A weapon capable of firing a heavier projectile, than a *gun* of similar calibre, and at a higher angle. Mounted on a mobile carriage and employing variable *charges* it fired at a relatively low velocity from positions behind cover.
LIFE OF A GUN	The calculated number of *rounds* which could be fired through a barrel accurately and safely. A gun reached the end of its life when its rifling was so worn as to render it inaccurate at which stage it required to be relined.
METEOR	Meteorological Report, then Meteorological Telegramme. See Annex K.
MORTAR	A low velocity weapon designed for firing relatively heavy shells or bombs at high angles of elevation (usually above 45°) and at short ranges.
NATURES	Types of ammunition; high explosive, shrapnel, smoke, gas etc.
PIECE	The barrel and breech assembly excluding the carriage or mounting as in the alternative definition of *gun*.
PREDICTED FIRE	A form of fire in which previous firings to adjust the fall of shot onto the target had not been carried out.
PREMATURE	The detonation of a shell inside the weapon firing it or at any point before that intended.
QF	QUICK FIRING. *Guns* and *howitzers* using brass cartridge cases for their *charges* and fast-acting breeches, e.g. 13-pounder QF gun, 4.5-inch QF howitzer, 13-pounder 9 cwt QF Anti-aircraft gun. A QF always used a non-variable charge and was usually so designed that its detachment were able to remain on or very close to it on firing and thus able to reload and re-lay the weapon quickly thus leading to a high rate of fire.
REGISTRATION	The ascertaining of the position of a target and its type and thus how it would be engaged when required. Registration could be 'silent' by obtaining information from the study of a map, and the ground as well if possible, or by firing at a target to obtain data for future use.
RFA	ROYAL FIELD ARTILLERY. The largest proportion of the Royal Regiment of Artillery, armed with field *guns* and *howitzers* and primarily concerned with the close support of infantry.
RGA	ROYAL GARRISON ARTILLERY. Armed with medium and heavy *guns* and *howitzers*, sometimes railway mounted. Their weapons could be equipped with wheeled carriages or with mountings placed directly on the ground. This part of the Regiment handled the largest equipments from the 60-pounder BL *gun* to the 15-inch BL siege *howitzer*. Its weapons were employed in siege warfare, counter-battery and coast defence and were usually under direct command at Division, Corps or Army level.
RHA	ROYAL HORSE ARTILLERY. Although most weapons were horse-drawn the RHA was required to be more mobile than the RFA and was primarily concerned with the close support of cavalry. It was armed with the 13-pounder QF *gun* which was somewhat lighter in weight than the RFA's 18-pounder. During the period of trench warfare the RHA served in a similar capacity to the RFA for most of the time.
ROUND	The projectile and its requirements; shell, fuze, propelling *charge* and the initiating explosion which fires that *charge*.

Index